DATE DUE			
NOV 2 3 1987			
DEC 0 5 1990			

D1597621

Perón's Argentina

"On the most exalted throne in the world, we are still seated on nothing but our arse."

MONTAIGNE

Perón's Argentina

By George I. Blanksten

THE UNIVERSITY OF CHICAGO PRESS

The University of Chicago Press, Chicago 60637
The University of Chicago Press, Ltd., London

Published 1953. Midway reprint 1974
Printed in the United States of America

International Standard Book Number: 0-226-05685-6

Preface

It is not difficult to justify bringing out a new book on Argentine government and politics at this time. During World War II, the people of the United States expressed considerable concern over Argentine affairs. It was felt then that Buenos Aires' orientation toward the Axis threatened the security of the United States and other nations actively involved in the war. Now that World War II is over, "North Americans," preoccupied with the "cold war," have tended to neglect the rest of the Western Hemisphere. This may be dangerous. It is still too early to forget Argentina.

Probably not much is generally known in the United States about Argentina beyond the impressions that President Juan Domingo Perón operates a dictatorship and that the Argentine government followed a pro-Axis policy during the late war. Both of these propositions are essentially correct. Although Perón has promulgated a constitution and wishes it to be thought that he governs according to its postulates, true constitutional government is certainly not one of the characteristics of the "new Argentina." Juan Domingo Perón is the law in that country, and his will dominates all public agencies on all levels of government. Opposition parties, while they still exist, are carefully hemmed in, and only the *Peronista* party, blindly loyal to Perón, is permitted to win elections when they are held. Moreover, both of the presidential elections conducted since the Perón revolution were held during states of siege, when even the ostensible civil and political liberties were suspended. These freedoms have been suppressed effectively through the Federal Police, the dreaded *Control del Estado,* and other agencies of Perón's Argentina. Political prisoners, until a short time ago, were herded off to concentration camps, and are still subjected to physical torture. Neither the press nor the schools are free; and radio and the theater have been placed under thoroughgoing censorship. A new alliance between Church and State threatens religious freedom, and Argentine nationalism, unleashed by Perón, has fostered an increasingly hostile attitude toward foreign countries, particularly the United Kingdom and the United States.

The "new Argentina" was identified with the Axis during World War II, when the influence of Nazi Germany was much in evidence at Buenos Aires. Since the end of the war, the Germans have remained powerful and influential in Argentina, although Perón has endeavored to dissociate his regime from naziism and fascism. To offset the onus of these defeated and discredited concepts, the *Peronistas* have created a new word—*Justicialismo.* Perón says that this is a new political theory, that *Justicialismo* represents a "Third Position" between capitalism and communism, and that the "Third Position" is anti-Soviet as well as anti-Yankee.

Yet all this is only a part of the strange story of the "new Argentina." The Perón revolution, after all, *is* a revolution. It has seized an essentially agricultural country which was traditionally ruled by the landowners, who expressed little concern for the welfare or grievances of the lower classes. Before Perón appeared on the national scene, landowner rule had bred fraud and corruption, and many Argentines had rejected the old order in search of something new. Perón *has* brought something new. He has attempted to in-

dustrialize the country at the expense of the rural landowners. This has shaken the economy of Argentina and may
well spell Perón's ruin, but it is new. The landowners do
not dominate the country as they did before 1943. Perón
has given Argentina a regime which at least *says* that it has
the interests of the lower classes—particularly organized
labor—at heart. A new class—"uncultured" folk, men of
little social status—has risen to political power in Argentina.
This class threatens the landowning "Oligarchy" with a social revolution curiously reminiscent of the Jacksonian
movement which struck the United States more than a century ago.

A case can be made for calling Perón's Argentina a dictatorship. A case can also be made for saying that Perón is the
first Argentine president in a generation to be elected by a
genuinely popular vote. Both cases are important to an understanding of the "new Argentina."

Whatever else might be said of President Perón, he is a
skilled political opportunist. He has straddled many Argentine national issues in a fashion that would put more than
one "North American" politician to shame. This is at once
the basic strength and the fatal weakness of Perón. His is
fundamentally an unstable and uneasy regime. It is beset by
tensions and uncertainties. Many of these have been created
by Perón's attempt to play all sides of questions which perhaps nobody can straddle successfully in Argentina. There
is, for example, the question of the "two Argentinas," the
historic struggle of Buenos Aires against the provinces of
the "interior." The Perón regime has not been entirely effective in being on both sides of that issue. And the "new
Argentina" of Perón rests on a strange alliance of the army
and militarism with the labor movement. This, too, is an unstable and uneasy arrangement, for these two pillars of the
Perón revolution harbor long-standing antagonisms against

each other. These and other considerations contribute to the fundamental instability of contemporary Argentine government and politics. In November of 1951, Juan Domingo Perón was re-elected president of the nation for a six-year term. Many observers of the Argentine scene doubt that his regime can last that long.

Perón's government is not to be counted as one of the more reliable friends of the United States in the Western Hemisphere. This is in part the logical expression of a long-developing duel between Argentina and the United States for the diplomatic leadership of Latin America. This struggle between the "Yankees of the South" and the "Colossus of the North" was intensified with the announcement of President Franklin D. Roosevelt's Good Neighbor policy, and the contest between the two states reached its apogee during World War II. That war has ended, but Argentine–United States rivalry has not. Perón's "Third Position" is in a sense his proclamation of continued resistance against the United States. The "Third Position" stands between the camps of the United States and the Soviet Union. *Justicialismo* is pro-neither. "Neither" is an important word. It can become "either." It is still too early to forget Argentina.

My particular interest in Argentine affairs is a decade old. I readily concede that this is not old enough. For four years —from 1942 to 1946—I was affiliated at Washington, D.C., with two agencies of the government of the United States: the Office of the Co-ordinator of Inter-American Affairs, and the Department of State. During those years much of my attention was consumed by what was then called the "Argentine Question." Since leaving Washington, I have continued to follow Argentine problems closely. In 1950 and 1951, I was in Argentina as an Area Research Training Fellow of the Social Science Research Council. My business there was to study the Perón government, and what appears in the following pages is the product of that year spent in Argentina. Much of the material in this book was gathered during the course of original field research in that country. A large part of what I offer here has never before been published in English—or in Spanish, for that matter.

This is the first time I have felt obliged to preface my writing about Latin-American politics with a word or two about objectivity. It may be that this is an indecent confession on my part, and perhaps it should not be made. I have heard it said that absolute objectivity in social science is impossible, valueless, or both. It has not been easy for me to be objective about contemporary Argentine politics, but I have tried. I have sought out the *Peronistas*, befriended them, and attempted to get their side of the story. I have done the same with the Radicals, the Socialists, the Conservatives, and the Communists of Argentina. I have attempted, by applying various field techniques to diverse sources, to frame my own independent interpretation of the significances of Perón's Argentina. Frankly—as long as confessions seem to be in order—this has turned out to be a much more honest book than I had thought I would be able to bring back with me from Argentina.

I have written this volume on the assumption that the reader will be more interested in *Argentine* than in *my* politics, and I have endeavored to prevent the latter from creeping into the manuscript. But the truth is that I do have my politics, and some of them are Argentine. I have been interested in Argentina for ten years, and I lived there for one of them. I like some Argentine political parties more than others. Today I count many Argentines among my close friends, and a number of them are politicians. In short, I am infected—I am afraid that it was impossible for me to live in Argentina for even as short a period as a year without forming friendships and associations there, without becoming involved myself in the problems vital to the people I lived with. My Argentine friends include some *Peronistas*, some Radicals, some Socialists, and some Conservatives. I was not very successful at acquiring friends among the Argentine Communists. I regret that. I had desired to achieve as intimate an understanding of all sides of Argentine politics as possible.

I arrived at Buenos Aires on July 1, 1950. Three months later, Perón's congress declared my work in Argentina—research in political science—to be "espionage," and outlawed my mission there. In the ensuing months, I had a few brief encounters with the Federal Police. But nobody was hurt, and I am not angry at anybody. I am not even angry at Perón, and this book is probably less hostile toward him than most of what is published about him in the United States. I would probably feel differently about Perón if I had to live in Argentina indefinitely, but only a year of cloak-and-dagger play did not miff me very much. Many of my Argentine associates will probably be upset when they see this book. I do not imagine that any of them will agree entirely with what I have written. Some of them may wonder why I did not accept the 20,000 *pesos* I was offered to write a pro-Perón volume. The answer is that I have not followed anybody's line except my own. As I indicated above, even I am a little surprised that this book has turned out to be as honest as I think it to be.

One more matter remains. I think that when Perón sees this book, there are two things that he will want to know about it. One of them is, how was I able to get my notes out of Argentina? The other is, who helped me? I will offer Perón a sporting proposition. I will tell him about these matters after the *Peronistas* no longer govern Argentina.

Meanwhile, I am left in a somewhat embarrassing position with respect to acknowledgments. I imagine that if anything belongs in a preface, acknowledgments do. I find that I cannot mention the names of the Argentines who helped me most with this book. This depresses me. Few things would please me more than to be able to name them all—the truth is that I would like very much to dedicate this work to at least two Argentines in particular. But life in Argentina is hard enough for them as it is now, without my making it any more difficult. My *Peronista* friends would suffer especially if they were named here. I should therefore like to advance one more sporting proposition. At Buenos Aires, I attended a function at which the impending marriage of one of my friends was celebrated. Another Argentine told him: "I would like to buy you a beautiful wedding present, but Perón's inflation has made that impossible." The answer was: "Considering the condition of the country, I will accept your I.O.U." I offer my I.O.U. to the Argentines whom I cannot name at this time.

I regret that I am also unable to name a few of the "North Americans" who assisted me. But not everybody is behind an iron curtain, and I should like to acknowledge the aid of the following "North Americans" who I hope will have no further business with Perón. Professor Willmoore Kendall of Yale University talked me into doing this Argentine study in the first place. Also, two persons who remained there after I left Argentina were able to cover for me the declaration of "internal war" and other matters associated with the election of November 11, 1951. These were Professor Russell H. Fitzgibbon of the University of California at Los Angeles, and Mr. Donald B. Easum, a graduate student at the University of Wisconsin. Professor Clifton B. Kroeber, likewise of Wisconsin, was at Buenos Aires when I arrived there, tried to persuade me to go home, and, when that failed, was of invaluable aid in the early stages of this work. And I wish to express my deep appreciation of the help given me by three members of the Department of Political Science at Northwestern University. These are Professors Charles S. Hyneman, who, expertly ignorant of Latin-American affairs, read much of the manuscript to point out to me what needed to be explained to the non–Latin-Americanist; Roy C. Macridis, who read critically the portions of the manuscript dealing with political theory, particularly the chapter on *Justicialismo;* and James N. Murray, Jr., whose advice on international law assisted me in the analysis of Argentine territorial claims. Dr. Howard F. Cline, now with the Library of Congress' Hispanic Foundation, helpfully criticized sections of the book touching on Argentine history. And my wife certainly deserves mention for both research assistance in Argentina and her later perseverance in aiding me with editorial work and the preparation of the index. I am, of course, deeply indebted to the Social Science Research Council for the fellowship which made it possible for me to travel to Argentina and work there. I am especially grateful for the helpful co-operation I received at various stages in this project from E. Pendleton Herring and Elbridge Sibley, president and executive associate, respectively, of the Social Science Research Council.

None of the people I have named here is responsible for such errors of fact or judgment as might appear in this book. They are mine, all mine.

G. I. B.

Northwestern University
Evanston, Illinois
October 1, 1952

Table of Contents

Table of Contents

Table of Contents

I.

A Book of Introductions

"The following pages are purely confidential."
DOMINGO FAUSTINO SARMIENTO

1.

The "Yankees of the South"

According to many Argentines, Latin America is a huge and loosely defined area bounded on the north by the United States and on the south by Argentina. This view, somewhat curious to "North Americans," shapes much Argentine thinking about the Western Hemisphere and in part underlies the United States–Argentine diplomatic friction of recent years. Argentina is in, but not quite of, Latin America, and has long exercised strong cultural and political leadership among the Ibero-American states. This circumstance has led many Argentines to resent the political pre-eminence of the United States in the American hemisphere. For their part, the people of the remaining states of the Americas have frequently regarded this United States–Argentine rivalry with a somewhat disinterested "plague-on-both-your-houses" attitude. These people have seen striking similarities between the United States and Argentina, and, on occasion, have had little objection to establishing the southern extremity of Latin America at the Argentine frontier. To citizens in many American republics, attitudes of superiority and domination bear the same stamp whether they emanate from the "Colossus of the North" or the "Yankees of the South."

Argentina and Latin America

The point that Argentina is one of the major states of
the Western Hemisphere needs no laboring. With an area
of 1,078,278 square miles,* the republic is the eighth largest
country in the world from the standpoint of territory, and
the second largest on the continent of South America. Argentina's area is about one-third that of the United States
and five times larger than that of France, and accounts for
16 per cent of the territory of South America. The country's population—16,107,930 according to the 1947 census,
and officially estimated in 1950 at 17,424,926—embraces
approximately one-seventh of the total population of the
South American continent. Although Argentine statistical
services are among the most reliable in Latin America,
many of their findings are not available for publication.
The present government at Buenos Aires ruled that "considerations of national defense . . . prevent the publication
of official statistics"[1] from some sections of the Fourth
National Census, conducted in 1947. It has, however, been
made known that in that year no less than 61.4 per cent of
the population of Argentina was urban, with all communities of more than 2,000 persons classified as "urban."

Unlike many other South American states, Argentina
counts relatively few Indians among its inhabitants. In pre-
Hispanic times, the Indians in what is now Argentina probably never numbered more than 400,000, and their cultures
were essentially undeveloped as compared with indigenous
civilizations elsewhere in the Americas. The Indian societies
in what later became Argentina tended to disintegrate upon
contact with the Spaniards, with the result that few Argentines—about 15,000, or 1.5 per cent of the nation's popu-

* This figure does not include Argentine claims to the Falkland Islands
and to a portion of the Antarctic. See pp. 431–32.

lation—live as Indians today. An estimated 89 per cent of the country's people are European in their cultural orientation and are thought of as "whites." Indeed, Argentina, especially Buenos Aires, the capital city, strikes the foreign observer as being more European than South American; and the country has received more European immigrants than any other American republic with the exception of the United States. "Almost everything we have today comes from Europe," an Argentine writer has said. "Although we proclaim with conviction that we will absorb the immigrants, it is evident that . . . the republic has changed—without losing its old habits—in order to offer to the foreigners here whatever they had in their countries of origin."[2] It has been estimated that about 3,500,000 immigrants settled permanently in the country during the past century. Although Spain is regarded as Argentina's mother-country, it is nevertheless worthy of note that of the immigrants some 1,500,000 were Italians; and it has been argued that Italy could be considered as a second mother-country.

Argentina does not suffer from many of the problems plaguing the majority of the American republics. Illiteracy, for example, is a serious matter in much of the Western Hemisphere: in at least eleven of the republics over 50 per cent of the adult population cannot read or write. The Argentine figure—about 15 per cent illiterate—while high compared with that of the United States (4.5 per cent), reflects a much less serious literacy problem than exists in most of Latin America. Poverty, to cite another example, is a far less severe matter in Argentina than in most of the other nations of the hemisphere. Argentina's per capita national income has been figured at 334 United States dollars, as compared with an over-all Latin-American average of 106 United States dollars; and in 1951 Argentina supported a national budget of over $274,000,000. The country has received 12 per cent of the total Latin-American investments of the United States. Again, problems of nutrition and food consumption, reaching tragic proportions in much of the Western Hemisphere, are not so serious in Argentina, where, according to United Nations figures, the per capita calorie consumption is second only to New Zealand among the countries of the world. And the per capita meat consumption is higher in Argentina than in any other nation on earth.

Despite these marked differences between Argentina and the other states of Latin America, the interests of the "Yankees of the South" have been tied to the rest of the Ibero-American states for more than a century. The Latin-American countries, including Argentina, have tended to operate as a unit, a bloc, in international affairs. This tendency of the twenty states to band together for their mutual defense against threats from the outside world is known by different names in the various republics of the hemisphere. Some have dubbed it *americanismo*, which one writer has defined as "a natural effort toward a family understanding between Latin Americans." He points out that "a Colombian and an Argentine, meeting abroad, although their homes are in effect more remote from one another than each from Europe, are not quite foreigners to one another, since both are *americanos*, speaking the same language, inheriting, in a broad sense, the same traditions and remembering united action in the War of Independence."[3]

Americanismo, thus understood, has been a significant political force in the American hemisphere for more than a hundred years. As it has developed, this tendency of the Latin-American states to band together against the outside world acquired two characteristics of significance here. First, Argentina has played a leading role in *americanismo*, achieving through it a major measure of political pre-eminence in Latin America. Second, the United States has never

6

been associated with the phenomenon and has more often been regarded by Latin Americans as a part of the outside world against which *americanismo* was directed.

South American power politics are less well known in the United States than European power politics. It is nevertheless true that the "A.B.C. states"—Argentina, Brazil, and Chile—emerged from the tides and fortunes of the nineteenth century as the dominant powers of South America. Moreover, in the early 1930's, Argentina was almost universally recognized among these as the most powerful state in South America. A survey made in 1938 of the hemisphere's military resources revealed that at that time Argentina was the only Latin-American nation which had sought to create military institutions adequate for its own defense. And in 1941 the A.B.C. powers were the best-armed nations of the southern continent, with Argentina's forces outstripping those of Brazil and Chile.

Argentina's leadership in Latin America is thus integrally tied to the concept and practice of *americanismo*. While Argentines stand apart from the other peoples of the hemisphere and usually resent being called "Latin Americans," they nevertheless regard their country as the "big brother" of smaller American states. They like to point out that it was an *Argentine* president—Bartolomé Mitre, in 1865— who first used the term "Good Neighbor." And it should be noted that subsequent Argentine presidents have clung doggedly to *americanismo*. No less a figure than Juan Domingo Perón himself has declared that his government "desires good understanding with her sister countries of the Americas. . . . There is nothing but cordiality in Argentina's attitude toward the nations of the continent."[4]

Argentina and the United States

Two Latin-American policies pursued by the United States during the last half-century or more furnish a background against which Argentine–United States diplomatic friction has developed in recent years. The first of these policies, Pan-Americanism, dates from 1889 and may be said to consist of the Washington government's attempts to organize all of the American republics in support of the foreign policy of the United States. In general, Pan-Americanism has been resisted by *americanismo*, frequently under Argentine leadership. Such events as the Spanish-American War, the acquisition by the United States, in 1903, of the Panama Canal Zone, and implementation of President Theodore Roosevelt's corollary to the Monroe Doctrine drove much of Latin America to seek refuge in *americanismo*. Intervention practices during the administrations of the "North American" presidents from William Howard Taft to Herbert C. Hoover gave rise to a veritable library of anti-United States literature in the other American republics. *Americanismo* was fed in this period by Latin-American antipathy toward, and distrust of, the United States. And during this time Argentina's star rose in highlighting that country's role as the "big brother" in the Americas, as the leader in *americanismo*.

The second United States policy, that of the Good Neighbor, had quite different consequences. In a sense, the Latin-American policy proclaimed by President Franklin Delano Roosevelt amounted to an attempt to fuse or combine certain elements of *americanismo* with some parts of Pan-Americanism. Shortly after his inauguration in March of 1933, the second Roosevelt outlined his hemisphere policy in these words:

> The maintenance of constitutional government in other nations is not a sacred obligation devolving upon the United States alone. The maintenance of law and orderly processes of government in this hemisphere is the concern of each individual nation within its own borders first of all. It is only if and when the failure of orderly processes affects the other nations of the continent that it becomes

their concern; and the point to stress is that in such an event it becomes the *joint concern of a whole continent in which we are all
neighbors. The Monroe Doctrine confers no superior position upon
the United States.*[5]

Implementation of this policy was not long in coming. The
Platt Amendment, which had given the United States a
controlling voice in Cuban affairs, was abrogated; Washington recognized Panama's full sovereignty; the United States'
earlier practice of intervening in Central America was re-
nounced; Washington signed non-intervention agreements
with all twenty Latin-American states; the United States
Marines were withdrawn from Nicaragua; and at the
Eighth International Conference of American States at
Lima, Peru, in 1938, the Monroe Doctrine was redefined
as a guarantee of the protection of all American republics
rather than—as had previously been the case—of the United
States alone.

In so far as the Good Neighbor policy affected the fusion
of *americanismo* with Pan-Americanism, it laid the foundation for a dramatic crisis in Argentina's relations with the
United States. In *americanismo*, to which the Buenos Aires
government clung stubbornly, Argentina's pre-eminence in
Latin America, particularly in South America, had been
virtually undisputed. Now, with the Good Neighbor policy, the United States seriously and successfully challenged
Argentina's leadership in the hemisphere. With states like
Mexico and Brazil reacting favorably to the over-all hemisphere policies of the second Roosevelt, Argentina faced
the prospect of displacement from her traditionally leading
role in the Americas.

The diplomatic tension between the United States and
Argentina during World War II gave marked emphasis to
the rivalry between the two states for hemisphere leadership. In general, Latin America tended to follow the lead

of the United States, supported by Mexico and Brazil; and Argentine resistance against this trend relegated the southern republic to a position of increasing isolation.

When the European war began in 1939, the United States endeavored through its hemisphere defense program to strengthen the armed forces of the Latin-American states against the possibility of an Axis invasion of the American hemisphere. It is true that German Reichsmarshal Hermann Goering told an unsympathetic war crimes tribunal at Nuermberg in March of 1946 that Adolf Hitler had never at any time contemplated an invasion of the Western Hemisphere, but there were many who questioned this statement. Moreover, in 1939 and the years immediately following, the possibility of an Axis onslaught against the Americas was regarded on the western side of the Atlantic Ocean as a real and ever-present danger. The pattern of the United States' hemisphere defense program, like the Good Neighbor policy before it, was resisted by Argentina. Not only was that state displaced as a diplomatic leader in the Americas, but now its military hegemony was likewise challenged. Washington's program, involving, among other things, military assistance to Brazil, operated to oust Argentina from her traditional position as the major armed power in South America. Buenos Aires' resistance to the hemisphere defense program was partially motivated by a desire to preserve Argentina's historic role as South American leader.

Argentina joined in the inter-American declaration of neutrality which emerged from the First Meeting of American Foreign Ministers at Panama in 1939, but hemisphere conferees experienced greater difficulty at the Second Meeting of American Foreign Ministers at Havana, Cuba, a year later when they attempted to secure Argentine cooperation in anti-Axis measures. Buenos Aires' delegates reluctantly joined in the Act of Havana, pledging all American governments to joint administration of British, French, and Dutch New World possessions should the Axis endeavor to seize them; and more reluctantly Argentina agreed to participate in an inter-American program for the suppression of Axis fifth-column activities.

At the Third Meeting of American Foreign Ministers at Rio de Janeiro, Brazil, in January of 1942—held shortly after the Japanese attack at Pearl Harbor brought the United States into World War II—frequent crises resulted from the position taken by the Argentine delegation, led by Foreign Minister Enrique Ruiz-Guiñazú. He at length agreed to sign an emasculated Final Act, and the "Argentine Question" found its way into hemisphere headlines with increased regularity in the months following the Rio conference. At Buenos Aires the problem was clear enough: the hemisphere defense program of the United States was reversing, inverting, the power picture in South America, and Argentine military and diplomatic officials desperately sought a formula whereby their nation's traditional role in South America could be saved.

When the Perón revolution of 1943 occurred in Argentina,* the rest of the hemisphere was alarmed as the new rulers at Buenos Aires expanded their co-operation with the Axis and developed a pattern of government disconcertingly similar to the regimes then presided over by Adolf Hitler in Germany and Benito Mussolini in Italy. In the months after June of 1943, the Americas learned of Argentine-Nazi negotiations for German military assistance to Buenos Aires and of Argentine-inspired efforts to overthrow the governments of Bolivia, Brazil, Chile, Paraguay, Uruguay, and other neighboring republics. Reports of political and social collaboration between Argentina and Nazi

* See pp. 45 ff.

Germany startled the Western Hemisphere. Buenos Aires failed to repatriate Nazi agents engaged in espionage, protected and even assisted pro-Axis newspapers, and allowed Nazi schools and organizations to continue operating in Argentina. Pointing to police terrorism and repression in Argentina, government control of organized labor and the nation's educational system, censorship of the press, and a huge Argentine armament program, the governments of the United States and many other American republics seemed convinced that Argentina had entered into a partnership with Axis interests in support of totalitarian practices.

Despite the fact that the Argentine government severed diplomatic relations with Germany and Japan on January 26, 1944, dictatorship and collaboration with the Axis persisted at Buenos Aires. The conviction grew in the United States and other American nations that nothing short of a new conference of foreign ministers could cope with the "Argentine Question." In October of 1944, Mexico's Foreign Minister Ezequiel Padilla, supported in his action by the United States, branded the Argentine government as "fascist" and called for a hemisphere conference to deal with the situation. "We are applying economic sanctions against Argentina now," Padilla revealed, "isolating her from the rest of the world."[6]

But Argentine diplomacy was not to be outmaneuvered. On October 27, 1944, the government at Buenos Aires addressed to the Pan-American Union a request that a conference be called to consider the "Argentine Question." During November the situation appeared to be hopelessly confused. Those who had advocated a conference before Argentina joined in the request now opposed it; and those who had been lukewarm in the matter before the Argentine move were now utterly divided. In the midst of the confusion, Cordell Hull resigned as the United States Secretary of State.*

Hull's successor, Edward Riley Stettinius, proceeded to reorganize the State Department, and on December 4, 1944, Nelson Aldrich Rockefeller, until then Washington's Co-ordinator of Inter-American Affairs, was named Assistant Secretary of State for Latin-American Affairs. As the Stettinius-Rockefeller "team" viewed the conference problem, what was involved was not one conference, but rather *two:* the one desired by the United States and by Mexico, and the other requested by Argentina. Thus enlightened, the Governing Board of the Pan-American Union announced on January 8, 1945, its decision to postpone action on the Argentine request. Simultaneously, the United States Department of State revealed that an inter-American conference, to which Argentina would not be invited, would be held in mid-February to consider—*not* the Argentine matter—general postwar problems. And on January 11 the Mexican Foreign Office, with Washington's approval, invited all American republics except Argentina to attend an Inter-American Conference on Problems of War and Peace. The agenda was to be devoted to ways and means of intensifying the Americas' war efforts, and to consideration of postwar problems. The conference was to convene on February 21 and adjourn on March 8. If any time remained between the exhaustion of the agenda and the latter date, the delegates would discuss the Argentine problem informally.

According to Secretary of State Stettinius, the Inter-American Conference on Problems of War and Peace—popularly called the "Chapultepec conference"—achieved

---

* Secretary Hull's resignation on November 27, 1944, was motivated by considerations essentially unrelated to the Argentine problem.

six major objectives. These were: (1) agreement to stamp out the last vestiges of Axis influence in the Americas; (2) inter-American indorsement of the Dumbarton Oaks plan as the basis for the Charter of the United Nations, to be framed later at San Francisco, California; (3) the "Act of Chapultepec," a temporary war-time instrument designed to stifle aggression within the Western Hemisphere; (4) reorganization and strengthening of the inter-American system; (5) a series of economic agreements to raise standards of living in the hemisphere; and (6) the "formulation of a united policy toward Argentina."[7]

The "united policy toward Argentina" was said to be contained in Resolution LIX of Chapultepec's Final Act, which declared:

> The conference hopes that the Argentine nation will co-operate with the other American nations and identify itself with the common policy pursued by the latter, guiding its own policy until it achieves its incorporation among the United Nations as a signatory of the joint declaration drawn up by them. . . . [All the resolutions of the conference] are open to adhesion by the Argentine nation, provided always that it be in accord with the criterion of this resolution.[8]

Stripped of its diplomatic jargon, Resolution LIX meant that the United States and other American republics offered the Argentine government a two-point formula for solving the "Argentine Question." The first point involved Argentina's adherence to all of the decisions made at the Chapultepec conference. If the Argentine government were to take that step, then the second point would call for support, by the United States and the other hemisphere republics, of Argentine admission to the United Nations Conference on International Organization to meet later at San Francisco. The Argentine government expressed its willingness to accept this solution.

The first point was relatively simple. Argentina declared

war against Germany and Japan on March 27, 1945, forty-two days before the shooting war ended in Europe and five months before the Japanese capitulation. The Governing Board of the Pan-American Union agreed on March 31 that Argentina was now eligible to sign the Final Act of the Chapultepec conference. This signature took place at the Mexican capital on April 4, amid fitting ceremonies.

The second point was more difficult. Admission to the United Nations Conference on International Organization, which opened at San Francisco on April 25, 1945, was contingent upon invitation by the four powers sponsoring the conference. These were the United States, the United Kingdom, China, and the Soviet Union. Under Chapultepec's Resolution LIX, the United States was already committed to endorse Argentine admission; and British and Chinese acceptance of Argentina was readily obtained.

However, some difficulty—to put it mildly—was involved in securing Soviet acquiescence in admitting the new member to the United Nations. Foreign Commissar Vyacheslav M. Molotov, heading Moscow's delegation, observed when the parley opened that the Argentine case was "a new question to me;"[9] and Padilla of Mexico and Chile's Guillermo del Pedregal undertook to educate Molotov on the subject. The Soviets had expected to encounter strong Latin-American opposition to Moscow's desire that independent admission to the United Nations be accorded to the White Russian and Ukrainian Socialist Soviet Republics, but Molotov was informed that Chile's Foreign Minister Joaquín Fernández y Fernández and other Latin-American delegates, believing that Argentina was eligible for admission to the conference, would be pleased to support the seating of White Russian and Ukrainian representatives. And Padilla, Fernández, and Brazilian Foreign Minister Pedro Leão Velloso assured Molotov that Argentina was progressing satisfactorily toward fulfilment of her Chapultepec obligations.

On April 28 the *Polish* and Argentine issues were linked when Molotov told the parley's steering committee that he would consent to Argentina's admission to the United Nations if the Poles' Lublin government were likewise accepted—that is, if the United States and the United Kingdom would abandon the rival Polish group which had maintained a government-in-exile at London throughout the war. Stettinius, Britain's Sir Anthony Eden, and China's T. V. Soong met in executive session with Molotov, who was quoted as telling them: "You can have Argentina if we get Poland."[10] At length, the way was cleared on April 30, 1945, for the admission of Argentina and the Lublin Poles to the international organization.

Argentina had become a member of the United Nations.

Although United States–Argentine rivalry for leadership in the Western Hemisphere persists as a basic fact in inter-American relations, it is nevertheless true that the celebrated "Argentine Question" which crashed to a close at San Francisco in 1945 was primarily a war-time problem. While the heat of World War II and Argentine collaboration with the Axis was fresh, the United States Department of State declared that the "Argentine Government and many of its high officials were so seriously compromised in their relations with the enemy that trust and confidence could not be reposed in that Government."[11] However, Argentine–United States relations have since become more cordial, and the time has come for a new and less passionate evaluation of affairs in the country which caused the Americas such deep concern during World War II.

2.

Until Perón

Today it is not difficult to find Argentines who maintain that General Juan Domingo Perón presides over a bitterly divided nation. This is, no doubt, true. But it is also true that this division was not invented by Perón, and that acrimonious strife among the people of Argentina has been a constant factor in the history of the country.

Two Argentinas

Argentine politics is essentially dualistic. Two Argentinas have long existed side by side in a relationship lacking in cordiality. One of these Argentinas is Buenos Aires, the capital city; the other is the "interior" of the country, frequently referred to as "the provinces." Juan Bautista Alberdi, a celebrated Argentine statesman of the nineteenth century, observed with dismay that "they are not two parties, they are two countries; . . . they are Buenos Aires and the provinces."[1] And the remarkable Domingo Faustino Sarmiento noted that, upon traveling westward from Buenos Aires, "everything changes in aspect: the man of the field wears other clothes; . . . his ways of living are different; his needs peculiar to him; two separate societies appear, two peoples foreign to each other."[2]

This basic and tragic schism in Argentine national life

underlies much of what has been called the "Argentine riddle." The hostility between Buenos Aires and the "interior" is mutual and starts afresh every day. Buenos Aires, sophisticated and oriented toward Europe, regards itself as "civilized" and looks with disdain upon "the provinces"; for their part, the folk of the "interior" have little love for the *porteños*, as the residents of Buenos Aires are called. A recent student of Argentine problems has summed up "the *porteño* mentality" as "the inner conviction that Argentina exists for Buenos Aires, and that all outside the limits of Buenos Aires is outside the limits of civilization."[3] And the people of "the provinces" have their own view: they "are imbued with localism and firmly believe that the world ends at their boundary. Go to Buenos Aires? Just for a few days, long enough to have a good time. See Europe? A magnificent idea, but it is so far, so expensive, and after all, one can find out all about it from books. Visit other Spanish-American countries? Too typical, too native, too poor. Go to the United States? Why? What could one learn there? . . . What did they teach you in those universities with steam heat?"[4] The folk of Buenos Aires themselves feel that they are traveling in a foreign country when they visit "the provinces:" a recent Argentine President, General Pedro P. Ramírez, declared upon escaping from the *porteño* capital to the "interior" that he was "glad to be among the real workers, unaffected by the exotic ideas which contaminate the life of the city."[5]

The historical roots of this division run as far back as the first decades of the Spanish exploration and conquest of the area that was to become Argentina. Two separate and distinct streams of conquest and colonization explored and settled the region; and in some ways these two streams represented basically different civilizations. One of them, coming directly from Europe, settled Buenos Aires and its environs; the other, based on Peru, entered Argentina from the northwest and bore a culture and civilization at least as Peruvian as European.

Bloody Precedent

The two Argentinas were only superficially united when the Spanish Emperor Charles III signed, on August 8, 1776, the royal decree creating the Viceroyalty of the Plata River. This entity, which embraced not only what later became Argentina but also the future republics of Paraguay and Uruguay, together with a portion of the later Bolivian state, endeavored to join the two Argentinas, but succeeded only in housing rival spirits. At Buenos Aires the *porteño* liberals absorbed the atmosphere of the French Revolution and were stimulated by the new republican ideas. In the "interior," the *provinciano* civilization, based at Córdoba, Tucumán, and Mendoza, knew little of the French Revolution and rejected as much of it as made its way to "the provinces." General José María Paz wrote from his *cordobés* stronghold that "violently agitated elements of dissolution and anarchy are preparing for a conflagration which will not be slow in coming."[6] The prediction was substantially correct: the French Revolution touched off a violent battle between the two Argentinas, and this tragic struggle set the stage for the coming of Perón.

Napoleon Bonaparte undoubtedly played a greater part in the Argentine conflict than he realized or cared. During the course of the Napoleonic Wars, French and Spanish sea power was weakened by the British Navy at the decisive Battle of Trafalgar in 1805. The British then proceeded to attack the Spanish overseas empire, and twice invaded the Viceroyalty of the Plata River, occupying Buenos Aires in 1806 and again in 1807. The enraged *porteños* amazed the British and even themselves when, under the leadership of

Santiago de Liniers y Bremond and of Juan Martín de Pueyrredón, Buenos Aires rose to expel the invaders in an action known to the Argentines as the *Reconquista*, or the Reconquest. The affair, epic in the life of Buenos Aires but of little concern to the indifferent "interior," shocked the *porteños* into a sudden realization of their own strength and of the weakness of Spain. When Napoleon's forces overran Spain in 1808 and drove the Emperor Charles IV from his throne, the time had come for the liberation of Buenos Aires from colonial status. The *Reconquista* proved to be a dress rehearsal for the achievement of Argentine national independence.

Buenos Aires proclaimed its political independence of Spain on May 25, 1810. This celebrated "May Revolution," like the *Reconquista* before it, was the work of the *porteños* alone; the "interior" played no part in it. Moreover, other sectors of the old Viceroyalty of the Plata River moved rapidly to dissociate themselves from the "May Revolution." Asunción announced in July, 1810, that it was not involved in the movement, laying the basis for the eventual establishment of the separate republic of Paraguay; and Montevideo, controlled by 1811 by General José Artigas, likewise went its own way, becoming the nucleus for the later Uruguayan state. Thus Buenos Aires stood alone in revolution, and regarded the conquest of the "interior," the second Argentina, as a pressing necessity following the "May Revolution." The "interior," oriented to Peru and, with it, loyal to Spain, was not yet convinced that its lot lay with the *porteños*.

Military action was necessary to free the "interior" from Spanish Royalist forces, and General Manuel Belgrano led the troops charged with tying the second Argentina to Buenos Aires. Meeting with initial successes, Belgrano advanced as far into the "interior" as Tucumán, where he defeated the Royalists in September of 1812. A military stalemate followed, with the revolutionary forces unable to progress from Tucumán until January of 1814, when Belgrano was relieved by the redoubtable General José de San Martín, today Argentina's major national hero. Under San Martín's leadership, the "interior" at length joined the revolution and issued its own declaration of independence at Túcumán on July 9, 1816. Thus each of the Argentinas has its own independence date: May 25, 1810, for Buenos Aires, and July 9, 1816, for "the provinces." The Royalist forces were at length overcome in both Argentinas by the end of 1817, when San Martín, bent on "Americanizing" the revolution, crossed the Andes to participate in the liberation of Chile, Peru, and Ecuador.

Though the revolution had given the Argentines a new name, the old division between the two Argentinas persisted. Each saw the revolution in a different light. To Buenos Aires it was essentially a liberal movement imbued with the spirit and much of the doctrine of the French Revolution. The *porteños*' desire for order and to dominate the "interior" led them to demand a centralized form of government for the new-born Argentine republic, in opposition to insistence by "the provinces" that the infant nation be organized along confederate or decentralized lines. This issue divided the two Argentinas sharply: the folk of Buenos Aires became the nucleus of the Unitary party, seeking centralized government for all of Argentina under *porteño* hegemony; whereas the *provincianos* of the "interior" spearheaded the so-called Federal party, demanding a decentralized arrangement providing for considerable regional and provincial autonomy. The Unitaries of Buenos Aires called for a centralized constitution under which representative government would prevail. "Any constitution which does not bear the stamp of the general will is arbitrary," Bernardo Monteagudo declared as early as 1812; "no reason, no pretext, no circumstance can justify it. The people are free and they never err if they are not corrupted or intimidated."[7] Bernardino Rivadavia became the leader of the Unitary party and later (1826–27) Argentina's first president. Determined to give the country centralized, representative government, he symbolized the "May Revolution" for many *porteños*.

But the Federals of the "interior" rejected Rivadavia. The "provinces," their leadership based at Córdoba, Tucumán, and Mendoza, "had to fight against Buenos Aires as much as against Spain for their emancipation."[8] Deaf to the French Revolution and other events in Europe which had profoundly influenced Buenos Aires, the "interior" remained dominated by a colonial spirit still likewise cultivated in Peru; and the conservatism of the *provincianos*, characterized by a pious Catholicism and strong localistic regionalism, underlay the Federal party of "the provinces." The separatist nature of the politics of the "interior" combined with a species of feudalism to give the second Argentina its peculiar character. Regional landowners, strongly reminiscent of feudal lords, assumed political control of their provinces and were dubbed *caudillos*. Many of them acquiring dictatorial powers, these regional barons of the "interior" were, on the whole, physically courageous, cruel —"it was a savage age"[9]—and politically independent. In a sense the *caudillismo* of the Argentine "interior" was but the political expression of an essentially feudal economic system; and the *caudillos*, the provincial warlords, became the leaders of the Federal party, symbolizing the "interior's" struggle against the Argentina of Buenos Aires and the Unitary party. Few were misled into thinking that the difference between the Federals and the Unitaries was merely the difference between two views on how constitutional authority should be distributed in the form of the new government. The difference between the Federals and the Unitaries was the entire difference between the two Argentinas; it was, as Sarmiento said, the difference between barbarism and civilization. "This great faction of the republic which formed the Federal party does not fight only for a form of government, but also for other interests and other sentiments," Córdoba's General Paz wrote. "First, it is the fight of the more enlightened against the ignorant. In the second place, the men of the fields are opposed to those of the cities. In the third place, the lower classes wish to overpower the upper classes. Fourth, the provinces, jealous of the predominance of the capital, wish to level it. In the fifth place, democratic tendencies are aligned against the aristocratic and even monarchical. . . ."[10]

The pampa acquired a unique significance in the provinces' chaotic struggle against Buenos Aires. The broad, limitless, and almost treeless plain produced a peculiarly Argentine social type, the *gaucho*, who, identified with the "interior" against Buenos Aires, served effectively as cavalryman in the provincial armies. The Argentine *gaucho*, frequently compared to the "North American" cowboy, was the peculiar product of social conditions on the pampa. Essentially a nomad, the *gaucho* roamed the immense plains, his character formed by the frequently oppressive and deadening isolation of the pampa. Today the *gaucho* has become legend in Argentina, and his story has been immortalized in José Hernández' classic, *El Gaucho Martín Fierro*. The halo with which legend has crowned the *gaucho* as a hero of romance has led many to forget that those who knew him were convinced that he had "done little for civilization,"[11] and that "an inclination to maltreat animals, . . . a dislike for any work that cannot be done on horseback, playing cards, drunkenness, and thievery"[12] were among his primary vices. The *gaucho's* "great characteristic is his lack of necessities," a foreign visitor remarked years ago. "He is accustomed to living in the free air and sleeping on the ground. . . . He does not believe that money has much value: in effect, he is contented with his lot. . . . One cannot avoid feeling that there is as much philosophy as ignorance in the *gaucho's* determination to live without necessities."[13] This observer likewise noticed that "the habits of the women are very curious. Literally, they have nothing to do; the great plains which surround them give them no reason to travel, rarely do they ride horses, and their lives are certainly very indolent and inactive. All of them have children, whether or not they are married; and when I asked a very pretty young girl who her baby's father was, she replied: '*¿Quien sabe?*' "[14]

Inseparable from his horse, the *gaucho* was the centaur of the interprovincial wars. As a fighting man he was formidable, and *gaucho* armies ranged the pampa in the turbulent years of the second quarter of the nineteenth century. To such conventional weapons as firearms and knives the *gaucho* added the lasso and the *boleadoras*, the latter a group of two or three leather-covered stones tied together with thongs. This weapon, whirled rapidly over the head and shot at an enemy, had lethal effect within a range of twenty-five to thirty feet. The *gaucho* cavalryman was singularly effective in the provincial armies of the "interior" and blindly loyal to the *caudillo*, or warlord, of his province. The *caudillos*, provincial dictators, dominated an epoch in the life of the "interior," and many of them acquired key places in the history of Argentina. The most celebrated of the *caudillos* was General Juan Manuel de Rosas of the Province of Buenos Aires. Also notable were General Juan Facundo Quiroga of La Rioja, the *cordobés* General José María Paz, Santa Fé's Estanislao López, and

General Bernabé Aráoz of Tucumán. In desultory fashion they rose against the first Argentina, the Europeanized city of Buenos Aires of Rivadavia and the Unitary party.

The Argentinas descended into anarchy when Rivadavia promulgated in 1819 a unitary constitution which would have suppressed provincial autonomy. The *caudillos* of the "interior" rebelled against this move of the *porteños'* Argentina, and the nation embarked upon a generation of tragic civil war and anarchy. The chaos gave eventual form to the original fourteen provinces of the "interior." Corrientes and Entre Ríos had been formed in 1814, and La Rioja a year later; a separatist "Republic of Tucumán" was proclaimed in 1820, and Santiago del Estero hastily seceded from this so-called republic. San Luis emerged in 1820, as did the Andean Province of San Juan, the first in all of Argentina to proclaim religious freedom. And, in 1821, the Province of Catamarca bolted from the "Republic of Tucumán" to go its own way. During the anarchy of the 1820's the relations among the provinces were, in effect, international relations. Treaties of trade and mutual assistance were entered into by the provinces; and the major treaties created regional blocs in linking strategically situated provinces.

General Juan Manuel de Rosas rose from the chaos to dominate Argentina and become its first dictator. "Bloody Rosas" ruled the nation from 1835 to 1852, and his regime represented a victory of the second Argentina, the Federals of the "interior," over the Unitaries of Buenos Aires. The most aristocratic of the *caudillos*, Rosas was born on March 30, 1793, the son of an *estanciero*, the owner of a large landed estate. Rosas had little schooling—he was thirteen years old when his school was closed down—and he fought for the Province of Buenos Aires in the interprovincial wars of the anarchic 1820's. He turned against Bernardino Rivadavia and the Unitaries in 1826 and 1827,

when Rivadavia endeavored to "federalize" the city of
Buenos Aires, that is, separate it from the province of the
same name. Rosas regarded Rivadavia's move as destructive
of the Province of Buenos Aires, and joined the Federals of
the "interior" in a death struggle against the Unitaries of
the city of Buenos Aires. On December 8, 1829, Rosas was
named Governor of the Province of Buenos Aires, a post
which he held for three years. In 1833 he stepped down
from the governorship to lead a military campaign in the
south against the Indians. During his absence, political chaos
engulfed the Province of Buenos Aires; and upon his return in 1835, Rosas was welcomed as a savior, as the "Restorer of the Laws." Resuming the governorship on
March 7, 1835, he remained in power until February of
1852, and his celebrated dictatorship remained unequalled
in Argentine annals until the coming of Perón in 1943.

Juan Manuel de Rosas was loved by the *gauchos* of the
"interior," with whom he was closely associated, and these
plainsmen followed him unquestioningly. Their armies were
a major sector of his strength, and the *gauchos* worshipped
him. Indeed, it was said that Rosas was more of a *gaucho*
than the *gauchos:* he could throw the *boleadoras* and break
horses, and his physical courage inspired awe and respect
among his hardy followers. Rosas was the "interior," the
second Argentina, personified. "His government was a return to the old order which had existed in colonial society,
and the defeat of all the principles and ideas which had inspired the revolution," José Ingenieros has said. "Rosas
was, above all, a restorer of the old system against the new
one advanced by the 'May Revolution.' "[15] Although he was
himself a landowner, he knew and understood the lower
classes of the "interior," and he captured their imaginations.
"I . . . have always had my own system," Rosas once confided to a friend. "I know and respect the talents of many

of the men who have governed the country; . . . but it seems to me that all committed a great error; they governed very well for the cultured people but scorned the lower classes, the people of the fields, who were the men of action. . . . They did nothing against the rich and the upperclass: I believe that it is important to establish a major influence over this class to contain it and direct it, and I propose to acquire this influence at any cost; for this I will work constantly, with many sacrifices. I will be a *gaucho* among the *gauchos,* I will talk as they do; to protect them I will be their attorney, I will care for their interests."[16] Such words were not again spoken by an Argentine ruler until 1943.

The dictatorship of "Bloody Rosas" was the dictatorship of the "interior" over Buenos Aires. Declaring himself a Federal bitterly opposed to the Unitaries, Rosas prevented the writing of a constitution. He imprisoned, exiled, and executed his political enemies, many of whom suffered cruelly at the hands of the *Mazorca,* Rosas' combined secret police and terroristic private army. Newspapers and books were censored during his regime: "The forty-three newspapers of 1833 were reduced to fifteen in 1834 and were only three in 1835. Why would Rosas want newspapers?"[17] The Church was closely allied with Rosas' terroristic dictatorship, which represented an intellectual reaction in Argentina. "The tyrannical system and every crime inspired by Rosas merit the condemnation of history," Ricardo Levene, Argentina's leading historian, has said. "Under his system of government there were no guarantees for personal liberty or life," and during his rule the nation experienced "continuous revolutions, violent government crises, the change of political parties from principles to personal parties, and the disintegration and agitation of the society of his time by phenomena of moral and political dissolution."[18]

Opposition to Rosas, bitter among the *porteños*, grew as his regime progressed. Foreign interests, particularly British and French, intrigued against the dictator, although the political opposition was centered in two political parties headquartered at the city of Buenos Aires. These were, first, the old Unitary party, composed of Rivadavia's political heirs, and, second, a group known as the "May Association," led by the poet Esteban Echeverría, who became a precursor of Argentina's Socialist party. "The tyrants have sown dissension and erected their iniquitous thrones on the debris of anarchy," Echeverría wrote. "For us there is neither law, nor rights, nor country, nor freedom. . . . Our heritage is obscurity, humiliation, servitude."[19] But civilian organizations could do little against Rosas. Military action was necessary to destroy the dictatorship, and it was by military action that Rosas was at length overthrown. General Justo José de Urquiza of the Province of Entre Ríos defeated Rosas in the historic Battle of Caseros on February 3, 1852, and the long and bloody dictatorship ended.

The "interior," the second Argentina, had had its day. With the passing of Rosas, the Argentine nation stood at the brink of a new era.

Constitutional Government

The long nightmare of the Rosas regime ended, the Argentina of Buenos Aires raised its head. The followers of Urquiza, in power after 1852, regarded themselves as liberals, as the inheritors of the political tradition of the *porteños'* "May Revolution." Though they stood triumphant over the Federals of the "interior," the *urquistas* realistically recognized that Argentina's salvation lay in compromise between the two Argentinas. The nation's Constitution of 1853 was written in this spirit of compromise; and with this document the country experienced a measure of stable and prosperous constitutional government which endured until 1930.

Under Urquiza's leadership, the provinces were invited to send delegates to a congress which convened at Santa Fé in November of 1852 to write the constitution which was promulgated on May 1 of the following year as the fundamental law of the land. The writers of the Constitution of 1853 were profoundly influenced by the constitutional system of the United States, and copies of *The Federalist* and other "North American" documents were much in evidence at the Congress of Santa Fé. Since 1853, Argentine and United States constitutional usages have been strikingly similar; and the explanation of this lies in large part in the fact that the constitution-writers at Santa Fé in 1852–53 consciously copied much of the work of those who had convened at Philadelphia in 1787. Perhaps no Argentine exercised a greater influence in shaping the Constitution of 1853 than did Juan Bautista Alberdi, a professed admirer of the Constitution of the United States. Alberdi had written prolifically—his collected works occupy no fewer than eighteen volumes—and his ideas shaped much Argentine constitutional thinking. "What is the best type of a constitution for a desert?" Alberdi asked. "The type which will make the desert disappear; the type which will cause it to cease to be a desert in the shortest possible time. . . . This must be the political goal of the Argentine constitution. . . ."[20]

No exhaustive discussion of the governmental structure established by the Constitution of 1853 will be undertaken here.* It is sufficient to note at this point that the constitution, closely following the model laid down by the "North

* The present writer feels justified in foregoing such a discussion because a detailed description of the structure of the Argentine government provided for by the Constitution of 1853 has already been published in English. See Austin F. Macdonald, *Government of the Argentine Republic* (New York, 1942).

American" system, provided for a separation of powers on the national level of government among three branches—legislative, executive, and judicial—similar to those existing in the United States. A further aping of the northern constitutional arrangement was evidenced by the creation in Argentina of a federal system apportioning governmental authority between the national government, on the one hand, and, on the other, the governments of the original fourteen provinces. This was the federalism of the United States rather than the decentralization demanded by the old Federal party of the Argentine "interior"; what the Federals had sought was a quasi-separatist decentralization more confederate than federal. Indeed, the *urquistas* of 1853 regarded the importation of "North American" federalism as the most important feature of the Constitution of 1853. This provided the vehicle of compromise between the two Argentinas; it was a method of blending the centralism of the Unitary party of Rivadavia and the *porteños* with the centrifugal separatist tendencies of the "interior." To the partisans of the Constitution of 1853, this new federalism was a formula for compromise, for the achievement of eventual peace between the two Argentinas.

Theoretically, the constitution remained Argentina's fundamental law until it was replaced by Perón in 1949; in fact, the nation experienced constitutional government under the document only until 1930. The period from 1853 until 1930 was, on the whole, auspicious for the progressive development of the Argentine nation; and the republic was favored, especially in the early portion of the period, by a succession of outstanding statesmen occupying the presidency. Chief among these in the first years of the constitution were General Justo José de Urquiza (1854–60), Bartolomé Mitre (1861–68), and Domingo Faustino Sarmiento (1868–74).

In the years after Sarmiento faded into history, Argentina was transformed slowly by broad social and economic changes. The large landed estates of the "interior" became less feudal and were devoted increasingly to stock-raising; the *caudillo* was transformed into the *estanciero*, or ranch-owner; and the *gaucho* faded from the Argentine scene to give way to the rural workers and the *colonos* (settlers or planters). European immigrants continued to flock to the country in large numbers, and the circulation of Argentine produce in the trade channels of the world gave the republic a place of significance in international commerce. The rivalry between the city of Buenos Aires and the "interior," though less chaotically acute than in the old days, continued to plague Argentines; and a major step toward meeting that problem was taken during the administration of President Nicolás Avellaneda (1874–80). In the last year of his presidency, the city of Buenos Aires was "federalized." This action removed the capital city from the jurisdiction of the Province of Buenos Aires. It was, in essence, what Rivadavia had endeavored to accomplish in the chaotic 1820's, but the Argentinas were not prepared to accept "federalization" as a solution until 1880. Again "North American" influence was much in evidence: the city of Buenos Aires acquired a constitutional status patterned after that of the capital city of the United States. As Washington was located not in any of the states but rather in the District of Columbia, subject to the immediate jurisdiction of the national government, so the city of Buenos Aires was placed in 1880 not in any of the provinces but rather in a newly created Federal Capital, under the immediate jurisdiction of the central government.

Although the years after 1853 were, on the whole, years of constitutional government and a measure of democracy, it was also true that during this period the national life continued to be dominated by the landowning class. Less privileged Argentines, though they possessed many civil and political liberties, remained essentially removed from the processes of government. Politics seemed to be the monopoly of a social class, the *estancieros;* and perhaps no more than two hundred families exercised the controlling voice within this class. Toward the end of the nineteenth century the landowners acquired the name of "Oligarchy," and the first attempts among the discontented to unseat this group became evident in the 1880's.

The protests of the Oligarchy's enemies resulted in two attempts to overthrow the government—in 1890 and again in 1893. Although both rebellions were stifled, they were followed by the resignations of the presidents against whose administrations they were directed—President Miguel Juárez Celman resigned in 1890 and Luis Sáenz Peña did the same in 1895. Social transformations—the emergence of a more articulate opposition to the landowning Oligarchy and the appearance of an industrial working class—could not be met, however, simply by the resignations of presidents. In the 1890's, two new political parties were formed to give articulate expression to opposition to the Oligarchy. One of these was the Radical Civic Union, popularly known as the UCR* or the Radical party, and the other was the Argentine Socialist party. Of the two, the Radicals were stronger, and carried on a spirited campaign against the governing group. The Radicals became more militant in their opposition as the twentieth century opened, but met with little success at the polls. Electoral fraud robbed the Radicals and the Socialists of many of their votes as the Oligarchy's determined struggle to retain power was reflected in a marked deterioration in the integrity of the electoral process.

Himself a representative of the Oligarchy, President

* Formed from the initial letters of *Unión Cívica Radical* (Radical Civic Union).

Roque Sáenz Peña (1910–13) came to the *Casa Rosada*, Argentina's White House, convinced that fraud in elections had become a national problem requiring immediate attention. Sáenz Peña directed his energies toward the framing of legislation which would give the country more fair and free elections. His efforts were successful: on February 13, 1912, Law No. 8,871—the celebrated "Sáenz Peña Law"— entered into force. This legislation rendered voting secret and obligatory and assured minority parties representation in Congress.[21] The law did much to terminate the previously existing electoral fraud; indeed, the election of 1916—the first presidential election held under the "Sáenz Peña Law" —has been called "the first and only honest election ever held on Argentine soil."[22] While this might be too strong a claim for the 1916 balloting, it is nevertheless true that that year's election did inaugurate a significant departure in the progress of Argentine government and politics.

The opposition Radical party won the election of 1916. Thanks largely to the operation of the "Sáenz Peña Law," the Radicals received 372,810 votes as against 351,099 cast for all other parties; and Radical presidents occupied the *Casa Rosada* from 1916 to 1930. The first of these was Hipólito Irigoyen,[23] who remains one of the most controversial figures in recent Argentine history. Beginning a six-year term in 1916, President Irigoyen became the storm center for political squabbles coalescing around three issues—his domestic policies, foreign affairs, and the president's leadership of the Radical party.

The election of 1916 had, in effect, ousted the Oligarchy from political power, and Irigoyen encouraged the rise of the nascent Argentine middle class to positions of respectability. His administration sponsored a number of mildly pro-labor measures, and organized labor came to be a political force of consequence during his presidency. Moreover, a tendency toward governmental centralization appeared during Irigoyen's time, and the government at Buenos Aires exercised greater control over the provinces than it had while the Oligarchy was in power. These economic and political trends signified social dislocations and were heatedly debated in Congress and in other Argentine forums.

President Irigoyen's foreign policy was also the subject of protracted controversy. World War I was two years old when he assumed office, and Irigoyen steered a course of careful neutrality. This policy became increasingly difficult after the United States entered the war in April of 1917; but Irigoyen insisted that "Argentina cannot be dragged into the war by the United States and the nation must take the place it deserves on the American continent."[24] Once the war was ended, Irigoyen, ably assisted by his foreign minister, Honorio Pueyrredón, maintained that Argentina must co-operate with the states of the world in the League of Nations; and Argentina entered the League on July 29, 1919. This policy—neutrality in war, and peacetime participation in international organization—was bitterly debated by Irigoyen's contemporaries. However, in later years some Argentines argued that Irigoyen's foreign policy had become in effect "traditional" Argentine policy. In the 1940's this line of reasoning was used to justify Buenos Aires' policy toward World War II and the United Nations.*

Irigoyen's position within his own political party was a constant source of intra-Radical strife. His opponents in the party believed that President Irigoyen was exercising excessive personal control over the party, and they protested what they called his *personalismo*. This conflict became so severe that a group of Irigoyen's rivals bolted the party to

* See pp. 10–16, and pp. 400–409.

form their own *antipersonalista* Radical organization in opposition to the regular Radical party, which remained loyal to the president. When Irigoyen's term expired in 1922, he was succeeded in the *Casa Rosada* by Marcelo T. de Alvear, the leader of the *antipersonalista* Radicals. President Alvear (1922–28) conducted an essentially uninspired administration, and Argentina was restive when he departed from the executive office.

The election of 1928 precipitated a major crisis in Argentine annals. Irigoyen, determined to resume the presidency, ran for re-election. Most Argentine political observers now agree that this was a tragic error. Irigoyen was successful in his bid for re-election, but he was seventy-six years old and "painfully and publicly senile"[25] when he began his second term as president of Argentina in October of 1928. His leadership was weak and almost nonexistent; the *Casa Rosada* was disastrously unable to cope with problems associated with the Great Depression of 1929; and it seemed that the government of the republic had already disappeared before the administration was overthrown by a military revolt on September 6, 1930. "The military uprising pushed doors which were already open," said a political leader of the time. "On September 6, there was no ruler in the *Casa Rosada* except the doorman, who gave the keys to the first people who presented themselves as occupants."[26] Constitutional government, auspiciously begun in 1853, came to a definitive end in Argentina on September 6, 1930.

Strange Interlude

The thirteen-year period which began on September 6, 1930, and ended on June 4, 1943, prepared the Argentine nation to receive Juan Domingo Perón. During this time the country had its first tastes of dictatorship since the days of Rosas, institutional decadence settled on the republic, and the country's foreign policy oriented the nation, during World War II, toward the Axis and fascism.

Though these developments were of major consequence, the Revolution of 1930, which set them in motion, seemed to be hardly a momentous affair. "My personal impression was that the so-called revolution consisted of a twelve-hour parade of cadets from the Military School," an eye-witness recorded. "With the exception of a bloody incident at the *Plaza de Mayo*,* where two cadets and a civilian lost their lives, the parade met with no resistance. The troops at the *Campo de Mayo* [garrison] did not move; the regiments stationed in the [Federal] Capital declared themselves neutral; and the police remained passive."[27] The uprising was led by General José F. Uriburu, who declared himself president of the republic; and for three months Argentines could only guess at the social content of the revolt.

The aims of the nation's new rulers at length became clear on December 14, 1930, when President Uriburu delivered what proved to be a sensational speech. He denounced the minimum wage law and other pro-labor measures enacted during the Irigoyen administrations and declared that the "Sáenz Peña Law" was a pernicious piece of legislation. Demanding changes in the constitution and in the electoral laws, Uriburu called for a system of corporate representation of economic groups similar to the arrangement then in force in the Italy of Benito Mussolini. Argentina's new president asserted that government should be conducted by an elite, by a selected minority within the country; and he proclaimed that the democratic system was evil. Uriburu's declarations electrified Argentines: "The speech fell like a bomb charged with conservative reaction and with fascism!"[28]

* This is the huge open square faced by the *Casa Rosada*, Argentina's White House.

36

It became clear in the months after December that the Revolution of 1930 was supported by the Oligarchy, the landed gentry out of power since 1916, and by a number of the major banks in Argentina. President Uriburu himself had long been associated with the Oligarchy. A patrician of sorts, "he preferred to deal with the people of his class or of his environment, whose merits he knew how to appreciate, but whom he perhaps over-estimated," one of Uriburu's close friends has said of him. "He was noticeably influenced by some ideas of a corporative tint which he took from more or less fascist publications. . . . I do not believe that he proposed to transplant these European regimes to our country, but the fact is that some of their institutions seduced him. . . ."[29] It is also a fact that Italian fascism and, later, German naziism became increasingly influential and active in Argentina in the years after the Revolution of 1930. A Committee on Anti-Argentine Activities, established by the congress at Buenos Aires, declared in its report for 1941: "Uriburu attempted to unite all the reactionary forces, give them a program, and throw them into action against the democratic groups that had survived. He inaugurated the Argentine Civic Legion, organized on the pattern of European Fascist organizations. . . . The oligarchic caste that came to power had the intention of transplanting certain attitudes of Mussolini and Hitler. To get these powers, it tried to annul the rights and dignity of the citizens. Lacking a program that would permit it to attract the sympathy of the people, it appealed to the 'Jewish peril' and to the 'red peril' in order to disguise its real ends."[30]

General Uriburu remained in the presidency for less than two years. Pressures exerted by his associates combined with a desire to acquire the appearances of constitutionalism for the regime, and a presidential election was held in 1932.

The "Sáenz Peña Law" was not observed in this balloting, and the election of 1932 was characterized by fraud and violence. General Agustín P. Justo, a species of "official candidate," emerged as president, and during his administration (1932–38) the Revolution of 1930 moved toward consolidation. Justo, who had been a pacifist and a Socialist during the Irigoyen period, was closely associated with Uriburu at the time of the election of 1932. However, Justo broke with Uriburu in the following years, and the latter—observing that his "life began with one revolution [1890] and ended with another"[31]—fell from power and prestige.

During the Uriburu and Justo regimes, Italian fascism and, later, German National Socialism enjoyed some vogue in Argentina. It has already been noted that Uriburu had been "seduced" by some aspects of fascism, and Justo was not unlike him in that respect. Fascism appealed to some of Argentina's disgruntled intellectuals, to the impoverished scions of *estancieros* who had suffered financially during Irigoyen's time, to members of the clergy, and to important sectors of the Argentine Army. Fascism combined curiously with such aspects of Argentine life as *rosismo* (a semi-romantic nostalgia for the "good old days" of Rosas), a sensitive interest in events in the Spanish mother-country, and long-standing suspicion and distrust of the United States and the United Kingdom. Benito Mussolini had, of course, ruled Italy since 1922; but during Justo's stewardship in the *Casa Rosada* Adolf Hitler came to power in Germany and Spain was rent by civil war. Many Argentines followed these European developments with sympathetic interest. By January of 1938, the foreign office at Rome could report to Italian diplomatic missions that, thanks largely to the regimes of Uriburu and Justo, Argentina was counted among the "seven Latin-American republics . . . moving decidedly toward stabilization in accordance with the Fascist principles of Signor Mussolini."[32] In the 1930's, a significant difference emerged between Italian and German influences in Argentina. Italian immigrants had long flocked to the country in large numbers, and Italy was regarded as a second mother-country.* The Italians were easily assimilated into the Argentine culture and *were* Argentines within a few years after arrival. The Germans, on the other hand, came to the country later and were not so numerous. Moreover, they did not assimilate readily: they remained German in culture and orientation.

Thus most Argentine anti-Fascists regarded German influence in their country as more dangerous than the Italian. Some of them remembered that, as long ago as 1882, Sarmiento himself had warned his countrymen of German imperial aims in South America. And some resurrected the notorious "Tannenberg Plan" of 1911, in which the following proposed Anglo-German agreement was framed at Berlin:

Art. 13. Germany and England come to an understanding regarding their spheres of influence in South America. Germany takes under her protection the republics of Argentina, Chile, Uruguay, and Paraguay, the southern third of Bolivia . . . and the southern part of Brazil; German culture reigns in all these regions. For her part, England occupies Peru, Ecuador, the northern part of Bolivia, and the rest of Brazil. . . .

Art. 14. Germany and England agree to maintain, in all circumstances, their South American decisions against the eventual protests of the United States. . . .

Art. 15. Germany and England offer to the United States of North America, in exchange for her consent, the protectorate over Mexico, Nicaragua, Costa Rica, Honduras, El Salvador, Haiti, Colombia, Venezuela and Santo Domingo. The German protectorate in South America embraces 6,500,000 square kilometers and 12,000,000 inhabitants. The English protectorate is considerably greater: 9,720,738 square kilometers with 24,186,000 inhabitants. The part offered to the United States is of 4,580,000 square kilometers and 20,000,000 inhabitants.[33]

* See p. 5.

The first German Nazis arrived in Argentina in 1934, and by 1937 were coming in appreciable numbers. Some of them acquired the respect and admiration of many Argentines. The "Germans never treated the Argentines as 'natives,' as the patronizing British did. Nor did they count the days until they could 'go back to God's own country' with a lot of money, as did so many Americans. They came to stay. They learned Spanish. They married Argentines."[34] But Hitler's Germany claimed the loyalty of the Germans in Argentina: Berlin clung to the *jus sanguinis* theory of citizenship, in accordance with which the nationality of the parents determined the citizenship of a child, regardless of where he was born. Thus the German government claimed in 1939 that some 1,300,000 German nationals resided in Argentina, although only 43,626 of them had been born in Germany and the overwhelming majority of them had long since been naturalized as Argentine citizens. "We are one people, we are united by destiny and we will never cease to be united," the *Deutsche La Plata Zeitung*, a pro-Nazi German-language newspaper at Buenos Aires, declared editorially. "We are brothers, though our birthplace be on the banks of the Rhine, the Volga, the Danube, or the Plata."[35]

On January 30, 1937, Adolf Hitler signed a decree placing a branch of the Nazi party, dealing with Germans residing overseas, under the jurisdiction of the foreign office at Berlin. In accordance with this measure, a unit of the party—the *Deutscher Volksbund für Argentinien*—was established in the German Embassy at Buenos Aires. Under the direction of Fritz Küster, an embassy official, this entity assumed control of Nazi organizations and activities in Argentina. By December of 1938, no fewer than 1,629 registered members of the German National Socialist party were enrolled in Argentina, and 131 Nazi organizations had been set up at Buenos Aires alone. At that time, 203 German schools were counted in the country. These possessed an estimated 15,000 students, of whom 74 per cent were Argentine citizens according to Argentine law, 11 per cent Germans, and the remaining 15 per cent nationals of other states.

The first public note of this situation was taken early in 1938, when the governors of two Argentine territories— Governor Vanazco of Misiones and Governor Pérez Virasoro of La Pampa—charged that Germans in their areas, spreading Nazi doctrine, were engaged in "anti-Argentine" activities. The governors' accusations went almost unnoticed. But on May 18, 1938, Argentines were electrified by a speech in the national Chamber of Deputies. Deputy Enrique Dickmann, a Socialist from the Federal Capital, made a sensational and copiously documented public exposé of Nazi activities in the country. His speech was so startling to the Chamber that the body suspended its rules —unusual in Argentine parliamentary practice—to permit Dickmann to speak for two and one-half hours. He named Nazi leaders in the country and presented a detailed list of their organizations and membership. This speech proved to be but one out of four delivered by Dickmann in 1938 and 1939 in an attempt to rouse Argentina to face the Nazi menace. "The evil of Nazi-Fascist infiltration has acquired extension and depth," he asserted; "its venom is so subtle and so penetrating that many people in our country have succumbed to it."[36] Dickmann was soon joined in his crusade by Deputy Raúl Damonte Taborda, a Radical from the Federal Capital. Together they urged the Chamber of Deputies to establish a committee on anti-Argentine activities, to be patterned in structure and function after the Committee on Un-American Activities, which had been created by the United States House of Representatives on

May 11, 1938. The Argentine Chamber of Deputies was at first reluctant to form such a committee; and it was not until 1940 that a Committee on Anti-Argentine Activities was at last created under the chairmanship of Damonte Taborda. The "Damonte Taborda Committee" did what it could to expose and stem the rising tide of Nazi influence in Argentina.

As has been noted, Presidents Uriburu and Justo did little to discourage this influence. It was not until President Roberto M. Ortiz succeeded Justo in 1938 that the *Casa Rosada* was occupied by a chief executive who regarded naziism and fascism as evils menacing Argentina. World War II began in Europe during Ortiz' presidency. He watched Hitler's onslaughts against France and the low countries and was convinced that the Axis was a menace to the security of his own country. President Ortiz asserted that he saw "the necessity of recovering the popular sovereignty";[37] and he moved to obstruct Axis influences in Argentina. However, the move was short-lived. Ortiz, ill with diabetes, was forced to resign on July 3, 1940, and he died shortly thereafter. "When President Ortiz died, many understood that our country was politically bogged down," a Socialist leader declared. "It could not rise . . . [without] a new force, a great movement. . . ."[38]

That new force did not appear. Once Ortiz was removed from the scene, the policies of the *Casa Rosada* reverted to the Uriburu-Justo pattern. Vice-President Ramón S. Castillo, who succeeded Ortiz, sympathized with the Axis cause in World War II, and was convinced that Hitler's Germany would emerge from it as victor. Naziism became more powerful in Castillo's Argentina, and many Germans and pro-Germans acquired distinguished positions in his administration. "We began to see 'Argentinism' . . . and even Hispanism monopolized by the most rare personages, many of them of extraordinary and exotic origin, and some of them with names unpronounceable in Spanish."[39] Although Castillo's pro-Axis leanings were undisguised, he pursued a policy of official neutrality—in the "Irigoyen tradition"—toward World War II. "Outside problems should not disturb us, simply because Argentina is not and could not be other than Argentina," President Castillo asserted. "Everything else is another question; another ideal; another interest."[40] The "North American" Waldo Frank believed that Castillo "is keen enough to know that a democratic world will throw his crowd into the discard. On the other hand, Hitler's New Order might repay Argentina's neutrality by letting things stand as they are."[41]

Essentially, constitutional government had ceased to be a part of the Argentine system in 1930; Duncan Aikman once described the Argentina of the post-1930 period as "a modified democracy, flavored with a Chinaman's chance for overwhelming opposition majorities."[42] But even that chance disappeared during the Castillo administration. When the Japanese attack at Pearl Harbor brought the United States into World War II on December 7, 1941, the Western Hemisphere was plunged into crisis, and the governments of many American republics hastened to enforce emergency measures. In the midst of the excitement, President Castillo proclaimed a state of siege in Argentina on December 16, 1941. This step, not violating the letter of the Constitution of 1853, had the effect of dissolving the Congress and suspending what was left of constitutional guarantees in the country. Argentina has been ruled by dictatorship since December of 1941. During Castillo's state of siege, criticism of the regime was suppressed, and the pro-Axis orientation of the government became more dramatically open. Ray Josephs, a "North American" journalist stationed at Buenos Aires, described scenes typical of Castillo's Argentina: "For three hours this afternoon [May 1, 1943] I stood on the sidewalk in Calle Santa Fé. . . . Down Santa Fé marched 10,000 anti-United States, anti-democracy, pro-Nazi nationalists. They swaggered from Calle Pueyrredón down to Plaza San Martín, frantically shouting: 'Death to the British pigs! Death to the Jews! Neutrality and Castillo!' "[43]

Although no attempt has yet been made to test Argentine public opinion scientifically, most observers in the country during the Castillo period felt that the government was unpopular with the majority of the people. Josephs reported "plenty of grumbling in the cafés, in clubs and elsewhere" and was convinced that Castillo "would never have won any Gallup polls";[44] and another trained observer believed that "if the Castillo government had determined to make itself unpopular, it could not have gone about this more directly."[45] By the middle of 1943, the cycle of institutional decadence begun in 1930 had run a significant sector of its course. Many Argentines were convinced, for different reasons, that the time had come for a dramatic change.

And among them was an enterprising Argentine Army officer, Colonel Juan Domingo Perón.

II.

A Book of All That Glitters

"I can tell you now that the country is organized."
JUAN DOMINGO PERÓN

3.

Southern Colonel

"Urquiza, Awake! Rosas Is in Buenos Aires!"[1]

On June 4, 1943, the government of President Ramón S. Castillo "fell like a putrid fruit"[2] during the course of an uprising conducted by a sector of the Argentine Army. Some insight into what the insurrectionists had in mind may be obtained from the following manifesto distributed among the military men occupying key positions in the rebellion:

COMRADES:

The war has fully demonstrated that the nations are not able now to defend themselves alone. Hence the uncertain play of the alliances that lessen, but do not amend, the grave evil. The era of the NATION is slowly being substituted by the era of the CONTINENT. Yesterday the feudals united to form the nation. Today the nations join to form the CONTINENT. That will be the end achieved by this war.

Germany is making a titanic effort to unite the European continent. The strongest and best-equipped nation should control the destinies of the continent in its new formation. In Europe it will be Germany.

In America, in the north, the controller will be, for a time, the United States of North America. But in the south there is no nation sufficiently strong to accept this guardianship without discussion. There are only two nations that could do so: ARGENTINA and BRAZIL.

OUR AIM IS TO MAKE POSSIBLE AND UNQUESTIONABLE OUR POSITION AS GUARDIANS.

The work is hard and full of sacrifices. But we cannot make our country great without sacrificing everything. The great men of our independence sacrificed wealth and life. In our time Germany has given life a heroic meaning. All this should be an example to us.

The first step to be taken, which shall lead us toward a strong and powerful Argentina, is to get the reins of Government into our hands. A civilian will never understand the greatness of our ideal, we shall therefore have to eliminate them from the Government, and give them the only mission which corresponds to them: WORK and OBEDIENCE.

Once we have obtained power, our aim will be to be STRONG: STRONGER THAN ALL THE OTHER NATIONS UNITED. We shall have to arm, and continue to arm, fighting and overcoming difficulties, both internal and external. Hitler's fight in peace and war shall be our guide. The alliances shall be the first step. We already have Paraguay, and we shall have Bolivia and Chile. With Argentina, Paraguay, Bolivia, and Chile, we shall have no difficulty in bringing in Brazil, owing to the form of its government and the large nucleus of Germans. With Brazil on our side, the South American continent will be ours. Our guardianship will be a fact, a glorious fact, without precedent, realized by the political genius and the heroism of the ARGENTINE ARMY.

Mirages! Ideals! you will say. Nevertheless let us look again at Germany. Beaten in 1919 she was obliged to sign the Versailles Treaty, which was to keep her under Allied domination as a second-class state for at least fifty years. In less than twenty years she has had a fantastic career. By 1939 she was armed as no other nation, and in peace time she annexed Austria and Czechoslovakia. Then, in war she imposed her will on the entire continent of Europe. But it was not accomplished without a hard struggle. Strong dictatorship was necessary to make the people realize the sacrifices necessary to accomplish this great program. SO IT WILL BE IN ARGENTINA.

Our Government shall be a firm dictatorship, although at the beginning, in order to become firmly established, it will concede the necessary allowances. We shall attract the public, but eventually the people will have to work, make sacrifices, and obey. Work more and sacrifice more than any other country. Only thus will it be possible to carry out the armament program, indispensible for the domination of the continent. With Germany's example, the right spirit will be instilled into the people through the RADIO, by the CONTROLLED PRESS, by LITERATURE, by the CHURCH, and by EDUCATION, and so they will venture upon the heroic road they will be made to travel. Only in this way will they forego the easy life they now enjoy. Our generation will be a generation sacrificed on the altar of a high ideal. ARGENTINE PATRIOTISM will shine like a brilliant star for the good of the continent and of the whole of humanity.

¡VIVA LA PATRIA!³

In the first weeks after the uprising of June 4, 1943, the Argentine political scene appeared to be chaotic and uncertain. However, two central facts soon emerged—a military dictatorship had seized control of the government, and Argentine policy toward World War II, which was then in progress, was more openly pro-Axis than Castillo's policy had been. After the 1943 uprising, the Argentine presidency was occupied by four army officers: General Arturo Rawson, General Pedro P. Ramírez, General Edelmiro J. Fárrell, and Juan Domingo Perón, who was a colonel at the time of the revolt.

It was evident almost from the outset that none of the first three of these presidents was the real chieftian of what came to be called the "new Argentina." Some confusion reigned while Rawson was in the *Casa Rosada:* he was thought to be pro-British and anti-Axis in his sympathies. But speculation over Rawson's political orientation speedily became irrelevant—he was president for only twenty-eight hours before he was ousted.

Neither was General Pedro P. Ramírez, who succeeded Rawson in the presidency, the real power in the new dictatorship. Ramírez had enjoyed an army career of routine success: fifty-nine years old at the time he assumed the presidency, he had seen pre-Hitler Germany and Mussolini's Italy on military assignments, and had played a part in the Uriburu Revolution of 1930. "Among the troops, I have been designated the first soldier," Ramírez declared upon assuming office. "I face the situation shoulder to shoulder with my companions-in-arms, whose honor and mind I have solemnly pledged to the people."[4] He asserted that he intended to restore order, reorganize the administration, and "renew the national spirit."[5] He then proceeded to dissolve Congress permanently, "intervene"* the governments of the provinces, and postpone the presidential and vice-presidential election which had been scheduled for September 5, 1943. "We know that many are anxious to know when we will call elections," Ramírez confessed. "The people want to be interpreted and defended. . . . The people wish justice, they want government and not elections; but they will have elections anyway."[6] President Ramírez governed by executive decree, and these orders flowed from the *Casa Rosada* in amazing numbers. Ray Josephs calculated that the president signed an average of eighty decrees daily, and relayed the *porteños'* story of the man who had been "sitting in his bathroom . . . idly tearing off yards of toilet paper which he unwittingly let fly out the window and over nearby *Plaza [de] Mayo*. An hour or so later a detachment of soldiers knocked violently at his door. Admitted, they demanded to know if he had been responsible for the paper barrage. Meekly he confessed, apologizing: 'Sorry. I was careless.' But the colonel in charge was adamant. 'It is the concentration camp for you.' 'And why?' asked the amazed paper tosser. '*Caramba, hombre*, all that paper has floated in the window of the *Casa Rosada* and Ramírez has been signing it.' "[7] Ramírez, like Castillo before him, was unpopular with a probable majority of the Argentine people. Moreover, it was publicly obvious by November of 1943 not only that he was not a major force in the "new Argentina" but also that he was on his way out of the presidency. His departure was hastened on January 26, 1944, when one of the many decrees he signed severed diplomatic relations with Germany

* See pp. 136–43.

and Japan. This measure climaxed a major crisis within the governing clique, which forced Ramírez' resignation on February 24. "Fatigued by the intense tasks of Government which have obliged me to take a rest," said his letter of resignation, "I delegate on this date the position which I occupy to the person of His Excellency the Vice President of the Nation, Brigadier General don Edelmiro J. Fárrell."[8]

No more the chief of the revolution than Ramírez had been, President Fárrell remained in the *Casa Rosada* until June 4, 1946. Like Ramírez, he was an army officer who had enjoyed an assignment in Fascist Italy; and the military dictatorship was tightened during his presidency. "Everything done for the country may not be constitutional, but it is not contrary to the Constitution,"[9] President Fárrell declared in one of his more inspired moments; and he assured the army that the military would enforce its will "for the benefit of the people. . . . Let them call us tyrants and partisans of whatever ideology they compare to tyranny and we will continue our conduct. Our tyranny is precisely for the creation of liberty for all, and if we must be tyrants to make the people freer, we will be."[10]

In a sense, Rawson, Ramírez, and Fárrell were merely front men or puppets controlled by a powerful faction of the Argentine Army which engineered the revolt of 1943. Circumstance and accident pushed the three into the *Casa Rosada*—Rawson, because he happened to be senior officer at the strategic *Campo de Mayo* military garrison at the time its officers launched the uprising; Ramírez, because he had been minister of war in the Castillo cabinet and, as such, the ranking army chief; and Fárrell, because he was a convenient front man at the time of Ramírez' ouster. Indeed, it was noted during the Ramírez period that "people aren't blaming Ramírez directly. The talk is constantly of 'they.' . . ."[11]

Who were "they"? "They" were a small clique of army officers known as the G.O.U. These initials conveniently and interchangeably stood for either *Grupo de Oficiales Unidos* (United Officers' Group) or the clique's slogan, *¡Gobierno! ¡Orden! ¡Unidad!* (Government! Order! Unity!). This organization, popularly referred to as the "colonels' clique," was an outgrowth of the Uriburu Revolution of 1930. A strong sector of military opinion believed that Uriburu—and with him the army—had fallen from power because the military had not been sufficiently well-organized for the retention of political control of the Argentine government. This view gained ground among army officers in the decade after 1930, and in the year 1940, a group of young officers stationed with the Andean garrison in Mendoza established the G.O.U. for the purpose of giving political orientation to the army. The "colonels' clique" "is not a political party," an observer wrote. "It is a cult, almost like those of the Middle Ages. In some ways it is like the Japanese military Bushido."[12] Professing disgust with corruption in Argentine civilian administrations, the G.O.U. demanded military authoritarianism in government and strict control over most phases of national life. It sought a favored place for the army among Argentine institutions, demanded an "Argentina for the Argentines," and advocated a bloc of South American states to offset the influence of the United States in the Western Hemisphere. Thus the G.O.U. exhibited "patriotic, nationalistic, anti-foreign fetishes."[13] At the time of the 1943 rebellion, the organization controlled about 60 per cent of the 3,600 active officers on the army list. The "colonels' clique" tightened its control of the government after June of 1943: on July 12 it was noted that the G.O.U. "is more and more running things behind the scenes,"[14] and a report dated July 21 asserted that "no one is to have a say in the manage-

ment of the country—no one except the colonels. . . ."[15]
That the 1943 upheaval was primarily a military movement
was evidenced in the manifesto of the army to its officers
declaring that "if the June 4 revolution flounders, the army
will be lost with it."[16]

Although the G.O.U. dominated the government after
the 1943 revolt, a chaotic struggle for power raged within
the "colonels' clique" during the first two years after 1943.
"The first leaders of a revolutionary movement are almost
never in agreement as to its basic objectives,"[17] Perón himself said in later years. Until October 17, 1945—now celebrated as "Loyalty Day" in Argentina—these G.O.U. leaders struggled among themselves in a dramatic behind-the-
scenes contest in which the nominal presidents (Rawson,
Ramírez, and Fárrell) were but minor actors. On that
memorable date in October of 1945, Colonel Perón at
length emerged as the definitive victor in the contest and
as the master of the "new Argentina."

Success Story

Juan Domingo Perón was born on October 8, 1895, at
Lobos, located in the Province of Buenos Aires about sixty
miles south of the Federal Capital. From the time he entered
military school at the age of sixteen, he has led a basically
military life. "A personality-boy with a ready smile, a quick
wit, and a belief in himself,"[18] Perón was a sports enthusiast
and achieved considerable skill in fencing, shooting, boxing,
and skiing. He won fame as an army ski-instructor before
he was sent to Santiago, Chile, in 1936, as military attaché.
He became involved in an embarrassing scandal at Santiago
when Chilean authorities charged that he was engaged in
espionage there, and he was hastily withdrawn from the
Chilean capital in 1938. His next assignment—military attaché in Mussolini's Italy—found him in more congenial

circumstances. In Italy, Perón was associated with Alpine ski troops, studied Italian and German, and "caught the fever of fascism."[19] It has been said that his "pro-European attitude, suspicion of the United States, and sympathy for Nazi-Fascist totalitarian methods are easily explained by his background. . . . The most important foreign influences in his life have been Italian and German."[20] In later years, Perón readily admitted this. "In the War School and in the Military College I received valuable instruction from numerous German professors," he said in 1951. "I owe them perhaps a great part of the military education which I have acquired during my life, and I have a profound gratitude toward them."[21] Returning to Argentina in 1940, Perón was assigned to the garrison in the Andean Province of Mendoza, where he became one of the founding fathers of the G.O.U. In 1941 he was elevated to the rank of colonel, which he held at the time of the revolution of 1943.

The "colonels' clique" and the army dominated the "new Argentina," and control of the G.O.U. and the military were among Colonel Perón's chief objectives from the first days of the revolt. Named undersecretary of war in June of 1943, he moved swiftly to consolidate his power within the army; the dynamic colonel did not hesitate to tell a Chilean journalist that "we of the Argentine Army are playing a daring game, the most daring there is."[22] On February 28, 1944, President Fárrell appointed Colonel Perón to be acting war minister. In this post he proceeded to assure undisputed G.O.U. control of the army: he was soon able to say of 3,300 of the nation's 3,600 army officers that "their undated petitions asking for retirement are on file, and can be enforced at a moment's notice."[23] The dominant role of the "colonels' clique" within the military was further underscored on April 8, 1944, when Colonel Perón signed a measure promoting seventeen G.O.U. colonels to

the rank of brigadier general. From that date forward, the
G.O.U. officers were a majority of the general officers of
the Argentine Army. Perón, comfortably entrenched as *de
facto* army chief, was named permanent minister of war
by President Fárrell on May 4, 1944.

Although the army was the major pillar of the "new Argentina," Colonel Perón was not content with control of
the military alone. From the early days of the revolution,
he made a powerful bid for the support of the workers of
Argentina. He had been named director of the national department of labor on October 27, 1943, and he used this
position to organize labor in defense of the new regime. In
November of 1943, the national department of labor was
replaced by a new entity, likewise headed by Perón, known
as the secretariat of labor and welfare. "I have never been
able to accept the idea . . . that the problems in [labor-
management] relations were the private concern of the
directly interested parties," the colonel declared. "With the
creation of the secretariat of labor and welfare, the era of
Argentine social policy has been initiated."[24] As the "new
Argentina" progressed, Perón strengthened his endeavors
to win the favor of the workers, and his labor policies eventually became a major hallmark of the regime. "The day
we created the secretariat of labor and welfare is for me
the first day of our movement," he said in later years.
"From that moment the revolution acquired a new meaning
and began to travel down a road from which there was no
turning back."[25] Under the colonel's leadership, the secretariat of labor and welfare organized "spontaneous" pro-
Perón demonstrations in which workers participated, a
publicity and propaganda campaign was developed to win
the support of labor, and the pre-1943 union leaders were
driven from their positions to be replaced by henchmen of
the "new Argentina." The deposed labor leaders were

among the first residents of the newly-created concentration camps in the Chaco, in Patagonia, and in Neuquén. "What is going to happen only God can tell," Perón asserted. "I can only tell you that the workers are decided to defend their conquests, and if they do so, I am going to defend them."[26]

By mid-1944 Colonel Perón had succeeded, in his capacities as war minister and secretary of labor and welfare, in capturing the machinery for the mobilization of the military and of the workers in defense of the new regime. Thus his power—and the strength of the "new Argentina"—rested on an uneasy alliance of the army with captured labor organizations, and there was no doubting that "Perón is *the* guy in this government."[27] This *fait accompli* was formally and publicly recognized on July 7, 1944, when President Fárrell appointed Perón to be vice president of the nation. "I display only three titles with pride," the colonel declared upon his inauguration as vice president; "that of being a soldier, that of being considered the first Argentine worker, and that of being a patriot."[28]

He held three government positions simultaneously—the war ministership, the secretaryship of labor and welfare, and the vice presidency—from July of 1944 to October of 1945. This was a grim period for Argentines. With the press and most civil liberties curtailed during most of this time, the people leaned increasingly on rumor for their knowledge of events within the government. These rumors stressed continuing quarrels among the military leaders and told of frequently recurring crises. Many of the stories made their way to the ears of President Fárrell himself. "It is said that Colonel Perón and I quarrel every day," the president scoffed; "that he attempts to overthrow me at every moment and even that I had made him a prisoner.

. . . Also, that the chief of the armed forces at *Campo de Mayo* cannot come to Buenos Aires because we would put him in jail, while we cannot go to *Campo de Mayo* without being arrested."[29] These versions, Fárrell said, were non-sense; complete harmony existed within the administration and the country was at peace.

Believing that the "new Argentina" was sufficiently con-solidated to justify relaxation of the restraints on civil and political activities in the nation, President Fárrell on August 6, 1945, lifted the state of siege which—originally pro-claimed by President Castillo—had been in force since December 16, 1941. The results of this step demonstrated that the country was far from pacified and that many Ar-gentines were restive and resentful. Widespread popular disapproval and rejection of the regime found expression in many ways once the state of siege was lifted. By the end of August of 1945, the opposition Radical, Conservative, Socialist, and Communist parties had pooled their resources in a "Board of Democratic Co-ordination" to fight the regime. This board called upon the supreme court to as-sume the reins of government and call elections. In a des-perate attempt to mobilize the opposition, the Board of Democratic Co-ordination staged a mammoth "March of the Constitution and Liberty" at Buenos Aires on Septem-ber 19, 1945. The demonstration was memorable in Ar-gentine annals. Estimates of the number of participants ranged from 250,000 to 800,000 *porteños* as, for the first time in Argentine history, Radicals, Conservatives, Social-ists, and Communists marched together demanding an im-mediate termination of the dictatorship, and assumption of power by the supreme court. "Never before, by all ac-counts, had a demonstration such as this been staged in Ar-gentina," declared Arnaldo Cortesi, correspondent at

Buenos Aires for the *New York Times*. "Social barriers were completely down; class distinctions were forgotten; party jealousies were buried."[30]

The only lesson which the G.O.U. professed to draw from the "March of the Constitution and Liberty" was that the Argentines no longer knew how to make proper use of civil and political liberties. Fárrell thus reimposed the state of siege on September 26, asserting that the Constitution would remain suspended "until the government sees that the country . . . knows how to make good use of the citizenship rights which have been suspended."[31] A nationwide roundup of opposition leaders rapidly followed the resumption of the state of siege; the police dragnet produced an estimated 2,000 political prisoners by September 27, and all members of the Board of Democratic Co-ordination were imprisoned or driven into hiding. Cortesi felt that the renewal of the state of siege and the unprecedented wave of arrests "had intimidation as their only purpose. It is obvious . . . that the government is being forced on the defensive."[32] It was also obvious that the dictatorship's unpopularity increased significantly in September and the early part of October of 1945. "The undercurrent of dislike in the people's attitude toward the military is increasing," one observer wrote. "The provinces resemble occupied countries rather than free states."[33]

"Everybody is demanding my head, but thus far no one has come to get it,"[34] Colonel Perón defiantly asserted on October 2. He had spoken a week too soon; somebody came to get his head on October 9. Argentines, already rendered callous and cynical by more than two years of sensational and chaotic political changes, were stunned to learn on that date that Perón had resigned from his three government posts, that his henchman Colonel Filomeno Velazco had resigned as police chief at Buenos Aires, and that *Campo de Mayo* garrison commander General Eduardo Avalos had replaced Perón as war minister. Colonel Perón's ouster was followed by an anarchic series of cabinet reorganizations: by October 13, President Fárrell could boast a cabinet of only two members, General Avalos and Admiral Héctor Vernengo Lima. Amid the confusion it seemed clear that a group of army and navy officers, headed by Avalos, had directed a coup designed to remove Perón from power. The Avalos group, convinced that mounting popular opposition to Perón might result in the political destruction of the armed services, had moved to save the army and the navy. And, in their view, the road to military and naval salvation lay only in the removal of Perón. "I am not the boss," General Avalos insisted. "I am carrying out the orders of officers of the army."[35]

The exact whereabouts of Perón remained a mystery to most Argentines for four days after October 9. At length Colonel Aristobula Mittelbach, the new acting chief of the Federal Police, revealed that "Colonel Juan Perón was detained and taken to a naval vessel, where he is now confined."[36] And on October 14 a letter from Perón himself to War Minister Avalos was made public. "The minister is advised that I was detained by the Federal Police . . . , delivered to the navy, and confined at Martín García Island," Perón complained. "As I am still a senior army officer in active service and I do not know what crime I am accused of or why I have been deprived of my liberty and removed from the jurisdiction to which I am entitled by law and by my military status, I request that the details of the case be examined to clear up the facts and put me on trial or authorize my return to jurisdiction and liberty, if that be in order."[37]

The events of October of 1945 were crucial in the life of the "new Argentina." For a moment it seemed that

Perón—and with him the military dictatorship—was crushed. But it was only for a moment. The Avalos coup was a tragic failure. Avalos had believed that the public at large would support his move. But the coup had of necessity been planned and executed in secret, and the crowds which milled about in the *Plaza de Mayo* and the streets of Buenos Aires in those chaotic October days had little knowledge of the details of the palace coup. Some things were clear to the unorganized public at large—the Perón regime was a military regime, militarism was intimately bound up with the revolution of 1943. But the crowds did not and could not understand that *not all military men were Perón's men*. Avalos was not Perón's man, and Fárrell was willing to co-operate with Avalos. And those elements of the seething crowds who *did* understand that some army officers were *against* Perón had no way of knowing *which* military men opposed him. All wore the same uniform. And when enraged mobs attacked army officers indiscriminately, President Fárrell and his associates, watching from the windows of the *Casa Rosada*, came to a momentous conclusion. The Avalos coup had failed disasterously, they reasoned; what had begun as a military move against Perón had now become a popular uprising against the armed services in general. As *La Prensa*, the leading *porteño* anti-Perón newspaper, put it, "Everybody shouted and nobody listened."[38] The military, Fárrell thought, was ruined. It was ruined by Perón. Why should Perón relax in the safety of a prison while other army officers had to stand against an enraged multitude? Perón was responsible. Bring him back. Let *him* stand against the multitude. It would be his own medicine.

Colonel Perón, however, had other uses for medicine. He complained that he was suffering from pleurisy, that hospital treatment was necessary. He requested custody into Buenos Aires so that he might be hospitalized. And he was brought to Buenos Aires on October 17.

There were those who had forgotten that Perón's political strength rested on *two* legs. One of them, the army, was crippled, it was true; but the other was whole. Colonel Perón had, after all, been secretary of labor and welfare for a purpose. He had captured labor organizations, he had established machinery for "spontaneous" workers' demonstrations. He had said that the "workers are decided to defend their conquests, and if they do so, I am going to defend them." October 17, 1945, it was clear, was a date on which another "spontaneous" demonstration was needed. And it was a date on which Colonel Mittelbach had another disturbing communiqué to publish: "Groups of persons organized as a demonstration advanced today, through various streets, in the direction of the center of the city, coming from the Province of Buenos Aires, cheering Colonel Perón. A great part of these demonstrators have presumably come from Avellaneda and neighboring towns."[39] The Socialist party frantically denounced the demonstration "as a maneuver designed to confuse the opinion of the workers and to create factors of disturbance and anarchy."[40] But it was a futile warning. By mid-morning on October 17 the *Plaza de Mayo* was filled with shouting demonstrators cheering hoarsely for Perón.

The cheering neared mass hysteria when, at eleven o'clock in the morning, *Perón himself* appeared on the balcony of the *Casa Rosada*, accompanied by President Fárrell! The two men embraced before the shouting throng, and Fárrell declared that he and Perón had never felt anything but the closest friendship for each other. The cheering crowds chanted questions at Perón. "What happened?" "Where were you?" Perón knew how a great man would respond to such queries. "Do not ask me questions about things I have forgotten," he said; "men who are not capable of forgetting do not deserve to be loved or respected by their fellow-men."[41] And the crowds roared in admiration and understanding. This was magnanimity. This was statesmanship. This was the "new Argentina." Perón's Argentina.

"What was the 17th of October?" the Argentine news magazine *Qué* wondered. "For those who took part in it as actors or sympathetic witnesses, it was a widespread popular movement which involved large sectors of the working classes and youths . . . who aspired to play a role in that national hour. What did they want? To defend what they thought were their vital interests. . . . Who symbolized their hopes? Perón. . . ."[42]

What was the 17th of October? It was Colonel Perón's march on Rome. After October 17, 1945, Argentina belonged to Juan Domingo Perón.

4.

The Consolidation of Power

After October 17, 1945, Perón turned uncompromisingly to the task of buttressing his position as the chief of the "new Argentina." Among the major milestones in this process were the election of 1946, from which he emerged as president of the nation; the writing of a new constitution, which aided in the expansion of his control of the government; and the election of 1951, which legalized the prolongation of his power.

The Election of 1946

October 17, 1945, the date of Perón's march on Rome, was also the date on which his candidacy for the formal presidency of the Argentine nation was launched. Until that date he had dominated the scene only from behind the *Casa Rosada*. But now, he said, the memorable October days had at last unleashed "the program which I laid out for myself a long time ago—that is, to aspire to the presidency of the republic as a simple citizen, eliminating everything that might bear the appearance of official candidacy and undertaking my campaign with my own party."[1] His resignation on October 9 from the war ministership, the secretaryship of labor and welfare, and the vice presidency of the nation stood as definitive and final. And on October

18 his resignation from the army was accepted. He was no longer a government official. What was the 17th of October? It was the day that Perón became a simple citizen.

The machinery for holding an election was soon set in motion. President Fárrell decreed in October that balloting would take place on April 7, 1946, and was later convinced that there was little point in waiting that long. On November 14, 1945, the election date was changed to February 24, 1946. On that date, Fárrell said, the Argentine people would vote for presidential and vice-presidential electors, and members of the congress, on the national level; and in each of the fourteen provinces a governor and a legislature would be elected. The officials chosen on February 24, 1946, would assume office on June 4—the third anniversary of the revolution of 1943—on which date constitutional government would at last be resumed. President Fárrell assured the nation that the state of siege reimposed in September of 1945 would in no wise interfere with the conduct of the campaign and the election.

Perón formally announced his presidential candidacy on December 11, 1945. He was supported by two political parties—a "Labor party" and a group known as the "Collaborationist" Radicals. The "Labor party" was, in essence, the group whose representatives had poured into the *Plaza de Mayo* on October 17 to save Perón. Now they were to fight for him again: the ex-colonel's beloved workers—*descamisados*, the shirtless ones, he called them—stood ready to ratify the march on Rome. Organized as a political party, this workers' group on December 28, 1945, announced its platform calling for shorter working hours, labor participation in commercial and industrial profits, and political rights for women. And on January 15, 1946, the Labor party formally nominated its candidates—Perón for the presidency and, for the vice presidency, Colonel Domingo A. Mercante, Perón's henchman in the secretariat of labor and welfare.

Perón sought to widen his electoral support by attempting to woo the Radicals, the party of Irigoyen. The main body of the Radical organization stubbornly resisted the ex-colonel's overtures, but some members of the party succumbed. The Radicals—a small minority of the party— who at length joined Perón came to be known as "Collaborationists." Chief among them were Juan Hortensio Quijano, Armando G. Antille, and Juan Isaac Cooke. All three found posts in the Fárrell cabinet (Quijano as interior minister; Antille, finance minister; and Cooke, foreign minister) and were expelled from the main Radical organization on charges of collaborationism. "I do not care what a few party leaders do with me," Quijano declared. "The people are with the government, and especially the Radical people are with me."[2] The expelled "Collaborationists," led by Quijano, opened their own campaign headquarters on November 8, 1945, and their nominating convention opened at Buenos Aires on January 17 of the following year. This body named Perón and Quijano as its candidates for president and vice president, respectively. Ten days later, Colonel Mercante, who had been nominated by the Labor party, withdrew his vice-presidential candidacy, and the Labor and "Collaborationist" Radical organizations joined forces in support of the Perón-Quijano ticket.

Thus the Labor party and the "Collaborationist" Radicals were the two chief civilian sources of Perón's electoral strength. Other non-military organizations made their way into the ex-colonel's camp. Many Church officials, until then politically doubtful, read in November of 1945 a pastoral letter urging Catholics to vote against candidates who advocated the separation of Church and state, secular education, or legal divorce. This measure added new flocks to the already faithful, and expanded Perón's following. Additional support came from Argentine nationalists and from German Nazis, the latter contributing an estimated $13,500,000 to Perón's war chest during the campaign of 1945–1946. The former colonel's civilian following, then, included the Labor party and its *descamisados*, the "Collaborationist" Radicals, many sectors of the Church, domestic nationalists, and German Nazis and other foreign groups which had been pro-Axis during World War II.

Meanwhile, the opposition had not been idle. The main Radical organization, together with the Conservatives, the Socialists, and the Communists—these four parties had staged the spectacular "March of the Constitution and Liberty" in September of 1945—moved to pool their resources in an anti-Perón coalition for the election. The Socialists and the Communists assumed the initiative in inviting the other two parties to join the alliance. The decision was difficult for the Radicals and Conservatives: both had long pursued traditional policies of abstention from electoral alliances with other parties. The tradition had, however, been weakened by Radical and Conservative participation in the "March of the Constitution and Liberty"; and the Radical party formally agreed on November 14, 1945, to join again with the parties of the left against Perón. The coalition, called the Democratic Union, was organized on the following day, although the Conservatives had not yet made their decision. Much soul-searching and dissension characterized the debate among the Conservatives as their party considered the question of affiliation with the Democratic Union. Many Conservatives followed the lead of Dr. Rodolfo Moreno, former governor of the Province of Buenos Aires. "Although I have been a Conservative all my life, I affected a rapprochement with the extreme left,"

Moreno had said. "If they are willing to co-operate, we will march together to obtain our common objective."[3] However, the majority of the Conservative leaders eschewed affiliation with the left; and on November 23, 1945, the Conservative party formally decided against entering the Democratic Union. Nevertheless, the Conservatives made no nominations for the 1946 election, thus freeing their affiliates to vote for Democratic Union candidates. As the Democratic Union stood, then, it was composed principally of the Radical, Socialist, and Communist parties, with the nonformal support of the Conservatives.

The platform of the Democratic Union demanded restoration of constitutional government and resumption of civil and political liberties. On December 31, 1945, the coalition nominated Dr. José P. Tamborini and Dr. Enrique M. Mosca, both Radicals, for president and vice president, respectively. Tamborini, who was sixty years old, was a physician who had been in politics since the days of Irigoyen. He had served in congress intermittently since 1918 and had been interior minister in the cabinet of President Alvear. Mosca, the Democratic Union's vice-presidential aspirant, was a more colorful politician and a more driving campaigner than his running-mate. The sixty-six-year-old *santafecino* had been active in the politics of Santa Fé since 1912. He had been governor of that province from 1920 to 1924, and had run unsuccessfully for the vice presidency in 1937.

The campaign of 1945–46 was characterized by terror and violence. The army and the Federal Police—though both had suddenly become theoretically nonpolitical for the election—were openly employed to further Perón's candidacy. Many political demonstrations were accompanied by extensive rioting, and anti-Semitism assumed startling proportions as Argentines prepared for their first presidential and vice-presidential election since 1937. "Alarm and even terror are beginning to spread in the Jewish quarter," Cortesi reported in November of 1945. "For some time all gatherings of Colonel Perón's followers have been a signal for some action against Jews."[4] Although Perón himself denounced the anti-Semitic demonstrations, many agreed with the *New York Times* correspondent at Buenos Aires that "it is hardly possible to doubt any longer that anti-Semitism forms a part of Colonel Perón's political stock-in-trade."[5] Violent disorders were almost a daily occurrence during the campaign. A Democratic Union rally held at Buenos Aires on December 8 ended in chaos when nationalists, assisted by the Federal Police, attacked the estimated 200,000 *porteños* attending the rally, killing 4 and injuring 33 of them. A "North American" correspondent reported early in January that "half the downtown section [of Buenos Aires] is crying from tear gas bombs;"[6] and street fights were daily events in the capital by January 14. During the violence, Alejandro Jorge Gallardo resigned his post as assistant inspector of the Federal Police at Buenos Aires. "In the streets of Buenos Aires and several towns in the interior, I have witnessed *Peronista* gangs of hoodlums attacking our women and mistreating our brethren, shouting '*viva*' for an impossible candidate and counting on the passiveness of officials charged with keeping order," Gallardo asserted in his letter of resignation. "I have seen members of the Federal Police actively working in the Labor party's committees."[7] By January 28, it was unofficially estimated that sixty-eight Argentines had thus far been killed during the presidential campaign.

The violence reached its apex in January. The Buenos Aires stock exchange was bombed shortly before Tamborini and Mosca departed from the capital on January 21 to campaign in the provinces of the "interior." The Tamborini-Mosca campaign tour became something of a saga: the Democratic Union candidates' train was shot at and stoned in three towns before the train was set afire on January 24. The blaze destroyed campaign literature valued at $100,000. But Tamborini and Mosca pushed on to be attacked in Salta and Jujuy before they were at last peacefully received in Tucumán and Córdoba. "We want to remove from Argentine public life this impudence which sells the public offices of the state as electoral arsenals, which converts them into recruiting offices for street rioters," Tamborini told the *cordobeses*. "We desire order, peace, the ability to live together, and respect for law."[8] Tired and disheveled, Tamborini and Mosca returned to Buenos Aires on January 30.

Perón and Quijano also toured the country, but were exposed to little violence. Perhaps the most effective of campaign measures on behalf of the ex-colonel was the celebrated bonus law decreed by President Fárrell on December 20, 1945. This measure required all Argentine commercial and industrial establishments to pay their employees not only a minimum wage established by the decree but also an annual bonus in the amount of one month's salary. "The measure was clearly designed by its author to win the labor vote," said a foreign correspondent. "It brings Perón closer to the presidency than he has ever been before."[9] On January 13, 1946, Argentine commercial and industrial concerns began a three-day lockout in protest against the bonus law. The stoppage was virtually complete, but it served to confirm the *descamisados'* belief that Perón was their man.

One of the most spectacular developments in the closing weeks of the campaign was provided by the Government of the United States. On February 12—just twelve days before the election—the State Department published a memorandum entitled *Consultation among the American Republics with Respect to the Argentine Situation.* This document, popularly called the "Blue Book," was primarily the work of Assistant Secretary of State Spruille Braden, who had been the United States Ambassador at Buenos Aires from April to September of 1945. The "Blue Book," published at Washington after Braden and Undersecretary of State Dean Acheson had conferred with the diplomatic representatives of nineteen other American republics, reviewed the war-time record of the "new Argentina." The "Blue Book" asserted that since 1943 Argentina had been governed by a fascist-like military dictatorship which collaborated with the Axis during World War II. The publication of the "Blue Book" was intended, among other things, to influence the Argentine voters against Perón. It is, of course, impossible to measure the "Blue Book's" exact effect on the voters. If the document influenced the election at all, it was probably in the direction of *adding* votes for Perón, as many Argentines resented what they regarded as foreign intervention in their domestic affairs. Between February 13 and 22, the "Blue Book" was a major issue in the Argentine election campaign.

By law, all campaigning ceased on February 22, two days before the election. The outcome was "virtually determined beforehand by the government," declared a foreign observer. He compared the campaign to "the election which legally brought Adolf Hitler to power in 1933 and to the plebiscites which subsequently were held to confirm it. The election and plebiscite are being held simultaneously in Argentina, whereas they were held separately in Germany."[10] The leaders of the opposition Democratic Union were in substantial agreement with this view. Américo Ghioldi, the Socialist party chieftain, complained of the "lack of liberties for the parties and for individuals, and the conversion of the state, the army, and the police into an official political party with great monetary and material resources devoted to victory, 'cost what it will cost and fall who will fall. . . .' "[11]

The election was held on February 24, 1946. The state of siege was lifted for forty-eight hours—from midnight of February 22 to midnight of election day—to permit the balloting. Election day itself was peaceful and orderly, one foreign observer remarking that "after such an efficiently unfair campaign, there could be a free—and legal—election."[12] The official results of the voting indicated that 2,734,386 Argentines, or approximately 17 per cent of the nation's population, had cast ballots for presidential and vice-presidential electors. To nobody's surprise, the contest was won by the Perón-Quijano ticket. Its margin of victory, however, was unexpectedly slim: Perón and Quijano received 1,527,231 popular votes as against 1,207,155 for Tamborini and Mosca. The Argentine electoral college system, like that of the United States, frequently distorted the range of victory. Thus the Perón-Quijano combination received 304 electoral votes as against only 72 for the Democratic Union's candidates; and Tamborini and Mosca obtained the electoral votes of only four provinces—Corrientes, Córdoba, San Luis, and San Juan.

The inauguration of the victorious candidates took place on June 4, 1946, the third anniversary of the revolution. On that date, Juan Domingo Perón—now reinstated in the army with the rank of brigadier general—became Argentina's twenty-fifth president since the adoption of the Constitution of 1853. "The splendid decision of the people authorizes me to request and hope for the co-operation of all," President Perón declared in his inaugural address. "I request it with such sincerity and humility as is commensurate with the dignity of a governor. . . . I am not guided by hidden motives. . . . My purpose is high and my emblem is clear: my cause is the cause of the people; my guide is the flag of the nation."[13]

The Constitution of 1949

Theoretically, President Perón's inauguration marked the resumption of constitutional government. Argentines had lived in what was euphemistically called "constitutional abnormality" from December 16, 1941, when President Castillo declared a state of siege,* until Perón formally assumed the presidency on June 4, 1946. The constitution had remained suspended throughout this four-and-one-half-year period with the exception of two brief episodes: President Fárrell had lifted the state of siege from August 6 until September 26 of 1945, and again for the forty-eight-hour period beginning at midnight of February 22, 1946. But now, with Perón at last in the *Casa Rosada,* the state of siege had slipped into history, and the Constitution of 1853 was ostensibly in force once more.

The picture of Perón governing in accordance with the constitution staggered the imaginations of many Argentines as early as 1946. Some of them formed a "Club of 53" in a feeble attempt to defend the document against the new administration. When the club was closed down by Buenos Aires municipal authorities on November 5, 1947, many were convinced that Perón had permanent designs against the constitution of Alberdi and Urquiza, and that the president would remove the 1853 charter from Argentine national life.

These fears were justified. Early in 1948, Perón's followers began to demand what they called constitutional reform. They charged that the constitution was antiquated and, specifically, urged four basic changes in the Argentine

* See p. 43.

constitutional system. In the first place, they objected to the 1853 document's prohibition against the immediate re-election of the president. Under the constitution, the chief executive was elected for a six-year term and, at the end of that period, was ineligible for re-election. Secondly, they protested against the electoral college system which the constitution-writers of 1852–53 had copied from the Constitution of the United States. The *Peronistas* advocated direct election of the president and the vice president. Moreover, it was urged that the government's economic powers be expanded to allow it to intervene constitutionally in the national economy. Lastly, the *Peronistas* argued that the social and economic program of the revolution of 1943 should be written into the constitution.

When the congress convened on May 1, 1948, President Perón told that body that the time had come for constitutional reform. "The amendment of the National Constitution is a necessity imposed by the times and the convenience of a greater perfection of the institutions and organizations," the president declared. "Amendments must be considered in order to: (1) bring [the constitution] up to date, and adjust it to the evolution of the world; and (2) make it complete in the different aspects in which it evidently is not, in accordance with the life we lead today."[14] Perón coyly remarked that he supported all of the reforms urged by his followers with the exception of the change that would render him eligible for re-election to the presidency. Although he observed that the prohibition against the immediate re-election of the president "is one of the more wise and prudent provisions of our great charter,"[15] his followers had come to know that when Perón said "no" he occasionally meant "yes." And this was one of those occasions.

Perón was anxious that the legalistic forms be observed

in altering the constitution. According to the 1853 charter, the document could be amended in whole or in part once the necessity for constitutional reform had been declared by two-thirds of the members of each house of the congress after which a constitutional convention would meet to write the amendments. This was a provision with which Perón could afford to comply: in 1948 the senate was already 100 per cent *Peronista*, and his followers controlled over two-thirds of the members of the 158-man chamber of deputies.

The project met with little opposition in either house of congress. Although the opposition Radical party was theoretically represented in the Chamber of Deputies by forty-two congressmen when that body considered the question of constitutional reform, the opposition deputies were not present when the chamber voted on the matter. The Radicals had stalked out in protest against the expulsion of their floor leader, Deputy Ernesto Enrique Sammartino, from the congress early in August, and had temporarily left the Chamber of Deputies almost completely in the hands of the *Peronistas*.* When the forty-two Radical deputies returned to the chamber on August 13, they found that the constitutional issue had already been decided in their absence. The *Peronistas* had obtained the overwhelming vote of the deputies present for a bill declaring constitutional reform to be a necessity. The measure called for the election of a 158-man constitutional convention, in which the Federal Capital and the provinces would be represented by as many deputies as they sent to the congress, and authorized the president to call an election for the convention within 180 days of the measure's promulgation.

The remainder of the process was relatively simple. The *Peronista*-dominated Senate, receiving the deputies' bill,

* For a discussion of the Sammartino episode, see pp. 118–19.

74

passed it with little debate and forwarded it to the *Casa Rosada*. And President Perón dutifully signed and promulgated the measure on September 3. The Constitution of 1853, the president said, "served well when the Argentine Republic was a small agricultural community, but it cannot also serve a nation of 16,000,000 inhabitants already in the advanced stages of modern industry, with all the economic and social problems that new situation proposes."[16] He set December 5, 1948, as the date on which the constitutional convention would be elected.

Opposition to the impending change was immediate and widespread. The Argentine Bar Association went on record against constitutional reform, and the Radical party staged a mass meeting in which ex-Deputy Sammartino and defeated presidential candidate Tamborini were the featured speakers. "The president has said . . . that the Argentine constitution is of the time of the horse and buggy and that today we live in the air age," a Radical manifesto asserted. "The constitutions of the United States and England are also of the time of the horse and buggy in those countries. No jurist, no statesman, no thinker has yet confused mechanical progress with the stability of the cultural process reflected in political and social institutions. . . . The worst aspect of the reform with which we are menaced is its mystery. . . . Does anybody know what will happen to freedom of the press, to the federal system, to the judiciary?"[17] And the Socialist party urged its affiliates to vote "against the fascist reform."[18]

The campaign for the election of the convention repeated a pattern which was becoming increasingly familiar. Pro-administration demonstrators "spontaneously" intimidated the Radical-led opposition with the tacit permission of the theoretically neutral Federal Police; the laws regulating political activity were enforced in an openly partisan manner; and the opposition's campaign posters and literature were defaced, destroyed, and in some cases suppressed. When the results of the December 5 balloting indicated that the 158-member constitutional convention would contain 109 *Peronistas* as against only forty-eight Radicals, President Perón was cheered. The constitutional reform, he said, would be a "blank check" for his government; this, "which some have criticized, is for us the highest badge of honor, because the people do not give this type of blank check to men who do not deserve it."[19]

The *Peronista*-controlled constitutional convention opened at Buenos Aires on January 24, 1949, under the chairmanship of Perón's close friend and comrade Rear Admiral Alberto Teisaire, who has been called "a sailor at sea, a politician ashore."[20] It was obvious from the outset that the new constitution would be tailored to the president's wishes. The convention labored for two and one-half months to produce the document. In the closing days of the conclave, the forty-eight Radicals walked out of the convention, charging that it had no other object than to legalize Perón's re-election. The assembly terminated its labors on March 11, 1949, presenting the nation with a new constitution. Perón took an oath of allegiance to it on March 16, on which date the Constitution of 1949 officially went into force. The 1853 charter, "in spite of its intrinsic value at the time of its promulgation, was antiquated in many respects and hampered the national activities," the president declared. "If responsibility must be taken for proclaiming its reform, I take the full responsibility on my own shoulders. . . . I am prepared to be judged by my contemporaries and by history."[21]

Inasmuch as the reader will have ample opportunity to become acquainted with the major features of Argentina's new constitution in later chapters of this book, no analysis of the document will be undertaken at this point. Suffice it to say here that the Constitution of 1949 gave the *Peronistas* essentially what they had wanted: President Perón was now eligible for re-election, direct election of the president and vice president replaced the old electoral college system, the government's economic powers were expanded in the constitution, and Perón's social and economic program was written into the text of the document. On March 16, 1949, the Constitution of 1853 faded into the past and the Perón regime took a long step toward the consolidation of its power.

The Election of 1951

Once the new constitution had rendered President Perón eligible for immediate re-election, he faced the prospect of the 1952–1958 term much as any available presidential candidate in the United States would. "Not only am I not going to accept a second term," Perón said early in 1949, "but I do not believe my health would allow it."[22] When, in July of 1950, newsmen inquired after the president's plans for 1952, he said: "I suggest you address that query to the next president. I don't intend to run again, although I am the only one who believes it."[23]

The *Peronista* party formally launched its campaign for Perón's nomination for re-election on February 24, 1951, the fifth anniversary of his first election. By March of that year his re-election was publicly demanded not only by his own party and its women's branch, but also by the government-controlled General Confederation of Labor and by various smaller organizations which had fallen into the president's orbit. *Peronista* congressmen stumped the country in March and April to stimulate enthusiasm for a second term for Perón. In the early months of 1951, however, the president continued to play the part of the coy, noncommittal candidate. He declared that he was "a man who at this stage in life has no further ambitions of any kind. . . . I believe that it is premature to speak of these things."[24] And in April he told the *Peronista* bloc in congress that "I am not one of those men who believe themselves to be indispensable. . . ."[25]

The Constitution of 1949 fixes no definite date for presidential elections. That document provides only that the balloting must take place at least three months before the new presidential term begins. That new term was to commence on June 4, 1952. Congress had originally provided that the election would be held on February 24, 1952— exactly six years after Perón's first triumph at the polls— but on July 6, 1951, the legislators decided to change the election date to November 11, 1951. After the middle of that year, Perón left no doubt that he intended to occupy the *Casa Rosada* for an additional six years. At length, the *Peronista* party planned a mammoth mass meeting for August 22. Administration circles had hoped for a turnout of some 2,000,000 Argentines at the rally. They were disappointed: about 250,000 attended the meeting. The throng hoarsely demanded the re-election of Perón, who then assured them that he would seek another term in the *Casa Rosada*. Five days later, the *Peronista* party formally nominated Perón for re-election.

Speculation over the *Peronista* nomination for the vice-presidency of the nation had been spirited and widespread among Argentines for more than a year. Vice-President J. Hortensio Quijano, who had been elected with Perón in 1946, was a relatively colorless if useful figure; and by 1951 *Peronistas* had come to expect drama and color in their politics. Moreover, the most colorful of all *Peronistas* seemed available for the vice presidency. Rumors that the president's wife, the fabulous Señora María Eva Duarte de

Perón,* might be a candidate had been in circulation since September of 1950; and an organized movement for a Perón-Perón ticket had taken shape as early as February of 1951. The first "Perón-Perón" posters adorned the walls of the streets of Buenos Aires and other Argentine cities in mid-July, and the movement was in full force when the *Peronistas'* mass meeting was staged on August 22. Eva (her followers called her "Evita") Perón publicly agreed at that time to run for vice president on the ticket headed by her husband, and the nomination was formalized on August 27.

A few days later, Evita dramatically announced a reversal of her political plans. "I want to communicate an irrevocable and definite decision to my people," she declared in a radio address on August 31, "a decision I have taken by myself, to resign the noted honor given me by the open forum of the 22nd."[26] Evita withdrew her vice-presidential candidacy, giving two reasons for quitting the race. In the event that she were to succeed to the presidency, she would be commander-in-chief of the armed forces, a post which she said she thought improper for a woman; and she remarked that she was too young to meet the constitutional requirements for the vice presidency.† The real reasons for her withdrawal ran more deeply than those. She had only hinted at army opposition to her candidacy, which was a major factor in her "irrevocable and definite decision." Moreover, the delicate state of her health at the time—she was already fatally ill with cancer—likewise figured in her withdrawal from the campaign. To

* Chapter 5 is devoted to the life and works of Eva Perón.
† The Constitution of 1949 requires the vice president to be at least thirty years of age. Despite the fact that Evita said in 1951 that she was only twenty-nine years old, the record shows that she was born on May 7, 1919. According to this official information, she would have been thirty-three years of age when the vice-presidential term began on June 4, 1952.

these factors should be added the fears within the *Peronista* party that too many traditions were being broken too rapidly, and official concern over the fact that only one-eighth of the expected multitude had attended the rally which on August 22 demanded her nomination. Evita's brief bid for the vice presidency thrilled Argentines; in withdrawing it she asked that history record that "there was a woman alongside General Perón, who took to him the hopes and needs of the people, and her name was Evita."[27]

With Evita out of the running, the *Peronistas* turned again to the incumbent vice president, J. Hortensio Quijano, whose leadership of the "Collaborationist" Radicals had aided President Perón's victory in 1946. Quijano was accordingly nominated for re-election in September, and *Peronistas* again campaigned for a Perón-Quijano ticket, with both candidates running for re-election to the posts which they had held since June 4, 1946.

In 1951, the opposition parties were in a much more weakened condition than they had been in 1946. The Radical, Socialist, Conservative, and Communist organizations were still in existence, it was true; but eight years of restrictions on political activity had had a marked effect. Moreover, the opposition was forced in 1951 to operate under legal requirements which had not been in effect in the earlier election. By 1951, political parties were forbidden to form coalitions or alliances. Unable to duplicate the Democratic Union coalition of 1946, the opposition parties were required in 1951 to nominate their own individual slates of candidates and to campaign separately.* Accordingly, the Radicals chose ex-Deputy Ricardo J. Balbín and Deputy Arturo Frondizi for the presidency and vice-presidency,

---

* For a discussion of the status of Argentine political parties, see pp. 357–66.

respectively; the Socialists nominated former Senator Alfredo L. Palacios for the presidency and ex-Deputy Américo Ghioldi for the vice presidency; the Conservatives named Deputies Reinaldo A. Pastor and Vicente Solano Lima for the two posts; and the Communists nominated Rodolfo Ghioldi (brother of Américo Ghioldi, the Socialist leader) for the presidency, and the Señora Alcira de la Peña for the vice presidency.

Though the opposition was scattered by law in 1951, there was no doubt that the major anti-Perón presidential candidate was Ricardo J. Balbín. Not only was his party, the Radical organization, the strongest of the opposition groups, but also Balbín himself had become something of a martyr during the two years before the election of 1951. He attracted national attention in August of 1948, when he rose in the Chamber of Deputies to oppose unsuccessfully the *Peronista* drive to expel Deputy Ernesto E. Sammartino, the Radical leader, from the congress. "I say what I feel," Balbín had asserted when his remarks on the floor of the chamber drew ominous smiles from the *Peronista* majority. "I will be ridiculed today; I have already been ridiculed in other countries: Germany and Italy, Hitler and Mussolini. In that epoch other men spoke as I do now and the same smiles were on the faces of the powerful."[28] Shortly after these remarks, President Perón had asserted that Deputy Balbín was guilty of expressing contempt of the government, and that he should be deprived of his congressional immunity so that he might be subjected to judicial proceedings. Under the Argentine system, a legislator may lose his congressional immunity if the majority of the members of his chamber vote to deprive him of this protection; and the *Peronista* majority dutifully moved against Balbín. "My statements are clear and clean, decided and categorical," the latter affirmed during the debate over his immunity. "They are my fight, my mode of living, my modest contribution to the Republic. . . . I have expressed my ideas . . . because I have never devoted one minute to defending only myself. I have always placed all my energy at the service of the collectivity, of a cause which I thought honorable."[29] But Balbín's argument was futile. On September 29, 1949, by a vote of 109 against forty-one, the Chamber of Deputies deprived him of his congressional immunity, and he was forced to stand trial on charges of expressing contempt of the government.

The celebrated Balbín case will long remain a classic illustration of the workings of many aspects of Perón's Argentina. The courts were slow to move against Balbín. During the delay, provincial elections were scheduled in his home Province of Buenos Aires, and the Radicals nominated Balbín as their candidate for governor. The *Peronista* candidate was Colonel Domingo A. Mercante, long a close friend and cohort of Perón. On March 12, 1950, provincial election day, Balbín was at last arrested on the contempt charge; the election ended with Balbín in jail and with Mercante as Governor of the Province of Buenos Aires. Balbín remained confined until January of 1951. After a prolonged and frequently interrupted trial, he was at length, on November 22, 1950, declared guilty of contempt of the government and sentenced to five years' imprisonment. During the trial his name became a symbol around which much of the opposition to the regime had begun to coalesce; and by the end of 1950 it was obvious that the Balbín affair had become embarrassing to the government. In an effort to prevent him from acquiring the stature of a martyr, President Perón pardoned Balbín on January 2, 1951. Seven months later—on August 6—Balbín, now a species of quasi-martyr, received the Radical nomination for the presidency, and his long-embattled attorney, Deputy Arturo Frondizi, was selected as his running-mate. Together they campaigned on a Radical platform calling for the resumption of civil and political liberty, a re-emphasis on agriculture, the establishment of a new minimum wage, full employment, and nationalization of the oil refineries and meat-packing plants.

Much of the campaign of 1951, like that of 1946, was conducted during a state of siege, in which constitutional guarantees were suspended. On September 28—in the midst of the presidential campaign—the government announced that it had discovered a plot against it, and a new state of siege was declared. Asserting that a coup had been planned by "internal and foreign elements against the sovereignty of the nation and against its economic independence," the Perón regime stated flatly that "a state of internal war exists. Army officers taking part will be shot."[30] Former Senator Alfredo L. Palacios, the Socialists' presidential candidate, was imprisoned, as were ex-General Arturo Rawson, who had initially led the revolution of 1943, and former General Benjamín Menéndez. On September 29, approximately seventy army officers fled to Uruguay in seven airplanes.

In the atmosphere of general tension and crisis following the declaration of "internal war," the government imposed restrictions which made campaigning virtually impossible for the opposition parties. The government declared in October that Argentine radio stations were to be used for informational rather than political purposes. As this measure was interpreted by administering officials, *Peronista*-oriented broadcasts were "informational" while programs endorsed by the opposition groups were "political" and therefore forbidden. Permission to use radio broadcast time was specifically denied to the Radicals, the largest of the opposition organizations. On October 9 the Federal Police declared that permits to hold rallies and mass meetings would be issued to opposition parties under extremely restricted circumstances. At the same time, the courts ruled that the state of "internal war" meant that the right of habeas corpus would be suspended until "normality" was resumed.

Fighting against such odds, the opposition forces progressively crumbled during the course of the campaign. The Socialists ceased campaigning on October 6, and three days later the Conservatives complained that 250 of their leaders and candidates were in prison. Of the four opposition candidates for president, two were driven out of the race before election day. One of them, Palacios, the Socialist candidate, had been imprisoned in connection with the "internal war" declared on September 28. On October 22, Palacios formally withdrew his candidacy, charging that the government had made the campaign impossible for his party. The other, the Communist leader Rodolfo Ghioldi, was jailed on October 4. Released some days later, he continued his bid for the presidency. The Communist candidate's efforts carried him on a tour into a number of provinces, among them Entre Ríos. At a Communist rally at Paraná, the capital of that province, rioting terminated Ghioldi's bid for the presidency. Among the twelve casualties—two killed and ten wounded—was Ghioldi himself. He fell at Paraná, a bullet in his lung, on November 1.

Thus only two opposition presidential candidates, the Radicals' Balbín and the Conservatives' Pastor, remained in the race at the time the voters went to the polls on November 11. Of these, Balbín commanded the stronger electoral support. A Radical rally at Buenos Aires drew a crowd variously estimated at between 50,000 and 80,000 *porteños.* "The Argentine man no longer is intimidated," asserted Balbín, cheered by the size of the turnout. "Perón no longer is ruling this country; the pressure of the opposition already is forcing decisions on this government."[31] But this was a statement of courageous faith rather than of fact.

Meanwhile, Perón conducted his own campaign for re-election in a curious fashion. He declared that he did not wish to use his position as president of the republic to influence the results of the election, and that he would give evidence of scrupulous fairness if he were to step down from the presidency during the last weeks before the balloting. Accordingly, he called a special session of the congress and on October 9 presented that body with his request for a leave of absence. The legislators, characteristically subservient to Perón's wishes, granted him leave until April 30, 1952: Perón on October 23 signed the measure providing for his own leave of absence. Rear Admiral Alberto Teisaire, a trusted leader of the *Peronista* party, became acting president of Argentina, charged with the impartial administration of the election.

The unorthodox manner in which Perón conducted his own campaign gave rise to confused and sensational rumors during the two weeks before the balloting. Perón made no campaign tour, and delivered only four speeches. Among the stories circulated at Buenos Aires was a prediction that the election would be postponed; another had it that Perón and his wife—she was then fatally ill—were planning to flee Argentina and go to Switzerland for their health. Rumors such as these were fed by the fact that almost no pro-Perón posters were exhibited during the closing days of the contest. However, none of these rumors materialized: the election was indeed held on November 11, and the victorious Perón emerged from it with over sixty per cent of the votes and a mandate for a second term in his pocket.

Thus the "new Argentina" moved a long way toward consolidation in the years between "Loyalty Day" in 1945 and the election of 1951. The opposition had been scattered and intimidated, the Constitution of 1853 had been replaced by one inspired by Perón, and the *Peronistas* were able to carry all of the provinces in the 1951 election. When Perón was inaugurated for the second time on June 4, 1952—the ninth anniversary of his revolution—it was obvious to most Argentines that in the years since 1943 their country had traveled a major sector of an essentially irrevocable course.

5.

Once There Was a Lady

History has been asked to record that "there was a woman alongside General Perón, who took to him the hopes and needs of the people, and her name was Evita." Let the entry be duly made. There was indeed a woman named Evita.

Naughty Story

Los Toldos is a small rural community located at the extreme northwestern corner of the Province of Buenos Aires. World-shaking events rarely occur at Los Toldos; and the *provincianos* there can be forgiven for failing to recognize one if it took place on May 7, 1919. On that day an illegitimate child was born. Her name was María Eva Duarte, and most people who knew her called her Evita. Her mother was Juana Ibaguren, the daughter of a coachman. The father was Juan Duarte, a small landowner who had left his legal wife to live with Juana.

Evita learned about Argentine social problems the hard way. She was the youngest of five children—one boy and four girls—all of whom had been born out of wedlock. "Nice" children were not allowed to play with the Duarte youngsters, for reasons it was, for many years, difficult for the hapless Evita to understand. These were cruel and bitter years for her. They were years of ostracism and stigma. They were years in which Juan Duarte grew ill and died, and Evita and her brother and sisters were not permitted to attend their father's funeral. Then they became years of poverty and misery. They were years in which Evita learned that there were two kinds of people. The first included the wealthy owners of land, the "nice" folk who would not permit their young to associate with the Duarte brood and forbade them to watch their father buried. This class of people was called the "Oligarchy." The second kind were more friendly and generous. They were poor, like Evita, and they accepted her and her brother and sisters. This second group was called "the people of Argentina." Others could read it in books, but Evita knew from her own early life that "there are Argentine provinces where the infant mortality rate is as high as 300 per 1,000. . . . There are hundreds of thousands of our children who are hungry . . . without education, without hygiene, without homes. . . ."[1]

After the death of Juan Duarte, Juana Ibaguren and her children moved to the city of Junín, also in the Province of Buenos Aires. Although social ostracism at Junín was not so strong and cruel as it had been at Los Toldos, life in the new city continued to be difficult for the impoverished Duarte family. However, the hardships, for Evita at least, lessened as she grew older. Entering her 'teens, Eva Duarte developed into an unusually attractive girl; and—as she and men came to learn about each other—Evita realized that it was not absolutely necessary for a beautiful woman to live indefinitely in poverty. True, the opportunity to exploit one's charms was limited at Junín. But, as it had not been imperative to stay at Los Toldos, neither was it necessary to remain at Junín. One could go to the big city, to Buenos Aires. There was much a beautiful girl could do at Buenos

Aires that offered promise of a happier life than she had
known at Los Toldos and Junín. There were cafés and
night clubs at Buenos Aires, there were theaters and opportunities in radio and perhaps the movies. And, of course,
there were men at Buenos Aires. Naturally, there had also
been men at Junín; but those at Buenos Aires were more
wealthy and powerful.

Much as hopeful young women of the United States ar-
rive at Hollywood in search of a colorful career, so Eva
Duarte came to Buenos Aires as a sixteen-year-old seeking
a less drab and miserable existence than she had known in
the "interior." Evita's early years at Buenos Aires, though
she found them more satisfying than the Junín period, were
not especially successful. Today Argentines violently disagree on many matters in which Evita figured, but on one
point her countrymen were almost unanimous—she was a
beautiful woman. She has been described as "a 5-foot-2,
pale-skinned, dark-eyed, dazzling blonde,"[2] although her
hair was different colors at various stages of her career. At
Buenos Aires she sought work as an actress in radio, the
theater, and the movies. She discovered, however, that
physical beauty alone was not enough for success in these
fields. It was also necessary to be able to act, and the critics
said that Evita, despite her attractiveness, was not a very
good actress. Nevertheless, she did find steady work with
Radio Belgrano, and even took part in some motion pictures. She played bit parts in a number of photoplays, and
eventually was able to achieve featured roles in two motion pictures. One of them, *La Cabalgata del Circo*, was not
reviewed as a success, despite the fact that it starred Hugo
del Carril and the gifted Libertad Lamarque. The second,
La Pródiga, was never shown to the Argentine public, primarily because Evita was already in politics by the time the
picture was ready for release in 1945. The San Miguel

studios, rather than incur the wrath of the government, presented the print of *La Pródiga* to Perón as a gift in 1946.

When the revolution of 1943 occurred, Evita was working at Radio Belgrano. She had become friendly with a number of army officers, some of them G.O.U. members; and, although she insisted she knew nothing of politics, she did have a gift for sensing which of the officers would be powerful and important in the "new Argentina." There was, for example, General Ramírez, who became president of the nation: Evita won his favor and dazzled her co-workers by dining publicly with him while he was in power.

And, of course, there was Colonel Juan Domingo Perón. Evita met him at a Radio Belgrano party in October of 1943. He was undersecretary of war in the Ramírez government then, and, from their first meeting, Perón and Evita found much to admire in each other. The actress captivated and fascinated the colonel, as she had many another before him; and Evita said that the colonel was a man of destiny. Although he was twenty-four years older than she, he had been a widower since 1936 and was fair game for Evita. Soon after the October meeting, Perón and Evita moved their respective living quarters to Buenos Aires' fashionable Calle Posadas. They maintained separate residences, it is true—she lived in Apartment A and he in Apartment B—but Argentines understood that Perón had acquired a mistress and that her name was Eva Duarte. Among the first to realize the political significance of the event was the management of Radio Belgrano, which immediately increased Evita's salary from $35 to $350 per month.

Evita lived as Perón's mistress from January of 1944 until October of 1945. Although her relationship to the colonel was the subject of much rumor and gossip—malicious and otherwise—during this period, very little was published about her. This is in part due to a custom of the Argentine press. Questions of censorship aside for the moment, the tradition of Argentine journalism had long been to regard a man's personal life as his own private affair. If he was a figure in political life, as Perón unquestionably was, his public activities were a fit subject for press discussion, but his relationship to the lady in Apartment A was an item eschewed by the press as a matter of custom and tradition. Accordingly, Perón's mistress was only rarely mentioned in print until October of 1945.

As has already been indicated, October 17, 1945, was a date of crucial significance in the life of the "new Argentina," and the anniversary of that occasion is today celebrated as "Loyalty Day." A coup against Perón had removed him from power on October 9. The officers who came to arrest him then found him with Evita, and discovered that it was much easier to overthrow Perón than to dislodge his mistress. Perón, as is perhaps proper on such occasions, frantically begged his captors not to kill him. Evita was another matter. She flew into a trantrum, screamed and spat at the conspirators, and shouted defiant obscenities at them. The plotters regarded themselves as gentlemen in the best Argentine tradition: they knew how to arrest Perón, but they were not schooled in techniques of handling his apparently hysterical mistress. On October 9 they captured the colonel but left Evita free.

She then proceeded to play a major role in frustrating the coup against Perón. She alerted his political lieutenants, and the machinery for restoring the colonel to power was rushed into operation. What happened on October 17, 1945, is now an old story in Argentina. Perón was rescued in a dramatic movement which was climaxed by his historic "march on Rome." Though public attention was focused almost exclusively on Perón during those chaotic October events, there were those who recognized that much of the credit for saving the regime belonged to Evita. Perón himself realized this, and said so publicly. What was October 17, 1945? It was the day on which the principal figures in the Argentine drama realized that Evita had a valid claim to recognition as something more than Perón's beautiful mistress. It was the day on which their marriage could no longer be delayed.

On October 21, 1945, Juan Domingo Perón, age fifty, and Eva Duarte, age twenty-six, were married in a secret civil ceremony at Buenos Aires. On December 9, the union was confirmed in a church ceremony at La Plata, with Colonel Domingo A. Mercante serving as best man. After Perón's inauguration as president in June of 1946, the obscure but comely Evita of Los Toldos and Junín was known throughout the world as the Señora María Eva Duarte de Perón, Argentina's first lady.

Embattled Feminist

As the wife of the president, Eva Perón presented Argentines with a spectacle never before seen in their country. The glamorous Evita soon acquired "the furs of a czarina, the jewels of a maharani,"[3] and came to spend an annual average of $40,000 on gowns and dresses fashioned by such Paris designers as Balmain, Dior, Fath, and Rochas. By the time of her death in 1952, Evita had traveled a long way from Los Toldos: not even the story of Cinderella could provide a parallel to the meteoric career of Argentina's late first lady.

Although she asserted that she did not understand politics, Eva Perón became a major political power in the "new Argentina." Shortly after her husband's installation in the *Casa Rosada*, she was given "a desk and a few chores to do"[4] in the ministry of labor and welfare. Before many weeks had passed, not only this ministry but also other government agencies were running her errands. Perón and Evita soon developed a team which, to outward appearances at least, functioned smoothly. She built up her own political organization and slowly surrounded the president with politicians subservient to her. Lacking a sense of humor, Evita harbored vicious grudges against those she considered her enemies; and many of her reprisals were ruthless. She engaged actively in politics, and frequently demanded the resignations of cabinet ministers and ambassadors. Perhaps her most spectacular bid for increased power and prestige came during the election campaign of 1951, when she made a dramatic but futile attempt to become vice president of the nation. This was frustrated in part by opposition within the army to her ambitions,* but the poor condition of her health added a tragic side to the story. Evita had long suffered from a disease the exact nature of which the government was reluctant to make public. It was officially admitted in September of 1951 that she was "rather seriously ill"[5] of anemia, but the full truth could not be suppressed indefinitely. Cancer was her disease, and it was cancer that eventually killed Evita on July 26, 1952. Her death at the age of thirty-three electrified Argentines and occupied newspaper headlines throughout the world. During her brief and hectic life she had risen to the status of a political force of no mean magnitude. And her seven-year partnership with Perón had been a husband-and-wife dictatorship with few parallels in history, modern or otherwise.

In her early years as first lady, Evita turned her huge energies to an element of Peronism—the emancipation of Argentine women—which became her program at least as much as Perón's. Indeed, it has been said that "in the future

* See pp. 79–80 and 313–14.

it will never be possible to speak of feminism and woman suffrage in Argentina without referring to Perón and to his wife Eva. If the first is the inspiring brain and the creator of national feminism and woman suffrage, the second is the living thought and the incarnation of the will of Argentine women."[6]

Although the country is in many respects atypical of the Latin-American states,* the position of women in Argentina has long been similar to the prevalent situation elsewhere in the Americas. Legally and socially, Argentine women have traditionally been assigned a distinctly subordinate status. They have had limited property, civil, and political rights. Until 1947, Argentine women were not permitted to vote. Traditionally, they have not had the benefits of higher education: in 1945 only 13 per cent of the country's 62,700 university students were women. Characteristically, the female sector of Argentina's population has lived in the Hispanic tradition. "Woman, almost always industrious, but intellectually deadened by the action of a society which thinks it dangerous . . . for her to be able to read and write," is the picture painted by a contemporary Argentine feminist leader. "Capable of understanding and being a part of a great collective movement, of sharing the aspirations of men. . . . Strongly dominated by religious beliefs, molded by archaic prejudices, impregnated by a spirit so Spanish that it led man to treat woman with gallantry and at the same time to deny her personality; to value her grace and her beauty but to exploit her weakness and her ignorance, and to have no confidence in her intelligence; to fight a duel when he thought his own woman offended . . . but to shower any woman he passed in the streets with insolent remarks. . . ."[7] This is a picture known to anyone familiar with Hispanic-American life. It

* See pp. 4–6.

irked many Latin-American women, including Eva Perón. "Because I have seen that women have never had material or spiritual opportunities—only poetry took them into account—and because I have known that women were a moral and spiritual resource of the world, I have placed myself at the side of all women of my country," Evita said, "to struggle resolutely with them not only for the vindication of ourselves but also of our homes, our children, and our husbands."[8]

It cannot be denied that Evita played a major part in the history of the Argentine feminist movement. On the other hand, neither should it be denied that the movement *had* a history, and that much of it antedated Eva Perón. Unlike similar movements in Britain and the United States, Argentine feminism had been characterized by an essentially apathetic and inarticulate feminine populace reluctant to follow the lead of the few women in the nation's history who have had the courage and the determination to espouse the cause of rights for women. The earliest of these was Dr. Cecelia Grierson, who in 1889 became Argentina's first woman physician and thereafter endeavored to secure political rights for her female countrymen. Her movement was basically ineffective, due largely to the lack of anything like mass support for her objectives. The same problem frustrated Raquael Camaña's subsequent campaign for co-education and sex instruction in Argentine schools. Indifference on the part of the mass of the nation's women likewise condemned to failure Carolina Muzzili's struggle for legislative protection of female workers; and Sara Justo had only a scant following when she founded the Association of Argentine University Women.

A niche for Argentine feminism was provided in the First International Congress of Free Thought, which met at Buenos Aires in 1906. This conclave's "Feminist Center" endorsed resolutions looking toward the civil and political emancipation of women, but the resolutions went un-implemented in Argentina. Four years later, the Association of Argentine University Women sponsored the First International Feminist Congress, which made similar proposals and urged the liberalization of Argentine divorce laws. Between 1910 and 1918, three feminist organizations appeared in the country—the Argentine Feminist Party, led by Dr. Julieta Lanteri; the Juana Manuela Gorriti Society; and the League for the Rights of Women, founded by Dr. Elvira Rawson de Dellepiane.

World War I gave a major impetus to the movement for woman suffrage in Argentina. Although the country was neutral throughout the war, the tendency in the belligerent states for women to take war jobs found its social repercussions in Argentina. For the first time the nation's women began to assume positions in commerce and industry on anything like a large scale, and with this development came increased demands for votes for women. The post-World War I drive for woman suffrage was stimulated by the adoption in the United States of the Nineteenth Amendment to that republic's constitution, giving the ballot to "North American" women, and by similar developments during this period in other countries of the world. In 1920, the new Argentine National Feminist Union sponsored a mock election to demonstrate the ability of women to cast ballots as well as men. A major victory for the Argentine feminists was achieved in 1926, when the congress enacted measures raising the legal status of women. This was rapidly followed by the foundation of the Argentine Union of Women, the Argentine Association for Woman Suffrage, and various feminist groups sponsored by the country's Socialist party. Moreover, the formation in 1930 of the Inter-American Commission of Women served as a stimulus for feminist movements not only in Argentina but also in other American nations. And, as the example of women in belligerent states taking wartime employment had influenced Argentine females during World War I, so a similar pattern developed in World War II, during which women even entered the armed services of some of the warring countries.

World War II was in progress when the Perón revolution occurred in 1943. It is a curious and significant fact that the Argentine dictatorship—especially during the presidency of General Ramírez—at first endeavored to halt the feminist movement. Ramírez, in his campaign to "renew the national spirit," discouraged commerce, industry, and the government from employing women, and urged the female portion of the populace to concentrate its attention on the home, the raising of children, and religion. "There is a great commotion among the numerous women employees in all government offices," Ray Josephs recorded during the Ramírez period. "The new regime is evidently opposed to women in business or public life. Although they are allowed to retain their salaries and to continue to work . . . they are being eased out of positions of trust. The Castillo administration* had no objection to women, and [Agriculture Minister] Amadeo y Videla especially had such an eye for a pretty *señorita* that the Ministry of Agriculture had been achieving the proportions of a Billy Rose whoop-to on a gigantic scale. All these gals are being summarily cleaned out."[9] The anti-feminism of the "new Argentina" reached its apogee during the presidency of General Fárrell. When, during the course of World War II, Paris was liberated from the Nazis by anti-Axis military forces, the Fárrell regime endeavored to prevent Argentines from celebrating the emancipation of the French capital.

* See pp. 42–44.

Such celebrations nevertheless took place at Buenos Aires in August of 1944, and President Fárrell noted with concern that the demonstrations involved "outside elements . . . directed against the authorities with the object of making a public display of political and extremist ideologies." Fárrell declared with alarmed disapproval that "some impromptu demonstrations . . . were led by persons of the feminine sex"[10] who impeded the work of the police, exploiting the circumstance that the latter were gentlemen.

Then came Evita, and Perón became a feminist. In a dramatic reversal of one aspect of the social content of the revolution of 1943, Eva Perón assumed the role of the nation's foremost feminist. The more acceptable elements of Evita's background were paraded before the Argentine public as illustrations of what woman could really accomplish once she was emancipated and pursued a career. Eva was pictured as the country's model career girl. She had, after all, been an actress, she had been on the radio and in movies. Moreover, by 1948 she was even in the newspaper publishing business. She owned three Buenos Aires papers—*Democracia*, *El Laborista*, and *Noticias Gráficas*—and for a time she was credited with the authorship of a daily column in *Democracia*. The lesson, as outlined by Evita, was clear: *all* Argentine women could accomplish such feats if they would join in the feminism of Eva Perón.

Her movement centered at first on the achievement of woman suffrage. This had already been urged for a number of years by the opposition Radical party, but it was not Evita's business to remind anybody of that. When President Perón's five-year plan was presented to the congress in 1946, woman suffrage was included among the many provisions of the project. Enthusiasm for votes for women was stimulated throughout 1946 and the early portion of 1947, and—for reasons peculiar to the "new Argentina"—Evita's movement did not suffer the same problems and difficulties as had the feminism of Cecelia Grierson and Raquael Camaña, of Carolina Muzzili and Sara Justo, of Julieta Lanteri and Elvira Rawson de Dellepiane.

The Peróns' woman suffrage bill was passed by the Chamber of Deputies on September 9, 1947, approved by the Senate on September 21, and signed and promulgated as law by the president on September 23. The law provided that from that date forward Argentina's woman citizens would have the same political rights as men, that women over the age of eighteen years* could vote and run as candidates for public office. In a ceremony on September 23, 1947, President Perón handed a beribboned copy of the woman suffrage law to Evita. "The vote which we have won is a new tool in our hands," she declared on that occasion. "But our *hands* are not new at struggling, at working, at the repeated miracle of creation. . . . [Women] have an important task to carry out in the coming years. . . . In this battle for the future, our country has given us a dignified and just position which we can occupy with honor. With honor and with conscience. With dignity and with pride. With our right to work and our right to vote."[11] *Peronistas* were eloquent in their tribute to Argentina's leading feminist. "Eva Perón . . . united Argentine women by her own heroic example; she showed them, like a compass, the route," one of her admirers wrote. "Eva Perón gave Argentine women . . . her messianic message of emancipation of their sex. . . . From the shop to the university—worker, teacher, Samaritan, or professional—Argentine woman is now free. . . . The revolution . . . has recognized her inalienable right to all forms of social justice. If Christianity

* A curious amendment enacted on October 13, 1948, provided that woman voters would not be required to disclose their ages to polling officials, who would be required to accept these voters' oral statements simply that they were over eighteen years of age.

dignified her as a wife and sanctified her as a mother, the revolution has placed her on the pedestal of citizenship."[12]

With woman suffrage written into law, Evita then called upon Argentine womanhood to display "the most strict loyalty to the doctrine, the work, and the personality of General Perón."[13] For the purpose of mobilizing this female loyalty, she founded on July 26, 1949, the *Peronista* Feminist party, designed to serve as a militant women's branch of the larger *Peronista* organization. The formal objectives of the female party, of which Evita became president, were to create a unified feminist movement as a political force, to found educational and cultural centers for women, to strengthen the family as a quasi-political institution, and to obtain the assistance of Argentine women in the consolidation of the revolution of 1943. Many of her followers enthusiastically joined Evita in this new endeavor. "We Argentine women have the honor of collaborating with Eva Perón in the formation of a great political party; and, because we have an unequaled leader, we aspire to go down in history as an example of organization and discipline," one of the officials of the new party declared. "We must give all our support . . . in this new Argentina created by the marvelous brain of the revolution. Working for the good of the country and of our party, . . . we can contribute to the greatness of the country."[14] Said another *Peronista* feminist leader: "The only thing that we Argentine women want is that Perón and Eva Perón continue governing for many years, because in this way we can consolidate the conquests which only the . . . government of General Perón has been able to give us."[15] By the election campaign of 1951, the *Peronista* Feminist party was a significant factor in Argentine political life. An estimated 2,000,000 women voted at that time. Moreover, the election of 1951 brought women into the congress for the first time in Ar-

gentine history. Six female senators and twenty-four
woman deputies—all thirty were *Peronistas*—were among
the members of the national legislature when that body
convened in May of 1952. It was against such a background
that Evita was convinced at the time of her death that the
feminist movement over which she had presided had been
a major success which would perform a profound function
in the political evolution of Argentina. "We began, as a
small group of enthusiastic women, to carry out a gigantic
task in this country where women had been not only relegated to a secondary position but also used as instruments of
mixed ambitions," Evita said proudly. "Never before had
they been given the opportunity to undertake a constructive work in the service of their country and people."[16]

Sister of the Downtrodden

The late Eva Perón was a woman of humble origins, and
her background, of course, colored the social content of
much of her work as Argentina's first lady. It is only necessary to remember the poverty, obscurity, and ostracism of
the years at Los Toldos and Junín to appreciate a large part
of her activities. "For many years I have had a limitless
quantity of illusions and dreams," Evita said. "I felt most
deeply that the anguish, the grief, and the sadness of our
people could not be eternal; and that some time a new day
would dawn in this land of ours and that on that new day
the people . . . would break forever the chains of the
hateful slavery and the painful misery in which they had
been kept by the old oligarchy which had been sold to
bastard, anti-national interests. So when I saw Perón take
the flag of the workers to carry it to victory, . . . and
when I saw that the people had decided to fight with Perón
. . . I, a humble woman of the people, understood that it
was my duty to take my place with the workers, with the

*descamisados,** to help Perón realize our hopes so that all could see the great Argentina of which I had dreamed."[17] There is no doubt that much cynicism and insincerity is widespread among Perón's followers: one member of the president's cabinet has gone so far as to say privately that he did not know if every Argentine liar were a *Peronista*, but that he was convinced that every *Peronista* was a liar. Nevertheless, there is considerable justification for the observation that "other *Peronistas* may be in the movement for what they can get out of it, but Evita [lived] as one convinced that her husband's regime [was] a new and revolutionary force in the world."[18]

The most spectacular symbol of Evita's identification with the problems of Argentina's economically under-privileged folk was the mammoth María Eva Duarte de Perón Social Aid Foundation, popularly known simply as "the Foundation." This organization, originally headed by Evita, was established on June 23, 1948, with a capital investment of $2,092 of her own money; by the time of her death in 1952, the Foundation was operating on an annual budget of approximately $100,000,000. According to Evita's statement when the enterprise was begun, it was to have two major sources of revenue—her own personal donations, and voluntary contributions from other Argentine persons and private organizations. In September of 1950, the congress approved a measure permitting the Foundation to participate in the government's budget, although administration officials were careful to point out at the time that the organization was to remain essentially Eva's privately operated project, and that it was not to be regarded as a government agency. "The Foundation of the Señora de Perón is a civil institution, with which the state has nothing

* See pp. 316–18.

to do," President Perón himself explained. "It is, without a doubt, the first great experiment of its kind in the country."[19]

Techniques of financing the María Eva Duarte de Perón Social Aid Foundation have long been a matter of spirited discussion among Argentines. Theoretically, the organization derived its resources from (1) Evita's personal funds, (2) voluntary contributions, and (3) occasional government subsidies. Since the Foundation was not regarded as an agency of the state, its financial records were not open to public scrutiny, and many agreed that Evita operated the enterprise "as casually as a bride's personal checking account."[20] In July of 1949, the Foundation was exempted from taxation, and thereafter public funds were frequently transferred to the organization in the form of state contributions to assist the Foundation in carrying out a number of its operations. Twenty per cent of the annual income of the national lottery went to Evita's project for the same purpose.

Many labor unions affiliated with the government-controlled General Confederation of Labor (C.G.T.)* made regular contributions to the Foundation in the form of "voluntary" donations of the country's workers. These contributions were frequently "voluntary" only in a Pickwickian sense. At its national convention in August of 1950, the C.G.T. voted to deduct thenceforth two days' pay per year from its members' wages for delivery to the Foundation as a voluntary contribution of the workers. This measure added an estimated $6,000,000 to the organization's yearly intake. The following December, the Foundation announced that it would return the "contribution" to the workers, who then spent the Christmas season under the

* See pp. 319–328.

impression that Evita was making the refund to them as a magnificent holiday gesture. However, the C.G.T. protested after Christmas that the bookkeeping difficulties involved in making the refund would be insuperable; and on January 16, 1951—when the holiday spirit remained alive only in the hardiest of Argentines—the Foundation at length graciously accepted the "voluntary" contribution. The entire procedure was branded by the opposition Socialist party as unconstitutional.

Some techniques of financing the Foundation were reminiscent of the work of a number of "protection" rackets in the United States involving "voluntary" payments as the alternative to painful reprisals. Variously effective pressures were applied to force "contributions," and few Argentines were able to withstand these pressures successfully. The notorious Massone incident was a case in point. Long one of South America's leading manufacturers of biochemicals, the Massone Institute—under the direction of Arnaldo Massone, well known for his anti-*Peronista* leanings—had refused to make "voluntary" contributions to the Foundation. At length, in October of 1950, Evita took steps to force the Massone Institute to donate funds for the Foundation. When Massone stubbornly refused to make a contribution, he and other directors of his institute were indicted on charges of falsifying the chemical descriptions of a number of biochemical products. Justice was swift: on December 27, 1950, the Massone Institute was fined $54,268 and its directors were sentenced to from forty-five to ninety days' imprisonment. Massone himself escaped to Montevideo, but a cerebral disease soon prevented him from appreciating fully his Uruguayan haven. And on December 29, the newspapers of Buenos Aires reported that the Massone Institute was in bankruptcy.

As originally conceived, the Foundation's purpose was to give financial aid and assistance in finding employment to the needy of Argentina; and to construct housing units, schools, and hospitals. Evita said that she hoped "to supply necessities and to improve and consolidate the home life of all Argentines who suffer. . . . We wish also to supplement the action of the state by solving individual problems."[21] In a very real sense, the appearance of the Foundation represented a revolution in the Argentine approach to social assistance. Before the rise of Perón, the problem had been handled primarily as a matter for charity, the administration of which was almost exclusively the concern of the venerable and aristocratic Society of Philanthropy. Traditionally, the honorary president of the society was, on an *ex officio* basis, the wife of the nation's chief executive. But, when Eva Perón became the first lady in 1946, she was not invited to head the Society of Philanthropy. To her this was but another chapter in the Los Toldos–Junín story of the Oligarchy and ostracism: "When the [Society's] haughty dowagers decided that Evita was not good enough, Evita set out to show them."[22] By 1950 the Society of Philanthropy was no longer in operation, and social assistance had become the monopoly of the huge and sprawling bureaucracy of the María Eva Duarte de Perón Social Aid Foundation, Argentina's largest single enterprise.

While the Foundation's program seemed ambitious when it was first announced in 1948, the agency after only three years' work had not only an impressive record of performance toward its initial goals, but had also expanded into other fields of endeavor. Homes for children, workers, the aged, and transients were built, as were hospitals, clinics, and schools; food and clothing were distributed among the needy; and emergency relief was rushed by Evita to disaster victims not only in Argentina but also in other countries of the world. She said with much truth that her "work is in plain sight and anybody can see it."[23]

She espoused an especial interest in the orphaned and uneducated children of her country and liked to quote her husband, who once said: "In Argentina, the only privileged people are the children."[24] The late Evita not only made emotional speeches about "thousands of little ones, without schooling, without hygienic care, without any home life, herded together in sordid huts and falling ready prey to illness of every kind,"[25] but she also did something about them. Consider, for example, statistics on school construction. Between June 4, 1943, and December 31, 1950, some 4,000 schools were built in the "new Argentina." Of these 1,000 were erected by the María Eva Duarte de Perón Social Aid Foundation. Evita said she wanted to aid the "abandoned child, the child who has no home,"[26] the child who has no Christmas. In Argentina, Christmas is observed somewhat differently than in the United States: there are toys for the children, to be sure, but the holiday season in Argentina is not complete without the traditional *pan dulce* —a kind of sweet bread—and cider. During the 1950 Christmas season, Eva's Foundation distributed 5,000,000 toys, 4,000,000 loaves of *pan dulce*, and 4,000,000 bottles of cider among impoverished families with children, many of whom would not otherwise have had an Argentine Christmas. "The country which forgets its children and does not supply their needs is a country which denies itself a future," Evita asserted, perhaps remembering Christmas at Los Toldos or Junín. "To fight for the well-being, the physical and moral health, the education and the life of the child is, essentially, to fight for the grandeur of the country and the future welfare of the nation."[27]

The record was similar in other areas of the Foundation's work. In the expansion of medical services available to the less wealthy of Argentina, statistics are again impressive. In 1943, when Perón came to power, the country boasted 57 hospitals with 15,425 beds. At the end of 1949, there were 119 hospitals with 23,395 beds, much of the real and movable equipment bearing the imprint of the María Eva Duarte de Perón Social Aid Foundation. In 1951 the Foundation's nursing schools were training 1,300 nurses, and Evita's organization opened 35 clinics in that year alone. And the Foundation likewise operated as a species of Red Cross, sending emergency aid to the scenes of disasters and accidents throughout the country. Let an airplane crash in Tierra del Fuego or a railroad train overturn in Córdoba: the Foundation was on hand within hours of the calamity, with blood plasma, doctors, nurses, medical supplies, food, and clothing for the surviving victims of the tragedy.

Nor was Evita's emergency relief work limited to Argentina alone. When, in August of 1949, South America's most catastrophic earthquake in a decade struck the small republic of Ecuador, the Foundation immediately went into action. An estimated 8,000 Ecuadorans died in the disaster: many of the survivors were aided by medical personnel, supplies, and equipment, and by food and clothing sent by Evita. The story was repeated in many other places outside of Argentina—in the Colombian earthquake of July of 1950, in the Venezuelan tremor of the following month. And the hand of the Foundation reached far outside of South America: in August of 1950, there arrived at Tel Aviv a shipment of food and clothing for needy immigrants entering the youthful state of Israel. The source of the aid was conspicuously stenciled on the shipment: the María Eva Duarte de Perón Social Aid Foundation.

Even some "North Americans" had the politically embarrassing help of Evita. The Children's Society, Incorporated, of Washington, D.C., found to its consternation in January of 1949 that it was the recipient of a gift from Eva's Foundation, clothing for 600 children to be distributed within the District of Columbia. The alarmed directors of the "North American" society had several misgivings as to whether or not to accept the shipment, and at length referred the question to the Department of State at Washington. When this department indicated that it had no official objection to receipt of the Foundation's donation, Mrs. Fay Vawters, codirector of the Children's Society, somewhat unhappily announced that "we are going to accept [the gift] with all the grace that God in His mercy can bestow upon us."[28]

More recently, the Foundation went into business, selling many of the items it had previously distributed gratis. In 1951, Evita's organization opened a chain composed initially of twenty-four stores at Buenos Aires which handled a vast range of commodities. The Foundation's stores undersold other Argentine grocers and clothiers and seriously threatened to drive many of them out of business. There was no point in arguing that this menaced private enterprise: theoretically the Foundation itself was a private enterprise; and, besides, Perón had said that he had no love for capitalism.*

Evita was anxious to distinguish between charity and social assistance as dispensed by her foundation. "Charity humiliates and social aid dignifies and stimulates," she said. "Charity is given discreetly; social aid, rationally. Charity prolongs the situation; social aid solves it. . . . Charity is the generosity of the fortunate; social aid remedies social inequalities. Charity separates the wealthy from the poor; social aid raises the needy to the level of the well-to-do."[29] The program of her Social Aid Foundation, she pointed

* See p. 289.

out, emerged from conditions in which thousands of Argentines lived "with starvation wages, without security of employment, without rights to self-improvement, without a single guarantee for themselves, their families, and their future. . . . I hope that, as the word 'impossible' has disappeared from the language of the Argentines, . . . so the word 'charity' will disappear from all the languages of the world."[30]

Evita devoted much of her own time and energy to the work of the Foundation. She was at her desk in the ministry of labor and welfare by seven o'clock in the morning of every working day, and usually put in what her admirers called a day of "intense humanitarian labor." Three days a week she received the poor and distributed impressive quantities of food, clothing, money, and advice among them. One of the characteristic sights of the "new Argentina" during Evita's time was the long line of shabbily dressed Argentines waiting at the Peru Street entrance of the ministry of labor and welfare for their opportunity to see *la señora,* the "woman of the people." Hers was a fatiguing pace, a staggering working day, which she maintained steadily until approximately a year before she lost her fight with cancer. She said that she spent "every hour of the day looking after the needs of the *descamisados,* to show them that here, in the Argentine republic, . . . the gulf which had separated the people from the government no longer exists; that here we are all one, working night and day for the greatness of the country and for the happiness of its people."[31] Her work was deeply appreciated by many Argentines and by citizens of other lands as well. Indeed, she was honored and decorated by many governments in addition to her own. She held the Spanish government's Grand Cross of Isabella the Catholic, and Colombia's Cross of Boyacá; Peru's Grand Cross of the Order of the Sun, and

Mexico's Order of the Aztec Eagle; the Netherlands' Grand Cross of the Order of Orange Nassau, and Ecuador's Grand Cross of the Order of Merit, the last-named bestowed in recognition of "the spontaneous and generous manner in which she contributed to the relief of the grief of the victims of the earthquake of August of 1949."[32]

The late Eva Perón was thus much more than merely the beautiful wife of the president of Argentina. She was a major South American politician and a partner in dictatorship, a leading feminist and an outstanding social worker. Late in 1952, Argentines were reading that Evita's body would lie in state at Buenos Aires much in the fashion of Lenin's at Moscow, and that many monuments would be erected in her memory. In death, as she had during the last seven years of her short life, Evita provoked bitter controversy among Argentines. Some regarded her as a vicious and immoral woman. Others ranked her with Mrs. Franklin D. Roosevelt and with Madame Chiang Kai-shek to say that these were the three greatest women the twentieth century had thus far produced. Still others sought sainthood for Evita, and said that it was unfair to class her with only the *norteamericana* and the *china* when there was also Joan of Arc.

6.

Institutionalized Lockstep

Perón's Constitution of 1949 provides for the presidential system of government, complete with a three-way separation of powers on the national level. This division of authority among executive, legislative, and judicial branches —the Argentines call them "powers"—is, of course, familiar in the United States. The writers of the Argentine Constitution of 1853 consciously borrowed this arrangement from the "North Americans"; and the *Peronistas*, in writing the 1949 document, retained the form of the separation of powers. Whereas the system had some substance in Argentina during the life of the Constitution of 1853, government under the new constitution preserves the external form and little more of this division of authority. Perón's control of the Executive Power has already been noted; his domination of the Legislative and Judicial powers, though more indirect, is no less effective.

Congress

The so-called Legislative Power has had an irregular existence in the "new Argentina." The bicameral congress—composed of a senate of 30 members and a 158-member chamber of deputies—was totally inoperative for the four-and-one-half-year period from December of 1941 until

June of 1946. It will be remembered that, in the immediately pre-Perón era, President Ramón S. Castillo declared a state of siege on December 16, 1941.* The dissolution of the congress was among the constitutional effects of this measure. Thus, the Legislative Power had already been in a state of suspended animation for a year and a half when the Perón revolution occurred on June 4, 1943. Within forty-eight hours of that rebellion, President Ramírez signed a decree reaffirming the dissolution of the Legislative Power; and the congress remained nonexistent until 1946.

With the election of February 24 of that year—Peron's first election—new senators and deputies were chosen; and June 4, 1946, the date of Perón's first inauguration, was also the date on which the congress convened for the first time since December of 1941. In the years before Castillo, the congress under the Constitution of 1853 effectively exercised legislative authority.† Since 1946, however—and especially since the adoption of Perón's new Constitution of 1949—the national legislature has been an essentially subservient body. To the extent that the opposition Radical party has been granted minority representation in the Chamber of Deputies, that chamber has served in part as one of the few rostrums from which the opposition might speak in the "new Argentina"; since 1946 the opposition has not been represented in the Senate.

Under the Constitution of 1949, the 192-member bicameral congress meets for one five-month regular session per year. This session opens on May 1 and adjourns on September 30. Special sessions may be called by President Perón. The Senate may meet alone for the purpose of confirming presidential appointments; this is the only circumstance in which one legislative chamber may meet for a period

* See p. 43.
† Cf. Austin F. Macdonald, *Government of the Argentine Republic* (New York, 1942).

of more than three days while the other is out of session.

THE SENATE. The constitutions of both 1853 and 1949 provided for a federal principle of senatorial representation, in accordance with which the Federal Capital and each of the provinces would send two members to that chamber. This arrangement resulted in a thirty-member senate so long as the Argentine provinces were fourteen in number. However, two new provinces were created in 1951 and 1952;* and, since the latter date, the total number of senatorial seats has been figured at thirty-four. The Senate is presided over by the vice president of the nation. Senators are required to be at least thirty years old, Argentine citizens for at least ten years before their election to the Senate, and residents of the provinces they represent (or of the Federal Capital, in the case of the two senators from that entity) for at least two years before the election.

With respect to the structure of the Senate, two major differences between the constitutions of 1853 and 1949 should be noted. In the first place, the *Peronistas* have changed the method of electing senators. Under the older constitution, the legislatures in each of the fourteen provinces elected twenty-eight of the senators, and the two senators from the Federal Capital were chosen by an electoral college unit which met at the city of Buenos Aires. Since the adoption of the Constitution of 1949, the senators are directly elected by the voters in the provinces—now sixteen in number—and the Federal District. In the second place, the senators' terms of office have been altered. During the life of the Constitution of 1853, senators had nine-year terms and one-third of the Senate was renewed every three years. The writers of Perón's new constitution felt that this arrangement called for too many elections; accordingly the 1949 document provides that all senators are

* See pp. 145–46.

to have six-year terms and that the entire body is to be elected at the same time. A transitory article stipulated that all senators who were in office at the time the change was made (1949) would have their terms extended until April 30, 1952; thereafter, the Senate was to be entirely renewed once every six years. Both the 1853 and 1949 constitutions declared that senators were indefinitely eligible for re-election.

Very little free debate occurs in either chamber of the congress in the "new Argentina"; and far less debate is to be heard in the Senate than in the Chamber of Deputies. The Senate has been composed entirely of *Peronistas* ever since 1946. Opposed views almost never clash on the floor of that chamber, and when they do it is generally in consequence of differing interpretations among *Peronistas* as to what their leader wants. In Perón's Argentina the Senate is neither a deliberative body nor a debating society.

THE CHAMBER OF DEPUTIES. Such congressional debate as does occur in the "new Argentina" is to be found in the Chamber of Deputies, the so-called lower house. The membership of this chamber totals 158 under the Constitution of 1949, which did not alter the size of the body as it stood during the closing years of the 1853 instrument. Theoretically, representation in the Chamber of Deputies is determined on a distribution-by-population basis, but this constitutional requirement was not scrupulously enforced under either the Constitution of 1853 or the new document. Both of these constitutions stipulated that a census would be taken once every ten years, but this was done only four times—in 1869, 1895, 1914, and 1947—during the life of the Constitution of 1853, and as yet no census has been conducted since the adoption of the new charter. The present size of the chamber—158 deputies—stems from Law No. 10,834 of September 26, 1919, which, based on the 1914 census, stipulated that the provinces and the Federal Capital would elect one deputy for every 49,000 inhabitants and one additional deputy for each remaining fraction of that figure, provided that the fraction was larger than 16,500. The Constitution of 1949 provides that there shall be one deputy for every 100,000 inhabitants (and one for each remaining fraction larger than 50,000) in the provinces and in the Federal Capital. But the total size of the chamber remains fixed at 158 deputies. Each province and the Federal Capital are divided into as many congressional districts as deputies they send to congress, with one deputy then being selected from each of these districts.

Deputies are required to be at least twenty-five years of age, Argentine citizens for at least ten years before their election, and residents of the provinces they represent (or the Federal Capital, where that is the case) for at least two years before the election. Their terms of office have been altered by the Constitution of 1949. Under the older charter, deputies had four-year terms, with one-half the chamber renewed every two years; since 1949, they have had six-year terms, with the renewal by halves occurring once every three years. As in the case of the senators, deputies in office at the time the change was made had their terms extended until April 30, 1952.

The "Sáenz Peña Law" of 1912* introduced the requirement that at least one-third of the seats in the Chamber of Deputies be held by members of minority political parties. This stipulation was observed in the composition of the chamber until an electoral law passed in 1951 reduced the minimum number of seats to be held by opposition deputies to ten. Thus, the Chamber of Deputies has not yet been 100 per cent *Peronista*, as the Senate has since 1946; and debate in the lower house has been more spirited and lively in

* See p. 33.

Perón's Argentina than discussions have been in the Senate. The chief opposition party, so far as the Chamber of Deputies is concerned, has been the Radical organization. The Radicals acquired forty-three seats in the chamber after the election of 1946. After the 1951 election, the Radicals—with fourteen seats—were the only opposition party represented in the chamber. This stubborn minority conducted a bitter criticism of the Perón regime in the congress, often subjecting the administration to severe embarrassment. Thus, Perón's opponents had smaller representation in the congress during his second term; but it remained true that the Chamber of Deputies was the only legislative organ in the "new Argentina" in which an anti-Perón voice might be raised, albeit cautiously.

According to the text of the constitution, the powers of the Argentine congress closely parallel those of the Congress of the United States. In actual practice, however, the Argentine national legislature has no effective autonomy in Perón's Argentina. With a Senate that is 100 per cent *Peronista* and a Chamber of Deputies containing only fourteen opposition congressmen, the congress of Argentina plays the supine role of a rubber stamp for the wishes of the chief of the Executive Power. Let the President of the Nation let his wishes known, and the congress places them on a statutory basis. Such is the role of the Legislative Power in Perón's Argentina.

Insofar as the opposition is represented in the Chamber of Deputies, that body performs a function of some significance in that it provides a platform from which anti-*Peronista* spokesmen may at times operate. Radical deputies have upon occasion been sufficiently effective in embarrassing the regime to inspire the *Peronistas* to seek ways and means of silencing even the little opposition that raises its head in the Chamber of Deputies. The *Peronista* deputies, an overwhelming majority in the chamber, have developed two parliamentary weapons which have been effective in terrorizing and in "disciplining" the opposition. The first of these is to deprive a legislator of his congressional immunity, which according to Argentine law can be done by a vote of a simple majority of the chamber of which the legislator in question is a member; and the second is to expel a congressman from the legislature altogether, which can be done by a vote of two-thirds of the members of the chamber involved. The *Peronista* majority is sufficiently large in the Chamber of Deputies to muster the number of votes needed for either of these punitive measures, and they have been felt by many an outspoken Radical deputy. When, for example, Deputy Agustín Rodríguez Araya, a Radical from the Province of Santa Fé, made a speech on April 19, 1949, in which he compared the *Peronistas* to the fabled villains of *Ali Baba and the Forty Thieves*, the majority in the Chamber of Deputies came to the conclusion that the comparison was so unfortunate that Rodríguez Araya needed disciplining. The *Peronista* machine swept into operation: the requisite two-thirds vote was produced, and the offending Radical was expelled from the congress on June 9, 1949. "Already the voice of men means nothing," Rodríguez Araya observed with some dismay; "I also know in what climate and in what epoch I live."[1] Or consider the case of Deputy Atilio E. Cattáneo (Radical, Federal Capital) who was reckless enough to venture aloud the opinion that Perón's personal wealth had not diminished during the latter's presidency: Cattáneo was on December 7, 1949, deprived of his reserve commission in the Argentine Army because "his conduct [belies] good conduct and education";[2] and on December 12 Cattáneo was expelled from the congress. Or take Deputy Mauricio Yadarola (Radical, Córdoba), who was in June of 1950 expelled from the chamber because he had introduced a bill providing for the resurrection of civil liberties; its text had intimated that such liberties did not exist in Perón's Argentina.

The two most celebrated cases of punishment of opposition congressmen who dared to speak out against the regime are the instances of Deputies Ricardo J. Balbín (Radical, Province of Buenos Aires) and Ernesto E. Sammartino (Radical, Federal Capital). The Balbín affair has already been discussed in another connection.* Sammartino was the leader of the Radical bloc in the Chamber of Deputies when, in mid-1948, he criticized Perón for writing a series of articles for the "North American" press. When Sammartino publicly assailed Perón as "a president who alienates all his political adversaries; a president who believes that history begins and ends with him,"[3] *Peronista* Deputy José Conte Grand rose to propose Sammartino's expulsion from the chamber. The motion was eventually carried, but the debate on the Sammartino ouster gave Argentines some of the most daring and thrilling oratory they had heard throughout the life of the "new Argentina." Sammartino lashed out desperately at his tormentors. He charged that Perón and the late Evita were attempting to "train the press to fear dictators. . . . We have not come here to bow reverently before the whip or to dance jigs to please a Madame Pompadour. This is not a fashionable night club or a social club or the anteroom of a palace. This is the chamber of a free people, and it is necessary to say here, so that those who should know this will know it, that this chamber should never again listen to the voice of command of old colonels dressed in long shirts, or to the orders embraced in perfumed invitations from the boudoir of any ruler. It is only necessary to add that we are repeating the

* See pp. 81–82.

example of the senate of Rome's decadence, which maintained that Caesar had the right to take for himself any woman in the Empire."[4] Sammartino's was a bombastic but immediately fruitless defense: the question of his expulsion was put to a vote when Deputy Dávila (*Peronista*, San Juan) declared with alarm that "today the Fascist state is in crisis."[5] By a vote of 104 *Peronistas* against 42 Radicals, Sammartino was expelled from the Chamber of Deputies on August 5, 1948. Incensed and angered by their leader's ouster, the remaining 42 Radicals stalked out of the congress in protest, returning on August 14 only after they had been urged to go back by the Radicals' formal leadership and by Sammartino himself, who had fled to Montevideo. "The fact that I am going underground is only the beginning," Sammartino told them from his Uruguayan exile. "Tomorrow all of you will have to join me."[6]

Peronista-dominated congressional investigating committees have undergone since 1946 a significant evolution as one of the regime's major tools of repression. It has been said that the "new Argentina's" congressional committees "make the United States House Un-American Activities Committee in the days of J. Parnell Thomas appear mild."[7] The case of the Chamber of Deputies' committee to investigate torture is illustrative. It had long been charged that the Perón regime was subjecting some of its political prisoners to physical torture,* and in 1949 a congressional committee was established to investigate these charges. The committee, headed by José Emilio Visca and Rodolfo P. Decker, both *Peronistas*, discharged its task by subjecting the *newspapers and wire services* which had carried stories of torture to a most thoroughgoing inquisition! Before the committee completed its work, it had taken over the account books of the Buenos Aires offices of the Associated Press and the

* See pp. 181–85.

United Press, the Argentine branches of the National City Bank of New York and the Bank of London, and seven Argentine newspapers, including the two leading anti-Perón papers of the capital, *La Prensa* and *La Nación*. As for torture of political prisoners, the Visca-Decker committee declared in 1950 that it was not "convenient" to report on that matter; and the committee was forthwith dissolved.

The Legislative Power in Perón's Argentina is an obedient tool of the Executive Power and little more. A group of carefully disciplined *Peronistas*, many of them fanatically loyal to their leader, dominate the congress and have dedicated themselves to giving Perón whatever he wishes. The eclipse of the Legislative Power in contemporary Argentina has been a major feature of the Perón era. *Peronista* congressmen work closely with, and at the bidding of, the Executive Power; and the opposition deputies are cowed and intimidated. The decline of the once effective Argentine congress has been a tragic if spectacular story; and few documents tell it more effectively than the *Diario de Sesiones de la Cámara de Senadores* and the *Diario de Sesiones de la Cámara de Diputados*, which together constitute Argentina's *Congressional Record*. There is little significant debate in the Senate, where all members are *Peronistas*; as for the Chamber of Deputies, witness these excerpts from the official record:

CASAL [*Peronista*]: The author of the bill does not understand the fundamentals of the problem.
SAMMARTINO [Radical]: I at least do not come with my speech written by the Secretariat of Public Health.[8]

Or again:

ROCHE [*Peronista*]: This law is to punish traitors.
SANTANDER [Radical]: The traitors can be in the *Casa Rosada*.
DECKER [*Peronista*]: You must retract those words.

The Presiding Officer [HÉCTOR J. CÁMPORA, *Peronista*]: Mr. Deputy from Entre Ríos: the deputies of the majority bloc invite the deputy to retract the words which he has just spoken.[9]

Although an opposition deputy occasionally dares to voice criticism of the Perón administration, the reprisals for these indiscretions are so swift and merciless that only the most courageous or reckless defy them. As elsewhere in the "new Argentina," opposition in congress has been progressively cowed and intimidated. Pointing to "the suppression of freedom of speech in the congress," Sammartino has declared that "without freedom of speech, no Legislative Power, no congress, is possible. A meeting of popularly elected persons never was a Legislative Power, a congress . . . without freedom of speech. . . . No deputy can effectively carry on his work in this congress so long as the majority stands ready to discipline him, no deputy may work here if his soul is sensitive to the abuses of dictators and if his conscience commands him to defend liberty."[10] The *Peronistas* themselves have spoken little about their own inner feelings on the matter, but it may be that the Radical Deputy Uranga had some insight into them when he said: "None of the deputies of the majority are proud, satisfied, or happy after voting as we know they will vote, after a vote as mechanical as the *vivas* and the *mueras* dictated to them through the microphone at the *Casa Rosada*. . . . We know that there will not be a dissident deputy here, or a strong voice raised in opposition to this brutal and unjust dictatorship."[11] And hear Sammartino's last speech in the chamber of deputies: "We all know— why should we deceive ourselves?—who governs the country. There is a will which is above the law, and this implacable will has decreed my expulsion from this chamber. . . . I have seen the fallen commemorative columns in Rome, along what was once called the Via Mussolini."[12]

The Courts

The same pattern of executive control is to be found in the Judicial Power. The Argentine court system, originally patterned after the "North American" judiciary, enjoyed a large measure of independence and power during the life of the Constitution of 1853. "The principal and most powerful of the functions of the Judicial Power is to interpret and decide upon the validity of laws enacted by the Legislative Power," Argentina's foremost constitutional lawyer said of the pre-Perón arrangement. "The Judicial Power is supreme, and only it has the authority to declare a law of the congress unconstitutional."[13] Since the coming of Perón, however, the Argentine judiciary has adhered to this precept only in form: the substance has been the substance of executive dictatorship.

The formal structure of the Argentine court system resembles strikingly its prototype in the United States. Theoretically, federalism exists in Argentina,* and this means, among other things, that there are two systems of courts— the national tribunals and the judiciaries of each of the sixteen provinces. The basic Argentine principle distinguishing the jurisdiction of the national courts from that of the provincial tribunals is the proposition that the former handle only those cases arising under the national constitution and laws, and that all other litigation lies to the provincial courts. This principle was stated by Argentina's Supreme Court of Justice in a celebrated 1873 decision involving an attempt to assassinate the president of the nation, then Domingo F. Sarmiento. The court ruled that, inasmuch as no provisions regarding such a case were to be found in the national constitution or laws, the national tribunals were not competent to try the alleged culprit. "Offenses—such

* See pp. 133–49.

as this attempt against the life of the Supreme Chief of the Nation—which ought to be under the protection of the national tribunals but are not, because of an imperfection in the laws, should be subject to the ordinary jurisdiction of the courts of the province in which the offense was committed," the Supreme Court of Justice declared at the time. "This is preferable to allowing the national judges to assume legislative power, a usurpation which would bring within itself more evils than the criminal acts which it would attempt to punish."[14] It is a curious fact that, despite the tenor of this opinion, the general effect of Argentine practice—even in the years before Perón—has been such that a much smaller proportion of the litigation falls to the Argentine provincial courts than is heard by the state courts in the analogous situation in the United States.

As the hierarchy of the Argentine system now stands, national courts exist on five levels. Little purpose would be served by an exhaustive analysis here of all these tribunals. A discussion of the status of the Supreme Court of Justice, Argentina's highest judicial body, would suffice to demonstrate the position of the Judicial Power in the Perón era.

The Supreme Court of Justice is composed of five judges. Members of this tribunal must be native-born Argentine citizens, hold graduate law degrees conferred by Argentine institutions, have at least ten years' experience in the legal profession before their appointment to the court, and be at least thirty years of age. Inasmuch as Argentine judicial proceedings are largely written and rarely oral, the five members of the Supreme Court of Justice very seldom sit as a body.

The jurisdiction of this tribunal extends only to actual controversies brought before it. The court will not hand down declaratory judgments; that is, it will not rule on a question unless it is actually germane to a case which the tribunal must decide. Although the jurisdiction of the Supreme Court of Justice is largely appellate, the court does have original jurisdiction over three types of cases: controversies between the national government and a provincial government, or between an Argentine province and a foreign state; between two or more Argentine provincial governments; and litigation involving ambassadors, public ministers, and consuls. So far as its appellate jurisdiction is concerned, the court may take appeals either from lower national courts or from the highest provincial tribunal in each of the sixteen provinces. Theoretically, the Supreme Court of Justice may take an appealed case from a provincial supreme court only if the national constitution and laws are alleged to be involved in the case; in theory, the provincial courts are the final judges of the constitutions and statutes of their respective provinces.

In Argentine practice, the Supreme Court of Justice has been the only tribunal in the country with even a modified form of the power of judicial review, that is, the authority to decide on the validity of the acts of the Executive and Legislative powers. As in the United States, judicial review in Argentina was established by court decision rather than by constitutional texts. The two Argentine cases establishing judicial review were handed down in 1875 and in 1884. The latter case introduced the doctrine of separability into the Argentine system, providing that if only a part of a legislative enactment is declared unconstitutional, that part may be separated from the remainder of the enactment, which would continue in force.[15]

The Argentine Supreme Court of Justice exercises a large measure of control over the other courts in the country. The Constitution of 1949 declares: "The interpretation which the Supreme Court of Justice makes of the Constitution . . . must be applied by lower national and by provincial courts."[16] Moreover, the highest Argentine tribunal exercises administrative supervision of the lower national courts. This power involves control of such matters as their internal organization, budgets, and personnel policies.

When the revolution of 1943 occurred, the five members of the Supreme Court of Justice were Chief Justice Roberto Repetto, Antonio Sogarna, Luis Linares, Benito Nazor Anchorena, and Francisco Ramos Mejía. These gentlemen were not in sympathy with the methods or objectives of Perón and his collaborators, and in the early years of the "new Argentina" the court conducted a spirited opposition to the regime. Although the tribunal did recognize the Ramírez administration as a de facto government on June 7, 1943, other actions of the court left little doubt as to its attitude toward the political situation. On April 3, 1945, in what was described as an "unprecedented blow to Argentina's military rulers,"[17] the Supreme Court of Justice declared three of their decrees unconstitutional. Perón, then vice president, war minister, and secretary of labor and welfare, charged that the tribunal had "judged men and not the excellence of the measures."[18] The rejoinder of the Supreme Court of Justice was not long delayed: on May 23, 1945, it invalidated a labor and welfare decree of which Perón himself had been the author. When, two months later, a series of labor courts was established with Perón's sponsorship, the Supreme Court of Justice refused to swear in the new labor judges. And, in September of 1945, the tribunal ordered the release of twelve retired army officers whom Perón had ordered imprisoned on charges of conspiracy to overthrow the government. Later in the same month the court annulled a fine of $270 which had been imposed on the All-American Cables Company because it had allegedly violated censorship regulations. A few weeks later, the Supreme Court of Justice secured the release of Rodolfo Barraco Marmól, a federal judge at Córdoba, who had been jailed for freeing six political prisoners.

Thus, though the members of the court argued that they were dispensing impartial justice and not engaging in politics, it was evident by September of 1945 that the Supreme Court of Justice was centrally involved in Argentina's acrimonious political turmoil. Few were surprised on August 28 of that year when a group of 208 professors of the University of the Littoral addressed a formal petition to the tribunal, urging it to retract its earlier recognition of the regime and take over the reins of government itself. Though the court on September 10 declared that the professors' petition was out of order, the lines were clearly drawn: the Supreme Court of Justice was opposed to Perón, and opposition political groups began to use the tribunal in their struggle against the regime. When Perón temporarily fell from power in October of 1945, a group of navy officers formally requested the court to assume the power of government and call elections; and four days later the Radical party endorsed this request.

Though the tribunal took no decisive action on those appeals, its enmity toward Perón was clearly apparent when the latter became president on June 4, 1946. Those who listened to the new president's inaugural address saw in it indications that the Supreme Court of Justice would soon be among Perón's victims. "I place the spirit of justice above the Judicial Power," Perón said; and added that the tribunal "does not speak the same language as the other branches of the government."[19]

Shortly after President Perón's inauguration, Argentines witnessed an impressive spectacle: the *Peronistas* embarked upon the ambitious task of *impeaching the entire Supreme*

Court of Justice! Impeachment procedures in Argentina are similar in form to those in the United States: the Chamber of Deputies brings the impeachment charges, and the Senate sits as a court to try the accused officials. The impeachment project began in the Chamber of Deputies in September of 1946. Chief Justice Repetto, rather than endure the ordeal, resigned from the court in October. The remaining four judges—Sogarna, Linares, Nazor Anchorena, and Ramos Mejía—stayed at their posts to be impeached by the Chamber of Deputies and removed from office by the Senate.

The affair was both spectacular and instructive in the ways of Perón's Argentina. His well-disciplined machine in the Chamber of Deputies produced five decisions of the Supreme Court of Justice which were cited as evidence that Sogarna, Linares, Nazor Anchorena, and Ramos Mejía were guilty of misdemeanors and hence unfit for membership in their nation's highest tribunal. The first such decision was the ruling of June 7, 1943, recognizing the revolutionary regime as a de facto government. Such recognition, the *Peronistas* charged, was a political and not a judicial function, lying beyond the competence of the judiciary. Exhibit B—invalidation of a labor decree—was submitted as proof that the four justices were reactionaries incapable of keeping their class bias separate from their work as judges. In the third place, the Supreme Court of Justice had prevented the establishment by executive decree of a national tribunal in the Chaco, evidence to the *Peronistas* of the high court's systematic political sabotage of the administration. Fourth, the justices had freed Córdoba Judge Rodolfo Barraco Marmól, who, Perón himself said, belonged in prison. Exhibit E: rent control had been declared unconstitutional. Ex-Chief Justice Repetto had retired from the struggle, but his moral support went to his embattled former colleagues when, from his haven, Repetto branded the five charges as "imaginary crimes" and warned that "a new state power has been instituted above the constitution and above the law. This power has risen on the ruins of public liberties."[20] The contest in the Chamber of Deputies was hectic: twenty-three orators took part in an eighteen-hour debate before the chamber at last, by a vote of 104 against 47, approved the impeachment of Sogarna, Linares, Nazor Anchorena, and Ramos Mejía.

Once the four were impeached by the Chamber of Deputies, the drama was transferred to the Senate, which sat as a court to determine whether or not the four should be removed from office. *Peronista* prosecutors stressed the point that the removal of the judges would be entirely constitutional, not only on the basis of the impeachment provisions in the text of the Constitution of 1853 (then theoretically still in force), but also because of precedent established in the United States, after which the Argentine constitutional system was patterned. Argentines were told that Perón was only trying to do in 1946–47 what the "North American" President Franklin D. Roosevelt had attempted in 1937–38 in his own struggle with the Supreme Court of the United States. Their press censored,* most Argentines had no way of knowing what the differences were between Perón's removal of all of the members of the Supreme Court of Justice and Roosevelt's unsuccessful attempt to enlarge the membership of the "North American" high tribunal. Not all of the oratory in the senate was authored by *Peronistas*: Justice Sogarna was defended in the proceedings by the remarkable ex-Senator Alfredo L. Palacios, veteran Socialist leader and skilful constitutional lawyer. "I affirm that this impeachment has been brought about at the evident suggestion of the present president of the republic,

* See pp. 202–16.

leader of the party to which two-thirds of the accusing deputies and all of the judging senators belong," Palacios asserted. "We are dealing, as Jefferson said, with a terrible weapon placed in the hands of the dominant faction."[21] But the Senate was 100 per cent *Peronista* and the Supreme Court of Justice was 100 per cent removed from office: the Senate voted so to do on May 1, 1947.

Argentines who cared to witness the postscriptum gathered curiously around Buenos Aires' *Tribunales* buildings on August 1, 1947. Those who made their way inside could see a new Supreme Court of Justice sworn in: Chief Justice Tomás D. Casares, and Justices Felipe S. Pérez, Luis R. Longhi, Justo Lucas Alvarez Rodríguez, and Rodolfo Guillermo Valenzuela. Thereafter, President Juan Domingo Perón had no difficulty with the Supreme Court of Justice.

The same story can be told on less spectacular scales so far as the lower courts of the so-called Judicial Power are concerned. All federal judges are appointed by the president of the republic and the appointments are confirmed by two-thirds of the senate. These judges theoretically hold office for the duration of their good behavior. The reader has already been instructed as to the method of removing members of the Supreme Court of Justice; lower federal judges are removed by a special tribunal composed of five other judges. The power to separate judges from their benches has been used freely during the Perón era. Nine days after the revolution of 1943, eight judges were removed simply by executive decree. The regime was interested in "restoring to the judiciary powers that majesty and prestige necessary to the fulfilment of duty," the decree said. "Many judges were lacking in integrity and equanimity—elementary conditions for a judge."[22] The adoption of the Constitution of 1949 provided new techniques for the removal of judges. In declaring that judicial appointments must be confirmed by the senate, that document rendered the requirement of confirmation retroactive; that is, judges holding office before 1949 were forced to have their appointments again confirmed if they desired to retain their posts. Senatorial refusal to reconfirm such appointments resulted by the end of 1949 in the dismissal of seventy-one federal judges.

In view of the foregoing, perhaps little need be said here about the nature of the judicial process in Perón's Argentina. In general, the work of the judiciary tends to be of a high level of competence so long as political issues are not involved in matters undergoing litigation. Also, it should be remembered that, although much of the Argentine system—even since the introduction of the Constitution of 1949—is patterned after "North American" usage, still Argentina is a Roman Law or code law country. Much of what has been written on the subject has conveyed the impression that a sharp contrast exists between common law, as developed in the United States and the United Kingdom, and Roman Law, as practiced in the Latin-American countries. This distinction, insofar as Argentina is concerned, is much greater in the books written by jurists than it is in "the law" as developed on a non-political basis by the judges. The similarities between Argentine and United States judicial practices are striking. In both countries many decisions are based on precedents established by earlier cases; members of courts write opinions in handing down their decisions; and judges who do not agree with the majority of their colleagues write dissenting opinions. The similarities are, of course, heightened by the fact that many Argentine usages have been consciously copied from the United States. This excerpt from an 1887 decision of the Argentine Supreme Court of Justice is certainly worth noting: "The system of government that rules us is not our creation. We have found it in action, tested by long years of experience, and we have appropriated it. And it has been said with reason that one of the great advantages of this adoption has been the existence of a vast body of doctrine, a practice and a jurisprudence that illustrate and fulfil the fundamental rules, and that we can and must utilize with regard to everything that we do not wish to alter because of our peculiar circumstances."[23]

Yet Argentina's Roman-Law orientation does account for some differences from usage in the United States, questions of Peronism aside for the moment. Consider, for example, the matter of trial by jury. The Constitution of 1853 provided for trial by jury; Perón's 1949 constitution does not include this provision. Some "North American" writers have been quick to conclude from this circumstance that Perón has abolished trial by jury in Argentina. This accusation, in the form in which it is usually made, is unfair to Perón. The truth is that trial by jury scarcely existed in Argentina: the Constitution of 1853 *permitted* the use of juries, but the initiative for their establishment rested with the governments of the provinces. In the entire ninety-six years of the life of the Constitution of 1853, juries actually appeared only in three provinces—Buenos Aires, Córdoba, and San Juan—and were rare even there. The effect of the elimination of trial by jury from the text of the 1949 constitution is to make juries still more scarce in those three provinces. That is a different matter from what is connoted when it is stated flatly that Perón has abolished trial by jury. Roman-Law procedures as they developed in Argentina *before* Perón never did lend themselves to the institution of the jury.

Other differences from common law procedures are to be found in Argentina, for reasons lying at the door of the Roman Law rather than of Perón. It has been noted that most court proceedings in Argentina are written rather than oral. Again, it should be pointed out that judicial codes, generally associated more with Roman than with common law, are used in Argentina. These codes deal principally with civil, commercial, penal, mining, aeronautical, sanitation, and "social" law. Each code is a relatively comprehensive statement of the law of the subject with which it deals. While the codes are lengthy, they are not even theoretically complete treatments of their subjects, and are employed by the courts in conjunction with other statutes, previous court decisions, and the constitution. The use of this codification is an area of some significance in which Argentine judicial usage differs from the "North American." It is, however, worth bearing in mind that only the Argentine code of "social law" can be attributed to Perón.[24]

On balance, however, the Judicial Power is hardly a reality during the Perón era. The separation of powers has been written into the text of the Constitution of 1949, it is true; but in the "new Argentina" this division of authority is a legalistic fiction. President Perón's control of the Legislative and Judicial Powers is as complete as his domination of the Executive Power. The voice of the Constitution of 1949, whether it comes from executive, legislative, or judicial lips, is the voice of Juan Domingo Perón.

7.

Institutionalized Lockstep (Continued)

Argentines frequently compare the Perón regime with
that of General Juan Manuel de Rosas.* The comparison
is intriguingly significant, and not merely because "Bloody
Rosas" was a dictator. It will be remembered that there are
two Argentinas, and that the history of the nation is in large
measure an account of the bitter struggle between Buenos
Aires and the provinces of the "interior." "Until the two
Argentinas are brought together," a recent student of the
country has declared, "that nation will have no peace."[1] As
the Rosas era was meaningful in terms of its place in the
schism between the Argentinas, so the Perón epoch will
find its niche in the tragic story of the conflict between the
porteños and the *provincianos*. In the legalistic usages of
contemporary Argentine politics, Perón's influence on the
century-old division among Argentines has been expressed
in the language of federalism.

"Practical Federalism"

Argentina is constitutionally divided into three types of
territorial units. The first of these is the Federal Capital,
which embraces the huge city of Buenos Aires, and is under
the direct control of the national government. The second

* See pp. 25–28.

includes the sixteen provinces,* most of which have long conducted an acrimonious political struggle against the capital. And the third embraces the eight national territories,† which, largely politically inarticulate, have played virtually no role in the contest between the Argentinas. The city of Buenos Aires has been distinguished throughout the history of the nation as a force making for centralization in government and has generally been thought of as liberal. The provinces of the "interior," on the other hand, have been centers of secessionism and separatism. The "interior" was frequently labeled as conservative in consequence of its caste-like social hierarchy presided over by a comfortably aloof ruling class of landowners, and in view of the strong position in the "interior" of the Roman Catholic Church.

With the exception of the Province of Jujuy, which was created in 1834, all of the original fourteen provinces were established between 1813 and 1820. These were anarchic years dominated by the struggle between the Argentinas. The Rosas regime crystallized and gave course and character to the conflict; and the Constitution of 1853 was written in an attempt to compose the struggle by compromise. Federalism was the vehicle of compromise: the constitution-writers of 1852–1853 looked to the Constitution of the United States for a formula within which the two Argentinas could live peacefully. As the "North American" federal system had divided authority between a central government and the administrations of the various states, so the Argentine arrangement, consciously following the northern example, distributed constitutional power between the national government at Buenos Aires and the governments of

* Buenos Aires (province), Corrientes, Entre Ríos, Santa Fé, Santiago del Estero, Córdoba, San Luis, Salta, Jujuy, Tucumán, Catamarca, La Rioja, San Juan, Mendoza, Presidente Perón, and Evita Perón.

† See pp. 144–46.

the provinces. Perón's Constitution of 1949 has retained the legalistic form of this federalism, but, as has already been noted in other connections, the retention is largely a matter of form and little else.

According to the law of the Constitution of 1853, the original fourteen provinces were not constitutionally equal in power. It is to be borne in mind that in the years before the adoption of the 1853 document the relations among the provinces were in effect international relations. During those years the provinces wrote their own constitutions and entered into agreements not only with each other but even with foreign states. Many of the provinces acquired from these constitutions and agreements rights and powers which they were reluctant to relinquish in 1853. The national constitution adopted in that year accordingly made allowance for this situation by recognizing five legal sources of the powers of the provinces—national laws promulgated before 1853; earlier treaties with foreign states; pre-1853 inter-provincial treaties; provincial constitutions and laws adopted before 1853; and customs, practices, and traditions developed in the preconstitutional period. Thus, the provinces did not in theory acquire powers from the Constitution of 1853; and that document expressly stipulated that "the provinces retain all the power not delegated by this constitution to the federal government, and that which they may have expressly reserved by special covenants at the time of their incorporation."[2] Accordingly, Argentine federalism resembled that of the United States in that the provinces had inherent or residual rather than delegated powers, but different from the "North American" proto-type in so far as all of the provinces were not constitutionally equal in authority.

Although their powers were not exactly the same, all of the provinces under the 1853 charter were in general charged with the provision of primary education, the colonization of provincial lands, the establishment of municipal and other local governments, a number of public-works functions, and the defense of civil liberties. Each province was required to grant full faith and credit to the public acts of the other provinces, and to extradite criminals escaping from other units of the federal union. The provinces were expressly prohibited from engaging in interprovincial compacts dealing with political matters, coining money, and raising armies except in cases of invasion. The national government at Buenos Aires possessed, in general, more power vis-a-vis the provinces than did the Federal government of the United States with respect to the states; and, as the years passed, the Buenos Aires government tended gradually to expand its powers at the expense of provincial autonomy. The basic national agency for the conduct of the central government's relations with the provinces was the ministry of the interior.

In recent times, the curious "interventor system" or "system of national intervention" has been foremost among Perón's techniques of dominating the provinces. Although Argentines have known the interventor system ever since 1853, its retention in the 1949 constitution provides an effective tool for the control by national authorities of government on the provincial and local levels.

The Argentine interventor system has had a constitutional history of its own for the past century, and has been the subject of many learned discussions and treatises.[3] The constitution-writers of 1852–1853, it will be remembered, derived much inspiration and many ideas from the Constitution of the United States; among them was federalism, which became an Argentine as well as a "North American" feature. In reviewing the relationships between the government at Washington and the "North American" states, Argentines of the mid-nineteenth century were interested in the obligations owed by the Federal government to the states. According to the Constitution of the United States, the central government "shall guarantee to every State in this Union a republican form of government, and shall protect each of them against invasion; and on application of the legislature, or of the executive (when the legislature cannot be convened) against domestic violence."[4] Argentines, in writing this provision into their own Constitution of 1853, felt that the "North American" version was defective. It was duly noted that the courts in the United States experienced difficulty in defining a "republican form of government" within the meaning of their constitution, and that those courts at length refused even to venture a definition. Moreover, the Constitution of the United States was silent as to the specific procedures and techniques to be used in preserving the states' form of government.

Convinced that these considerations added up to defects in the "North American" approach to federalism, the Argentines in 1852–53 wrote an "improvement" on the system into their own constitution. While it is true that the Argentines were no more specific than the "North Americans" in defining a "republican form of government," still the Argentines *were* more exact in so far as they wrote into their basic law the procedure to be followed in guaranteeing the provinces a "republican form of government," whatever that might be. The procedure was the interventor system, and, as finally included in the 1853 text, was to be used not only to preserve provincial republican forms, but also to maintain peace and justice in the provinces and to assert national supremacy as a principle of Argentine federalism. The interventor feature of the 1853 constitution—which Perón has carried over into the 1949 document—provided that the "national government may intervene in the territory of the provinces to guarantee the republican form of government, or to repel foreign invasions, and, on requests of their constituted authorities, to support or re-establish such authorities, if they have been overthrown by sedition or invasion from another province."[5]

As developed in the years after 1853, national intervention was regarded as in order whenever there existed in any province a political situation which both impeded the execution of national laws and could not be destroyed by ordinary judicial procedures. Intervention in a province always meant the suppression of the provincial constitution and the removal of all provincial and local government. "When the Federal government intervenes in a province, that government, in the name of national sovereignty, exercises full and extensive authority within the territory of the province," an Argentine official has explained. "The Federal Interventor displaces the local officials and, as the representative of the supreme authority of the nation, assumes all power necessary to carry out his mission."[6] Theoretically, national intervention is a temporary measure, to be terminated as soon as "normality" is restored in the affected province or provinces. Moreover, the Argentine courts long ago ruled that it was not within their domain to pass judgment on the wisdom, necessity, or proper duration of national intervention in any instance. "National intervention, in all cases in which the Constitution permits or requires it, is by its nature a political act, to be carried out exclusively by the political powers of the nation," the Supreme Court of Justice said long before the coming of Perón. "These are the congress and the Executive Power, with no participation by the Judicial Power."[7] Questions of intervention, then, have traditionally been regarded as political questions, with which the judiciary has no constitutionally proper concern.[8]

When intervention is decreed in a province, its legislative, executive, and judicial authorities* are automatically removed from office. The president of the republic appoints an official, known as the Federal Interventor, to take over all powers of government in the intervened province. The Federal Interventor is the president's representative, and acts only on orders and instructions received from the national Executive Power. The interventor, as "a direct representative of the president of the nation," carries out "a national [as distinguished from a provincial] function."[9] Moreover, the Supreme Court of Justice has ruled that the Federal Interventor's appointment "does not derive from any provincial law, and his acts are not subject to . . . local laws, but rather to . . . the national power in whose name he functions."[10]

Obviously, the interventor system, already provided for by the constitution, stood as a ready-made instrument of dictatorship at the disposal of the military men who made the revolution of 1943. Perón and his associates made widespread and free use of national intervention to consolidate their hold on the Argentine nation. However, it should in fairness be pointed out that Perón is by no means the first Argentine president to employ the interventor system on a liberal scale. Indeed, every president since the adoption of the Constitution of 1853 has intervened in at least one province; and by 1930 there had been a total of 131 interventions, of which 87 were undertaken on presidential initiative and 44 on the basis of congressional recommendations. And some presidents—for example, Hipólito Irigoyen (1916–22, 1928–30) and Roberto M. Ortiz (1938–40)—were noted for the excessively large number of interventions decreed during their administrations.

But, as might be expected, intervention has been used on

* See p. 143.

a much grander scale in Perón's Argentina than at any previous period in the nation's history. Consider the pattern of
intervention in the "new Argentina." President Ramón S.
Castillo had already intervened in Tucumán and Corrientes
when the Perón revolution took place on June 4, 1943. The
nation's new military rulers made short work of the governments in the remaining twelve provinces. Mendoza was
intervened by President Ramírez on June 9, 1943; Buenos
Aires and Entre Ríos, on June 11; Santa Fé, Santiago del
Estero, and Jujuy, on June 14; San Juan, the following day;
and Córdoba, Salta, La Rioja, Catamarca, and San Luis on
June 18. Thus, all provincial and local government was destroyed within two weeks of the revolution of June 4, 1943.
A "North American" correspondent reported at the time
that "the provinces resemble occupied countries rather than
free states."[11]

The Federal Interventor looms as a major figure and a
key instrument of dictatorship in Perón's Argentina.
Though the interventors have in general been able men,
they have long been among Argentine satirists' favorite
subjects for political caricature. The Federal Interventor
"is a personage created by decree," Alfredo R. Bufano has
said in his delightful book on what he calls "Political Zo-
ology." "Yesterday he was simply Parménides Chirimoya,
an obscure landowner from Calamuchita or Chelforó. Today, without warning, he is His Excellency the National
Interventor, Doctor don Parménides Chirimoya. Only God
knows the fright and the consternation of don Parménides
when he heard the news that he would represent the president of the republic, his old friend! Also, only God knows
the offense for which don Parménides was punished when
the president offered him the position of Interventor with
the assurance that he should accept it in the interests of the
august vitality of the party and the sacred interests of the
country!"[12] During the Perón era, the interventors have

been military men to a greater degree than in the earlier period. In the first months after the revolution of 1943, civilian interventors were rare; since 1946, the military-civilian ratio among interventors has been roughly equal.

Since the Perón revolution, the interventor system has been used to assure the "new Argentina's" control of all of the provinces. They were under intervention from June of 1943 until Perón's first inauguration as president in June of 1946. That event in theory signaled the resumption of constitutional government in the provinces as well as on the national level. Provincial governors and legislatures were elected with Perón in 1946. It is significant that thirteen of the provinces emerged from that election with pro-Perón governors and legislative majorities. The one province with an anti-Perón governor—Corrientes—did not keep him long. Corrientes was intervened on September 4, 1947, and that province's entire constitutional machinery was suppressed at that time. "The intention was clear," *La Nación* of Buenos Aires editorially remarked of the intervention in Corrientes. *Peronistas* "could not admit that a provincial government could exist with an affiliation opposed to the dominant group."[13] Theoretically, intervention remains a temporary measure. Actually, it is continued in each province as long as is necessary to assure *Peronista* domination of the province after the intervention has terminated. Some of the "temporary" interventions have impressive longevity. Take Catamarca, where the intervention was in its fourth year in 1951. A Buenos Aires newspaper observed late in 1950 that "this is the moment in which the interventor—who is also the court system—announces a vast plan of public works requiring months or years in office. There is reason, therefore, to discount [protestations that the purpose of the intervention is to] re-establish the autonomy of the province."[14]

In the Perón epoch, the interventor system has been put

to unique uses. All interventors were ordered on July 5, 1943, to prevent the newspapers in their provinces from making "malicious comments" about Argentine foreign policy. In a circular instruction issued on October 30, 1945, Interior Minister Bartolomé Descalzo ordered all interventors to refrain from commenting on the progress of World War II, Argentine foreign policy, or domestic politics. And consider this interior ministry order to the interventors: "Not only are you to proceed directly against all organizations even vaguely suspected of communist affiliation, but arrest all communist leaders and their principal followers, gather all possible information about their connections, however distant."[15]

Occasionally the interventor system has been used to satisfy one of Perón's personal grudges. The story of the Catamarca intervention is instructive. In the election of 1946, Vicente Eli Saadi was chosen senator from Catamarca. When the Senate held an executive session which outsiders were ostensibly prohibited from attending, Senator Saadi rose to protest against the presence of an outsider at the session. The only circumstance that gave Saadi a place in history and in the pages of this book was the fact that the outsider whose presence he objected to was none other than Eva Perón. Evita had broken men for lesser insults, and Saadi was broken. He was called to the *Casa Rosada* and told that he was now the *Peronista* candidate for governor of Catamarca. When the election was held in that province, Saadi was the victor. But he remained governor of Catamarca for an even shorter period than he had been a senator. Upon the inauguration of Governor Saadi, Perón announced that the new governor was guilty of fraud in his election and mismanagement of his province. Intervention was forthwith decreed in Catamarca, and Saadi was removed from office and imprisoned. Personal

insults are highly priced in Perón's Argentina. One of them
cost the people of Catamarca an intervention which was in
its fourth year in 1951.

Each of the provinces is authorized to write its own constitution, which is ostensibly in force whenever the province is not under intervention. With the adoption in 1949
of Perón's new national constitution, the provinces were
given ninety days in which to rewrite their individual constitutions in conformity with "the principles, declarations,
rights, and guarantees"[16] of Perón's document. By mid-
1949, each of the provinces accordingly had a new constitution which contained the social and economic program
of the "new Argentina." Today each of the provincial constitutions provides for a form of government embodying
the three-way separation of powers.

Each constitution establishes an executive, a legislative,
and a judicial "power." The chief executive in each province is called the governor; he is elected for a six-year term
which begins and ends at the same time as Perón's. All of
the provinces except San Luis and Santiago del Estero also
have a lieutenant governor. The provincial governors are
"natural agents of the federal government,"[17] and are
charged with the execution of the laws in their respective
bailiwicks. The provincial legislatures are all composed of
members elected for six-year terms.

The legislatures provide for the internal administration
of their provinces, manage provincial property, and enact
national budgets. Finally, the provinces have court systems;
the names of the tribunals and the individual patterns of the
court hierarchies vary considerably from province to province.

Peronista control of the provincial governments is complete. In the first place, the arrangement outlined in the
foregoing paragraph may at any time be swept away by

national intervention. Secondly, even in the absence of intervention Perón dominates the provinces. Every governor is a *Peronista;* and techniques of removing recalcitrant provincial legislators and judges from office are similar to what has already been noted with respect to the national level. A few cases may illustrate the provincial pattern. On July 26, 1946, Pacífico Rodríguez, the *Peronista* governor of the Province of Catamarca, dissolved the entire provincial legislature when opposition elements in it launched an attempt to impeach him. A year later, the governor of Córdoba did the same for a similar reason. In October of 1949, the *cordobés* legislature expelled José A. Mercado from its membership because he made an anti-Perón speech. And witness the pattern of politics in Santiago del Estero: when *Peronista* provincial legislators proposed that the name of a street be changed from *"Libertad"* ("Liberty") to "Perón," provincial deputy Eduardo Rotondo rose to speak in defense of the retention of *"Libertad."* He was immediately expelled from the legislature, and on November 2, 1950, Rotondo was imprisoned on charges of expressing comtempt of President Perón! And, a month later, Teobaldo José Giménez, a Radical member of the San Juan legislature, was jailed for a similar cause.

The national government's control of the eight national territories[*] is less indirect than its domination of the sixteen provinces. Two of the territories are administered by the armed services: Tierra del Fuego became a naval command on August 18, 1943, and Comodoro Rivadavia was made a military zone on May 31, 1944. Each of the six remaining territories is administered by a governor appointed by the president of the republic. Although the governors have three-year terms, Perón has the constitutional authority to

[*] Misiones, Formosa, Río Negro, Neuquén, Chubut, Comodoro Rivadavia, Santa Cruz, and Tierra del Fuego.

dismiss any of them at any time. Existing laws permit the establishment of legislatures in the larger territories, but no legislative body has yet—before or since 1943—been created in a territory. Six of the territories are administered through the national ministry of interior; Tierra del Fuego is governed through the navy ministry; and Comodoro Rivadavia is administered through the ministry of the army.

Legally, a territory is entitled to be advanced to provincial status when its population exceeds 60,000. There were ten territories when the cenus of 1947 was taken, and the resultant figures indicated that five of the territories had passed the 60,000 mark.* Considerable Argentine sentiment —and not all of it *Peronista*—in favor of elevating some of the territories to provincial status was evident in the country by the middle of 1950. "The creation of new provinces from the territories with populations of more than 60,000 . . . would not be an institutional adventure with uncertain results for the republic," *La Prensa*, then the leading anti-*Peronista* newspaper of Buenos Aires, declared editorially. "Some national territories have not only greatly surpassed this figure but have also demonstrated an economic capacity and social and cultural development sufficient for the recognition of their right to determine their own destinies."[18] At length, President Perón indicated that he supported the conversion of two of the territories into provinces, and the legal machinery for this transformation went into action. The two territories singled out for constitutional advancement were the Chaco and La Pampa. The first acquired its new status in December of 1951, and has since been called Presidente Perón Province. La Pampa became a province on January 5, 1952, when it was christened Evita Perón Province. Since the latter date, the

* Misiones, 244,123; the Chaco, 443,922; Formosa, 112,056; La Pampa, 167,582; and Neuquén, 85,601.

provinces have been sixteen in number, and the territories, of course, reduced to eight. In general, the remaining territories tend to be politically inarticulate and to carry small weight in Argentine politics.

Not the least of the significances of the Perón regime is its long-range effect on Argentine federalism. It must be admitted in all fairness that the question of whether or not a true federalism ever existed in Argentina, even before Perón, is an issue which can be debated, with honest and sincere folk taking either side of the question.[19] Let those who hate Perón recall that the interventor system was not his invention, and that it was freely used many times before 1943 to destroy the governments and the powers of the provinces. Let those who are quick to damn remember that Argentine federalism—if such there ever was—always involved a greater degree of national supremacy than was admitted into the federal system in the United States.

If there is a question as to the pre-1943 existence of Argentine federalism, there can be no doubt that a true federalism has not operated in the country since the Perón revolution. Perón disputes this. He claims that his is still a federal system, although he concedes that its nature has changed in the "new Argentina." His federalism, he says, is a "practical federalism." What is "practical federalism"? Let Perón himself explain that. "Our provinces were formed on the basis of *caudillos'* rivalries, and in each was enthroned a family oligarchy whose only and major preoccupation was to maintain itself in power, the better to protect its own private interests," President Perón has said in surveying the course of Argentine federalism. His political opposition, he has contended, "continues to talk about federalism because it cannot talk about its lost personal interests now that its members have been turned out

146

into the streets as citizens. . . . Political federalism was
always a lie. . . ."[20] That was the past.

But what of the present? Hear the voice of Perón: "Our
movement has had from its first moments one basic objective: *national unity.* . . . The people want a centralized
government."[21] Listen to the man who is God for the *Peronistas*: "For the national government, provinces or national territories do not exist; every part of the country,
every zone of its territory, deserves equal attention and the
government has the duty of lending it this aid, whether by
its own effort, or its sacrifice, or with the effort and sacrifice of all the Argentines inhabiting this land of ours."[22]
What is "practical federalism"? Hear the boss: "We have
laid the basis for a *new federalism:* a practical federalism.
. . . In other times the federal system was a good topic for
political speeches. Some of our provinces owe their present
backwardness to this oratorical federalism of yesteryear.
. . . The federalism which we desire for ourselves and our
children, and which we are practicing, is that which will
bring about national unity through the integration of the
provinces. . . . In our concept of practical federalism, the
central government plans for the entire country . . . and
the provinces have the task of carrying out their sector of
the general plans without prejudice to the full liberty which
they possess for the achievement of goals peculiar to themselves."[23]

There can be no doubt that provincial autonomy has
been crushed in Argentina, at least for the duration of the
Perón era. But let not the loudest mourners for the corpse
be those who did not know it when it had life. The Perón
regime cannot be understood without an understanding
of Argentina; and those who know Argentina realize that
there are two Argentinas. They know, too, that provincial

autonomy has long been the vehicle for bitter and acrimonious civil war between the Argentinas. "There are two Argentinas, and the whole history of the nation is the story of their struggle," it has been pointed out. "Until the two Argentinas are brought together, that nation will have no peace."[24]

Has Perón brought that peace to Argentina? Has a divided nation been sewn together by wholesale intervention, by the multiplication of Doctor don Parménides Chirimoya, by the incarceration of a governor who insulted Eva, by the imprisonment of a deputy who loved a street named "*Libertad*"? *Peronistas* will shout "yes," but let it be noted that *Peronistas* are paid for shouting "yes." And, lest it be dubbed immoral to be paid for shouting, let it be recorded that there are also those who are paid for shouting "no."

And let it be further noted that those who are paid for their answer whether it is yes or no might well answer "yes" *and* "no." Only the unconscious can fail to tie Perón to "Bloody Rosas." What are the two Argentinas? They are Buenos Aires and the provinces of the "interior." And which was the Argentina of Rosas? His was the "interior." Which is Perón's Argentina?

The question is not merely intriguing. It is vitally significant. Its answer is the answer to the riddle of the two Argentinas. The truth is that Perón has endeavored to straddle the two, and that one of the major weaknesses of his regime lies in his inability to straddle them effectively. Has Perón brought peace to Argentina? Here is "peace" in the "new Argentina's" Buenos Aires: "Half the downtown section is crying from tear gas bombs."[25] And the provinces of the "interior"—even those that bear his name and that of the late Evita—what of them? Hear a journalist's report on their "peace": "The situation in the 'interior' is much more rebellious than here in Buenos Aires. . . . In some prov-

inces the government Interventors and their staffs are os-
tracized by the people. The provinces resemble occupied
countries rather than free states."²⁶ No, Doctor don Par-
méndes Chirimoya has not done his job well. But it is not
really his fault.

For Juan Domingo Perón is not really Juan Manuel de
Rosas.

And the Least of These

The national government's control of municipal and local
administration is as thoroughgoing and complete as national
domination of the provinces. Argentine municipal government has a significance unparalleled in most of the Latin-
American states: it has already been noted that 61.4 per
cent of all Argentines live in urban communities, and that
the population has been moving increasingly to the larger
cities of the nation.* The growing urbanization of the
country looms as one of its major problems. And the hand
of Perón presses heavily upon the cities.

Historically considered, Argentine cities have played a
role in the nation's development standing in marked contrast to the typical Latin-American pattern. In Argentina,
as elsewhere in the Americas, the cities were the earliest
centers of Spanish civilization. The basic organ of municipal administration in the early colonial period was the
cabildo, a kind of town council. The *cabildos* have been
lauded as cradles of Latin-American democracy, but subsequent research indicates that what spent its tender years
in the *cabildo* was probably not very democratic. "The
famous *cabildos* . . . were oligarchical and caste institutions, constituted by the 'white' or 'almost-white' minorities of each neighborhood," Ingenieros has pointed out.
"Between them and the [lower classes] there never was any

* See p. 4.

community of interests or ideals."[27] Certainly, few would
pin a democratic label on the manner of constituting *cabildos:* "During the conquest [the founders of a city] appointed the members of the first *cabildo.* Afterward, the
incumbents designated their own successors."[28] Although
no case can be made today for calling the *cabildos* cradles
of democracy, it is nevertheless true that they *did* nurture
municipal autonomy in most of Spanish America, but not
in Argentina.

The explanation of this difference lies in large part in the
circumstance that the Argentine area was a late-comer into
the Spanish overseas empire. The Viceroyalty of the Plata
River was not created until 1776, as compared with the
Viceroyalty of New Spain (later Mexico), established in
1535; the Viceroyalty of New Castille (later Peru), created
in 1543, and the Viceroyalty of New Granada (later Gran
Colombia), established in 1717. Late in the eighteenth century, the Spanish empire reduced the *cabildo* form of overseas municipal government. The *cabildo* had, however, an
opportunity to take root and grow in the older viceroyal-
ties; and municipal autonomy continued to flourish there
largely in consequence of this circumstance. But in the
United Provinces of the Plata River—created only in 1776
—the *cabildos* had hardly been born before their powers
were reduced by royal decree in 1782. A result is that municipal autonomy is a political characteristic of almost every
Latin-American state except Argentina.[29]

After 1782, the primary unit of regional government in
Argentina was the intendancy. Whereas the old *cabildo*
had governed a more compact social unit, the intendancy
had jurisdiction over a more widespread area. "The old and
primitive municipal organization of the colony was succeeded by a territorial and regional organization, which
notably reduced the power of the *cabildos,* until then the

most important bodies in the transmission and execution of the royal will and the only ones which had in any way dealt with public opinion," an Argentine historian has explained. "From then on, the governor-intendant, as the executive official in charge of finance, war, justice, and police, was the supreme regional authority; the *cabildos* subordinated to him, were limited in their work to simply urban matters."[30] Indeed, some Argentines have felt that "the lack of a tradition of municipal government has been one of the causes of the instability of our political institutions"[31] In any case, the reduction of the *cabildos* and the introduction of the intendancies did contribute to the growth of provincial as opposed to municipal autonomy in Argentina. The role of interprovincial rivalries in the early nineteenth century has already been discussed; the final blow to the municipalities was dealt by Bernardino Rivadavia, who suppressed city government in 1821.

BUENOS AIRES. Central in the Argentine chaos of the first half of the nineteenth century was the problem of the relationship of the city of Buenos Aires to the "interior" of the nation. The *porteño's* city differed in many ways from the rest of the country. The culture and civilization of Buenos Aires were European rather than South American, while the "interior" provinces were more Peruvian than European in outlook. Buenos Aires was more densely populated, more literate—and its politics more radical—than the rest of the nation. Today the differences remain: Buenos Aires is the largest city in Latin America, the third largest city in the Western Hemisphere, and the ninth largest in the world. Buenos Aires is "a great metropolis—a world city with a world civilization. Its roots are in the Argentine soil, but the flower of its social life is largely European. It looks chiefly to Paris for its styles of dress and thought, but somewhat to London, New York, and even Hollywood."[32]

In a sense, the Argentine struggle of the nineteenth century was a struggle for the control of Buenos Aires. The province of the same name endeavored to retain the *porteño* metropolis within its jurisdiction; this was resisted by the other provinces and by the *porteños* themselves. Rivadavia in 1826 sought to solve the problem by "federalizing" the city of Buenos Aires—that is, by detaching it from the province of the same name and making the city directly dependent upon the national government. "Federalization" failed in the 1820s, but it was the solution finally agreed upon in 1880. On September 20 of that year, the congress approved Law No. 1,029, establishing the pattern for the government of the capital city; and the problem of the position of the city of Buenos Aires within the Argentine nation approached solution.

Specifically, the "federalization" law of 1880 removed the city of Buenos Aires from the jurisdiction of the Province of Buenos Aires. The measure declared the former to be the national capital and rendered all public property in the city national property. A Federal Capital was created for the government of the city—the Federal Capital was to be under the direct control of the national rather than of any of the provincial governments. The municipal government of the city of Buenos Aires is today divided into two branches. The chief executive officer of the municipality is called the intendant. He is appointed for a three-year term by the president of the nation. The other branch, a kind of municipal council, is called the Deliberative Council. It is composed of thirty members popularly elected for four-year terms.

In general, "federalization" and the constitutional system of Argentina have meant the control of the national capital by national authorities. Perón controls the city of Buenos Aires. Legally, this is as much due to the position of the

Federal Capital since 1880 as to post-1943 innovations. Let those who decry Perón's domination of Buenos Aires look to the position of Paris within the French constitutional system. Or to the status of Washington, D.C., after which the legal position of the Argentine Federal Capital was patterned. Whoever controls the national government controls the capital city. That has been the law in Argentina since 1880. Perón did not invent all of the legal arrangements by which he profits.

OTHER CITIES. With the growth of provincial autonomy during the first half of the nineteenth century, municipal authority declined. At length, the cities of the "interior" fell under the complete control of the provinces thereof; and today the cities of the "interior" are the creatures of the provinces in which they are situated This is a condition which runs parallel to the constitutional position of cities in the United States. As the forty-eight "North American" states have the legal power of life and death over the cities within their borders, so the sixteen Argentine provinces exercise similar authority over the municipalities within their domains. When the provinces are under intervention, there is no local government at all beyond the measures decreed by the Federal Interventors. To say that Perón dominates the provinces is to say that he likewise has the cities in his pocket.

Argentine authorities on municipal government have long expressed dissatisfaction with the nature and condition of city government in their country. This dissatisfaction has coalesced around two types of considerations. In the first place, nepotism and party favoritism have traditionally governed municipal personnel policies, and city administrations have been notoriously ridden with graft and corruption. The complaint of Carlos Alberto Pueyrredón, the last pre-Perón intendant of the city of Buenos Aires, is typical of other Argentine municipal situations. "In public departments, wherever one poked a finger pus was sure to emerge," Pueyrredón asserted. "The municipal departments had become a perfect teeming house of *recomendados*—persons for whom jobs had been found whether jobs were to be had or not. In the old days of the Deliberative Council, it used to be a standing joke that business offices could be wall-papered with the letters of introduction given to job applicants by the municipal councilors."[33] In Perón's Argentina, that particular joke is no longer current, but the condition which gave it point remains.

A second long-standing criticism of municipal government runs to the core of basic—and pre-Perón—Argentine theory and practice of the organization of cities. A "generalized belief that the system of municipal organization was a failure in the country"[34] is common among Argentine experts on problems of local government. While it has long been true that "the provinces are absolute masters of the organization of their municipalities,"[35] there is some danger in carrying the "North American" analogue very far. In the United States, the cities are legal creatures of the states; but there is a spirit of self-government on "North American" local levels not to be found in Argentina. There the cities are likewise creatures of the provinces, but there is virtually no tradition of municipal self-government in Argentina. Whether the *cabildo* would have provided it, if given a chance in the Viceroyalty of the Plata River, is, of course, a moot question. The point is that the *cabildo* never had such an opportunity in Argentina and that no substitute vehicle of municipal self-rule ever took genuine root in the country. Argentine municipalities have traditionally been administrative and fiscal subdivisions of the provinces and little more; particularism and regional autonomy have been carried by the provinces and not by the cities.

The basic proposition underlying Argentine municipal organization is the principle that the forms and powers of the city governments are to be determined by the provinces within which they are located. In general, the system of city government is uniform within each province, and "the right of a municipality to establish its own institutions does not exist."[36] Although the provinces decide the outline of city government, the basic Argentine form is that already seen in the case of the city of Buenos Aires—there is in each city in most of the provinces an intendant and a deliberative council. More specific provisions vary from province to province. In ten of the provinces the municipal intendants are appointed by the provincial governors; in the provinces of Buenos Aires, Tucumán, Córdoba, and Entre Ríos, the intendants are elected, in some cases by the appropriate deliberative councils, in other cases by the residents of the municipalities involved. Most Argentine experts agree that the systems of local government are most advanced in the provinces of Córdoba, Entre Ríos, and Santa Fé. The *cordobés* system resembles the "cafeteria" style of home rule which some "North American" cities enjoy: the provincial legislature has prescribed a number of forms of municipal government, and the cities of Córdoba may exercise a certain leeway in choosing among them. In Entre Ríos, the legislature has divided the cities into two classes: the larger ones have the intendant-council form, while the smaller municipalities have only an elective deliberative council and no intendant, the pattern resembling somewhat the commission form of city government to be found in some "North American" municipalities. In Santa Fé, cities with populations of more than 25,000 may write their own charters, while the provincial legislature determines the form of government for the smaller municipalities. In the remaining provinces, the intendant-council pattern, with the form prescribed by the legislature, is the prevailing style.

Perón's techniques of dominating the municipalities are perhaps inherent in the foregoing paragraphs. The Federal Capital and the city of Buenos Aires have been placed under his control by the constitutional system. Three weeks after the revolution of 1943, the Deliberative Council of the Federal Capital was dissolved and its powers delivered to the intendant, an appointee of the "new Argentina." The first intendant of Buenos Aires after the revolution was General Basilio B. Pertiné, a G.O.U. member and "a known 100 per cent Nazi."[37] When, some time later, Pertiné and Perón came to a political parting, the former was replaced by Lt. Col. César Caccia, who was as acceptable to the rulers of the "new Argentina" as Pertiné had been in June of 1943. The same story was repeated many times in the "interior": provinces were intervened, destroying all local government. In provinces not under intervention, virtually all intendants and the overwhelming majority of the members of the deliberative councils have been *Peronistas*. These have had ample authority—legal and otherwise—to depose, expel, and imprison any of their recalcitrant colleagues. Everywhere the hand of Perón can be seen; everywhere the pattern is the same, whether the level be national, provincial, or local.

Everywhere there is a lockstep, and the Constitution of 1949 has but institutionalized it. "North Americans" may find the Perón regime instructive. The model for its institutional structure was, after all, the Constitution of the United States. Argentines borrowed the separation of powers, and Perón came to dominate it. Argentines aped the federalism of the United States, and Perón came to make it "practical." In a sense, Argentine local government is similar to "North American" forms, and that likewise has fallen to the service of the "new Argentina." It is sometimes difficult to distinguish between a written constitution and any other piece of paper. Where the difficulty is especially great, a Perón may simplify the problem. It is simple in Argentina today. Hear a southern deity: "I can say without boasting that in this moment in Argentine political history the president of the republic really and effectively governs the country. . . . Our government is now organized in such a way that it operates only with an absolute unity of purpose."[38] And that purpose is the purpose of a man who is God.

III.

A Book of Ideology and Politics

"I have seen the fallen commemorative columns in Rome, along what was once called the Via Mussolini."

ERNESTO E. SAMMARTINO

8.

Peronism and Individual Liberty

If the café is sufficiently secluded and the *vino* is good, and if no stranger or other politically unreliable person is within earshot, Argentines may tell a story about two dogs, one Chilean and the other Argentine. The Chilean dog was disease-ridden and underfed, and left his native land to journey to Argentina. The Argentine dog was in good health and was well fed, but nevertheless traveled to Chile. The two animals met near Mount Aconcagua, along the rugged Andean frontier between Chile and Argentina. Like other travelers, they greeted each other and discussed their journeys. The Chilean dog said that he had heard that food was plentiful and of high quality in Argentina and that he was therefore traveling there in search of a good meal. Noting the excellent physical condition of the Argentine dog, the Chilean beast asked him why he was going to Chile. "Oh," said the Argentine dog, "I want to bark."

The story, and hundreds like it now circulating in Argentina, is indicative of a major aspect of the Perón regime. Civil liberty has virtually disappeared in the "new Argentina." Freedom of speech and action—once enjoyed by *porteños* and *provincianos* alike—has little place in the Argentina of Juan Domingo Perón.

Of Cloaks and Daggers

"We are living through dark days of Argentine political decadence," the Radical Ernesto E. Sammartino declared in his last speech in the chamber of deputies. "We live under the sign of fear. . . . An invisible electric current seems to paralyze the will and hide the conscience. Fear of losing one's employment, fear of being defamed, fear of being slandered, fear of losing one's privileges and property, fear of incurring the wrath of the president of the republic, who today is the owner of the land, the life, the destiny, and the liberty of the Argentines."[1] Intimidation and repression on a scale unprecedented in Argentina have gone hand in hand with the consolidation of the Perón regime. Arnaldo Cortesi, the *New York Times* correspondent who was transferred to Buenos Aires after years of covering Mussolini's Italy, reported in mid-1945 that Argentine repressive measures compared with the most severe he had seen in Italy.

Indeed, a general atmosphere of fear settled upon Argentines in the first months after the revolution of 1943. It was noted that people "ceased to discuss politics with strangers and withdrew unto themselves, afraid of those who had come as friends and had now taken over the house."[2] Ray Josephs was impressed by "the hush-hush attitude in front of uniforms, unknowns, or anybody you just don't like."[3] In the early days after the revolution, a seemingly endless flow of decrees and regulations reached into areas of Argentine life never before touched by government. A representative early decree prohibited all Argentines, unless they were government officials, from making public statements expressing "opinions that in any way bear on foreign policy";[4] and ensuing regulations curbed political expression even further. By mid-1944 the Socialist Nicolás Repetto remarked from exile that the regime "has abolished all liberties except the freedom to speak well about the government."[5]

When the present writer was in Argentina in 1950 and 1951, Argentines had already become accustomed to the necessity of avoiding discussions of government and politics in public places or in any situation in which there was a danger that the talk might be overheard by strangers or by politically unsympathetic persons. But in the early months of the "new Argentina," the experience was new and terrifying: "Plain-clothes men circulated in bars and public places, listening for public expressions of disagreement with the regime. For the first time since the rule of Juan Manuel de Rosas, people looked over their shoulders before expressing a critical opinion. The waiter might be a spy."[6] The government freely admitted that it held an ear to Argentines' private conversations. In January of 1945, Rear Admiral Alberto Teisaire, then minister of interior, told a Chilean journalist that "many people express opinions against [us] even in cafés." Asked how he knew this to be true, Teisaire said flatly, "we have people informing us. . . ."[7] And news items like the following remain a commonplace event in Perón's Argentina: "For spilling some loose political talk in a Buenos Aires café last week, eleven citizens were rounded up by the police."[8] The cafés are not the only dangerous places. Not even the telephone is safe for "loose political talk." Consider this government order published after widespread wire-tapping had been in force for some months: telephones "may not be abandoned to the thoughtless or irresponsible. Employing the telephone to insult or offend is a crime which deserves punishment by justice. . . . The long arm of the law and the Department of Posts and Telegraphs watch over the use of the telephone, that its noble and social purpose should not be misused. Such irresponsible criminals will be punished and their names published in the press."[9]

Individual liberty was once guaranteed in Argentina by the Constitution of 1853. Perón's 1949 document, on the other hand, takes a very different approach to the problem of freedom. The new constitution declares that "the state does not recognize the liberty to undermine liberty."[10] This proviso, as interpreted by a highly placed *Peronista* theorist, means that "individual liberty should not be absolute." According to this official spokesman, the regime "advocates the suppression of abuses of liberty without arriving at the collectivist extreme of abolishing liberty outright in the name of the state or the race."[11] Extreme individual liberty, it is held, vitiates the citizenry's ability to obey the laws. Hear another of the "new Argentina's" wise men: "States survive public disasters not so much because their rulers know how to govern as because their citizens know how to obey. . . . Many well-intentioned governments have fallen because of anarchy among the people, and others have achieved glory and fame because of the obedience of the governed."[12] If this smacks of Mussolini's fascism, let it be noted that President Perón himself has said that "Mussolini was the greatest man of our century, but he committed certain disastrous errors. I, who have the advantage of his precedent before me, shall follow in his footsteps but also avoid his mistakes."[13] And, according to Perón, the suppression of individual liberty was *not* one of Mussolini's mistakes. From the *Peronista* point of view, Mussolini was at his best when he observed that "nobody asks me for liberty, everybody asks me for bread."[14]

Among the "new Argentina's" first steps in the suppression of individual liberty—or, as the *Peronistas* would put it, the organization of obedience—was the requirement that all persons in the country register with the police so that the authorities might at all times know where individuals were and what they were doing. An order published on August 11, 1943—just two months after the revolution—required that "all adult male Argentines must register before October 31 and keep police advised of any changes in address or status."[15] The registration machinery has been elaborated and "improved" upon incessantly in the years since 1943: at length, on October 14, 1948, a National Registry of Persons, charged with keeping track of literally everybody in Argentina, was established within the ministry of interior. The requirement of registration, of course, means that all persons in the country must carry with them at all times the necessary documentation certifying that their business with the police is in order. On occasion the number of required documents makes for an almost ludicrously large bundle of papers.

In November of 1948, the government classified and listed the various papers persons must carry with them at all times. The official list established seven types of documents. (1) An *identification booklet*, issued by the Federal Police, must be carried by every Argentine citizen and by each foreigner resident in the country for an indefinite period of time. (2) A *credential*, issued by the same agency, must be borne by every government official and by each journalist. (3) A *passport* must be obtained by any Argentine intending to travel abroad, and by almost every foreigner in the country. (4) *Certificates of retirement* must be carried by persons claiming pensions. (5) *Certificates of release* must be held by all former prisoners as evidence that their exodus from jail was legally accomplished. (6) A *certificate of good conduct* must be carried by each Argentine citizen as evidence that he is in good standing with the government. This document, popularly called a *buena conducta*, is a matter of extreme importance to the average

Argentine today. When it is realized that a citizen loses his *buena conducta* if he is in trouble with the regime, the tremendous pressure exercized by this harmless-looking little booklet can be appreciated. Argentines must present their *buenas conductas* when they (*a*) return to the country after having been abroad, (*b*) apply for employment, (*c*) register as university students, and (*d*) marry. Some of these, it will be admitted, are important aspects of the day-to-day lives of all Argentines. He who has been in trouble with the police—whether the reason be his political opposition or any of a host of other considerations—and has therefore been deprived of his *buena conducta*, finds life difficult indeed. He may not legally obtain a job, he is deprived of an opportunity for higher education in the country,* and he must forego marriage and/or live in sin. The cost of being an anti-*Peronista* is high for the average Argentine citizen. "There are those who call this government tyrannical," President Fárrell once observed in the early years of the "new Argentina." "Yes, we are tyrants, but only against those who disturb order and oppose the progress of the nation."[16] (7) The tally is completed by the *police certificates*, which must be carried by all foreigners who are in Argentina as tourists.

The everyday administration of the multifarious restrictions on civil and political liberties is entrusted to two government agencies—the super-secret *Control del Estado* and the Federal Police. Although there is some jurisdictional overlap between the two organizations, the *Control del Estado* theoretically deals only with Argentine government employees, while the Federal Police handles everybody else in the country.

Very little has been published in English—or in Spanish,

* Of course, if he goes abroad for his schooling, he may not return to Argentina without his *buena conducta*.

for that matter—about the dreaded *Control del Estado,* popularly referred to in whispers as the *Control.* Its work is treated with the utmost secrecy: not even its budget is published. The *Control* is essentially Perón's confidential political police force. Argentines compare it with the *Mazorca,* Rosas' notorious "private army of terrorists and thugs."[17] Germans with Hitlerian experience—and there are many of these in Argentina*—frequently compare the *Control* with the Nazi *Gestapo.* Regardless of where the analogies are sought, the *Control* is primarily a military organization charged with the political policing of Argentines, with special attention devoted to government officials and employees. This agency is under the direct supervision of Perón, and is attached, for budgetary and other administrative purposes, to the presidential office.

The *Control del Estado* administers a huge loyalty program or security check, endeavoring to guarantee unquestioned loyalty to Perón on the part of every official and employee of the national, provincial, and local governments. To be a *Peronista* is a major qualification for public office in the "new Argentina": all persons "not identified with revolutionary ideals or imbued with the precepts of social justice"[18] were relieved of their government jobs in the early years of the regime. Since then it has been the function of the *Control* to assure the continuing loyalty of the holders of government office and the aspirants therefor. This has been a large-scale undertaking. It has already been noted that, although official figures are not published, there are approximately 1,000,000 government employees in Argentina.† These form, "with their respective families, an army of at least 4,000,000 citizens, or about one quarter of

* See pp. 418–22.
† National, provincial, and local officials and employees are included in this figure.

the population of the country."[19] This army is terrorized, intimidated, and kept "loyal" by the *Control*.

The methods of the *Control* range from the most obvious and summary to remarkably subtle and indirect tactics. Government workers may be simply dismissed, or they may be investigated, jailed—even tortured*—or driven into exile. On occasion the victims of the *Control* may be advised informally and indirectly that "justice" is about to fall upon them: if they make judicious and efficient use of this short notice they may be successful in absenting themselves from the country in time to avoid the more direct measures of the *Control*. The work of this agency is conducted in the utmost secrecy and the Argentine press is forbidden to mention its operations. It is, therefore, somewhat difficult to document the *Control's* activities. The reader may, however, obtain some insight into these activities from the case presented below. This case was delivered to the present writer by two of the principal figures in the affair. They are here called "Suárez" and "Gómez": the names are fictitious—to protect the principals from further harm when the *Control* reads this book, as it surely will—but the remaining facts in the case are based on the personal accounts of these two unfortunate gentlemen.

Both Suárez and Gómez were disloyal in the sense that they disapproved of many of Perón's methods and much of his program. Both, however, desired employment, and were able to secure government jobs. It is generally true that "every man employed by the government has lost his . . . independence and is forced to be, or appear to be, a *Peronista* in order to live."[20] This was the difficult situation of both Suárez and Gómez when they entered the government service; and it was not long before the *Control* be-

* See pp. 181–85.

came suspicious of their political unreliability. Suárez, a mature man of some reputation, became the chief of a division in one of the executive ministries; the younger Gómez was given a lesser position in the division headed by Suárez. They did not become acquainted with each other until after they had worked in the same office for some time.

Suárez was not only mature and reputable, but also a man of financial means. He bought stocks and, of course, was interested in the fluctuations of the stock market. It happened that the only Buenos Aires newspaper which carried market quotations was *La Prensa*, then the leading anti-*Peronista* daily. Primarily because of his financial interests, Suárez frequently bought *La Prensa*. He would, of course, read other parts of the paper in addition to the market quotations—occasionally he even looked at the editorials. Suárez felt that some of *La Prensa's* editorials made good sense. Once—once was enough—he made the tragic error of telling one of his government associates (let him be called Morales) that a particular *La Prensa* editorial was worth reading. In his capacity as a division chief, Suárez was a bureaucrat of some importance. Occasionally he was required to attend official functions and to sit on the platform with other government people while speeches were made. A frequent orator at such functions was Eva Perón. Suárez was probably less entranced by the late Evita's speeches than a government official ought to be: he felt that *la señora* was not very original in her thinking, and that when a man had heard two or three of her speeches he had heard all of them. Once, while Evita was making a speech—and once was enough for this, too—Suárez confided to the gentleman seated next to him on the platform that *la señora* seemed to say the same things every time she spoke.

One morning—or, as the Argentines like to put it, one

nice day—Suárez received a telephone call from the secretary of Colonel Alvarez* of the *Control,* and an appointment was made for an interview. The very mention of the *Control* has a connotation of terror for most Argentine government workers, and it had this effect for Suárez as well. He faced his meeting with Alvarez with considerable apprehension, and was already making plans to leave the country when he called at Alvarez' office. The colonel proceeded to tell him that the *Control* had received *laudatory* reports of his work, and that Perón was considering giving him a more responsible government position. This remark put Suárez at his ease, and he freely answered the colonel's questions about the work of his division.

During the questioning, the colonel asked Suárez for an evaluation of Gómez, who worked in Suárez' division. The latter was generally complimentary with respect to Gómez, saying that he was a conscientious worker devoted to his job. Alvarez' manner stiffened suddenly, and he told Suárez that the *Control* had information to the effect that Gómez was a Bolshevik. This sudden change in the atmosphere of the interview caught Suárez unexpectedly. His reaction was a mixture of incredulity with sudden fear. He remained somewhat defiant, however, and told Alvarez that he knew of no evidence to the effect that Gómez was a Bolshevik, and asked whether any proof of that existed. Alvarez replied by placing a document before Suárez. It was an affidavit declaring that Gómez was a traitor to Argentina; at the foot of the affidavit was a space for the signature of Gómez' division chief. Suárez, of course, was the division chief; with an ominous gesture, Alvarez provided the pen for signature. Terrified but still defiant, Suárez announced that he would refuse to sign the affidavit in the absence of proof that Gómez was indeed a Bolshevik.

* This name is also fictitious.

Alvarez then proceeded to produce the proof. The evidence was a record of *Suárez'* activities! It was duly noted that Suárez was an habitual reader of *La Prensa*, an antigovernment organ. It was further stated that on one occasion—Alvarez cited the date—Suárez had told one Morales that a particular *La Prensa* editorial was worth reading. And—worse than that—the *Control* had evidence that Suárez had once (again the exact date was cited) told a colleague that Eva Perón's speeches were not very good. Q.E.D. Gómez was a Bolshevik. Suárez would please sign the affidavit. Perspiring and thoroughly terrorized, Suárez signed. The rest of the story is simple: Gómez was imprisoned, and Suárez fled to exile.

Let it be noted that the *Control del Estado* polices only one quarter of the population of Argentina. The remaining three-fourths is left to the Federal Police. This entity has a constitutional position of some interest to "North Americans." During the latter part of the nineteenth century, Argentines borrowed many practices they found already in operation in the United States. Several of these have been discussed in earlier sections of this book. One such "North American" usage was the police power. Like the *norteamericanos*, the Argentines generally defined the police power as the authority to protect the health, safety, morals, and general welfare of the population. However, one significant difference distinguished the Argentine from the "North American" versions of the police power: in the United States, this was generally held to be a function of the state rather than the federal government, whereas in Argentina the central government rather than the provinces traditionally exercised the police power. Lest this be interpreted to mean that this authority was more rigorously applied in the southern republic, it should be pointed out that until the coming of Perón no single, centralized national agency existed for the implementation of the police power.[21]

This condition was altered in the first months after the revolution of 1943. Leopoldo Lugones, who had been a police official during the regime of President Uriburu (1930–32), was likewise highly placed among the rulers of the "new Argentina." He proposed that a federal police force be created for the unified and co-ordinated exercise of the police power. The proposition was enthusiastically received by the first rulers of the "new Argentina," among them Colonel Emilio Ramírez,* who was then one of the leaders of the G.O.U. Together, Lugones and Ramírez worked out a detailed project for the establishment of a federal police agency. The project was approved by the regime on November 17, 1943, and on December 26 a decree was published announcing the creation of the Federal Police, to have jurisdiction throughout Argentina for the preservation of internal security, the supervision of immigrants, and the prevention of sabotage and espionage. Colonel Ramírez became the first chief of the Federal Police, which was under the direct supervision of the president until March 15, 1944, when it was placed within the ministry of interior.

Since its creation in 1943, the strategic Federal Police has been headed by a curious parade of chieftains. Ramírez remained the head of the agency for only a few weeks after his appointment in December of 1943. He was replaced early in 1944 by Eugenio H. Saltero, who had studied police methods in Britain, France, and Italy and was regarded as something of a scientist in the field. Saltero remained at the post for a year, and was replaced in 1945 by Colonel Filomeno Velazco, who acquired a major reputation for bru-

* No relation to General Pedro P. Ramírez, who was president of Argentina at the time.

tality. Velazco was compared by the Radical ex-Deputy Julio González Iramain to Heinrich Himmler, one-time chief of Hitler's *Gestapo*. During Velazco's stewardship, the Federal Police achieved a political role of lasting significance in Perón's Argentina. The police developed a species of political rivalry with the army, and the resultant tension was a principal factor in the later removal of Velazco. The Federal Police remains, however, in an essentially non-cordial relationship with the army; and Velazco, now retired, is frequently regarded as a potentially powerful enemy of Perón. Political observers often point to the mutual hostility in which the police and the army operate, and count this as one of the more dangerous threats to the stability of the Perón government. Under the leadership of General Arturo Bertollo, the Federal Police is more subservient to Perón than it was during the Velazco period, although the police force may still bear watching as a possible source of trouble in the peculiar pattern of Argentine politics.*

Like the *Control del Estado*, the Federal Police is essentially military in its organization and orientation. As now organized, the Federal Police contains five major units of significance here. (1) The division of *Federal Co-ordination* is Perón's counter-espionage group, and is charged with tracking down such agents of foreign powers as might be operating in Argentina. (2) The *Political Order* section maintains a running surveillance over all Argentine political parties and groups with the exception of the Communists. (3) The *Special Section* performs this function with respect to the Communists. (4) The division of *Social Order* maintains a watch over Argentine social clubs and societies lest they develop political overtones. (5) The *Labor Order* section polices Argentine labor organizations

* For a discussion of the political role of the military, see pp. 306–16.

with a view to the preservation of their politically "correct" position.

On Law and Order

The question of constitutional guarantees interferes very little with the work of the Federal Police. Two constitutional stipulations—provisions for a state of siege and for a "state of prevention and alarm"—protect the police from the possibility of entanglement in a mesh of constitutionalism. The state of siege, originally contained in the Constitution of 1853 and carried over into the 1949 constitution, legalizes the suspension of constitutional guarantees "in case of internal commotion or foreign attack."[22] The president may declare a state of siege throughout the nation or in the Federal Capital alone or in any affected province or territory. At the time this book was written, much of the history of the "new Argentina" had been lived under states of siege. The siege declared by President Castillo on December 16, 1941, was still in force when the revolution of 1943 overthrew his administration. That condition— Argentines called it "constitutional abnormality"—persisted until it was suspended by President Fárrell on August 6, 1945. Expressions of political protest convinced Fárrell that his action had been premature, and the state of siege was reimposed on September 26, to be lifted only for the forty-eight hours necessary to hold the election of February 24, 1946. The state of siege was at length terminated in connection with President Perón's first inauguration in June of that year. There was no state of siege during the major portion of Perón's first term, but one was declared on September 28, 1951. Like its predecessor, this was lifted for the two days required for the election of November 11, from which Perón emerged with a second term.

The Constitution of 1853 said nothing about a "state of

prevention and alarm": this is new in the Constitution of 1949. At the time these lines were written, the "state of prevention and alarm" had not yet been used, and Argentine constitutional lawyers could only guess at what it meant or what it theoretically permitted. The new constitution provides that "a state of prevention and alarm may be declared in case of an alteration of public order which threatens to disturb the normal course of life or the fundamental activities of the population. The juridical effects of such a measure will be determined by law, but it will not suspend constitutional guarantees, although they may be temporarily limited if necessary. With reference to persons, the powers of the president will be limited to detaining them or transporting them from one point to another, for a period of no longer than thirty days."[23] After studying this passage, the reader is as competent an authority on the "state of prevention and alarm" as any Argentine, probably including President Perón himself.

Even in the absence of a state of siege or a "state of prevention and alarm," there is little legal frustration of policing activities. A host of decrees and laws restricts the liberties of Argentines whether or not the constitution is theoretically suspended. Two pieces of legislation are of primary importance in this field—the "contempt" law of 1948, and the legislation of 1950 tightening the restrictions against treason, sabotage, and espionage.

The first of these, a remarkable law from several points of view, prohibits the public utterance—whether by publication or otherwise—of expressions of "contempt" of the "new Argentina" or its officials. The law defines "contempt"* as "anything which offends the dignity of any public official, whether the statement refers directly to the

* The Spanish word is *desacato*, which may be translated as either "contempt" or "disrespect."

person or by allusion to him or the governmental organization of which he forms a part."[24] At the time this measure was debated in the congress during the closing months of 1948, the opposition Conservative Deputy Reinaldo Pastor warned that "once this law is passed, it will be difficult to criticize any act of the government . . . or the misconduct of any government official; it will be impossible for the Argentine press to exercise this function, so essential to democracy."[25] But this warning and others like it went unheeded, and overwhelming *Peronista* majorities in the Senate and the Chamber of Deputies placed the "contempt" law on the books in October of 1948.

What is "contempt"? According to the statute, the crime of "contempt" has been committed when a public statement is made or an article is published which does any of three things. (1) The statement is contemptuous if it is alleged to endanger Argentine neutrality with respect to any war. The punishment for this type of "contempt" ranges from six months' to one year's imprisonment. The present writer was privileged to watch this aspect of the law in operation. He was in Argentina in mid-1950, when the United Nations' police action began in Korea. When the United Nations Security Council addressed a communication to all members of the international organization—including Argentina—urging assistance in the action, Perón magnanimously announced that he would take whatever steps the people of his country desired. The Argentine public was thereupon urged to express its wishes with respect to their government's policy toward the Korean affair. Argentines were significantly silent: nobody would publicly advocate active involvement in the police action—Perón *could* call it a war—unless it was his ambition to spend the ensuing six months to one year in jail. The silence was interpreted to mean that the people of Argentina uniformly opposed their nation's active participation in the Korean fracas, and Perón complied with this interpretation.* (2) Also, the crime of "contempt" is committed if the statement in question is alleged to constitute an attack on Argentine sovereignty or an invitation to overthrow the government. This likewise carries a penalty of six months to one year in prison. (3) And the crime of "contempt" is involved if the statement is alleged to offend the dignity of a government official. If the official is the president, the vice president, any member of congress, a federal judge, a provincial governor or legislator, or a national cabinet member, the punishment ranges from six months to three years in jail; if the offended official is any other government employee, the penalty is two months' to two years' imprisonment. The fact that these penalties apply only to the authors of the offending statements does not mean that the publishers thereof are immune. Any person who publishes an allegedly contemptuous statement is subject to two months to a year in jail or a fine of from $67 to $334.† Moreover, whether or not the offending statement is factually true is a consideration which, according to the law, may *not* be introduced in defense of persons—be they the authors or the publishers of the offenses—apprehended for "contempt."

Since its promulgation in 1948, the "contempt" law has kept the Federal Police busy making arrests. The most celebrated "contempt" case is that of the Radical Deputy, and later presidential candidate, Ricardo J. Balbín, whose affair is elsewhere discussed.‡ Others—normally opposition political leaders—include the Radical Deputies Atilio E.

---

* It should be stated in fairness that a probable majority of the Argentine people were in opposition to sending their armed forces to fight in Korea. See pp. 427–28.

† That is, 1,000 to 5,000 *pesos*, here converted at the rate of 15 *pesos* to the United States dollar.

‡ See pp. 81–83.

Cattáneo, Luis R. MacKay, Eudoro Patricio Vargas Gómez, and Moisés Lebensohn. The Lebensohn case is illustrative of one pattern of enforcement of the law. He commented adversely on a speech made by President Perón, and was forthwith sentenced to a year in prison for "contempt." However, Lebensohn was freed and told that he would not be required to serve his sentence unless he committed additional "contempt" within the ensuing five years.

A second major measure expanding the work of the Federal Police is the 1950 law tightening prohibitions against treason, sabotage, and espionage. This measure was passed by the congress in September of that year, and served to strengthen Perón's hold on the nation. The law divides into three sections. (1) *Treason* had already been defined in the constitution as bearing arms against Argentina or giving aid and comfort to the nation's enemies.* The 1950 statute, with respect to treason, served only to fix the penalty for this crime at death or life imprisonment. (2) The law defined *sabotage* as applying to any person who "by whatever means provokes public alarm or depresses the public spirit, thereby causing damage to the nation."[26] It will be readily apparent that the very elasticity of this definition permits conviction on charges of sabotage for actions not considered by anybody but a *Peronista* to be sabotage. Since the passage of the law in 1950, nobody in Argentina has been exactly certain of what sabotage is. Obviously, it is whatever Perón says it is. And—whatever it may be—the penalty for it ranges from one to eight years in prison. (3) And the most sweeping of the provisions is the 1950 definition of *espionage*. Article 6 of the law declares that this crime is committed by any person who "without authority [from the

* This provision is similar to that contained in the Constitution of the United States, with the exception that the "North American" version requires two witnesses to the same overt act. This stipulation is dispensed with in Argentina.

Argentine government] hands over, remits, communicates, publishes or divulges economic, political, financial, military, or industrial data which, even though not secret, are not yet intended [by the government] for publication."[27] According to this definition, espionage was engaged in by the present writer when he did research in political science in Argentina, and by the Argentines—many of them *Peronistas!* —who aided him. This book is the product of espionage. The punishment for it ranges from one month's to four years' imprisonment. Does freedom of investigation exist in Argentina? Not for the research scholar who is interested in economic, political, financial, military, or industrial matters. That is, not if he is caught by the Federal Police while committing the crime of research.

It should be obvious from the foregoing that the Federal Police is one of the most overworked agencies of the "new Argentina." With or without a state of siege there is ample ground for the arrest of Argentines whose ideas and activities are not consonant with Perón's. Since the revolution of 1943, the number of political prisoners held in Argentine jails has been greater than at any other time in the nation's history. The government, as might be expected, has never published the number of persons held in confinement. However, unofficial but well-informed estimates placed the number of political prisoners at 2,000 in August of 1944, 3,000 in October of the same year, and at *14,500* a year later. In what was described as a magnanimous gesture, Perón celebrated his first inauguration as president on June 6, 1946, by signing Decree No. 7, which ordered a general amnesty for political prisoners. A month later—on July 3—he signed Decree No. 1,515, rescinding the amnesty. It is typical of Perón's propaganda techniques that Decree No. 7 was given wide publicity by the newspapers of Argentina, whereas Decree No. 1,515 was not mentioned in the press.

It is characteristic of the "new Argentina" that many of the people who now spend significant portions of their lives in jail are criminals only in the eyes of a *Peronista*. The crimes of a high percentage of them are political activity, "contempt," or seeking employment after having lost their *buenas conductas*. Many of the prisoners are labor leaders, politicians, writers, publishers, and members of various professions. On December 11, 1950, the Córdoba Bar Association released a statement pointing with alarm to the large sector of the nation's legal profession then in prison.

The process of political arrest has become virtually ritualized in the "new Argentina." If the intended victim has strategically placed connections, he may be informed that his arrest is about to take place, and he may have time to escape to safety—usually Montevideo, Uruguay, or the embassy of some foreign state. If he does not have that much time, or if he lacks the strategically placed connections, then he may be surprised when the agent of the Federal Police calls upon him at home or at his place of business. The affair is usually quite gentlemanly, in the best Argentine tradition. The policeman announces that his superior officer desires to see the victim—the announcement is made much as though it were an invitation to join the officer at tea. The ritual then requires that the victim ask whether the message is an invitation or a command, and the policeman normally replies politely that it is his fond wish that it be regarded as an invitation, but if it is not so regarded he regrets that it will have to be considered as a command. The two then depart for the prison, and, upon their arrival, tea frequently *is* served. The reactions of many of the political prisoners to the intriguing experience of arrest and confinement range from anguish to an intellectual, semi-morbid interest in what is happening to themselves and to the world of the Argentines. One has time in prison to con-

template broad and even philosophical questions, whereas
his previous life had been too rushed or routinized for that.
And many—especially if the duration of their imprisonment is short—may agree with the Socialist Deputy Enrique
Dickmann, who said of his arrest during the Uriburu revolution of 1930: "I must confess that I harbor no grudges
and I am not sorry that I spent a week in the penitentiary.
It was a new experience in my life. It put me in contact
with men and with things I had not known before."[28]

For others, imprisonment may be a physically painful ordeal. Shortly after the revolution of 1943, concentration
camps were established in the Chaco, in Neuquén, in Patagonia, and on the island of Martín García. In the first
months of the "new Argentina," the existence of the concentration camps was difficult to document. Stories of them
came from "North American" journalists like Ray Josephs,
who, on August 11, 1943, reported: "Every day I hear
more tales of trains loaded with persons summarily arrested without trial, departing with alleged Communists
headed for Neuquén and Tierra del Fuego concentration
camps. To avoid attracting attention, the prisoners are
loaded early in the morning at southern suburban stations.
. . . Machine gunners are posted on the roof of each car in
case somebody should try a 'rescue attempt.' "[29] And later in
1943: "The few letters smuggled out [of the concentration
camps] tell horrible tales; tales of prisoners being kept
standing naked while their clothes are taken away and thin
prison garments given them. The weather down there [in
Neuquén] has been particularly bad, facilities especially in-
adequate. Prisoners get little to read, only the barest medical
attention and many have become ill with pneumonia. Few
know where to turn or what they can do. . . ."[30] Official
confirmation of the existence of the concentration camps
came in October of 1943, when 25,000 striking packing-

house workers returned to work after the government agreed to release 47 of their union leaders from confinement in Patagonia. And on November 29, 1943, the regime published a warning that persons distributing anti-government propaganda would be sent to concentration camps. The chief inmates of these institutions from 1943 to 1946 were labor leaders who were confined during the course of Perón's campaign for the conquest of Argentine organized labor. As this program neared consolidation the use of concentration camps for the control of union leaders tapered off.* After Perón's inauguration in 1946, the government slowly abandoned these camps. So far as the present writer was able to determine, concentration camps no longer existed in Argentina when he was in the country in 1950 and 1951.

However, the practice of torturing political prisoners continues in Argentina. Torture was outlawed in the country in 1813, but it was resumed shortly after the revolution of 1943. The first reports of this were circulated in November of that year. Detailed exposés were published by the Communist leader Rodolfo Ghioldi in May of 1944, and by the exiled Radical Deputy Silvano Santander in February of 1945. In the latter year, 60 inmates of concentration camps in the Chaco were reportedly subjected to physical torture, and 200 released political prisoners jointly accused the Buenos Aires police of using methods of extreme torture. And on November 25, 1949, a documented account of the use of torture by Argentine police was submitted to the United Nations by the International League for the Rights of Man.

Very little has been published about the *picana eléctrica*, or electric goad, which is the contribution of the Argentine

* The course of Perón's capture of organized labor is traced on pp. 319–27.

Control del Estado and Federal Police to techniques of
modern physical torture. The *picana eléctrica* is an electric
rod which was originally used in Argentina for the purpose
of herding cattle. The rod, when touched against a sensitive part of an animal's body, delivers an electric shock
which inspires the beast to move rapidly in the direction desired by the herder. When applied to sensitive sections of
the human body, the *picana eléctrica* is also effective. It
produces a painful, burning shock, and has been known to
induce nervous disorders and sexual impotency. From the
standpoint of the *Control del Estado* and the Federal Police, a major advantage of the *picana eléctrica* is that it
leaves no bruises or identifying marks on the body of the
victim, who therefore finds it difficult to prove later that
he had been tortured.

The writer is acquainted with several Argentines who
have had experience with the *picana eléctrica*. This, too, has
its ritual. The *Control del Estado* or the Federal Police, as
the case may be, submits the intended victim to a medical
heart examination before applying the *picana eléctrica*. If
the result of the examination indicates that the victim's
heart might not withstand the shock, the use of the electric
goad is foregone. If, on the other hand, the medical verdict
is otherwise, the victim is not to be congratulated on his
sound health. Nobody has emerged from *that* experience
saying, "I must confess that I harbor no grudges and I am
not sorry." The writer's acquaintances who have known
the *picana eléctrica* are convinced that they have deep-
running scores to settle; they will not be dissuaded from this
easily.

The first recorded use of the *picana eléctrica* as an instrument of human torture occurred in November of 1943
in a concentration camp in the Chaco. By 1945, charges
were widespread that the device was being applied on a

large scale against political prisoners, and the *picana eléctrica* was in that year the subject of editorials carried by *La Prensa* and *La Nación*, the two leading anti-Perón newspapers of Buenos Aires. The government at first denied the accusations, but at length announced on June 27, 1945, that an official investigation of the matter would be undertaken. The investigation proved to be a farce. It was not until July 26, 1949, that the congress established a joint committee to look into the question. This committee was under the co-chairmanship of José Emilio Visca and Rodolfo P. Decker. Both were *Peronista* congressmen, as were the majority of the other members of the body. The Visca-Decker committee investigated many matters, but the use of the *picana eléctrica* never really came to be one of them. The closest the committee came to that was to probe into the financial affairs of the newspapers and wire news-services which had carried reports of torture: the hard-working Visca-Decker group took over the account books of not only the Buenos Aires bureaus of the Associated Press and the United Press, and of seven *porteño* newspapers, but also of the Buenos Aires branches of the National City Bank of New York and the Bank of London. "The committee, formed as a face-saving gesture by the *Peronista* congress, went off on its tangent just as the biggest torture case was submitted to the United Nations Secretariat by Walter M. Beveraggi, one of the victims," a political observer reported. "But the majority of the committee of an administration signing all United Nations and inter-American documents defending civil liberties has not found it 'convenient'—often a decisive Latin-American condition—to report on the matter."[31] However, appeal to the United Nations has had its effect. Perón would like to eschew renewed possibilities of foreign or international intervention. Since 1950 there has been a noticeable tendency to restrict the *picana eléctrica* to political prisoners who are Communists or alleged Communists. This operates on the theory that nobody would publicly denounce the torture of such persons unless he wished himself to be branded as a Communist, or at least as a fellow-traveler.

There is, in short, something of a dearth of individual liberty in Perón's Argentina. The nation lives in an atmosphere of intimidation, in an *ambiente* or political climate where habeas corpus comes and goes while the *Control del Estado* and the Federal Police are ever-present. Whether there is a state of siege or a "state of prevention and alarm" or "constitutional government," life is essentially the same. One dare not discuss politics in public lest "politics" turn out to be synonymous with "contempt," "treason," "sabotage," or "espionage." Those who do not fit in well with the "new Argentina" are strong candidates for political imprisonment and even for cruel physical torture. Argentines with short-wave radios able to pick up the *Voice of America* on occasion hear themselves included among the "free peoples of the world." Some of them find this difficult to understand; other Argentines simply shrug their shoulders and smile cynically. After all, their constitution *does* provide that "the state does not recognize the liberty to undermine liberty."

9.

On the Mind of Man

Perón's Argentina has, as might be expected, sought to indoctrinate and educate the citizenry in the ways of its rulers. This objective has been central in a number of measures representing significant attempts to harness the thinking and the ideas of Argentines. These measures, frequently sweeping in scope and far-reaching in ramification, have extended to regulation of such matters as the nation's educational system, the Argentine press, and radio, theater, and motion pictures. All of these today bear the stamp of Perón and are organized as salesmen of the "new Argentina."

Of the Educative Process

The Argentine school system, long regarded as one of the most successful in Latin America, was among the first victims of the revolution of 1943. The reader has already seen illustrations of the tendency of pre-Perón arrangements to "set up" relatively easy conquests for the governors of the "new Argentina." One of these was the national school system. Long before the coming of Perón, the monopoly of public education by the national government had become settled practice; and the military men who came to power in 1943 found that the nation's public schools were already in their hands.

They made use of this situation to inject a curious combination of nationalism, militarism, and religiosity into the curricula of Argentine schools. In August of 1944, Alberto Baldrich, then the regime's educational administrator, asserted that the country's institutions of learning "must be absolutely Argentine. We must not allow ourselves to be corrupted by foreign ideas."[1] And Perón himself has contributed to a strange nationalism in pedagogy. "Argentine students must be taught by Argentine methods," the president has said. "We do not need to resort to Pestalozzi or any other of the great pedagogues. . . . We must create everything for ourselves."[2] What were the educational theories that the men of the "new Argentina" created for themselves? Hear one-time Education Minister Oscar Ivanissevich, speaking in 1948: "We will teach first that children learn to live, afterward that they should learn to know. That they should know less and want more. That they should know less and think more. That they should know less and feel more. That they should have more time for well-conducted animal spirits. . . . We will not place in the fertile soil of their intelligence more seed than their natural capacity can nourish effectively. We will fight with all our might against parasitic . . . intellectualism."[3] How have these precepts been implemented? A few illustrations may suffice. In September of 1946, the *Peronista* Senators Alberto Teisaire, Vicente Saadi,* and Sosa Loyola introduced in the congress a bill requiring that only one textbook be used for each course taught in Argentine secondary schools. The measure as finally passed provided that the book selected for each course would be approved and printed by the national government. Moreover, the nation's schoolrooms are used for the proselytization of projects

* Readers desiring to refresh their memories on the further adventures of Senator Saadi may care to turn to pp. 142–43.

supported by the regime. A case in point: during 1948 and the early part of 1949, when *Peronistas* were preparing the country to receive a new constitution, all public-school teachers were directed to imbue their students with a desire for constitutional reform.

Militarism, a basic component of the revolution of 1943, soon worked its way into the schools. A decree published on September 27, 1943, directed all Argentine primary-school teachers to "take advantage of every opportunity to exalt the sentiment of the fatherland . . . [and] to give to military glory and deeds of arms the preferred place which they deserve."[4] Implementation of this decree and others like it proceeded apace in the first years of the "new Argentina." By the time that Perón was inaugurated as president in 1946, the country's military schools were organized so as to teach "the spirit of sacrifice," "the wealth of our soil," "the wealth of our language," and "the work and action of the heroes of our country."[5]

But perhaps foremost among the early educational measures of the "new Argentina" was the celebrated Decree No. 18,411* of December 31, 1943. This decree resumed compulsory religious instruction in Argentine public schools. In so doing, the measure reversed a long-standing Argentine solution of the characteristically Latin-American problem of the relationship of the Roman Catholic Church to public education. The Church played a major part in the Argentine educational arrangement until Domingo Faustino Sarmiento, the remarkable "schoolmaster-president, entered the *Casa Rosada* in 1868. He inspired a host of projects for educational reform. One of them did not become law until a decade after Sarmiento left the presidency. This measure, enacted by the congress in 1884 during the administration

* Law No. 12,978 of April 17, 1947, placed this decree on a statutory basis.

of President Julio A. Roca, provided for what Sarmiento had called "religious neutrality" in the public schools. The law, buttressed by enforcing legislation passed in 1888 and 1904, established secular education in Argentina based on the proposition of a separation of Church and state so far as the public schools were concerned.

This separation remained a controlling educational principle until the revolution of 1943. In that year, Argentine public policy with respect to this matter reverted to a pre-1884 position with the promulgation of the decree of December 31. The text of this significant measure is perhaps worth quoting here:

> In all public schools . . . instruction in the Catholic religion will be imparted as a regular section of the respective courses of study.
> Respecting liberty of conscience, exempted from this requirement are those students whose parents manifest express opposition because of affiliation with another religion. These students will be given moral instruction.[6]

Official proponents of this decree pointed out that the president and vice president of the nation were required by the constitution to be Roman Catholics, and that compulsory religious instruction would have the effect in future years of rendering a greater proportion of the nation's population eligible for these offices. "The official school without religion is anti-democratic and unconstitutional," it was said. "It does not train the child for the supreme honor to which every Argentine may aspire, that is, to become president of the nation."[7]

Perhaps more immediately important was the tendency of the decree to encourage a somewhat political alliance between the "new Argentina" and the Roman Catholic Church. In a message to General Ramírez, who was nominal president at the time the compulsory religious education decree was promulgated, Monseñor Capello, the Cardinal of Buenos Aires, declared: "The patriotism shown by Your Excellency in fulfilling one of the deepest hopes and greatest ambitions of the Argentine people has recuperated for them the morality of our country's great destinies, the path of which was shown by the great thinkers and heroes who forged its nationality."[8] And, in a message to Perón himself, none other than Pope Pius XII said, "We are pleased by this recognition of the rights of the Church in the field of Christian education."[9] It should be noted that the relationship between Church and state in the Perón era is a complex and somewhat contradictory matter; it is explored more fully in Chapter 10 of this book.

Argentine teachers and professors who did not agree with the educational and other policies of the post-1943 regime were, of course, dismissed from their posts. The mass exodus of Argentina's educators, begun in 1943, was still under way at the time these lines were written. This has been a spectacular tragedy: Argentina, whose scholars and teachers once set high standards for the Americas, has witnessed a large-scale departure of her more competent contributors to most fields of knowledge and thought. This has been an especially acute condition with respect to the social sciences —much research in these fields was branded after 1950 as "espionage"*—but other fields have suffered as well. Certainly very few of the students who heard the last words— "And now I have delivered my last lecture. . . . The next must come from a colonel"[10]—of the dismissed distinguished medical scholar, Dr. Bernardo A. Houssay, will soon forget that occasion. Houssay, deprived of his position at the University of Buenos Aires in October of 1943, continued his work abroad. In 1947, he became the first Latin-American scholar to receive the Nobel Prize in the field of medicine. The replacements for Houssay and the thousands of other

* See pp. 178–79.

dismissed Argentine educators have been of a quality which has very seriously lowered the standards of competence once proudly maintained by Argentina's institutions of learning. Public notice of this development has produced formal statements of protest by prominent educational leaders in many countries of the Western Hemisphere. For example, on November 2, 1943, a group of twenty outstanding "North American" scholars—including Dr. Albert Einstein of Princeton University; the late Dr. Clarence Dykstra, then at the University of Wisconsin; and Dr. Francis McMahon of the University of Notre Dame—protested what they called the Argentine "dictatorial edict" which dismissed Houssay and other educators who had expressed political opposition to the "new Argentina." "When books are burned in one country, all freedom of objective scholarship is threatened everywhere," the twenty "North Americans" asserted. "When a man takes a stand against despotism in any country he is at the service of all humanity."[11]

Making the country's six universities fit the Procrustean bed of the "new Argentina" has not been an easy task, even for Perón. It was one thing to dismiss intransigent administrators and faculty members; it was quite another problem to bring the 62,700 students of the Universities of Córdoba, Buenos Aires, the Littoral, La Plata, Tucumán, and Cuyo to heel. For the truth is that Argentine university students never were very docile, not even in the years before Perón. "The Argentine university, traditionally, is a miniature battleground of national politics," one observer has written. "Students strike, riot, and stage political demonstrations on the slightest provocation."[12] This has been the traditional pattern of Argentine student behavior. Hear a *cordobés* recalling his student days at the University of Córdoba: the students' readiness to launch a political strike "becomes a passion that invades and confuses everything. I myself remember many postponed examinations; many study hours disturbed; countless meetings, speeches, discussions; strikes—a whole year lost in them—elections that ended with gunfire. . . ."[13] Against the background of such a tradition, it could not be expected that the "new Argentina" could be saddled on the nation's university students without a fight.

The revolution of 1943 was greeted by a mood of frank hostility and rebellion on the part of most of the students attending the country's six universities. They had gone on strike and conducted political demonstrations for causes much lighter than the coming of Perón; and in 1943 the students again prepared to do battle. The Argentine University Federation, with which students on all six campuses were affiliated, launched a general strike in October of 1943 in protest against the wholesale dismissal of their professors. The government responded by closing all of the universities on October 27. The schools were reopened a few days later, and the Argentine University Federation was ordered dissolved. The federation, however, had not learned the lesson of obedience. It continued to operate as a species of committee of co-ordination and correspondence for the six universities, and in July of 1945 it directed its affiliates to wear black in mourning for the "loss of public freedom and rights."[14] A month later, the student federation joined with 208 professors in formally requesting the Supreme Court of Justice to withdraw its recognition of the military regime as a *de facto* government. And on September 30, 1945, the Argentine Student Federation called another general student strike.

The turmoil following this strike call was memorable. Argentines who were university students in 1945 still talk excitedly about those stirring "October days." They were curious and hectic days; they were in a sense heroic days, days in which the attention of the entire Western Hemisphere was drawn to the struggle of Argentina's university students against their military rulers. On many previous occasions, the students had barricaded themselves in university buildings, it is true; but those had been isolated, local affairs involving small numbers of students. The ordeal of October of 1945 was different: no fewer than *30,000* students rose in opposition against the regime! They stubbornly resisted the Federal Police; they threw marbles under the hooves of the horses of the mounted representatives of the "new Argentina." And they barricaded themselves in the buildings of the universities while the Federal Police milled about outside. The first to barricade themselves were the students at the University of La Plata, who shut themselves in on October 2; the example was soon followed at Buenos Aires and at other schools. While the frustrated Federal Police laid siege to the barricaded students and endeavored to cut off their communications and their sources of food, water, and electricity, the sit-down strikers drew the eyes of the Western Hemisphere to themselves and to the regime against which they struggled. The resourceful besieged students established loud-speaker systems, through which they broadcast encouragement to the sympathetic sectors of the populace beyond the academic walls; the strikers organized systems of communication and supply; they established a press. "Argentine youth is united both within and without the occupied buildings," the beleaguered students at the University of Buenos Aires proclaimed through their amplifiers and their press, "and solemnly declares that it will fight for constitutional normality with the one weapon available to an unarmed people—civil disobedience."[15] At the University of La Plata the situation was more desperate but no less gallant. "We have converted our island into a bastion, and we will stand guard in it for the republic until the *Mazorca** overcomes us," asserted Aquiles Martínez Civelli, the acting president of the University of La Plata, who was barricaded with his students. "We number 230. Our arms: a recording of the National Anthem, a microphone, and some loudspeakers. . . . We number 230. . . . We are all proud."[16]

But it was a losing battle. The Federal Police forced their way into one university and then another; by October 9 the last of the six universities was subdued. The affair, though hopeless from the students' side from the outset, was an epic in university annals: it created a tradition, it built an *esprit de corps*. Though the Federal Police eventually forced the buildings and arrested the students and some of their professors, the "October days" served in large part to kindle a spirit of resistance among the students which was still very much alive when the present writer visited the Universities of Buenos Aires, La Plata, and Córdoba in 1950 and 1951. The casualties of the "October days" may not impress some: at the University of Buenos Aires, 2 students were killed, and 1,445 men and 149 women students were jailed, together with 6 of their professors. Also imprisoned at Buenos Aires were 39 "agitators"—that is, persons who were not students or professors but who were nevertheless involved in the fray. The figures for each of the remaining five universities were smaller than those for the University of Buenos Aires; the over-all total number of imprisoned students came to approximately 2,000.

Observers spent years writing post-mortems on the "October days." Many persons were impressed by the unity and solidarity among the students during the crisis. "Perhaps for the first time in all their history, the Argentine universities have presented to the country the most complete

* See p. 27.

unity of thought and action," a participant in the strike wrote. "All division among the students disappeared. In some schools the students had been accustomed to divide themselves into a half dozen parties and centers. But in October of 1945—spontaneously and almost without exception—from some nationalist groups to the Communists, all had the same desire, the same fervor, and made the same sacrifices."[17] Even "North Americans" took notice. The strike was "an example of how democracy and liberty can be fed by the schools; of how they can constitute a citadel of liberty while other institutions of free government, because of timidity or cynicism, have abandoned the cause of liberty," the *New York Herald Tribune* said editorially. "The spirit of the Argentine universities proved superior to the political vagaries of that country's government and stood out against armed tyranny. The Americas have reason to be proud of this sturdy intellectual growth on their soil."[18] But it took an embattled Argentine university professor to make this point: "Unfortunately, the Argentine university does not 'educate' us. . . . The instruction it gives us can be an ingredient of education, but evidently it is not 'education' in itself. I therefore believe that the experience the students lived through in October of 1945 is more important for their lives as men than many examinations and many years of study."[19]

The "October days" of 1945 marked the apogee of university resistance to the "new Argentina." Thereafter organized opposition weakened, although the spirit of rebellion remained alive. But with the crumbling of organized academic resistance, the regime moved to consolidate its conquest of the universities. "Interventors," charged with the management of academic administration, were installed on all six campuses in May of 1946; later that year, it was decreed that all students who refused or failed to take their examinations would be suspended from school for the ensuing two years.

The Perón regime's basic measure for the control of the institutions of higher learning is the "University Law," which went into force on October 4, 1947. That legislation undertook the administrative reorganization of the universities and set forth a *Peronista* statement of what the proper function of a university should be within the context of the "new Argentina." The law provided that thenceforth the rectors (roughly equivalent to presidents) of the six universities would be appointed for three-year terms by the president of the nation. The duties of the rectors would be to serve as the legal representatives of their respective institutions, to appoint their administrative and academic personnel, and to direct the over-all administration of their respective universities. Moreover, the "University Law" of 1947 established a National University Council, composed of the six rectors and the minister of justice and public instruction, the last-named a member of Perón's cabinet. The task of the National University Council, according to the law, would be to maintain liaison between the government and the universities and to "co-ordinate" the curricula and the administrations of the six campuses.

The "University Law" limited the lawful functions of the universities to (1) the development of a national historic conscience, (2) the conduct of research, (3) the accumulation and diffusion of knowledge, (4) the advancement of technical and applied sciences, and (5) the preparation of students for positions in the liberal and other professions. A later measure required the universities to offer obligatory courses in Perón's social and economic doctrine* to guarantee the proper "political formation" of the students. The text of the "University Law" made it clear that

* See pp. 276–93.

the universities were to serve the foregoing purposes to the total exclusion of any others. "The universities should not, in any case or for any reason, detract from the value of their specific functions," the law said. "The professors and students must not take direct or indirect part in politics in their capacity as members of a university, nor formulate group declarations constituting political militancy or intervention in questions not related to the specific function [of the universities] . . . ."[20] For the purpose of making the government's supervision of the campuses more effective, a secretariat of education was established as a government agency by decree of February 14, 1948. With the adoption of the Constitution of 1949, this secretariat was elevated to the status of a ministry, and the minister of education replaced the minister of justice and public instruction as an *ex officio* member of the National University Council. The last of Perón's major university reforms was promulgated on June 20, 1949, when the six institutions became tuition-free.

Two aspects of the role of educational institutions in Perón's system are significant. In the first place, it is true that education is now thoroughly controlled by the government, and that the schools now lie at the political service of the "new Argentina." The teachers and professors must be politically acceptable to the regime, the curricula preach the glory of Perón and the late Evita, research—especially in the social sciences—has been tightly curbed, and liberty of teaching and investigation does not exist. But on the other hand, while the quality of instruction and research has declined seriously since the revolution of 1943, what education the schools are still permitted to impart is open to a much greater percentage of the population than was true before the coming of Perón.

All Argentine public schools—be they primary, secondary, or universities—are now tuition-free. In 1951 alone, 401 new primary schools were opened, 984,297 children were enrolled in the elementary schools, and 281,954 students were in the secondary, normal, and technical schools. "I can declare with legitimate pride," Perón said in 1951, "that my government has constructed more schools in five years than the total erected in the one hundred preceding years."[21] Literacy, traditionally high in Argentina when compared with the other states of Latin America, probably will not suffer statistically in the Perón period. Censorship has prohibited the publication of the full results of the Fourth National Census, conducted in 1947. But those who are willing to take Perón's word for it might find the following statement significant. "The Argentine republic at the present time has no illiterate children," President Perón asserted in 1951. "Among the adults there exists illiteracy of only 8 to 12 per cent."[22]

Although more Argentines go to school in Perón's system than was the case before 1943, there can be little doubt that the nature of formal education is changing in the "new Argentina." The mood of frank rebellion still persists in the universities, but each year it grows weaker. Generations of students change more rapidly than other types of generations; Argentines in school in 1952 knew the heroic "October days" of 1945 only by story and subversive legend. As the years progress, it can only be expected that the schools will fall more completely into the place set for them by the Perón regime. "Until a very short time ago, the aims of the Argentine school were to acquire wealth, wisdom, and a retirement pension," President Perón declared in a recent speech. "Today its aims are: to be ever conscious of the glory of God, placing the spiritual above the material . . . ; to put an end to class conflicts in order to form only one class of Argentines . . . ; to unite all Argentines in

one aspiration, one will . . . ; [to make] each Argentine
. . . a perfected value with a high level of technical capacity and strong creative impulse . . . ; [to establish]
the ambition of each citizen . . . to own a plot of land in
the fatherland, and a part of the sky above it . . . ; to dis-
seminate the doctrine of economic and political independence in order to consolidate national and international peace
through the rule of justice."[23]

Domingo Faustino Sarmiento, the fabulous "schoolmaster-president" of the nineteenth century, was never one to
eschew strong language when the occasion seemed to justify it. "Idiots!" he once asserted. "Ideas cannot be killed!"[24]

The Public Prints

Censorship of the press became an integral part of the
"new Argentina" from the very first day of the revolution
of 1943. This aspect of the Perón regime has attracted
widespread attention outside of Argentina, and has frequently been the object of "North American" press attack.
Press censorship "is the classic first step by which dictatorship is imposed upon a people," the *New York Times* has
said editorially. "By its very nature, dictatorship moves
inexorably to stifle the voice of a free press and to destroy
the sources of trustworthy information. . . . In following
in this respect the pattern endorsed by Stalin and Hitler,
Mussolini, and Franco, Señor Perón has embarked on a
course of infinite danger to his country."[25]

In a curious sense, the history of freedom of the press in
Argentina has been the history of a circle. In the first years
of the Spanish colonial period, the sale of books—*all* books
—was prohibited in what later became Argentina. No printing press existed there until one was established by the Jesuits in the eighteenth century. This press was confined to the
publication of books on Church doctrine and to the pro-

duction of Spanish-Guaraní* dictionaries. Even this publishing activity dwindled into insignificance with the expulsion of the Jesuits from the Spanish Empire late in the eighteenth century; and it was not until the eve of independence of Spain that periodicals appeared. The first of these was *Telégrafo Mercantil* (founded in 1801), which was soon followed by *Seminario de Agricultura* (1802). With the launching in 1810 of the war for national independence, a larger group of periodicals was born: prominent among them were Belgrano's *Correo de Comercio, El Censor, La Gaceta,* and *La Crónica Argentina.*

Freedom of the press was proclaimed as one of the principles of the Argentine revolution of 1810. A royal decree of August 22, 1792, which had forbidden publication anywhere in the Spanish Empire of news items concerned with the French Revolution, was suspended by the revolutionary *junta* at Buenos Aires in a measure dated April 20, 1811. This act announced that the press was thenceforth to be free in Argentina, but six months later censorship of religious information was decreed, and a law of December 3, 1817, required the press to use "moderation" at all times in treating of all subjects. Fuller press censorship was resumed with the coming in 1820 of the anarchic interprovincial wars. Severe punishments for "abuses" of liberty of the press were promulgated on May 9, 1828. And a most thoroughgoing censorship remained in force throughout the regime of "Bloody Rosas," which came to an end in 1852. "With the press law of 1828 and its amendments, the opposition press was silenced and the rest was domesticated," an Argentine student of the press has written. "The

* Guaraní is the language of the Indians inhabiting much of Paraguay and a portion of the Argentine Chaco.

forty-three newspapers of 1833 were reduced to fifteen in 1834 and were only three in 1835. Why would Rosas want newspapers?"[26]

With the writing of the Constitution of 1853, liberty of the press again became an Argentine principle. Substantial freedom was enjoyed by the nation's newspapers for the ninety-year period which ended in 1943. Although it is true that this liberty suffered minor threats and interruptions during that era, it was nevertheless a golden age for Argentine journalism, and the country produced a number of newspapers whose standards were rated highly throughout the world. Notable journals existed in the provinces of the "interior" as well as at Buenos Aires; but the *porteño* papers acquired more widespread reputations and exercised greater influence over Argentine national affairs.

Of the leading Buenos Aires newspapers established between 1853 and 1943, ten might be mentioned here. Foremost among them were *La Nación* (founded in 1862) and *La Prensa* (1869), which became the *porteños'* only leading morning newspapers.* The appearance of *La Epoca* (1875) was followed by *El Diario* (1881). *La Vanguardia* (1894) became the major organ of the Argentine Socialist party,† and *El Pueblo* (1899) was a strongly Catholic journal. *La Razón* (1904) was regarded in its early years as a "serene" newspaper which made an elaborate point of avoiding sensationalism. *Crítica* (1913) shocked *porteños* at first—a uniquely "uncultured" journal, it specialized in sensationalism and developed an unprecedentedly large circulation, becoming the nation's first "newspaper of the masses."[27] *El Mundo* (1927) gave Argentines their first glimpse of a domestic tabloid. *Noticias Gráficas* (1930) endeavored

* *La Nación* and *La Prensa* are further discussed on pp. 208–14.
† *La Vanguardia* is considered further on pp. 214–16.

with some success to strike a middle position—with respect to sensationalism—between *Crítica* at one extreme and *La Razón* at the other.

A number of newspapers serving minorities and foreign colonies at Buenos Aires are also worthy of note. At the disposal of the British colony are two English-language journals, *The Standard* (1860) and the *Buenos Aires Herald* (1876). *The Standard* is the oldest newspaper in any language still functioning in Argentina; the *Buenos Aires Herald* was the first Argentine paper to carry cable services from Europe. The French colony is served by *Le Courrier de la Plata* (1864), the only French-language paper published anywhere in South America; and the Argentine Spanish colony has *El Diario Español* (1871). The principal German-language journals are *Argentinisches Tageblatt* (1888) and *Deutsche la Plata Zeitung* (1870): and the Italians have *L'Italia del Popolo* (1917) and *Il Matino D'Italia* (1929). Finally, the Argentine Jewish group* is served by *Di Presse* (1915), published in Yiddish; *El Diario Israelita* (1914), in Yiddish; and *Israel* (1916), in Spanish. In general, all of the journals serving minority and foreign groups—with the notable exception of the German papers†—have endeavored to abstain from participating editorially in Argentine politics.

Press censorship was imposed within hours of the revolution of June 4, 1943. "In order to prevent the diffusion of rumors, news, and editorials which might contribute to the creation of an atmosphere of inquietude in the population, or which might affect the international prestige of the nation," a decree of June 4 declared, "the press of the country will abstain from publishing items related to the recent public events, with the exception of material released by the

* See pp. 224–28.
† See p. 404.

chief of the armed forces or previously authorized by him."[28] On July 5 the ministry of interior instructed all Federal Interventors to prevent the newspapers in their provinces from making "malicious comments" on foreign relations or the governmental organization of foreign states. "Journalists . . . must be reminded," the ministry of interior said, "that the constitutional guarantees and privileges protecting our free government are irreconcilable with abuse or calumny directed against representatives of authority."[29]

A flood of decrees and laws has established the machinery for the control of the press. A Subsecretariat of Information—at first called the "Subsecretariat of Information and Press"—was created on October 21, 1943. The subsecretariat was originally attached directly to the presidency, was placed within the ministry of interior on March 10, 1944, and returned to direct presidential supervision on May 31, 1946. The Subsecretariat of Information serves as the point of liaison between the government and the Argentine press. The agency is the administration's chief propaganda center. As such, it releases all official statements and announcements of the government. The subsecretariat is the administrative headquarters for press censorship, being required to "supervise the conduct" of the press and other media of information and opinion. Argentine news transmitted abroad must be cleared through the Subsecretariat of Information, which also controls foreign publications distributed in the country. Lastly, the agency administers the rationing of newsprint and raw film consumed in Argentina. Throughout its history, the Subsecretariat of Information has been headed by an army officer. The basic press law administered by the subsecretariat was promulgated on December 31, 1943. This measure required all publishers and journalists in the country to register with the Subsecretariat of Information. Publication of all official press releases was made mandatory for all newspapers. And the nation's press was prohibited from publishing any items which were held by the regime to (1) be "contrary to the general interest of the nation"[30] or disturbing to public order; (2) undermine Christian morals or good customs; (3) upset Argentina's relations with other states; (4) injure government officials; or (5) be untrue. This basic press law authorized the Subsecretariat of Information to close down any newspaper which violated any of these provisions.

Thus armed, the government exercised a free and heavy hand in suspending and suppressing newspapers throughout the country. In September of 1943, *La Unión* of Tucumán, and *Diario de Mendoza* and *Los Andes*—the last two in the city of Mendoza—were suspended, leaving only one newspaper functioning in the latter city. The dearth of newspapers in the entire Province of Mendoza was aggravated by the end of September, when *La Tarde* and *Crónica* were suppressed on charges of publishing "false rumors" and "pretended humor" dealing with "army officers, public officials, and respectable citizens."[31] *El Intransigente* of Salta also fell in September. At Buenos Aires, José W. Auguisti, the editor of *Noticias Gráficas,* was imprisoned on September 14 for the "propagation of false and tendentious rumors."[32] He was released on October 7; two weeks later, he arrived at Montevideo for an "indefinite stay" in exile.

The censorship was not limited to materials originating in Argentina. When, on October 26, 1943—World War II was still in progress—the "North American" and British governments added to their proclaimed lists of blocked nationals ("black lists") the names of additional Axis firms operating in Argentina, the press was "requested" by the regime not to publish the names of the black-listed firms. On November 18, one hundred and thirty foreign and domestic magazines were excluded from the Argentine mails. The "North American" news magazine *Time* was included among the banned periodicals. *Time* was allowed on December 10 to re-enter Argentina. In 1947, however, *Time* carried a cover story on Eva Perón; the magazine was again denied circulation in the country, and that ban was still in force when this book was written. On March 19, 1944, the United Press was prohibited from transmitting news to or from Argentina; this restriction was lifted on April 4 of the same year. A month later, the newspapers of the Province of Entre Ríos were warned that they "would be closed permanently if they mentioned such subjects as freedom, the constitution, or religion."[33] Within two months of the warning, six newspapers in that province were closed. *Momento Argentino* fell on September 22, 1944;* *Argentina Libre* in December; and *El Día* of Jujuy and *El Diario* of Paraná in March of 1945. Eight more newspapers were suppressed two months later. By mid-1951 no fewer than one hundred Argentine newspapers and magazines had been destroyed during the course of the consolidation of the Perón regime.

The rationing of newsprint in the "new Argentina" has been developed into a refined and subtle technique of indirect press censorship. Since virtually no newsprint is produced in Argentina itself, the nation's press must depend almost exclusively on imported paper. The government has controlled the importation of newsprint in such a manner that a newsprint shortage has been a chronic and continuing problem faced by the Argentine press. In the decade before Perón, the country's publications consumed between 144,000 and 170,000 tons of newsprint per year. And

---

* The charge against *Momento Argentino* was that it lied in falsely reporting the overthrow of Brazilian President Getulio Vargas. *Momento Argentino* did in fact lie: Vargas was not deposed until a year later.

consider these figures for more recent years: Argentina imported 140,900 tons of newsprint in 1947, 121,000 tons in 1948, 117,000 tons in 1949, and 140,000 tons in 1950. Pleading the chronic newsprint shortage as grounds, the regime in 1945 inaugurated a system of rationing of newsprint, with the government alocating the paper among the nation's publications. Along with newsprint rationing—and also justified by the chronic shortage of paper—has gone a system of governmental regulation of the number of pages each newspaper may include in each of its editions.

Thus, the administration announced on October 8, 1948, a decree limiting the number of pages per full-sized (as distinguished from tabloid) newspaper to eight pages if it sold for five *centavos*, fourteen pages if it sold for ten *centavos*, and sixteen pages if the price was higher than ten *centavos*. Most of the major newspapers of the country fell in the last of these categories. Tabloids were permitted twice as many pages as the full-sized papers in their respective price brackets. Each newspaper—full-sized or tabloid —was allowed to publish one eight-page supplement per week. All persons and firms possessing newsprint were required to register with the government on November 24, 1948; "surplus" newsprint held by these registrants was confiscated on December 1. On March 5, 1949, additional newsprint was confiscated and the newspapers were again cut down in size. Papers selling for five *centavos* were cut to a maximum of four pages; ten *centavos*, ten pages; more than ten *centavos*, twelve pages. A decree published seven months later rendered printing ink subject to expropriation. Finally, all newsprint owned by all newspapers was confiscated on February 16, 1950—thereafter, the entire Argentine press was totally dependent on the government's rationing system for paper. After March 5, 1951, no full-sized newspaper—regardless of the price for which it sold —was permitted to publish an edition of more than eight pages. The system of forced newsprint shortages and government rationing, *La Nación* asserted editorially, "has placed the entire Argentine press on the verge of disappearing."[34]

The progressive suffocation of Argentine newspapers has been the subject of widespread discussion and comment, both in Argentina and abroad. "The present restrictions on liberty of the press in our country demonstrates a variety of criteria and procedures which have become even more arbitrary," *La Nación* has said. "We are living through sad years for the independent press. Its will to continue . . . faces great obstacles. . . . Confiscation of paper, rationing of editions, reduction of the number of pages, and limitation of the circulation, augmented by known tacit restrictions and frequent infamous reprisals, are indications of a technique in the process of perfection."[35] The Radical Deputy Sammartino once charged that Perón was endeavoring to "train the press to fear dictators."[36] And the Radical Deputy Uranga has pointed out that "the police . . . have damaged the buildings in which papers were published, they have threatened their editors with death; . . . there are constant 'contempt' suits against the publishers of opposition newspapers; . . . all this, I say, undermines freedom of the press."[37] Beyond Argentine frontiers, the other American republics have frequently deplored the plight of Argentine newspapers. At its meeting at Quito, Ecuador, in July of 1949, the Inter-American Press Association approved a resolution protesting "the vicissitudes of the papers published at Buenos Aires or in the 'interior.' "[38] The same organization, when it held its 1950 meeting at New York, branded Argentina as one of the six American nations restricting press freedom.*

Fighting against virtually irresistable pressures, the Ar-

---

* The other five: the Dominican Republic, Colombia, Guatemala, Peru, and Venezuela.

gentine press has slowly succumbed to the "new Argentina." Of the Buenos Aires papers, one after another joined Perón until only three—*La Prensa, La Nación*, and *La Vanguardia*—remained in opposition. *La Prensa* and *La Nación*, outstanding journals, were generally recognized as the leaders of the press opposition to the regime. Their intransigence irked Perón: he declared that these newspapers were "not enterprises of public opinion but financial enterprises . . . supported by those who always were at the service of foreign capitalism. . . . As yet, the 'serious' press of the country has not been able to understand us."[39] Perón has, on occasion, found the opposition of these "serious" newspapers useful. For example, in 1950 he received a delegation of visiting "North American" newsmen. To their inquiries after Argentine press censorship he replied: "There is none. It is against the constitution. The greatest dailies of this country belong to the opposition—which is all the evidence you need. I get the same kind of treatment President Truman gets in the United States."[40] The "serious" press, however, has been disappearing. *La Nación* of Buenos Aires is the only major opposition paper still functioning at the time these lines are written. The great *La Prensa* was conquered in 1951, and *La Vanguardia* fell in 1947.

La Nación, the sole remaining major opposition newspaper, was founded in 1862 by José María Gutiérrez. Originally called *La Nación Argentina*, the paper began its distinguished career by lending editorial support to the administration of President Bartolomé Mitre (1861–68). In 1870, Mitre himself became the editor of the paper, and its name was changed to *La Nación*. Under Mitre's guidance, the daily made a noteworthy contribution to the development of Argentine journalism. Regarded in its early years as a "new form of expression,"[41] *La Nación* was remarkable for the moderation of its language and its emphasis on "culture," devoting an impressively large portion of its space to poetry, literary articles, and book reviews. The paper developed an energetic editorial policy—President Sarmiento said that *La Nación* called things by their names, that it "put its hand where the pain was"⁴²—and it exercised an influential voice in Argentine affairs. The paper continued this role after the revolution of 1943, and has been a major enemy of Perón. The bulk of *La Nación*'s struggle against the "new Argentina" was carried on under the editorship of Alberto Caprile, who furnished the journal with courageous guidance during the most difficult chapter in its history. Caprile's editorial policy angered the *Peronistas* and drew ominous threats from them. Hear a recent *Peronista* warning: "*La Nación* . . . has placed its columns at the entire disposal of all the unfounded and capricious calumnies which could be imagined. . . . [we] warn this newspaper that if its policy is inspired by the intention to appear . . . as a martyr to the old story about the absence of freedom of the press, we will not think it inconvenient to give it a taste"⁴³ of such martyrdom. Alberto Caprile died on April 5, 1951; under its new editorship, *La Nación* has continued its role as the sole remaining major opposition newspaper.

The death of *La Prensa*, also of Buenos Aires, will long remain one of the greatest tragedies in the history of modern journalism. Founded on October 18, 1869, by José C. Paz, *La Prensa* never was an ordinary newspaper. "Our credo," Paz said, "is based on independence, respect for man as a citizen, and reasoned discussions of the public acts of men rather than their individual personalities."⁴⁴ Throughout its life—from 1869 to 1951—*La Prensa* attempted to abide by this credo as successive editors understood it, and the paper had achieved an international reputation for high journalistic standards by the eve of the revolution of 1943. "When *La Prensa* first appeared, it was only one more newspaper, but even in its first numbers it demonstrated that it was 'something different,'" *The Standard* of Buenos Aires said in 1941, in observance of *La Prensa*'s seventy-second anniversary. "It had a soul of its own, and it was directed by men of an uncommon intelligence and force. . . . At seventy-two years of age, *La Prensa* is as young as—or younger than—it was in the first year of its life. The truth of its news, the courage of its editorial opinions, and its ability to adapt itself to prevailing conditions . . . have given it a distinguished place in world journalism. . . . [*La Prensa*] is no longer considered as the leading newspaper of the Argentine republic, but as one of the greatest organs of the world press."[45] This judgment has been supported by evaluations expressed in other nations of the world. Hear *The Times* of London: "*La Prensa*, with its high standing wherever newspapers are read and compared, has done much for the credit of Argentina in the world; its independent existence is a credit to the regime that allows it, and though irritations may come to authority through the reporting of unpalatable truth, authority—in any country—is wise to bear them gracefully."[46]

When Perón came to power, *La Prensa* was a mighty institution with a daily circulation of 460,000 copies, and 570,000 on Sundays. Perhaps the truth is that Argentina never was big enough to contain both Perón and *La Prensa*. The daily, under the uncompromising leadership of Alberto Gainza Paz, lashed out against the regime. "We do not need mentors or tutors or prophets or redeemers or protectors or saviors," *La Prensa* said defiantly. "Let nobody govern or try to govern unless he has been freely and spontaneously called by the people to govern."[47] This, and other editorials like it, were enough for Perón. "For a hundred years," he asserted, "*La Prensa* has pontificated with endless lies and imbecilities."[48] Thus one more battle line was drawn in the "new Argentina." On April 26, 1944, the paper was suspended for five days for "distorting the truth and misleading public opinion."[49]

When *La Prensa* resumed publication in May of 1944, it took up a campaign of editorial opposition to the regime which did not cease until the journal was definitely closed in 1951. This seven-year battle was marked by occasional violence and by increasingly restrictive measures applied against the newspaper. Pro-Perón demonstrators on January 24, 1947, attacked the *La Prensa* building, starting three fires. In March of 1948, both that journal and *La Nación* were required to pay retroactive duty allegedly due on all imported newsprint on which they had printed advertisements *since 1939!* And, in October of 1948, the government—pleading the paper shortage—confiscated 8,055 tons of *La Prensa*'s newsprint. In the following year, the Federal Police raided the paper's offices after it had published a story on the torture of political prisoners. The journal was ordered on March 9, 1950, to cease work on the installation of newly purchased press equipment; at the same time, *La Prensa* was removed from the list of Argentina's licensed importers.

The fatal blow fell on January 26, 1951, during the course of a railroad strike. *La Prensa*'s newshawks had discovered two pieces of information about the rail stoppage: serious violence was associated with it, and the politics of the strike reflected a deep schism within the ranks of the *Peronista* party.* Despite the fact that the government was seriously adverse to the publication of these items, they were indeed printed in *La Prensa*'s edition of January 26.

* See pp. 326–27.

That is, they were printed—but not circulated. The news-paper distributors' union, an affiliate of the government-controlled General Confederation of Labor (C.G.T.),* declared a strike against *La Prensa* and refused to distribute it, beginning with the edition of January 26. The strikers demanded that the newspaper close its branch circulation offices, give up its subscription lists, and turn over 20 percent of its revenue from advertising to the union's "social assistance" program.

A concerted official attempt was made to describe the affair as a labor conflict rather than as censorship of the press. In a ringing statement, the strikers declared that "we will continue the fight even though it molests the deter-mined clientele of this paper, who—as much abroad as here—urgently desire to see in its pages the dose of venom against the government of General Perón which they need every day to feed their hope that the greatness of today's Argentina might be lost."[50] *Epoca*, which had long before fallen into the *Peronista* camp, declared editorially: "Dedi-cated to the service of treason, *La Prensa*, which demon-strates a suspicious insistence in its editorials on diverse questions, . . . is today the victim of its own evil arts and perverse intentions."[51] But the disguise of a labor-manage-ment conflict soon wore thin. "The editing, administrative, accounting, shop, and distribution workers of *La Prensa* . . . wish their firm and complete adhesion to the paper to be clearly manifested," asserted a statement signed by more than 1,300 of *La Prensa*'s employees. "This adhesion is determined fundamentally by the ideals of liberty and of democracy which inspire the orientation of *La Prensa*. . . . [We] have no conflict with the newspaper."[52] When, on February 27, many of the journal's employees endeavored to return to work, they were met by armed guards—

* See pp. 319-23.

"pickets," the government called them—who opened fire, killing one *La Prensa* worker, Roberto Núñez, and wounding fourteen others. Two newsmen representing the "North American" magazine *Life* were imprisoned for covering the violence.

With *La Prensa* closed by the "strike," President Perón called a special session of the congress to deal with the affair. This session met on March 16, and adjourned after appointing a nine-man committee—composed of eight *Peronistas* and one Radical, Deputy Arturo Frondizi—to investigate the matter and recommend action thereon. The committee labored diligently until April 11, when the congress met again to consider the results of the investigation. The joint committee reported, among other things, that *La Prensa* had been paying $8,000 weekly for the services of the United Press, and that the paper was, accordingly, foreign-dominated. The United Press and the Associated Press, the committee asserted, control "all information and nearly all thoughts spread throughout the world. What *La Prensa* gives its readers, with the exception of a few editorials, is not the thoughts of *La Prensa* but the thoughts of the United Press. The thought-out news manufactured by the United Press . . . are the thoughts of bankers, industries, and powerful commercial interests. The people of the United States are also under this yoke, and their leaders are threatened by its enmity."[53] On April 11, the congress voted the expropriation of *La Prensa*. The government declared it would pay $1,366,915 for the property, although its former owners valued it at $20,458,650. Let it not be supposed, however, that the government paid even the $1,366,915: against this sum was assessed $5,733,334 in alleged retroactive import duties and severance pay for the paper's employees. *La Prensa* was dead. The affair found repercussions throughout the hemisphere. At Washington, United States

Assistant Secretary of State Edward G. Miller, Jr., declared that his government was "deeply worried by the situation";[54] and, acting on a resolution of the National Press Club of Washington, all newspapers in the United States, Canada, and all Latin-American republics—except Argentina—flew flags at half-mast in mourning for *La Prensa*.

Meanwhile, Alberto Gainza Paz, the paper's editor, was ordered arrested on March 21. Eluding his would-be captors, he made his way to exile in Uruguay. In September he journeyed to the United States, where he was awarded an honorary doctorate by a "North American" university. "The real democratic Argentina will survive," Gainza Paz declared at New York. "You can expropriate the machinery of a newspaper but not the spirit. Freedom always wins the last battle."[55] Proceeding to Evanston, Illinois, he received the honorary degree at Northwestern University on October 1.

There were ceremonies at Buenos Aires, too. "*La Prensa* will be handed to the workers in any condition they desire," said President Perón during a labor-day rally on May 1. "This paper, which exploited its workers and the poor and was an elaborate instrument of treason against the country, will expiate its guilt by becoming an instrument of the laboring class."[56] Under the management of the General Confederation of Labor, *La Prensa*, now one more *Peronista* organ, reappeared on November 19, 1951. The new *La Prensa*, Perón said, had sprung from a "colossus with a heart of mud; . . . the workers of the 'new Argentina' will impart to it a new tonic and a new soul which, coming from them, will be pure, great, and virtuous."[57] But *La Prensa* was dead.

Though *La Prensa* was the most celebrated and the most significant of the journalistic victims of the "new Argentina," it should not be concluded that this daily was the only one to fall before Perón. Mention should also be made of *La Vanguardia*, which was likewise destroyed by the "new Argentina." Let it be noted that *La Vanguardia* was a Socialist newspaper, and that it fought as gallantly against Perón as any newspaper of any political orientation. *La Vanguardia*, founded on April 7, 1894, by the great Socialist leader Juan B. Justo, had been in trouble with government all its life. Throughout its existence, *La Vanguardia* was an opposition newspaper, whether the administrations were Conservative, Radical, or *Peronista*; all its life *La Vanguardia* was a major contributor to the literature of Argentine social protest. Juan Domingo Perón was not the first to close down *La Vanguardia*: President Julio A. Roca did this in 1902, and President Manuel Quintana in 1905. President José Figueroa Alcorta closed the paper in 1909; later in his adminstration *La Vanguardia* was forced to cease publication for three months after rioters attacked the paper's offices and destroyed its equipment. President Uriburu suppressed the Socialist organ in 1931, and President Castillo did the same four times—twice in 1942 and twice the following year.

Then came the "new Argentina." *La Vanguardia* was suspended for one day on July 20, 1943, for five days beginning August 14, and for two weeks on September 23. Resuming publication on October 7, *La Vanguardia* struggled along for three months. Then—on January 6, 1944—the Socialist daily did an amazing thing: it suspended operations *voluntarily!* "In view of the impossibility of freely complying with our social duty, we cease publication as from today," the farewell edition said. "We will be back."[58] *La Vanguardia* did come back—on April 7, 1944, the fiftieth anniversary of its founding. But the resurrection was short-lived. Two weeks later—on April 22—the government closed the daily in a sweeping action which included

the arrests of Américo Ghioldi, the editor; Juan Antonio
Solari, then secretary-general of the Socialist party; Rómulo
Bogliolo and José Alejandro Rodríguez, administrative of-
ficers of *La Vanguardia;* and Luis Pan, an editorial writer.

Attempting a new tack, *La Vanguardia* reappeared as a
weekly on January 16, 1945. This arrangement lasted for
nine months, until the periodical was again suppressed on
October 8. Resuming publication some weeks later, the
weekly was again closed on August 27, 1947. Subsequent
sporadic attempts to revive the periodical failed. At length,
La Vanguardia gave up in September. "They took the pen
out of our hands and put wrenches in our press, but they
say that we have liberty,"[59] the paper asserted. It was, indeed, a losing struggle. *La Vanguardia* died in 1947.

Radio, Stage, and Screen

A similar system of government control dominates the
radio stations and the theaters—both legitimate and motion-
picture—of the "new Argentina."

Shortly after the revolution of 1943, the regime turned
its attention to the country's thirty-one radio stations, of
which twelve were established at Buenos Aires and nineteen in the "interior." It was observed two months after
the revolution that "the government is out to convert radio
into one vast propaganda machine for itself."[60] This conclusion was doubtlessly inspired by the stream of decrees
and regulations governing radio which issued from the
Casa Rosada soon after the revolution. On June 14, 1943—
only ten days after the uprising—a decree required that all
radio programs be subjected to previous censorship, that
no deviation from approved scripts be permitted, and that
the time consumed by news broadcasts be divided equally
between foreign events and domestic Argentine news. This
was followed by rules prohibiting the broadcasting of "soap

operas" after July 15, 1943, forbidding radio presentations of "jived" versions of classical music, and preventing foreign musicians from speaking on Argentine radio programs. Radio stations were required to emphasize native folklore, and broadcasting orchestras were ordered to be composed of the greatest possible percentage of Argentine musicians. A decree published on November 24, 1943—World War II was then in progress—forced the country's radio stations to broadcast pro-Axis propaganda. Some time later—on May 21, 1944—the rebroadcasting in Argentina of "North American" and British short-wave news programs was prohibited unless the programs had been previously recorded by the stations and edited by local censors.

At length, all stations were required to be wholly owned and managed by Argentine citizens. If naturalized, such citizens must have been resident in the country for at least ten years before participating in the ownership or management of the radio stations. A detailed and lengthy "Manual of Instructions for Radio Stations," promulgated on May 14, 1946, minutely regulated many matters. This decree determined broadcasting hours and the percentage of radio time each station was required to devote to each type of program. Article 51 of the manual obliged the stations to cut off any political speaker who might, during the course of his broadcast, depart from the previously approved text of his speech. And in July of 1949, it was stipulated that every musical program carried by an Argentine radio station must include at least one work by an Argentine composer. Moreover, political campaigns may no longer be conducted over the air. For the election of 1946, it had been agreed that the stations would make equal time available to all political parties. However, this was not possible when Perón ran for a second term in 1951: at that time, use of the radio was denied to all opposition parties. Thus, radio is as effectively muzzled as the press in the "new Argentina." This, too, has been a matter for hemisphere-wide concern. The Inter-American Association of Broadcasters, which held its 1948 meeting at Buenos Aires, declared at that time that Argentine stations "broadcast official propaganda and not the views of the legitimately recognized opposition political parties." Accordingly, the Argentine Broadcasters' Association was then expelled from membership in the Inter-American Association of Broadcasters, which asserted that "liberty of expression has been practically abolished in Argentine radio."[61]

With respect to the legitimate theater, the story is similar. Avenida Corrientes, the porteños' Broadway, was once the center of unceasing thespian activity, much of which was politically oriented. With the coming of restrictive measures, culminating in the "contempt" law of 1948, the treaders of the boards have been constrained to forego politics in the theater. It was noted as early as August of 1943 that "theaters have . . . had to eliminate all satirical political skits, long one of the brightest features of Buenos Aires' Broadway."[62] And by mid-1949 measures were in force requiring each legitimate theater company to present two native Argentine plays for every foreign play, and restricting foreign companies to Argentine engagements of no longer than six months.

Censorship of motion pictures has likewise been introduced in the "new Argentina." During World War II, such anti-Axis Hollywood productions as The Great Dictator and Edge of Darkness were banned from the country. A decree of December 31, 1943, required each motion-picture theater to include at least one Argentine-made newsreel in every program, and, beginning in January of 1944, a sliding scale was established to grant tax rebates to theaters based on the percentage of Argentine-produced films exhibited.

Seven months later, each motion-picture house was required to pay at least 35 per cent of its gross intake to local film producers, and to show at least seven Argentine-made feature pictures per month. And a ten-man cinema board was established in April of 1947 to regulate both the production and the exhibition of motion pictures in the country. This program was augmented by the creation in August of 1950 of the General Directorate of Public Spectacles, a government agency charged with the supervision of all pictures produced in the country, in order that they might "reflect faithfully the high culture, the customs, and the true ideology of the Argentine people."[63]

Thus, all media of communication of information and ideas—whether by the schools, the press, the radio, or the theater—have been chained in the "new Argentina" to the service of Perón. These media march on orders from the *Casa Rosada*, where dwells a firm determination to indoctrinate and educate the citizenry in the ways of its rulers.

10.

On Hating Foreigners

A recrudescence of Argentine nationalism has been one of the more significant developments in the country since the revolution of 1943. Official implementation of this trend has included the reduction of selected types of foreign influences in Argentina and attempts to foster an anti-foreign sentiment in the country. Perón's program in this area has been expressed in a cluster of policies characterized by Argentine nationalism, a somewhat tenuous alliance with the Roman Catholic Church, and a campaign of "economic independence" designed to cripple some forms of foreign economic influence in Argentina. The foreign elements singled out for restrictive treatment have been primarily British and "North American," both associated in *Peronista* pronouncements with imperialism.

The Fatherland and God

The people of the other Latin-American nations have their reasons—not readily apparent in Argentina or the United States—for calling the Argentines the "Yankees of the South." The "North American" who looks with disdain upon the other peoples of the Americas may well be among the first to condemn the Argentine who does likewise. Many Argentines have in fact long viewed the rest of the hemisphere with a condescending superiority similar to that prevalent in the United States. It has been observed that "probably in no place in the Western Hemisphere do common citizens announce their nationalism with greater pride than does the Argentine workman or farmer when he says, 'I am an Argentine.' "[1] This pride of nationality was not invented by Perón: Argentines, figuring the racial composition of their country at approximately 90 per cent "white," have for generations felt themselves to be superior to the peoples of the other American nations, where Indians and other ethnic groups live in large numbers.

As there are two Argentinas, so there are two Argentine nationalisms. The *porteños* and the *provincianos* each have their own ethnocentrisms. The folk of Buenos Aires ascribe a certain superiority to their cultural orientation toward Europe rather than to the rest of Latin America. "As far back as the seventeenth century," it has been recorded, "the people of Buenos Aires prided themselves that they were not like other men. . . . They were not conquistadors, but merchants and lawyers and notaries, and they had gone to the New World to trade in the products of the land that was opened by the adventurers they despised. They considered themselves infinitely superior to the new race of gauchos which was being born on the *pampa*, fathered by the conquistadors and mothered by the brown-skinned girls of the conquered Indian tribes."[2] Yet the nationalism of the *porteños* carried with it a species of ambivalence, of vacillation. While they derived a spirit of superiority from the Europeanization of their ways, they felt on the other hand that what they had was in essence a slavish imitation of the ideas and inventions of folk who were not themselves Argentines. "Our great transformations have been determined by imitation or imposed by force," a *porteño* has said. "Everything came to us from the outside. Almost all the elements of our present civilization bear the stamp of foreign manufacture."[3]

The *provincianos* of the "interior," for their part, nursed a nationalism which had been born in Indo-America and fanned by resentment of Buenos Aires. More than one generation of *provincianos* fought desperately against the *porteños* for a cause which the folk of the "interior" called "federalism." It took General Juan Manuel de Rosas to teach the *provincianos* that theirs was a pseudo-federalism and that "their interests lay not in provincial isolation but in nationalism."[4] But their nationalism was one which united them against Buenos Aires, which cultivated the view that the *porteño* capital was peopled by foreigners because it was oriented toward Europe rather than toward Indo-America.

The Perón revolution has been called the "nationalist revolution."[5] Perón indeed has sought to unite the two Argentinas. He declared that his "great ambition, as I have said over and over again, is for the aggrandisement of the Argentine nation."[6] His movement, he has asserted, "has had from its first moments one basic objective: *national unity*."[7] He declared that this unity was "one thing that is indispensable" to permitting the "new Argentina" to face "all personal ambitions or caprice with a united 14,000,000 of Argentines determined to die if necessary."[8] The revolutionists of 1943 carried an official slogan—"Argentina for the Argentines, because only they created it, defended it, and are worthy of it"[9]—based on nationalism. And Perón, in a spirit of nationalism, has pleaded for national unity. He has frequently made overtures to Argentines who were opposed to him, urging them to drop their hostility. Offering to "forget offenses and insults and consider all Argentines as brothers," he declared after his first election in 1946 that "from now on, our fundamental mission is to unite all Argentines, pardoning those who lied about us or insulted us, and forgetting that some of us forsook our flag for another."[10]

Nationalist political organizations had been in existence in Argentina for years before the revolution of 1943. These —many of them had already been given impetus by the Uriburu revolution of 1930—were among the first groups to come to the support of the military regime established after June of 1943. The various nationalist organizations played significant parts in Argentine politics—especially in the stormy period between 1943 and 1945—and seven of them are worth mentioning here. (1) The *Governing Board of Argentine Nationalism* operated as a co-ordinator of the political activities of the various nationalist organizations. This governing board was led in 1943 by General Basilio B. Pertiné, who became the intendant of Buenos Aires immediately after the Perón revolution.* The board was an essentially military organization. (2) The *Argentine Civic Legion*, founded by President Uriburu in 1930, was an armed terrorist organization which originally professed admiration of the Fascist system which Mussolini had constructed in Italy. It should be noted that the Argentine Civic Legion, in the days of the Axis, was consistently more oriented toward Mussolini's Italy than toward Hitler's Germany. (3) The *Superior Council of Nationalism*, founded in July of 1941 by General Juan Bautista Molina, was also pro-Fascist in its international orientations. In the months after the revolution of 1943, Generals Molina and Pertiné became rivals for the recognized leadership of the nationalist movement. (4) The *Argentine National Patriotic Union*, also founded in 1941, was led by Manuel Fresco, onetime governor of the Province of Buenos Aires. Under Fresco's leadership, this organization developed pro-Nazi,

* See p. 156.

anti-Semetic, and anti-capitalistic overtones. The Argentine National Patriotic Union published during World War II a frankly pro-Axis newspaper, *El Cabildo*, which was financed through the German Embassy at Buenos Aires.* (5) The *Nationalist Youth Alliance*, with a claimed membership of 10,000, was numerically the largest Argentine nationalist group in 1943. It maintained bands of rowdies, called *mazorqueros*, organized along storm-trooper lines, and, like the Argentine National Patriotic Union, was pro-Nazi and anti-Semetic. (6) *Afirmación Argentina* was less militant than the Nationalist Youth Alliance, but was indirectly supported by the German Embassy during World War II. (7) *New Order* was organized along military lines and advanced the proposition of military conspiracy as a basic technique in national politics.

All of these nationalist organizations came to the support of Perón after the revolution of 1943. They endorsed the notion of government by the military, and they responded actively to the nationalistic pronouncements made by the regime in the first months of the "new Argentina." "When the sword of the military is unsheathed it is not only a piece of shining metal but also a materialization of the spirit in which is present nothing less than the Fatherland itself," Justice Minister Alberto Baldrich asserted in May of 1944. "For this reason, to have a Fatherland and to be its soldier are one and the same thing."[11] In terms of this sort of orientation, the nationalist groups fell readily into line with the "new Argentina."

Anti-Semitism was much in evidence during the first two years after the revolution of 1943. Anti-Jewish feeling in Argentina antedated Perón—anti-Semitism rose perceptibly in the country in the years after World War I— and the roots of this prejudice were certainly not created by the

* See p. 404.

224

men who came to power in 1943. However, the phenomenon grew rapidly after that revolution, partly because of the pro-Axis orientation of the rebellion, and partly because of the anti-Semitic nature of the nationalist organizations supporting the new regime. It is important to point out that Perón himself never was celebrated as an anti-Semite. Although he tolerated and even encouraged anti-Jewish activities in the first two years after the revolution, he did not originate it, and he *did* terminate official anti-Semitism after 1945.

Between 1943 and 1945, officially tolerated and encouraged anti-Jewish outbreaks and demonstrations were frequent events in Argentina. The country's Jews—estimated at between 360,000 and 400,000—lived through anxious months during that early stage of the revolution. President Ramírez' inauguration on June 8, 1943, was made the occasion for an anti-Semitic demonstration sponsored by the Nationalist Youth Alliance, and Argentine Jews were greatly concerned by a cabinet reorganization four months later. That reorganization brought Gustavo Martínez Zuvería into the administration as minister of justice and education. Martínez Zuvería, a noted anti-Semite, remained in the cabinet until February of 1944. Under the pseudonym of "Hugo Wast," he had written a number of anti-Jewish novels, prominent among them *El Kahal, Oro, El Sexto Sello, 666, Las Espigas de Ruth*, and *Myriam la Conspiradora*. During Martínez Zuvería's stewardship, Jewish welfare associations were suppressed, Jewish teachers were dismissed from the schools, and kosher killing of cattle was prohibited in the municipal slaughter yards of Buenos Aires, Rosario, and Basavilbaso.

All Jewish newspapers were ordered closed in Argentina on October 11, 1943, on the official ground that the censors could not be expected to be able to read any other language than Spanish. This action brought condemnation from the President of the United States, then Franklin D. Roosevelt. In a White House statement, he declared that he "could not forbear expressing misgivings at the adoption in this hemisphere of action obviously anti-Semitic in nature, and of a character so closely identified with the most repugnant features of the Nazi doctrine."[12] The Argentine ban on Jewish newspapers was lifted shortly after Roosevelt's statement. Nevertheless, anti-Semitic activity continued. On October 23, 1943, the Federal Interventor of Entre Ríos announced that charters granted Jewish and Masonic benefit societies would not be renewed in that province; and in a demonstration at Buenos Aires in July of the following year, nationalists carried banners reading, "Let us kill one Jew today, tomorrow one Uruguayan."[13] When the Argentine Association of Israelites requested the ministry of interior to curb the demonstrations against Jews, *El Cabildo*, the organ of Fresco's Argentine National Patriotic Union, was ready with an answer. "What right have these people to ask for special favors?" *El Cabildo* demanded editorially. "This is the Jewish danger. We need only this to justify those who are so-called anti-Semites for convenience of language. If for nothing else, these demands made by the Jews entitle them to the kind of treatment we hope they will receive."[14] Anti-Semitic activity reached its peak in the "new Argentina" by mid-1945. Edward Tomlinson reported from Buenos Aires at that time that "I saw hoodlums paint 'Kill a Jew and be a patriot!' on the sidewalk while two of Perón's policemen stood approvingly by";[15] and Arnaldo Cortesi, the *New York Times* correspondent, wrote that "alarm and even terror are beginning to spread in the Jewish quarter because for some time all gatherings of Colonel Perón's followers have been a signal for some action against Jews."[16]

Throughout this turmoil, Perón himself remained silent on the Jewish question so far as his public statements were concerned. When he finally did discuss the matter publicly, it was to *condemn* participation in anti-Semitic demonstrations. "Those doing so," he said on December 11, 1945, "are outside all democratic standards and cannot be regular members of any Argentine political force."[17] Bartolomé Descalzo, then the minister of interior, declared that the government had no part in anti-Jewish activities. By the end of 1945, officially condoned demonstrations against Jews tapered off. "It being the intention of the government of the nation to encourage the tranquillity of all its inhabitants, without distinction of creed or ideology, it is proper to deny any opinion which attempts to picture the authorities as propagating ideas of racial persecution," said a full-dress policy declaration by General Felipe Urdapilleta, who had succeeded Descalzo as minister of interior. "The lamentable externalization of an anti-Semitic ideology has only achieved the repudiation of all responsible sectors and the most complete disapproval of the government, which considers it foreign to the atmosphere and spirit of the Argentines."[18] At length, in July of 1949, Henry Shosker of the Society of Hebrew Immigration and Manuel Sheinsohn of the Argentine Israelite Organization published statements affirming that official anti-Semitism no longer existed in Argentina.

The curious course of anti-Jewish activities in the "new Argentina" is instructive. In 1943, when it seemed likely to the pro-Axis revolutionists that Hitler would emerge triumphant from World War II, the Argentine military regime had no objection to the encouragement of anti-Semitism as a feature of the "nationalist revolution." By 1945, however, times had changed: Hitler and the Nazi cause fell in May of that year, and Perón saw the wisdom of dissociating his system from the Axis as much as he could. Continued anti-Semitism in a world in which the Axis had become defunct could conceivably bring foreign intervention in Argentina. Perón was and remains anxious to avoid such intervention, on the thesis that the "new Argentina" is safe so long as it does not provoke interference from abroad. After 1945, then, anti-Semitism fell from the cluster of official policies characterizing the Peróns' Argentina; indeed, President Perón acquired some reputation as the man who *terminated* anti-Jewish activities in the country!

Against this background, Perón since 1945 has been careful to avoid the incorporation of Nazi-like racist doctrine into his own system. While he espouses the cause of unity of Argentines and spreads the notion that Argentines are somehow superior to other peoples, *Peronistas* have not spun a Hitlerian racial myth to accompany those propositions. "For us, race is not a biological concept," Perón has said. "It is an aggregate of lofty virtues making us what we are and encouraging us to be what we should be."[19] *Peronistas* have appealed to "the Argentine people" and told them that they are "superior." But *any* Argentine is eligible for membership in this superior fraternity, regardless of his ethnic origin. The only requirements for membership are belief in the "new Argentina" and a conviction that what the *Peronistas* say is the truth from headquarters. Perón says that he serves "the Argentine people." These are not a "race." Perhaps the best *Peronista* definition of "the Argentine people" was advanced by none other than the late Eva Perón. "The people are not the proletariat of Marx," she said. "Neither can it be held that the people are the entire human multitude. Nor are they a race. . . . We, following the doctrine of Perón, maintain that the people are what they feel themselves to be. . . . The people do

not feel class . . . or proletarianism or race. . . . The
people feel themselves to be . . . a great community in
which there is no privilege. The people also feel themselves
to be a great entity made up of men and women whose primary function is to live and therefore to work. . . . The
concepts of solidarity, of fraternity, of equality, and of love
are inseparable from the concept of the people."[20] According to Perón, "the Argentine people" are all the citizens
who conform to these criteria and who support the regime.
And such folk are "superior" to other peoples.

The "nationalist revolution" has also had a vitally significant effect upon the political position of the Roman Catholic Church in Argentina. The relationship between Church
and state, of course, has traditionally been a problem
throughout the whole of Latin America, where the overwhelming majority of the people are Catholics. Prior to
1943, however, Argentina was regarded as one of the very
few Latin-American states in which the Church problem
was well on its way to definitive solution. Students who
surveyed the Argentine religious scene in the years before
Perón were generally convinced that the position of the
Church was no longer a political question among the Argentines. "The statesmen of Argentina displayed great
acumen in avoiding a sudden and radical break with the
religious past," the "North American" scholar J. Lloyd
Mecham wrote in a work published in 1934. "They
adopted, instead, the wise policy of disestablishing the
Church gradually; of gradually releasing the bonds. When
complete separation comes, it will find the state, the Church,
and the people prepared for, and willing to accept, the
change. Their mutual acquiescence will ensure the success
of the new status."[21] And the late Leo S. Rowe, writing in
the 1920's, said: "Not only is religious liberty freely guar-

anteed in every section of Argentina, but also the problem of the relation between Church and state has been solved in a manner which has eliminated the question from the field of public discourse. The question, for the time being at least, is considered settled."[22]

All that was before 1943. With the coming of the Perón revolution, the political position of the Church again became as lively a political issue as any known by Argentines. Any discussion which regards the Roman Catholic Church as a single, politically unified monolithic structure is unrealistic, at least as regards the Church position in Argentina. The Church is divided in that country: the schism is in part a reflection of the division between the two Argentinas. In the provinces of the "interior," Argentines tend to be more pious and devout, and the Church is more powerful there than at Buenos Aires. Most *porteños* are Catholics, to be sure; but their Catholicism is not the rigid religiosity to be found in Córdoba or, say, in Tucumán. Buenos Aires is Catholic in the same sense as Paris is—most of the people are nominally Catholics and they go to church on occasional Sundays, but their religion has been strongly tempered by the "modernity" of cosmopolitan life. The Church of the "interior" is reminiscent of the Church of late medieval Europe; the Church of the *porteños* is the Church of the larger cities of twentieth-century France or Italy. Argentines are not quite certain of which of the two Argentinas is Perón's. On some questions, it is evident that Perón has attempted to straddle the two; and religion is one of those questions.

The Church, of course, is a very important political plum in a country where the overwhelming majority of the people are Catholics. Any government with Church support derives therefrom widespread sympathy among the faithful. Perón has sought this sympathy. *Peronista* propaganda de-

signed for consumption in the "interior" has painted the
president as a very devout man, and official pronouncements published in the provinces are frequently strongly
religious in tone. Hear, for example, the Federal Interventor
of Tucumán: "Children must be taught that America must
realize its destiny within the framework of Catholicism.
Anything outside Catholicism is not American."[23] The people of Buenos Aires, on the other hand, are told that the
regime's is a *porteños'* Catholicism—sophisticated, emancipated, winking with "modern" cosmopolitanism at devi-
ations from formal religious doctrine and ritual.

In the early years after the revolution of 1943, Argentine
Church officials were divided in their stand on the "new
Argentina." They tended to align themselves into roughly
two camps. One of these, the so-called "left wing" of the
Church, was bitterly opposed to the military regime. This
group was led by such figures as Monseñores Miguel de
Andrea and Agustín Barrero, and by Padres B. de Eche-
verría and José María Dunphy. Monseñor Barrero did what
he could to warn his followers that elements of the "new
Argentina" ran counter to the teachings of the Church, and
Padre Dunphy likewise assailed the regime from his pulpit.
"It is true that I have spoken . . . against the regime,"
Padre Dunphy said in January of 1949, when he was relieved of his parish for criticizing Perón, "but I have always
spoken as a priest, as a Christian, and as a Catholic. Priests
all over the world today have taken up the fight against
communism on the same grounds—and of course I am
among them. But there is totalitarianism of the right and the
left, and from the moral and religious point of view they
are equally wrong."[24]

The recognized leader of the "left wing" of the Church
was Monseñor Miguel de Andrea. The rector of San Miguel
Arcángel since 1912, he became the Bishop of Temnos in

1920; and after the revolution of 1943, Bishop Andrea carried on a spectacular struggle against the "new Argentina." He appeared, in the early days after the revolution, to wield some influence at the *Casa Rosada,* but this influence —if it indeed was ever effective—was short-lived. By October of 1943, Bishop Andrea was an uncompromising enemy of the military rulers. "To dominate slaves is doubly ignoble; to reign over the free is doubly glorious," he declared at that time. "Your Excellency, Mr. President: let your authority be the guarantee of our liberty."[25] When the *Casa Rosada* turned a deaf ear to such petitions, Bishop Andrea continued his crusade, affirming that the revolution of 1943 had served only to immerse the country in a spirit of violence and hatred. Demanding an early return to constitutional government, he asserted that "the indefinite prolongation of an abnormal state of instability and uncertainty is a clear symptom of the evil which is a sad characteristic of our epoch."[26] He declared that it was his solemn duty to "recognize dangers, denounce them, and prescribe for them. .... We cite some now plainly in view. They are isolationist nationalism, Nazi liberticide, absorbing Caesarism, and atheistic communism."[27]

On the other hand, the Church's so-called "right wing" made common cause with the "new Argentina" soon after the revolution of 1943. This group was led by Cardinal Santiago Luis Copello, the primate of Argentina; Monseñor Gustavo Franceschi; Padre Wilkinson Dirube; and—later —Padre Virgilio M. Filippo. This faction eventually prevailed over the group led by Bishop Andrea, and did much to make the Church appear to be a political ally of the Perón regime. It was noted that this pro-Perón wing of the Church "tends to favor the authoritarian, anti-democratic tendencies prevalent among the Conservatives* and the

* See pp. 386–91.

small nationalist groups. . . . It is not mere coincidence that the most violently anti-democratic and anti-Semitic periodicals are those of the *clerico-fascista* groups."[28] It was said of Monseñor Franceschi that he had been "pro-totalitarian for years"; and Padre Wilkinson was described on July 14, 1943, as a "mouthpiece for the *Casa Rosada* since June 4th . . . reportedly writes many of the presidential speeches."[29]

Cardinal Copello undoubtedly did more than any other Argentine clergyman to assure the dominance of the "right wing" of the Church and to align it with the "new Argentina." He greeted the decree of 1943, providing for compulsory religious instruction, as "fulfilling one of the deepest hopes and greatest ambitions of the Argentine people,"[30] and this position was later buttressed by Pope Pius XII himself.* Under the leadership of Cardinal Copello, minor Argentine clergymen, like Padre Sepich, were encouraged to assert in 1944 that "we do not want elections. We want government."[31]

Elections were nevertheless called, and during the presidential campaign of 1945–46, the Copello wing of the Church entered the contest on the side of Perón. A pastoral letter distributed during the campaign urged Catholics to vote against candidates who advocated the separation of Church and state, secular education, or legal divorce; and some clergymen emerged from the campaign of 1945–46 as major *Peronista* politicians. Prominent among these was Padre Virgilio M. Filippo, parish priest of the Church of the Immaculate Conception at Belgrano, whose books—*Los Judios, El Monstruo Comunista*, and *La Religión en la Escuela Argentina*—had developed a strongly anti-Semitic and anti-Communist position. Playing a role in Argentine politics somewhat similar to that exercised by Father Cough-

* See pp. 188–90.

lin in the United States in the 1930's, Padre Filippo told his parishoners during Perón's first presidential campaign that "you must shut your mouths because Jesus Christ Himself was a great dictator."[32] Eventually, Padre Filippo won a seat in the congress as a *Peronista* deputy, and in that capacity devoted his energies to strengthening a Church alliance with the Perón regime. Representative of this activity was the publication in 1948 of *El Plan Quinquenal Perón y los Comunistas*, a book designed by Padre Filippo to demonstrate a harmonious parallel between Perón's entire program and various pronouncements of the Popes. The work made an elaborate point of citing Perón's propensity for planning his policies as conclusive evidence of his godliness. "The first planner is God," Padre Filippo asserted. "God created the heavens and the earth in six periods, or in a plan of six sections; not because it was necessary to do it that way, but rather to teach us to plan our work."[33]

Thus, nationalists, anti-Semites, and the "right wing" of the Church were quick and ready to align themselves with the "new Argentina." But a question of far-reaching significance remains to be asked. What of the regime? Should it be concluded that, since these elements supported Perón, he is therefore a nationalist, an anti-Semite, and a man of religion?

Fundamentally, Perón is a skilful politician. His primary objective—and the primary objective of the people in his entourage—is the retention of power. Perón is a nationalist, yes, for nationalism appeals to the bulk of the Argentines. But, so far as the government is concerned, such matters as anti-Semitism and extreme religiosity may be turned on or off, depending on whether they contribute to, or detract from, the domestic strength of the "new Argentina." Let it be remembered that the revolution of 1943 was first and above all a military uprising. The men who launched the rebellion were, after their fashion, in love with Argentina; some of them were anti-Semites, and some were men of religion. But their first loves were themselves, power, the army, and their own clique within it. When, after June of 1943, Argentina was governed by a group of army officers, it was noted that "this military clique considers *itself* deserving of absolute deification."[34] Later, when Perón rose to dominate the "colonels' clique," he himself became the object of that deification. The *Peronista* view that Perón "is God for us, so much so that we cannot conceive of heaven without Perón" needs no further elaboration here.

If any institution governs the country, it is the Argentine Army. The army is a nationalistic organization, but as an institution it is neither anti-Semitic nor religious. The politics of opportunism has been the chief determinant of the regime's position with respect to these questions. The reader has already seen that Perón discontinued official anti-Semitism when that step seemed politically wise from the standpoint of preserving his power. A similar pattern can be observed in the case of the Church. The government did revive compulsory religious instruction in the schools and write a constitution which declared that "the federal government supports the Apostolic Roman Catholic Church."[35] These and kindred measures were endorsed by the regime as vehicles for the transfer of some of the religious loyalty of the country's Catholics to the "new Argentina."

But, from the first days of the revolution, the governing clique has not permitted even the "right wing" of the Church to stand in its way. Consider, for example, the significant case of Padre Wilkinson. He was regarded as a "mouthpiece for the *Casa Rosada*" for a month or so after June 4, 1943. He enjoyed that position so long as it seemed that he put his love for the "new Argentina" above his loyalty to the Church. When it became evident that Padre Wilkinson was not that completely tied to the regime, his political star fell spectacularly. A report of July 21, 1943, noted that "the colonels are incensed and are insisting that such priestly influence be tempered and removed. . . . Father Wilkinson's soldierly figure . . . hasn't been seen so much at the *Casa Rosada* of recent days."[36] And, by November 11, 1943, that clergyman was "*persona non grata* to the *coroneles* and no longer around."[37]

There may be some utility in inquiring into the extent to which Juan and Eva Perón themselves could be regarded as Catholics. Neither was known as a religious person until Perón launched his presidential candidacy in October of 1945. Neither Perón in his capacity as an army officer and politician nor Evita in hers as night-club performer, radio and screen actress, and the colonel's mistress had been thought of as practicing Catholics. But then came October 17, 1945, and the emergence of Perón as a presidential candidate. The constitution required that the president be a Catholic, and Perón then married Evita and declared: "My Catholic faith places me within the constitutional requirements. I wish also to point out that I have always wanted to be inspired by the teachings of Christ."[38]

Perón's alliance with the Church has been primarily political, and the Catholic hierarchy has not been entirely blind to this point. In so far as Perón has entertained ideas of the supernatural, he has toyed somewhat with spiritualism. The Vatican has known this, and expressed its disapproval. Some Argentines found the politics of the Fifth Eucharistic Congress, held at Rosario in October of 1950, enlightening. Pope Pius XII sent a special delegate, Cardinal

Ernesto Ruffini, to represent the Holy See at the congress. The fluid nature of the union of Church and state in the "new Argentina" was already evident before Cardinal Ruffini arrived at Rosario. Perón had desired that the Pope, acting through Cardinal Ruffini, confer a Vatican decoration upon Evita at the festivities; this Pius XII refused to do. Moreover, the cardinal's ship put in at the harbor of Buenos Aires on October 16, the day before the fifth anniversary of Perón's "march on Rome." October 17— "Loyalty Day"—was a national holiday to be celebrated by the *Peronistas*. Cardinal Ruffini, realizing that if he left the harbor in time for that holiday he would be required to participate in it and contribute to an appearance of the Vatican's endorsement of "Loyalty Day," remained aboard his ship in the harbor until October 18. When he eventually arrived at the *Casa Rosada*, he was received by Vice-President J. Hortensio Quijano in the place of the chagrined Juan and Evita Perón, who had left Buenos Aires on a suddenly declared vacation.

Thus, while Church and state are more strongly allied in Perón's Argentina than they were before 1943, the union is essentially dynamic and fluid, and above all political. It should be remembered that Perón is God, and that is what is really important.

On the Imperialist

Many of the specific applications of the nationalism of the "new Argentina" have been economic in character. Foreigners, principally the British and the "North Americans," with a sizable stake in the Argentine economy have been branded as imperialists. President Perón has identified these interests as "the more dangerous international enemies beyond our frontiers."[39] His government has launched a major campaign for what is called the "economic independence" of Argentina. Since the revolution of 1943, the anti-British and anti-"Yankee" program of "economic independence" has risen from the cloak-and-dagger level to formal promulgation as a public policy of the Perón regime. Argentine employees of British and "North American" firms were approached some months after the revolution by the Federal Police, who offered rewards for bits of "interesting" information on the foreign employers' activities. In September of 1944, all persons employed in the country by non-Argentine concerns were required to register with the police. "The problem of achieving liberty for the country in which we live is not simple," Perón asserted. "To achieve it, it is first necessary to obtain the economic independence of the country, and for this it is indispensable to dislodge from it all the great international monopolies. It was these who enslaved us."[40]

By 1947, Perón was prepared to announce "economic independence" as a cardinal plank in the platform of the "new Argentina." Propaganda-wise, the step was taken in a grand manner. In July, the president journeyed to Tucumán. He reminded Argentines that it was at that very spot that no less a figure than General José de San Martín, the nation's George Washington, had on July 9, 1816, fathered the formal proclamation of Argentine political independence of Spain.* And Perón, following "the mandate of our history," sought to tie his bid for independence to San Martín's. "Following the course of conduct and the example of San Martín," Perón declared, "we have come to Tucumán, we have entered the historical house, we have endeavored to create a similar atmosphere, we have taken the same oath, and we are also ready to die, should it be necessary, to obtain our economic independence."[41] On July 9, 1947—the one hundred thirty-first anniversary of San

* See p. 21.

On Hating Foreigners

Martín's declaration of independence—Perón also signed a document at Tucumán. It was called the "Declaration of Economic Independence," and Perón hoped that it, too, would be an historic instrument. "We, the representatives of the people and the government of the Argentine republic," the document said, "invoking Divine Providence in the name and by the authority of the people whom we represent, solemnly declare . . . that the peoples and governments of the Argentine provinces and territories break the dominating chains which have bound them to foreign capitalism, and that they recover their right to govern their own sources of national wealth."[42]

It is not necessary to be a *Peronista* to appreciate the background from which the "Declaration of Economic Independence" sprung. Perón had long decried what he called Argentina's "colonial" economy, and it is true that, until the revolution of 1943, foreign capital, particularly British and "North American," exercised a major influence in Argentina. In 1940, foreign investments in the country totaled $2,141,878,000, of which $1,287,005,000 was British and $418,903,000 "North American." Fifty-five per cent of the individual owners of industrial establishments in Argentina were foreigners, and at least 28 per cent of the corporate profits made in the country belonged to foreign holders. The principal activities in Argentina controlled from abroad included railroad transportation, meat packing, the production of tires, the development of electric power, assembling automobiles, the operation of subways and streetcars, the maintenance of telephone systems, and the production of quebracho extract, used in tanning leather. Indeed, it has been said that in the pre-Perón period "foreign capital dominated decisively in all economic activities except agrarian."[43]

The British, who controlled approximately 60 per cent of

the foreign investments in Argentina, had long been accustomed to treating that country as a species of sixth dominion in their economy. British customs and ways accompanied their economic influence in the country. The five o'clock tea became an Argentine institution, and a number of curious colloquialisms worked their way into the language of the Argentines. When a man kept his appointment promptly, he was admired for his "English punctuality"; when an Argentine made a promise he sincerely intended to keep, he pledged his "British word"; and Argentine workers knew their beloved half-working day as the "English Saturday." But, much as some Argentines admired some British ways, the economic dominance of the *Ingleses* clashed with the national pride of the "Yankees of the South." Chagrined Argentines frequently told a story about a heated argument between an Englishman and a "North American." "You may take Canada from us," the Britisher told the *yanqui*, "but you will never take Argentina."

Such matters were no joke to Perón and his followers. The *Peronistas* swore that they would cleanse their country of British and "North American" economic influences, and some policies of the "new Argentina" have been directed toward that objective. The British-owned Primitiva Gas Company, which supplied the Federal Capital, was expropriated on April 17, 1944; and the United River Plate Telephone Company, Limited, was likewise taken over by the Argentine government on September 28, 1946. But Perón's largest British-owned targets were the railroads. The first of them established in 1857, nine British railways were in existence by 1943; and their expropriation became a major objective in Perón's program of "economic independence."

On November 16, 1943, the Argentine government named a three-man commission to study the financial situation of the British railroad companies. This proved to be the first step in a protracted series of transactions eventually culminating in the expropriation of the railways. The British were reluctant to surrender these holdings; but the United Kingdom, emerging from World War II in a financially weakened condition, was unable to resist the march of the "new Argentina." In 1946, two British officials, Sir Percival Liesching of the Board of Trade and Sir Wilfred Eady of the Treasury Ministry, arrived at Buenos Aires to negotiate the matter. Their bargaining position was poor: the United Kingdom was not able to liquidate approximately $750,-000,000 in Argentine credits which had been frozen in Britain during World War II, and Perón was willing to wipe out a portion of that account in exchange for the British-owned rail properties in Argentina. The extended negotiations centered on what percentage of the $750,000,-000 was to be traded for the railways. At length, an Anglo-Argentine agreement was signed on February 13, 1947, providing for the expropriation of the railroads in exchange for $600,000,000 of the Argentine credits already frozen at London. In a spirit of triumph, President Perón officiated on March 1, 1948, in a ceremony marking the Argentine government's formal acquisition of the rail properties. This was the most spectacular of the measures of "economic independence" directed against the United Kingdom, but it was not the entire story. British investments in Argentina, valued in 1940 at $1,287,005,000, had fallen to approximately $17,300,000 by 1952.

Although the British were the principal targets in the Argentine crusade for "economic independence," they were not the only ones. "North American" interests have also felt Perón's economic nationalism. The first such property to fall was the American and Foreign Power Company's Tucumán Traction Company, which was ordered expropriated by the Federal Interventor of Tucumán on December 11, 1943. The Argentine Telephone Company, a subsidiary of the International Telephone and Telegraph Company, was taken over shortly thereafter; and Perón eventually agreed to pay $95,000,000 for all of the Argentine holdings of the International Telephone and Telegraph Company. In May of 1944, the Federal Interventor of Entre Ríos ordered the confiscation of the East Argentine Electricity Company, until then held by the American and Foreign Power Company; and two months later, the concession of the Corrientes Electricity Company, a subsidiary of the same "North American" organization, was cancelled. Although not as hard hit by "economic independence" as the United Kingdom, the United States has nevertheless suffered measurably from the program. The income received by "North Americans" from their Argentine holdings, valued at $21,000,000 in 1946, had fallen to $8,000,000 by 1951. This is a record of which *Peronistas* are proud. "The 'Argentine miracle' of today has been achieved within Argentina," Eva Perón once said. "The days have passed when our destinies would be settled thousands of miles from our own shores; today we Argentines are the architects of our own destiny."[44]

Perón's program of "economic independence" is reflected not only in the expropriation of British- and "North American"–owned properties, but also in a system of state control of Argentina's foreign trade. A decree dated October 29, 1943, created the Argentine State Merchant Fleet, a government agency charged with the management of the country's entire merchant marine. Statistically, the Argentine State Merchant Fleet has thrived in the years since its creation. In 1947, it reported a net profit of $2,705,150, and the fleet has expanded its operations notably since then. Perón signed a measure on March 16, 1948, requiring that thenceforth the nation's seaborne foreign commerce be carried by the Argentine State Merchant Fleet whenever possible; and in his message to the congress on May 1, 1950, the president reported impressive figures in that field. He noted that, whereas only one-fourteenth of the country's seaborne foreign trade had been carried in Argentine bottoms in 1946, that figure had risen to one-eighth in 1949. The Argentine State Merchant Fleet has continued to grow. It carried 27.8 per cent of the nation's entire foreign trade in 1950, and the United States Maritime Commission reported the following year that the Argentine merchant marine was then ten times larger than it had been in 1936. In 1950, the Argentine State Merchant Fleet possessed 162 ships with a combined tonnage of 941,000; moreover, it had at that time let contracts for the construction in foreign shipyards of 35 additional vessels with an expected combined tonnage of 315,000.

Perón's ambition in this program has at times seemed boundless. In January of 1946, the Argentine State Merchant Fleet acquired an air arm called the Argentine Merchant Fleet of the Air, which was referred to colloquially as FAMA.* FAMA also grew: it inaugurated regular passenger service with Spain and Italy in 1947 and announced three years later the opening of regular flights between Buenos Aires and New York, with the journey scheduled within a record twenty-one hours. By 1952, FAMA had come to be a serious competitor of the major international airlines linking the Americas with western Europe.

The nature of Argentina's foreign trade is such that "economic independence," in so far as it is directed at the United Kingdom and the United States, is at best incomplete so long as the program is confined to the expropriation of some of the Argentine holdings of the British and "North

* Derived from the initial letters of *Flota Aérea Mercante Argentina*.

American" "imperialists." After all, these "imperialists" have continued to be the principal sources of the "new Argentina's" imports and the major markets for her exports, despite the expropriation program. In 1947, the United Kingdom bought 30 per cent and the United States took 10 per cent of Argentina's exports for that year; and 45 per cent and 8.4 per cent, respectively, of her imports came from the United States and Britain. Moreover, in 1950 Argentine exports to the United States were valued at $77,-430,000, representing an increase of 168 per cent over the corresponding figure for 1949. Perón has been among the first to realize that his economic nationalism was synthetic so long as Britain and the United States played dominant roles in Argentine foreign trade. From the *Peronista* point of view, it has not been easy to meet this problem. As much as he has said that he wanted to crush the "imperialists' " influence in his country, not even Perón would seriously consider carrying "economic independence" to the point of prohibiting trade with them. Yet, permitting that trade has meant that the British and the "North Americans" have continued to be the chief buyers from, and sellers to, Argentina.

Perón is not a man to face such a dilemma without attempting to do something about it. He could not prohibit trade with Britain and the United States, it is true; but he could control some aspects of it. Accordingly, two government agencies have been established with the objective of furthering Argentine economic nationalism through control of the country's trade and financial relations with other countries. These two agencies are the Argentine Institute for the Promotion of Trade and the National Economic Council.

The first of these, the Argentine Institute for the Promo-

tion of Trade—popularly called IAPI*—was created by a
decree of May 28, 1946. Perón's IAPI is strikingly similar
in function and objectives to the Soviet Union's *Amtorg.*
IAPI, like *Amtorg*, is a government agency controlling the
nation's foreign trade. IAPI fixes prices at which Argentines
may participate in international commerce, determines what
commodities shall be imported and which exported; de-
cides who the Argentine importers and exporters will be
and which foreign countries they may trade with. IAPI
is Perón's answer to the "imperialists" so far as trade with
them is concerned. Or, as Perón has put it, "IAPI had the
benefit of being able to offer a 'one and only seller' in opposition to the 'one and only buyer.' "[45] In actual operation,
IAPI has had little effect upon the "imperialists," although
it has been responsible for a rise in the prices of some Argentine commodities placed upon world markets. Perón
has, however, in general declared himself to be satisfied with
IAPI. The Argentine government has nationalized "the
systems of foreign commerce, abolishing the monopolies
which had dominated it," he has asserted. "We can say in
all truth that this achievement constitutes the point of departure in our reform of the economic order."[46]

The second government agency involved in this phase of
"economic independence" is the National Economic Council, which has led a bedraggled existence since its creation
on July 15, 1947. Introduced into the "new Argentina"
with considerable fanfare, the National Economic Council
was charged with no less a task than to co-ordinate all of the
financial and economic policies of the Perón regime. The
council is composed of eight members. When the agency
was launched in July of 1947, it was under the chairman-

* Derived from the initial letters of *Instituto Argentino de Promoción
de Intercambio.*

ship of Miguel Miranda, the president of the Central Bank of Argentina, who had acquired some renown as a species of financial wizard. The Miranda period—from July of 1947 until January of 1949—may be regarded as one of the more intense phases of Argentine economic nationalism.

With the passing of the Miranda period, Argentine financial and economic relations with the United States and other nations became somewhat less strained. A joint Argentine–United States committee was formed in May of 1949 to explore ways and means of increasing trade between the two countries; and by 1950, Argentine debts to "North American" creditors had been reduced from $250,000,000 to $125,000,000. However, the shortage of United States dollars remained a major problem for Perón. Miranda had said in 1948 that "I will cut off my two hands before asking for any loan."[47] This rhetoric, and perhaps the substance thereof, appealed to Perón. Smarting under the dollar shortage, yet clinging stubbornly to the defiant slogan of "economic independence," President Perón told the congress in May of 1950 that he, too, would "cut off my hands before I will put my signature on any document which means a foreign loan to my country."[48] The promise of amputation proved embarrassing when, two weeks later, the United States Export-Import Bank announced a loan of $125,000,-000 to Argentina. Perón still had his hands when he signed the agreement: by no coincidence, the loan covered the exact amount owed in the United States by Argentines. Although the trade relations remained difficult, Argentine–"North American" commerce improved considerably in 1950: in that year alone, the value of this trade surpassed the figure for the entire disastrous Miranda era. Moreover, after 1949 Argentina participated somewhat more fully in international economic arrangements. Late in 1950, the nation at length joined the United Nations Food and Agriculture Organization. "By this decision," a British observer commented, "Argentina has finally backed up her disavowal of the isolationist policy of Mr. Miranda."[49]

Also, the "economic independence" of the post-Miranda period has been tempered by a tendency of the "new Argentina" to invite the "imperialists" to invest their capital in the country again. Finance Minister Ramón A. Cereijo issued such an invitation when he visited Washington in April of 1950. And, five months later, Argentine Ambassador to the United States Jerónimo Remorino released the following statement to the "North American" press: "Argentina offers a fertile, ample, and solid field for the investment of foreign capital. Argentine authorities guarantee equality of treatment to domestic and foreign capital."[50] In short, the "imperialists" have learned that "economic independence," like other phases of Peronism, may be turned on and off as practical situations may demand.

Thus, nationalism—both ideological and economic—is a highly fluid and somewhat inconsistent aspect of the "new Argentina." The platforms of the nationalist organizations have been accepted and rejected, official anti-Semitism has come and gone, Perón's political alliance with the Church is not as solid and consistent a fact as some foreign observers have believed, and even "economic independence" has its weak moments. Opportunism ranks high among President Perón's arts, and one of his basic gifts is knowing when to turn policies on and when to turn them off. That he makes a philosophy of turning programs on and off is a thesis which will be explored more fully in Chapter 12 of this book.

11.

The Rich and the Poor

A large measure of the support among Argentines for the Perón regime has emerged from its announced position as the champion of the poor against the rich. Indeed, the president has sometimes been compared with Robin Hood, sometimes with Andrew Jackson, sometimes with Franklin D. Roosevelt. President Perón has said that the "new Argentina" has two types of enemies. The first of these is the "foreign imperialist," whose fortunes have already been discussed. The second is the domestic Argentine "Oligarchy," the men of wealth who have traditionally dominated the national economy. Perón has proclaimed his enmity against the country's large financial interests, sought to industrialize the nation, and endeavored to improve the economic conditions in which the lower classes have lived. "Until now, the economy has been in the service of capital," the *Peronistas* have said. "From now on, capital will be in the service of the economy."[1] Perón's widely publicized crusade against the "Oligarchy" has been a major factor in such support as his regime has among economically underprivileged Argentines.

Landowners and Capitalists

To Argentines, the "Oligarchy" is a significant political label. It has sometimes been applied indiscriminately to all the country's wealthy folk, but more traditionally it has been pinned on the older large landowning families. Although President Perón's speeches have expressed a strong antipathy for the landowners, the actual record indicates that the agrarian sector of the "Oligarchy" has not suffered at the hands of the "new Argentina" on anywhere near as large a scale as has been true of the urban commercial and small industrial interests. Perón has asserted his intention "to manage the economy of the country in such a manner that it may no longer be the privilege of a few, but the patrimony of all . . . ; to raise the economic standard of the citizens and to give all Argentines an opportunity to lead a worthier and better life."[2]

Presumably, such a program would embody a major economic revolution. If such a revolution is indeed taking place, it is *least* apparent in the pattern of landownership in the "new Argentina." The regime had been expected, in some quarters, to preside over a wholesale redistribution of Argentine agrarian holdings, but this has not yet materialized. Some analysts have even come to regard Perón as a champion of the interests of the country's *estancieros* or major landowners, although conclusive evidence of this remains to be established. In any case, the president has not altered the proposition that Argentina is primarily an agricultural and stock-raising country.

Throughout its history, the nation's wealth has lain chiefly in its crops and in its cattle. The first Spaniards who occupied the area, especially the "interior," believed that land was the only source of riches and that commerce was evil; and, on the eve of political independence of Spain, the Argentine economy remained predominantly pastoral. Moreover, landownership lay at the base of the power of the men who ruled the country during the century before the revolution of 1943. General Juan Manuel de Rosas was himself an *estanciero:* "This was the basic cause of his prestige among the conservative classes, militant enemies of the theoretical principles in whose name the Argentine revolution [of 1810] had been made."[3] Not only has the land been the traditional base of power and wealth in the country, but it has long been characteristic of the Argentine economy that a large percentage of the land has been owned by a small percentage of the population.

An increasing concentration of land-holding in fewer private hands had been a basic economic trend during the century before 1943. This development was accompanied by a tendency of Argentines to migrate from the rural areas to the nation's cities. In 1869 the national population was calculated at 67 per cent rural. This figure fell to 58 per cent in 1895 and to 42 per cent in 1914. And, according to the Fourth National Census of 1947, the population of Argentina was computed as 61.4 per cent urban.* With this progressive urbanization of the country, the rural land-owning "Oligarchy" grew in political and economic power. Although Perón decried this condition, it remained true after the revolution of 1943. In 1946 it was reported that "1,800 Argentine families still own an area greater than England, Belgium, and the Netherlands together. One clan, the Unzués, holds 1,000,000 acres in the single, fertile Province of Buenos Aires."[4] The problem of the concentration of large landed properties in the hands of relatively few owners is known to the Argentines as the *latifundio,* and the problem has been with them since the first years of their national life. Additional statistics may prove enlightening. In 1930, no less than 65 per cent of the combined area of the Provinces of Buenos Aires, Santa Fé, and Córdoba was composed of individually owned estates covering at least four square miles apiece. In the Province of Buenos Aires

* See p. 4.

alone, one-fifth of the total area of 118,467 square miles was owned in 1942 by only 300 persons or companies; and, in the ten national territories, 1,804 owners held as much land as the combined area of Italy, Belgium, the Netherlands, and Denmark. In the Province of Entre Ríos, only 600 people (the provincial population is 776,280) own 12,297 square miles, or more than 40 per cent of the total area of the province.

President Perón has promised to alter this situation, but thus far his policies in this field have been weak. "We are forming a new Argentina," he asserted shortly after his assumption of power, "so that there is no place for the outworn Oligarchy."[5] Nevertheless, the "outworn Oligarchy" has not been a major victim of the Perón regime. True, the large rural landowners wield less influence at the *Casa Rosada* today than before the revolution. But it is also true that the *latifundio* remains as much a problem of the "new Argentina" as it was of the old. It has been said that this pattern of landownership "will continue to flourish" in Argentina, and that "only large-scale expropriation under the state's power of eminent domain will accomplish a real change."[6]

Perón has declared himself to be no friend of the "Oligarchy," but he has not been willing to call for an immediate and thoroughgoing expropriation of rural landed holdings. In May of 1948, he announced that his government would subdivide a number of these holdings, but he has been reluctant to push such a program through to effectuation on a large scale. Some expropriation has indeed taken place, but the figures on it indicate that the regime has moved slowly and cautiously. Official statistics published in 1951 revealed that the number of individual landowners had increased somewhat since the revolution in consequence of the regime's policy of subdividing agrarian properties. Thus, while there has been some movement in the "new Argentina" toward expansion of the number of small individual landowners, the record of this phase of Peronism remained unimpressive at the time this book was written.

On the other hand, Perón's actions with respect to non-agrarian forms of wealth have been more vigorous. The urban capitalist has felt the effects of the "new Argentina," and it is in this area that the more significant aspects of the economic revolution can be seen. In a sense, Perón's policies toward urban merchants and industrialists reflect a traditional Latin-American attitude toward wealth which is not derived from the land. "A capitalist is not esteemed," Francis Herron wrote in his admirable *Letters from the Argentine*. "He is considered to be a schemer, an opportunist, at times even a thief. . . . A capitalist is not admired as one who promotes civilization; he is thought of as a plunderer. . . . This conception of the capitalist has been inherited from the Spanish colonial system, under which a capitalist had no social recognition."[7] Indeed, Perón has said that "the capitalistic system is an abuse of property,"[8] and, in his own inimitable manner, he has set about correcting this situation in Argentina.

During the Perón era, nationalization and expropriation of commercial and industrial properties have been carried forward to an appreciable extent. "It has been necessary for us to modify some liberal and bourgeois ideas about property," Perón told the congress in 1950. "In our economic view, property is not an absolute individual right, but rather a relative right in which property has not only an individual but also a social function."[9] The *Peronista* formula for distinguishing property with a "social function" from other types of property bears a resemblance to some "North American" criteria for defining a public utility. In

Peronista terms, if a given nonagrarian enterprise performs
a service declared to be in the "public interest," the property used by that enterprise is then held to have a "social
function" and is accordingly subject to expropriation, nationalization, or thoroughgoing governmental regulation.
This proposition was enacted into law in September of
1948, and vigorous action along these lines has been taken
since then. Indeed, Perón promised in May of 1949 that
all public utilities not already nationalized could expect to
undergo that process in the future; and a "North American" correspondent noted with some alarm that "no business structure, or private dwelling for that matter, in any
Argentine city is immune to expropriation or forced sale if
governmental officials decide they want or need it."[10]

Perón's record of performance in the nationalization of
public utilities has been substantial. The expropriation of
British- and "North American"–owned telephone companies has already been noted;* it remained only to deal
with the Argentine-owned telephone enterprises to bring
the entire utility under governmental administration. This
was handled in what came to be typical *Peronista* fashion.
In June of 1947, the director and sub-director of the Argentine Mixed Telephone Company were imprisoned on
charges of bookkeeping "irregularities" allegedly appearing in the company's accounts. Eight months later, the company was expropriated. Nationalization of the gas industry
followed a similar pattern. The British-owned Primitiva
Gas Company had been taken over as early as 1944, and the
domestic Argentine gas companies were nationalized during the course of five progressive steps taken between 1945
and 1948. Again, all public motor bus transportation was
placed under governmental control by November of 1950.

Thus the situation permits of considerable economic

* See pp. 240–42.

planning in the "new Argentina." The plan itself has not
been lacking. On October 21, 1946, President Perón presented the congress with a "Five-Year Plan." Largely the
work of Barcelona-born José Figuerola, an economic planner who had served the Spanish regime of Primo de Rivera,* the Five-Year Plan was a staggering instrument. Organized in no fewer than twenty-seven separate bills,
Perón's Five-Year Plan envisaged for the period 1947–51 a
collection of far-reaching governmental activities involving
numerous public works projects and the development of
civilian and military industries. While the actual performance on the plan by the end of 1951 fell below many of the
goals originally established in 1946, still the record of
achievement was such that the plan could not be called a
total failure. Indeed, J. G. Lomax, formerly the British
Commercial Attaché at Buenos Aires, has regarded the
Five-Year Plan as "the most important economic event . . .
possibly in all the history of Argentina."[11]

In so far as the regime sought through the Five-Year
Plan to industrialize a traditionally agricultural and stock-
raising nation, the project represented the "new Argentina's" bid for an economic revolution of some consequence.
To be sure, some attempts at industrialization had been
launched before the coming of Perón. These were especially evident in the years immediately following World
War I, when an Argentine textile industry of some magnitude appeared on the scene. On the whole, however, industrialization moved slowly before 1943. Many felt that
the obstacles to Argentine industrialization were insuperable: the country did not produce iron and coal in quantities
and qualities thought equal to the task, the economy was
fundamentally pastoral, skilled workers were rare, and the
Argentine public tended to regard manufactured products

* See p. 299.

The Rich and the Poor

marked *Industria Argentina* ("Made in Argentina") as inferior to imported goods. It was evident, however, from the first months after the revolution of 1943 that the rulers of the "new Argentina" were determined to do what they could to industrialize the country. Perón himself said, as early as July of 1944, that "we expect everything from our civilian and military industries because we believe that by the realization of this miracle Argentina thence need to rely only on its own forces."[12] And General Fárrell, then the president, asserted that "a country is proportionately more sovereign as it is able to supply its own needs."[13]

In a sense, then, the Five-Year Plan did little more than to state these objectives in terms of codified projects and specifically systematized goals. Many have felt that in attempting industrialization Perón is attempting the impossible in a basically pastoral country without important deposits of coal and iron. It is nevertheless true that the Five-Year Plan has met with a modicum of success. For example, if the index of the physical volume of Argentine industrial production be set at 100 for the year 1943, the index number for 1949 is 141.8. In the latter year, 16,039 new trademarks and 5,016 patents on inventions were taken out, as compared with 8,700 and 1,734, respectively, for 1943. The number of workers employed by Argentine non-agricultural industries rose from 732,799 in 1943 to 955,890 in 1949. "During my government," Perón declared in 1951, "30,000 new industries have been installed in Greater Buenos Aires alone, making a total . . . of more than 80,000."[14]

Moreover, the "capitalists" who participated in Perón's industrialization program did much better financially than the wealthy folk against whom the government said the revolution was directed. A study made in 1949 of 1,000 firms participating in the Five-Year Plan indicated that 87 of the concerns realized profits over 50 per cent, 213 of

255

them reported profits between 20 and 50 per cent, 528 of them realized profits up to 20 per cent, 28 broke even, and the remaining 144 suffered losses. Industrialists—and not all of them Argentines—have responded enthusiastically to figures such as these. The "North American" retired Major General Royal B. Lord, in Argentina in 1948 in his private capacity as an "imperialist," branded Argentine criticism of the Five-Year Plan as "exactly the kind of talk I heard [in the United States] in the first Roosevelt administration. . . . A company can now withdraw profits up to 12 per cent a year on its investment. Where else can you get 12 per cent on your money?"[15] It is easy, when writing for "North American" consumption, to damn all of Perón's policies. Somewhat more courage is required to write, as the *New York Times* correspondent Milton Bracker did in October of 1950, that "Argentina has made tangible progress under the regime of President Perón, and, particularly, some of his worst enemies affirm that it seems that the country is better off, in terms of its economy, in the long run. . . . Argentina leads the world in the increase in industrial employment and in industrial production between 1937 and 1949. It is possible, keeping one's eyes open, to see that President Perón has made great contributions to the national economy. . . ."[16] In short, while the Five-Year Plan fell short of its objectives when it was terminated in 1951, the failure was neither dismal nor complete.

Thus, Perón's policies as they affect the economy of the "new Argentina" embody a curious combination of measures ostensibly directed against the interests of the country's traditional patterns of wealth. The large landowners have suffered but little, but other forms of property, particularly public utilities, have been subjected to wholesale expropriation. Perón has embarked upon a program of industrialization which, although it had not reached the goals set for it in 1946, nevertheless had recorded impressive strides by 1952. In so far as this economic program had been pushed propaganda-wise in the name of the poor against the rich, the dispossession of the latter has by no means been complete. In the midst of World War II, Perón asserted in 1944 that "few capitalist countries will remain on the American continent after the war";[17] in 1950, he was still maintaining that "we cannot preserve anything that is capitalist, because to evolve we must move on to another form."[18] Much that is capitalistic nevertheless remains, and the outlines of "another form" continue to be nebulous.

On the Sore Beset

"North Americans" were quick to assert in the first years after the Perón revolution that the movement had little support among the people of Argentina. In 1945, John C. McClintock, special advisor to Nelson A. Rockefeller, then the United States Co-ordinator of Inter-American Affairs, wired with some glee from Buenos Aires that Perón had "lost the support of the right, the left, the workers, the farmers, and the capitalists, but the rest of the country is with him."[19] In the same year, a group of "North American" experts on Latin America, polled by Professor Russell H. Fitzgibbon, endeavored to rank the Latin-American states on the basis of a collection of criteria including the degree of popular acceptance and support of the various governments. Professor Fitzgibbon's experts believed in 1945 that, with the twenty Latin-American nations thus ranked, Argentina stood in fifth place; five years later, these experts altered their evaluations to drop the "new Argentina" to eighth place.[20] Some case may be made for drawing a curious negative correlation between the "North American" experts and Argentine political observers: as the former become more convinced that Perón is unpopular among Argentines, the latter retreat from this view. While some wishful thinkers might find solace in the thought that Perón has little support among the Argentine people, this attitude is essentially unrealistic. Of course, scientific measurement of public opinion has not yet been undertaken in that country, and Perón would doubtlessly regard such an endeavor as "espionage"; but this proposition lends as little comfort to the wishful as to others.

From the first days of the revolution, the governors of the "new Argentina" made a strong bid for the support of the lower classes of the country, of the economically under-privileged who firmly believed that throughout the history of Argentina very few administrations had expressed even an interest in the economic conditions in which the majority of Argentines lived. This belief has contributed to the emergence of a host of converts to Peronism. Argentine history, as understood by the enemies of the "Oligarchy," had been dominated by the landowning gentry; "during the nineteenth century," José Ingenieros wrote, "Argentine politics has been the monopoly of a social class, the landowners."[21] To most Argentines, control by the "Oligarchy" was a major principle in national politics, and as late as the 1940's a "North American" sociologist was told that "about two hundred families make up the Argentine social fabric."[22] Before 1943, very few opponents of the "Oligarchy" had achieved power. There had been a Rosas, to be sure, and there had been an Irigoyen; but Rosas had himself been a landowner,* and the Irigoyen period came to be remembered chiefly as an era of intra-party strife and senility. What had been fundamental was domination by the "Oligarchy." And, in the view of many of the enemies of the "Oligarchy," Perón made good sense when he said: "The conservative classes lost their instinct of self-preserva-

* See pp. 249–50.

tion. Their unrestricted ambitions to keep everything for themselves, their purpose of never sharing the advantages accumulated, blinded them to the evidence: whoever wishes to keep everything will lose everything. They did not understand that their adjustment to the tremendous changes suffered by the world was a question of life and death. The truly conservative thing to be was, precisely, to be revolutionary. But they did not understand this!"[23]

Whether or not the "Oligarchy's" enemies understood that point, many of them did understand that before 1943 most Argentine governments—dominated by the men of wealth—had not been chosen by an undisputed majority of the country's voters. Electoral fraud had repeatedly cheated the opposition in the elections of the late nineteenth and early twentieth centuries. It was not until the passage in 1912 of the "Sáenz Peña Law" that all Argentines could feel that the officially announced results of elections truly represented the way the voters had cast their ballots. And, before 1943, only two presidents had been elected in accordance with the "Sáenz Peña Law": Irigoyen and Alvear. Moreover, the situation deteriorated rapidly after the revolution of 1930. Nobody elected President Uriburu (1930–32), and Uriburu "elected" President Justo (1932–38). Charges of fraud likewise characterized the balloting which brought Presidents Ortiz (1938–40) and Castillo (1940–43) into the *Casa Rosada.* Most accounts support the thesis that Castillo was unpopular with a probable majority of the Argentine people. *Peronistas* will not object to italicizing this point, and their opponents can do worse than have their noses rubbed in it: *by the eve of the revolution of 1943, no Argentine president had been elected by an undisputed majority of the voters since Hipólito Irigoyen (1916–22, 1928–30)!* He, moreover, was overthrown by the "Oligarchy," which used armed force and not ballots in 1930.

It is not necessary to be a *Peronista* to understand Argentines who say that by 1943 "the country was tired of the predominant political Oligarchy. . . . If now [*Peronistas*] make mistakes and commit errors, it is the fault of those who had not raised politics from its level of dubious morality."[24] It is not very many steps further to the observation that the first Argentine president since Irigoyen to be elected by an unquestioned majority of the voters is Juan Domingo Perón.

Thus many Argentines who had long felt that the governments belonged to the "Oligarchy" rather than to themselves were quick to respond to the proposition that this condition had at last been terminated on June 4, 1943. The chieftains of the "new Argentina" assailed the "Oligarchy" and said that the new regime spoke in the name of the common people of the country. Perón himself said that "the rich should be less rich and the poor less poor,"[25] and that the state should give "preferential attention to the less protected and the more ignorant classes."[26] Many humble Argentines, long accustomed to calling the government "they," for the first time began to identify their own interests with the regime. A social revolution of no small significance seemed to be in the making.

Perón asserted that the revolution of 1943 was in part a revolt of the workers, although the rebellion was made by a sector of the army and not with labor participation. Acquiring status as the champion of labor, Perón was quick to point out that the workers had no political vision, no political direction. This phase of Perón's relationship to labor is of significance: if he were to bid for the votes and the support of the workers, their political action must be cast in terms of *personalismo*—loyalty to a particular politician, Perón, rather than formulation *by* labor of its own political and economic objectives. Thus, *personalismo* and

Perón's paternalism entered into a somewhat facile partnership. The workers were politically ignorant and inarticulate: Perón would tell them what they wanted, and they
would want it; labor would support Perón, but he would
do the deciding. As one *Peronista* put it, "the working class
. . . is incapable of determining its own role in the social
economy of the nation."[27] That proposition underlay much
of the "new Argentina's" operational relationship to labor.
Perón was the leader, the symbolic hero, of the workers—
he would decide what was to be done, and it remained for
labor only to be convinced that it was the beneficiary of the
revolution, and to fight and vote for Perón.

There is no longer any point in denying that the "new
Argentina" has captured the support of the bulk of Argentine labor. The gainfully employed numbered about 7,000,-
000 in 1951: some 5,000,000 of these were salaried workers.
The latter figure was divided roughly equally between government workers and industrial labor, and these 5,000,000
Argentines form the best-organized sector of the popular
support for Perón. In the years since 1943, he has presided
over the promulgation of decrees and laws declared to be
in the interest of the workers, and their rank-and-file has
moved demonstrably into the *Peronista* camp.

Labor measures constitute a major phase of Peronism.
The truth is that labor legislation had existed in the country before the coming of Perón: many such laws had been
put on the books during the Irigoyen period. But "put on
the books" is the important phrase in that sentence. Much
of the pre-Perón labor legislation had never really been
administered or enforced. Perón himself likes to tell a story
about his first days as a champion of labor. "When I first
went to the secretariat [of labor and welfare]," he has re-
called, "a very learned lawyer, with a profusion of legal
terms and methods of procedure, said to me, 'Colonel,

which law do you consider it is most important to include in labor legislation?' And I answered him, 'One which will insure that at any rate half of those already existing are obeyed.' In that lay our success; enforcing the observance of half the laws which already existed. That is something which everybody knows."[28] To that portion Perón added new labor measures. As now enforced under the aegis of the "new Argentina," the labor program includes such matters as paid vacations and holidays for workers, wage and hour regulation, protection of female and child labor, workers' housing projects, and educational programs designed especially for labor.

Paid vacations and holidays have served to endear the regime to many an Argentine worker. According to a scale established by a decree dated January 24, 1945, all commercial and industrial houses in the country are required to give their employees annual vacations with pay. Workers who have been in the same employ less than five years get ten-day vacations; employees with more than five years' service receive yearly vacations of at least fifteen days. Further, the network of holidays has been expanded in the "new Argentina" for most workers. In those sectors of the economy where the nature of the work permits these stoppages, there are seven nationally recognized holidays. Additional holidays are freely proclaimed from time to time. The seven standing holidays are Sunday of every week; Saturday afternoons (this half-working day is called the "English Saturday"); May 1, Labor Day; May 25, the anniversary of the *porteños'* "May Revolution" of 1810; July 9, the anniversaries of San Martín's and Perón's declarations of independence;* October 12 ("North Americans" call this "Columbus Day," Argentines and other Latin Americans call it the "Day of the Race"); and October 17,

* See pp. 21 and 238–39.

The Rich and the Poor

"Loyalty Day." Of these, only May 1, October 12, and October 17 became legal holidays after the revolution of 1943; the others had previously been "on the books," but not actually enjoyed by many Argentine workingmen until after the rise of Perón.

The enforcement of wage and hour legislation has been a standing feature of Peronism. "Labor is not a commodity, and poverty anywhere is a threat to the general prosperity," the *Peronistas* have said; wages should not fluctuate "because health and the stomach do not permit economies."[29] Although the forty-eight-hour working week had been written into law in 1933, it had not been generally enforced during the ten years that followed. Post-1943 maximum hour legislation combined by 1951 to give the average Argentine urban worker a forty-hour work week based on from six to eight hours of labor per day for five or six days out of every week.

Although the "new Argentina's" regulation of wages began in September of 1945, its most celebrated decree in this field was promulgated on December 20 of that year. That measure required all commercial and industrial establishments to pay their employees not only a minimum wage established by the decree but also an annual bonus in the amount of one month's salary. This famous step was taken at the height of the presidential campaign of 1945–46, and was undoubtedly designed to win the labor vote for Perón. While the opposition branded the decree as "only a device for buying support and crushing rebellion,"[30] it was nevertheless sufficiently effective as an election measure to inspire Perón to duplicate it when he ran for re-election six years later. On April 9, 1951, as another presidential campaign was launched, Perón, again a candidate, announced for government workers a general wage rise which was to be retroactive to January 1 of that year.

Other labor measures have endeavored to provide security of employment and protection for workers against the economic effects of industrial accidents and old age. A decree of December of 1945 consolidated a system which made it difficult for employers to dismiss workers and embodied a scale for the payment of severance sums. Under this arrangement, commercial and industrial firms were required to pay their dismissed workers severance money in the amount of one half of one month's wages for each year of the dismissed employees' service. Under the pattern of the laws, severance pay had to be provided in all cases except where the dismissed workers had damaged the employers' property, committed judicially determined acts of fraud, been unable to perform the tasks assigned, carried on their own personal business instead of the employers', or wilfully injured the latter's security or honor. A comprehensive social security system was moreover created on May 14, 1946, providing for old age pensions and payment of indemnities to workers injured on their jobs. As of the end of 1950, 3,438,000 Argentines were covered by this social security system, and approximately 23,000 of them were receiving old age benefits.

Several measures have also been newly enforced with respect to female and child labor. Expectant mothers may not be dismissed from their jobs because of pregnancy, and maternity benefits also provide that these women may not work within thirty days prior to, or forty-five days after, childbirth. With respect to child labor, persons less than twelve years old are completely prohibited from working, children between the ages of twelve and fourteen years may work only on projects in which older members of their families are also engaged, and youngsters between the ages of fourteen and sixteen years are limited to a four-hour working day. Moreover, no firm may maintain a labor force of which more than 15 per cent of the workers are less than eighteen years of age.

Perón's program in the field of the adjustment of labor conflicts is also worth noting. Shortly after the revolution of 1943, the regime assumed the authority to intervene in labor disputes, and a new system of labor courts was created in a series of decrees and laws the first of which was promulgated in November of 1944. The labor courts are empowered to use adjudication, arbitration, and conciliation in adjusting disputes. In contrast to the other courts of Argentina, where litigation is conducted in predominantly written form,* procedures in the new labor courts are largely public, oral, and immediate. Although most Argentine lawyers were still conducting a running attack against the labor courts when this book was written, the work of these tribunals has been impressive. In 1950, for example, these courts received 23,087 cases, of which approximately 14,000 involved controversies over severance pay, 3,721 were based on claims for back salaries, and 3,322 involved claims for compensation for injuries suffered in industrial accidents. Of the 23,087 cases, 8,184 were settled out of court by means of conciliation, while the remainder were handled through adjudication and arbitration.

Strikes were of dubious legality in pre-Perón Argentina. The government announced in 1946, however, that "strikes have lost their illegal character. . . . The right to strike constitutes an incontrovertible principle of labor legislation and an element of inestimable value in the struggle for dignified living and working conditions for the working class."[31] In general, the number of strikes has tended to decrease in recent years; this trend reflects in part Perón's expanding control of organized labor.† Official figures for

---

* See pp. 123 and 131–32.
† See pp. 319–27.

1949 indicated that only 29,000 workers had during that year participated in 36 strikes, as against 278,000 workers taking part in 103 stoppages the previous year. Although the right to strike is a generally proclaimed legal principle in Perón's Argentina, certain types of stoppages nevertheless remain illegal. A 1945 decree branding strikes against the government as "crimes against the security of the state" is still in force. Moreover, other types of strikes are illegal if they violate an existing contract, defy any decree or law, or disturb public order.

In accordance with the government's program to improve workers' living conditions, a National Housing Administration was created on May 29, 1945. This agency was expected to put large-scale slum clearance and housing projects into operation for the benefit of white-collar and industrial workers. As originally announced, this program was ambitious: the regime intended to spend $50,000,000 per year in slum clearance and construction scheduled to produce 20,000 new housing units per year. Like other aspects of Peronism, the record of achievement has fallen short of the original goal, yet the program cannot be branded as a total failure. As of the end of 1950, the government had constructed 35,000 workers' housing units since 1943, and 65,000 more were under construction.

Moreover, Perón has sought occupational education for workers. At the time this writer was in Argentina, about forty labor schools were in existence in the country, and plans had been made for a workers' university. Not only were workers to have occupational training, but students in all Argentine schools—labor and otherwise—were to be indoctrinated with a *Peronista* attitude toward labor. "The teachers must teach the children and the youths to love and respect men who work with their hands in the fields, in the shops, in the factories," Perón declared. "They do not know many laws or many sciences . . . but they have generous and honorable hearts."[32]

In general, *Peronista* labor measures have tended to be directed more toward urban than toward rural workers. Indeed, a basic characteristic of *Peronista* economics has been the regime's propensity for devoting especial attention to urban and industrial matters to the neglect of rural and agrarian problems. This is, of course, curious in a country with a predominantly pastoral economy, and Perón is frequently criticized on this score. The reader has already seen that the "new Argentina's" policies have been weak with respect to the rural landowning "Oligarchy."* This is accompanied by a complementary infirmity of policy toward the rural workers. Economists have held this official neglect of the countryside while concentrating attention upon the cities to be a fundamental weakness of the Perón regime. It has already been noted that Argentines are leaving the rural areas to flock to the cities in large numbers, and this trend has continued since the revolution of 1943. Perón has done little with respect to this problem. Neither has he done much to affect the economic situation of those workers who yet remain in the rural areas. His chief contribution in this field has been a piece of legislation called the "Statute of the Peon." This law, promulgated on September 3, 1949, provided for minimum wages, maximum hours, and vacations for rural workers; but in actual operation the statute has had only a minor effect on rural life. The regime's preoccupation with the cities to the neglect of the rural areas is a social and economic characteristic of the "new Argentina"; some economists believe that the economic ramifications of this pattern will be central among the factors spelling Perón's eventual collapse.

Price control, declared to be in the interests of the less

* See pp. 248–52.

wealthy, has been a feature of Peronism since 1944. The "new Argentina's" experiences and problems in connection with this program present an intriguing parallel to the tides and fortunes of the "North Americans'" attempts at controlling prices. On July 30, 1944—two and one-half years after price control was launched in the United States—Perón, then the vice president of Argentina, issued a decree endeavoring to roll prices of basic necessities back to their 1939 levels, and attempting to hold them there. Argentine labor, Perón declared at the time, would never be reduced to "rags in order that privileged groups may continue enjoying their luxuries, their automobiles, and pleasures."[33] As in the United States, Argentine price control was only semi-effective. Like the "North Americans," the Argentines were involved in a battle with inflation, and Perón could do little more than retard the steady rise in prices. The price levels of 1939 were never really achieved in 1944, and a new attempt was launched in the following year. A decree of May 30 attempted to hold prices at the levels prevailing between December 1 and 15 of 1944, but this goal was likewise not achieved. Since then, many laws and decrees have been announced in the attempt to stem the rise in prices. Inflation nevertheless continues in Argentina. The steps taken to police price control have sometimes been spectacularly extreme, but the cost of living has continued to mount in the country.

It is not easy to gauge the effectiveness of *Peronista* appeals to labor. In the first place, a distinction must be made between urban and rural workers. The latter have less reason to feel that they have benefited from the revolution of 1943, while the workers in the cities, especially Buenos Aires, are likely to feel otherwise. Within the ranks of urban labor, there is a strong identification of the workers with the Perón regime. Much of organized labor in the cities believes that it has profited greatly from the regime's economic measures.

Many urban workers *believe* that they have been the economic beneficiaries of Peronism. *Actually*, they probably have benefited economically. But the *extent* to which they have profited is another question. Its answer must depend in large part on wage and cost-of-living indices, and full official figures on these matters have not been available for publication. Perón has censored much of this information, and to seek it out is "espionage." Those who suspect that this writer engaged in such "espionage" while he was in Argentina operate on well-founded suspicions. However, the sources in collusion with this endeavor produced contradictory figures with respect to wage and cost-of-living indices. A composite picture of the wage index, based on the average income of Argentine industrial workers, suggests that if the wage index for 1943 be set at 100, the figure for 1950 was probably somewhere in the neighborhood of 500. If the average industrial worker made five times as much money in 1950 as in 1943, it did not follow that he was able to buy five times as much with his income. The cost of living had increased, of course, with mounting inflation. Opponents of the regime have not hesitated to point out that "whoever receives some *pesos* in the form of a wage increase or a bonus has more money in his pocket, but he cannot buy with it more things than before."[34] The extent to which this allegation is true is difficult to determine, as most of the data necessary for the construction of a cost-of-living index are censored. It would appear, however, that if the cost-of-living index be calculated at 100 for 1943, the index for 1950 would be somewhere between 350 and 400. Thus, Argentine workers probably *can* buy more with their money now than they could in 1943, but not as much more as the sums in their pockets lead many of them to believe. President Perón, careful to keep the full official figures secret, had this to say about the problem: "Things cost a little less before, but no one had the money to buy them. It does not matter that prices are high, but what does matter is that there should be money with which to buy things. It must be taken into account that deflation represents misery, poverty, and lack of employment. And it is the poor, the working classes, which suffer through it, not the rich, and that is why they want deflation. Thus the money they hold becomes more valuable and they gain greater profits, but the ones who have to suffer hunger, cold, illness and, in a word, misery, are the working classes."[35]

What can the average Argentine buy with his income? For one thing, food—he is not hungry in the "new Argentina." According to United Nations figures, the amount of food consumed by the average Argentine in a year weighs 48 per cent more than the *ideal* diet proposed by the United Nations Food and Agriculture Organization! He consumes more meat than anybody else in the world,* and his calorie intake is second only to the average New Zealander's. Even a bank traditionally associated with the Argentine "Oligarchy" has said that "the less fortunate are probably better off here than anywhere else in the world, because of the relative abundance and low cost of food. There is comparatively little poverty and unemployment."[36]

Thus the domestic pattern of *Peronista* economics follows the announced proposition that "the rich should be less rich and the poor less poor." In a sense this has indeed happened, but on a basically small scale. If the rich are less

---

* Nevertheless, weekly meatless days were decreed in Argentina in 1952. These were partially related to the imbalance in Perón's economic program between industry on the one hand and agriculture and stock-raising on the other, and partially to Buenos Aires' obligation to fulfil a meat contract with the United Kingdom.

The Rich and the Poor

rich, it is not by much less; if the poor are wealthier, they do not have a spectacularly larger real income. The government has proclaimed its enmity toward the large landowner, but he still has his lands and the *latifundio* remains a national problem. Industrialization has been carried forward to the economic benefit of both the rich and the poor. Labor legislation has been enacted and enforced to the greater profit of the urban than the rural workers. And all of this has been done in the name of the poor against the rich. Many Argentines of the lower classes support the Perón government because they believe it to be the first regime in the nation's history to speak for them instead of the "Oligarchy."

If there ever had been another such regime, it was that of Juan Manuel de Rosas. Indeed, Eva Perón once said that the lower classes to which Peronism made its appeal were the political heirs of the *gauchos* of the "interior" who clung loyally to "Bloody Rosas" a century ago. It is worth remembering that Rosas had said that "I know and respect the talents of many of the men who have governed the country . . . ; but it seems to me that all committed a great error; they governed very well for the cultured people but scorned the lower classes, the people of the fields, who were the men of action. . . . They did nothing against the rich and the upper class: I believe that it is important to establish a major influence over this class to contain it and direct it, and I propose to acquire this influence at any cost; for this, I will work constantly, with many sacrifices. I will be a *gaucho* among the *gauchos*, I will talk as they do; to protect them I will be their attorney, I will care for their interests."* Strikingly little editing would be necessary to convert this from a *rosista* to a *Peronista* policy statement. The revolution of 1943, Ysabel Rennie has ob-

* See pp. 26-27.

271

served, "is the gauchesque reaction. It is the poncho and the chiripá, the intensely indigenous—even, if you like, the barbarian. In its extreme form it is something at once terrible and pitiable. But the other extreme was an extreme, too, and on it was based nearly a century of exploitation."[37] Under other conditions, Perón could conceivably have reopened the war between the two Argentinas. But Perón has been more adept than Rosas at straddling the two, and, in the century since the Battle of Caseros, the *gaucho* has largely migrated to the cities. That the *descamisado*, Perón's beloved "shirtless" worker,* is the political heir of the *gaucho* is not merely *Peronista* propaganda.

Some "North Americans" might have been conscious while reading this chapter of a similarity between some of the domestic economic measures of Perón's "new Argentina" and the late President Franklin Delano Roosevelt's "New Deal" in the United States. Perón's "Oligarchy" wears the same mask as Roosevelt's "economic royalists," labor laws characterized both governments, both Roosevelt and Perón loom—each in his fashion—as champions of the poor against the rich. There is little point in silencing parallels between Argentine and "North American" social and economic development. Parallels certainly exist between the two, but if Juan Domingo Perón is to be compared with a president of the United States, the comparison lies not so much with Franklin D. Roosevelt as with Andrew Jackson.

The parallel between Peronism and "Jacksonian democracy" is intriguing and perhaps significant. In the United States more than a century ago, President Jackson forced the aristocratic New Englanders to witness the political elevation of their "uncultured" social inferiors, the men of the west. In Perón's Argentina, the "Oligarchy" likewise is faced with such a transformation. The lower classes, re-

* See pp. 316–19.

sponding to one of the very rare regimes in Argentine history to tell the humble and the "uncultured" that the country belongs to them, have begun to step out of what the "Oligarchy" calls their "place." Formerly social pariahs, the enemies of the "Oligarchy" form a species of *nouveau riche*, and many of them have acquired wealth and influence under conditions inconceivable in pre-1943 Argentina.

In a sense, the late Eva Perón was the prototype of the *Peronista* "uncultured" *nouveau riche*. Herself an illegitimate child, a "woman of the people" who rose, with little formal education, to wealth and to power, Evita's challenge to the "Oligarchy" typified a significant sector of the Perón revolution. So, too, did the achievements of a number of the military men who seized power in 1943. "To the wealthy, influential Argentines the new government is not something to be taken too seriously," Ray Josephs wrote shortly after the revolt. "The military, they believe, are upstarts, unknown people who've pushed their way into power and propose to stay as long as they can. The Jockey Club crowd [the 'Oligarchy'] consider the *militares* stupid, ignorant, incapable of governing. And the socialite wives, who know Paris as they know their own boudoirs, whose breeding is as pure as that of their own Palermo prize-winning shorthorns, laugh off . . . the new . . . crowd as pretentious and provincial."[38] The social context—the *ambiente*, as the Argentines say—of the revolution is surely reminiscent of the United States in the days of Jacksonian democracy.

Let the student of the Jackson era consider some aspects of Perón's Argentina. Hear the complaints of the "Oligarchy." Perón "is ruining the country," this writer was told by a representative of the traditional governing class. "Now *everybody* has money, and that is bad. *Everybody* can now go to the opera, the night clubs, the fine restaurants. But the new people who go there degrade these places—they do not know how to dress properly, they do not know how to behave in the elegant places. They are ruining the country." The *Peronistas*, conscious of, and sensitive to, this criticism, overcompensate, frequently, by pretending to a "culture" and even a literacy which, basically, is not theirs. The public expressions of this over-compensation are ludicrous proof to the "Oligarchy" that the Jacksonians of the south do not belong in power. Consider a few illustrations. Perón has promulgated a "decalogue" which contains more than ten points; this is conclusive evidence to the "Oligarchy" of the fundamentally "uncultured" illiteracy of Peronism. Or, hear Evita: "I like all music, concerts and operas—especially Chopin."[39] Again, a cabinet minister, on December 31, 1950, made a speech in observance of the passing of the old year. It, he said, had been the year of the three *S*'s—*Santo* (the Holy Year), San Martín,* and *Sincuenta* (fifty). The "Oligarchy" was not alone in pointing out that *cincuenta* begins with a *C*. This anecdote is widely circulated within the "Oligarchy": two *Peronistas*, each trying to impress the other, were discussing their recent rise to "culture." As the conversation turned to the artistic works of the great Wagner, the first *Peronista* felt constrained to say that he had recently purchased for his home one of Wagner's best *paintings*. The second *Peronista*, not to be outdone, retorted that he had met Wagner personally only the day before. The first *Peronista* would not believe this. "You met Wagner!" he exclaimed. "Where?" The second answered that while he was traveling on streetcar number twenty-four to the *boca*, the workers' quarter along the Buenos Aires waterfront,

* The one hundredth anniversary of San Martín's death, 1950 was celebrated throughout Argentina as the "Year of the Liberator General San Martín."

Wagner had boarded the car and sat beside him. The first *Peronista* scoffed. "That is impossible," he said. Affronted, the second *Peronista* demanded to know why the tale was questioned. "It is impossible," was the answer, "because I know for a fact that streetcar route number twenty-four does not go to the *boca!*"

Let the "North Americans" recall that one expression they gave to the world—"O.K."—might have come from a Jacksonian who understood that the letters stood for "Oll Korrect." In a sense, "O.K." could have been to Jacksonian democracy what the "year of the three *S*'s" is to the "new Argentina." In so far as the Perón revolution is a social revolution, it is corroding the "Oligarchy" as a social caste. New folk are rising to respectability in Argentina. They are, many of them, "uncultured" and unlettered; they are the southern counterpart of Jackson's men of the west. They are the humble ones, the lower classes. And many of these people worship the Perón regime because they believe it to be the first government in all the history of Argentina to speak in their name instead of the "Oligarchy's."

12.

Southern Dialectic

The reader has seen Juan Domingo Perón compared with Franklin Delano Roosevelt and with Andrew Jackson. This should not obscure the point that the more directly significant parallels to Peronism lie in the systems developed in Italy by Benito Mussolini and in Germany by Adolf Hitler. "North Americans" may remember that books about Argentina published in the United States during World War II bore such titles as *Argentina: Fascist Headquarters* and *The Nazi Underground in South America*. Before the fall of the Axis in 1945, Perón expressed admiration of Mussolini and suggested that the Nazis were right. Until mid-1945, Perón voiced little opposition to the labeling of his ideas and practices as "Fascist" or "Nazi"; after the defeat of the Axis, such labels fell into discredit and disgrace in Argentina and elsewhere in the world. To call Peronism "fascism" or "naziism" became "contemptuous," and it was necessary to find a new *word* for Perón's system. That new name has at last been found. The current label is *Justicialismo*. Although the word for it is new and different, Perón's system remains essentially what it was immediately before the forces of the United Nations entered Berlin and declared Adolf Hitler to be dead.

On Justicialismo *and the "Third Position"*

In 1951, a reputable "North American" periodical could say, as though it were not news to anybody, that "Perón operates a state essentially modeled on the classic Nazi-Fascist pattern."[1] The general tendency of non-Argentines to associate such a label with post-1943 affairs promotes a misunderstanding in so far as it encourages the belief that Argentina suddenly, overnight, became "Nazi-Fascist" on June 4, 1943.

It should be remembered that fascism had come into vogue in the country with the Uriburu revolution of 1930, thirteen years before Perón's rise to power.* Those Argentines—especially the *porteños*—who were culturally oriented toward Europe looked particularly to Spain and to Italy. If the former was the mother-country, Italy was a second cultural parent. Mussolini had ruled Italy since 1922; and in Spain, General Miguel Primo de Rivera (whose regime was not yet called "Fascist") had come into power in 1923. Although the Primo de Rivera government collapsed in 1930, Mussolini, of course, remained a dominant European figure for more than a decade thereafter. To many Argentines, the works of Primo de Rivera and Mussolini were an inspiration, an exhilarating challenge. It has been noted that President Uriburu (1930–32) seemed "seduced" by fascism; President Justo (1932–38) was a little less—but only a little less—so beguiled. During the latter's presidency, Hitler assumed power in Germany and General Francisco Franco launched a civil war in Spain.

So far as many Argentines were concerned during the Justo administration, the major figures on the international scene were Mussolini, Hitler, and Franco; and Argentines followed Italian, German, and Spanish politics with an in-

* See pp. 35–44.

tense and often sympathetic interest. Fascist and Nazi doctrines appealed to many of the "Yankees of the South." Indeed, Mussolini's diplomatic service reported that Argentina under President Justo was one of the seven Latin-American states "moving decidedly toward stabilization in accordance with the Fascist principles of Signor Mussolini."[2] * At Buenos Aires, the Socialist Deputy Enrique Dickmann rose in the chamber of deputies in 1938 to declare with alarm that "Latin America's interest in the Spanish civil war has given the Italian and German governments the opportunity to intensify [dissemination in the Western Hemisphere of] the totalitarian philosophies and policies which both are following. As a result of this very powerful propaganda, the names of Hitler and Mussolini receive more publicity in our papers than those of Justo, Alessandri, Benavides,† and Roosevelt."[3] Argentine sympathetic preoccupation with the doctrines and politics of the Axis, fanned during the Uriburu-Justo era, was discouraged by President Roberto M. Ortiz (1938–40), but stimulated anew by his successor in the *Casa Rosada*, President Ramón S. Castillo (1940–43).

When the Perón group came to power to establish a military dictatorship in 1943, Argentine concern with Axis doctrines, politics, and methods was notably intensified. Not only was the "new Argentina's" attitude toward World War II much more openly pro-Axis, but domestic measures likewise bore a rapidly mounting resemblance to those of Hitler's Germany and Mussolini's Italy. Four months after the revolution of 1943, Ray Josephs wrote from Buenos Aires that Argentina "gets more and more

* The other six: Brazil, Bolivia, Peru, Venezuela, Paraguay, and Uruguay.

† Arturo Alessandri was the president of Chile from 1920 to 1924, and from 1932 to 1938; General Oscar Benavides was the Peruvian chief executive from 1933 to 1939.

like Nazi Germany every day."[4] Sumner Welles, formerly the United States Undersecretary of State, called Perón "a fanatical Fascist";[5] and, in December of 1944, with the war still in progress, it was reported that the Argentine government, then nominally headed by General Fárrell, had entered into an agreement with Nazi Germany and Franco Spain for the transplantation of "Nazi-Fascist" ideology to the Western Hemisphere. "Mussolini was the greatest man of our century, but he committed certain disastrous errors," Perón declared. "I, who have the advantage of his precedent before me, shall follow in his footsteps but also avoid his mistakes."[6] Responding to widespread assertions that his ideas and methods bore a strong resemblance to Hitler's, Perón late in 1944 made this intriguing statement: "Some say that what I am doing follows the policy of naziism. All I can say is this: if the Nazis did this, they had the right idea."[7] This position alarmed many "North Americans": a wartime editorial assertion by the *Washington Post*—Argentina's government "stands for the opposite of everything that we are fighting for"[8]—was representative of the climate of opinion in the United States.

Moreover, the wartime leaders of the "North American" government were outspoken in their denunciation of the ideological position of the Perón group. On September 8, 1944, Cordell Hull, the United States Secretary of State, declared flatly that Argentina was fascism's headquarters in the Western Hemisphere. President Franklin D. Roosevelt observed that the "new Argentina" presented "the extraordinary paradox of the growth of Nazi-Fascist influence and the increasing application of Nazi-Fascist methods in a country of this hemisphere at the very time that these forces of aggression and oppression are drawing ever closer to the hour of final defeat and judgment in Europe and elsewhere in the world."[9] And Spruille Braden returned to Washington from his post as United States Ambassador at Buenos Aires to speak of the Argentine government as a regime "which in common honesty no one could call anything but Fascist, and typically Fascist."[10]

In April of 1945, the United States and other nations in the war against the Axis faced the problem of whether or not the "new Argentina" should be admitted to the United Nations organization, designed to preserve peace after World War II. Many "North Americans" opposed Argentine entry into the international organization. United States Representative John F. Coffee (Democrat, Washington), said that "we dare not let them into the society of free peoples, they are still Fascists";[11] and Representative Vito Marcantonio (American Labor party, New York) said eloquently, "keep the bums out."[12] But the "bums" were admitted to the United Nations,* and Perón soon found himself in an embarrassing situation with respect to the ideology and the methods of the "new Argentina." Hitler and the Axis had collapsed by mid-1945; Argentina had become a member of a world organization predicated on anti-naziism and anti-fascism; and Perón saw the necessity of dissociating his system from disgraced and fallen Axis symbols.

By the end of 1945, "naziism" and "fascism" had officially become naughty words in the "new Argentina," which felt a desperate need for a new name for an old system. The new word, *Justicialismo*, was not found until 1949; the preceding four years were spent in an endeavor to separate Peronism from the defunct Axis and to argue that Peronism was so thoroughly and distinctively Argentine that nothing like it could ever have existed in any other country on earth. "There cannot be one universal political doctrine, because conditions in the countries of the world are not universal," Perón said in one of his more clever

* See pp. 16 and 407–9.

speeches. "The doctrine which we preach in Argentina would probably be utterly unsuitable in Italy, or Germany, or Russia."[13] According to the statements made by the officials of the "new Argentina" between 1945 and 1949, Peronism was something new and something different. It was not naziism. It was not fascism. It was not communism. But obviously, talking about what Peronism was *not* had its limitations. Peronism needed to be positive. It had to be *something*.

What was it? It was *Justicialismo*, or the "Third Position." The first recorded use of the word *Justicialismo* was made by Perón in April of 1949. The occasion was memorable. A Congress of Philosophy, sponsored by the University of Cuyo, met at Mendoza. Some two hundred philosophers representing nineteen countries attended the affair. That in itself was not remarkable. What was remarkable was that one of the philosophers was President Perón himself! He presented a curious paper on a new philosophy which had been brewed at the *Casa Rosada*. His speech revealed him to be more familiar with nineteenth-century German philosophy than many observers had previously thought Perón to be. He talked facilely of the ideas of two Germans in particular—Georg Wilhelm Friedrich Hegel, and Karl Marx. Perón was critical of both. He said that Hegel's worship of the concept of the state was intellectually sterile, and that Marxism led to the "insectification of the individual."[14] Perón would accept neither equipping human beings with six legs nor "immoral individualism."[15] If extreme collectivism was wrong, so was extreme individualism. What was needed was something between the two, a "Third Position." The "Third Position" was *Justicialismo*. "What we have to search for," declared the philosopher Perón, "is the well-proportioned man."[16]

Justicialismo as an idea was not very well developed

when President Perón first spoke about it in April of 1949. Since then, however, *Peronista* thinkers and propagandists have devoted some energy to an attempt to fashion *Justicialismo* into something which might achieve the status of a political theory. By the end of 1951, three books on the subject had appeared—*El Justicialismo*, by Raúl A. Mende, who was minister of technical affairs in President Perón's cabinet; Julio Claudio Otero's *Ensayo sobre Doctrina Justicialista;* and Luis C. A. Serrao's *Justicialismo.* They endeavored to make systematic statements of *Justicialismo* as a political and social philosophy, and to divorce Perón's system from the ideological relationships it had maintained with naziism and fascism during World War II. In 1951, President Perón declared himself pleased with the progress made in the development of what he called justicialist thought. "I believe that a new political force has been born in the country," he said, "with a new orientation, a new doctrine, and new virtues."[17]

In 1950 and 1951, when the present writer was in Argentina, it was fashionable among anti-*Peronistas* to say that nobody knew what *Justicialismo* was. Most of Perón's opponents refused to regard it as a serious sortie into the realm of political philosophy. What is *Justicialismo?* Hear some anti-*Peronista* answers: "I am a very busy man. Do not disturb me with such nonsense." Or: "*Justicialismo* is that doctrine before, during, and after which nothing happens." Nevertheless, *Peronistas* have attempted seriously to create a justicialist doctrine, and that attempt deserves a hearing.

As cultivated since 1949, justicialist thought has acquired a curious inheritance from the ideas of Hegel and Marx. As the two nineteenth-century Germans had developed dialectical approaches, so *Justicialismo* has its dialectic. As the Hegelian and Marxist systems were theories of conflict, so there is a justicialist conflict theory. Hegel and Marx, it will be remembered, held that society was given life and meaning by the fact that forces were in conflict within it. The more abstract Hegel called his opposed forces within society "thesis" and "antithesis"; Marx called them "classes." And the dialectics held that society moved or progressed only through continuing conflict between the opposed forces. Hegel and Marx believed that there were only two societal forces in conflict—Hegel gave both his forces abstract names; Marx called one of his classes "capital" and the other "labor."

While many points of difference existed between Hegelian and Marxist thought, the two were in agreement on the basic proposition that there were *only two* opposed forces involved in the struggle within the social organism, and that this conflict was resolved by the achievement of a species of "Third Position" between the struggling elements. Thus Hegel believed that the "Third Position" between his opposed "thesis" and "antithesis" was a "synthesis" (his perfect "synthesis" was called the "State"); whereas Marx held that "socialism" was the "Third Position" between the mutually hostile forces of "capital" and "labor." On the other hand, *Justicialismo* maintains that there are not two but rather *four* basically conflicting forces in society. These are "idealism," "materialism," "individualism," and "collectivism." Two propositions are central to the justicialist interpretation of the four forces. In the first place, each of them has a necessary and desirable role to play in society. Secondly, a constant conflict rages among the four.

According to *Justicialismo*, what is the proper societal role of each of the four elements?

First, *idealism* is legitimate in so far as it leads man to his destiny, "the complete possession of happiness, which is God."[18] It is true that much idealism may be found in *Pe-*

ronista pronouncements. President Perón has said that "I have always believed that every human action, to be noble, must be based on an ideal";[19] and that his "doctrine is a doctrine of moral purity. . . . If it were an evil doctrine, I should be the first to oppose it, but being, as it is, nothing but good, we should aim at making it known everywhere and teaching it to every man and woman."[20] The late Eva Perón, too, spoke at some length of the position of idealism in *Justicialismo*. "Humanity is living through tremendous days," she said. "A cold materialism ridicules gentleness; a solemn hostility attempts to separate men from the human simplicity that gives hearts warmth and feeling. Mixed ambitions have made man forget . . . the humble things which surround us, and man, who needs to love, has been converted into an indifferent being."[21]

Second, *materialism* is necessary and proper in society to the extent that it provides man with the earthly necessities for the attainment of the goals of idealism. As one *Peronista* philosopher has put it, "man comes before the machine; the [Perón] revolution is not so much interested in the conservation and expansion of material wealth as such, but more in the preservation and perfection of the present and future human factor; in this sense the revolution is profoundly humanist and, as Perón himself has said in one of his speeches, involves a 'rise in the standard of living to a level compatible with the dignity of man and his general economic betterment, freeing man from economic slavery.' "[22]

In the third place, *individualism* is legitimate in so far as it permits man to attain happiness through knowledge of himself as distinct from other people. In the justicialist view, "the individual is the first and most important element in society";[23] indeed, "that the individual should meekly accept his elimination as a sacrifice for the sake of the community, does not redound to the credit of the latter."[24]

On the other hand, man, being a political animal, has need of society or the community, which is represented in *Justicialismo* by the fourth force, *collectivism*. This justicialist element aids man to achieve happiness in so far as he has need of the community or the collectivity. And the legitimate function of collectivism, in *Justicialismo*, is to preserve the community for the service of all men. "Man does not possess anything which belongs to the human community,"[25] a justicialist writer has said; and "when private interests are incompatible—or collide—with those of the community, then the authority of the state is applied to intervene directly."[26]

Thus, each of the four forces is held to have a legitimate and proper role in human affairs. But, like the Hegelian and Marxist systems, *Justicialismo* is a theory of conflict. In justicialist dialectic, the four elements are continually in combat with each other, and mutual hostility is the theoretically natural and necessary relationship among them. Idealism is always at war with materialism, and individualism is never at peace with collectivism. From this theory of conflict emerges the justicialist notion of evil and of tyranny. Injustice, evil, and tyranny arise whenever any of the four elements is subdued and not permitted to exercise its proper and legitimate role in society. In justicialist theory, this unfortunate circumstance may occur in either of two types of situations: one of the four forces may triumph over the other three, destroying them; or any two of the four may ally against the other two and demolish them. In either circumstance, according to *Justicialismo*, the result is evil and fraught with injustice and tyranny.

Consider the forms of tyranny. Suppose idealism were to destroy materialism, individualism, and collectivism. This is probably easier for the Latin American than the "North American" to imagine, for the Roman Catholic Church occupies a peculiar place in the Hispanic-American states. Clerical dictatorships have indeed arisen in the Western Hemisphere. South Americans need look no farther afield for their illustrations than to Ecuador, where the fabulous Gabriel García Moreno presided over a theocratic regime from 1859 to 1875. In this dictatorship, man was a citizen only in so far as he was a practicing Roman Catholic; individualism, materialism, and collectivism were smothered; and the name of the country was changed to the "Republic of the Sacred Heart." In the end, however, even idealism disintegrated, the tyrant García Moreno fell at the hands of an assassin, and man became demoralized and "tired of God."[27]

In the justicialist view, tyranny is no more tolerable if it results from a victory of materialism over the other elements. Materialism—property, the machine, the instruments of the "foreign imperialists"—can, according to *Justicialismo*, be as terrible a tyrant as any of the other forces. "One fine day, wise men, technicians, and teachers created the machine," said one justicialist writer, giving voice to a somewhat typically Latin-American antipathy for gadgets invented by foreigners. "The machine became a substitute for man. The machine was the instrument which permitted the organization of great commercial and industrial companies."[28] These, in turn, deified property, another form of triumphant materialism at its worst. "*Justicialismo* affirms—in the 'Third Position'—that property cannot be an absolute right of anybody, and that it is necessary to abolish, not the right to private property, but the abuses of that right when improperly used."[29]

So much for the tyrannical aspects of idealism and materialism. Individualism triumphant over the other forces can also bring despotism and injustice. In justicialist thought, anarchy is the rise of extreme individualism at the

286

expense of the other three forces. *Peronistas* have little desire for individualism they regard as extreme. President Perón has said that "we must do away with the individualistic mentality."[30] The reader need not be reminded at this point that individual liberty—a form of "extreme individualism," according to *Justicialismo*—has little place in the "new Argentina," and that the Constitution of 1949 stipulates, in approved justicialist fashion, that "the state does not recognize the liberty to undermine liberty."[31] As interpreted by President Perón, this provision means that "individual freedom cannot signify an unlimited right, not only because this right must be in harmony with all other rights, but because at no time must it be turned into a weapon to be used against the essence of freedom itself. Only the protection of an irresponsible, uncontrolled liberalism has made possible the successful propaganda of despotic regimes which have ended by implanting in a democratic type of nation systems of rightist or leftist tyranny."[32] Political individualism is bad enough to the *Peronista;* also intolerable is economic individualism. In justicialist terms, this involves "the resolve of the individualist to defend at all costs what he considers his inalienable right to make or sell whatever he likes, when and how he likes, and to engage in whatever business or industry he might think proper."[33] According to Perón, "individualism of this kind leads to a society of inhuman egoists who think only of getting rich, although to do so it may be necessary to reduce millions of their less fortunate brothers to a state of starvation, poverty, and desperation."[34]

Collectivism triumphant over the other forces is likewise tyrannical in *Justicialismo*. This is a point which the *Peronista* would probably have less difficulty in explaining to the "North American" than in elucidating on other aspects of the doctrine of Peronism. Spokesmen for the "new Argentina" say that they reject Hegel and Marx because both constructed systems providing for extremes of collectivism. "According to Hegel the individual is submitted to a historical destiny through the state, to which he belongs," Perón has pointed out. "The Marxists, for their part, would convert the individuals into beings all of the same pattern, with no landscapes or blue sky, part of a tyrannized community behind an iron curtain. What is very evident in both cases is the annihilation of man as such."[35] And *Justicialismo* eschews traffic with this class of annihilation.

Thus, one type of tryanny results from domination and destruction of three of the forces by any one of them. *Justicialismo* holds, further, that there is a second form of tyranny. This occurs when any two of the forces form an alliance against the other two, and are able to destroy them. What masks does this class of tyranny wear?

Suppose that idealism and collectivism were to unite against materialism and individualism, achieving their destruction. This is the current justicialist definition of naziism and fascism, which Perón since 1945 has said are evil. His postwar condemnation of naziism and fascism—he calls them "collectivist idealism"—stems ostensibly from his sudden realization that they are similar to communism. In the view of the manufacturers of *Justicialismo*, naziism, fascism, and communism are alike in that all three are collectivist: "the only difference is that naziism and fascism have an idealistic concept of the state."[36] But, since 1945, that difference has not been enough to save them. Since the end of World War II, fascism and naziism have been bad. Perón has said so.

Again, consider an alliance of materialism and collectivism, resulting in the elimination of idealism and individualism. This is Perón's definition of communism. Justicialist writers have no love for it. In communism, they say, "man has arrived at the lowest point in his history. This will be his most bitter hour."[37] *Peronistas* who know their doctrine say that they can imagine nothing worse than the destruction of idealism and individualism.

But what of a combination of materialism with individualism, to the exclusion of idealism and collectivism? This, according to Perón, is capitalism. And he does not like it. Capitalism, regarded within the justicialist framework as shorn of idealism and collectivism, is viewed by *Peronistas* as the "abuse of property." Perón calls capitalism "dehumanized capital." And "North Americans" may do well to note that Perón is a sworn enemy of capitalism as he understands it. Occasionally, when the United States is plunged into crisis, some "North Americans" complain that they had no forewarning of where the danger lay. They may do well to consider themselves forewarned by *Justicialismo*. *Peronistas* have asserted that "capitalism must be the enemy of this [that is, the Perón] revolution,"[38] and that *Justicialismo* "intends to abolish capitalism."[39] Hear President Perón himself: "We think that if we are against capitalism we cannot preserve anything that is capitalist."[40] He has said that "the political, social, and economic middleman must be eliminated,"[41] and that he "will not allow despotic capitalism to prevail in Argentina."[42] Time was when Hitler and Mussolini told "North Americans" that their system was decadent. According to Perón, that system is decadent again. "Capitalism, glorious perhaps in the eighteenth century in its constructive stage, is arriving at its final stage," he has said. "New forms—as has been the custom of humanity throughout the ages—struggle and contend in the world to replace capitalism in its final stage."[43]

Thus the high priests of *Justicialismo* have identified seven brands of tyranny. Four of them arise from the triumph of any one of the basic forces over the other three, whether the resultant evil be theocracy, all-inclusive materialism, anarchy, or complete collectivism. And three brands of tyranny spring from a victorious alliance of two of the elements to the exclusion of the other two, whether the product of the combination be fascism, communism, or capitalism.*

Can these tyrannies be avoided? *Peronistas* claim they have found a formula. Each of the seven tyrannies, it is argued, is a form of extremism, and what is needed is an arrangement which prevents extremism. This arrangement, says Perón, is *Justicialismo* or the "Third Position." Perhaps only a college professor would bother to point out that the "Third Position" is theoretically not "third," but rather eighth, in the sense that it is an alternative to the seven tyrannies. But—the dubious mathematics of *Justicialismo* aside for the moment—what is the "Third Position"?

It is an arrangement which guarantees each of the four basic forces the opportunity to exercise its proper role in society, neutralizes the conflict among the four, and prevents any one—or two—of them from dominating the others. In a sense, *Justicialismo* or the "Third Position" is the "new Argentina's" version of Aristotle's "Golden Mean," in so far as that concept sought the avoidance of extremes. The *Peronista* who knows his doctrine defines it thus: *Justicialismo* is "that doctrine whose objective is the happiness of man in human society achieved through the harmony of materialistic, idealistic, individualistic, and collectivistic forces, each valued in a Christian way."[44] Or thus: "It would be a concordant and balanced combination of the forces that represent the modern state, designed to avoid strife and the annihilation of one of these forces; en-

* Justicialist thinkers have said nothing about a combination of individualism with idealism. An alliance of materialism with idealism, or of collectivism with individualism, is held to be impossible in the nature of the system.

deavoring to conciliate them, to unite them, and to put them in parallel motion to be able to form . . . a common destiny with benefit for the . . . forces and without injury to any one of them."[45] *Justicialismo*, then, envisages a temperate social order compounded of "just the right amounts" of idealism, materialism, individualism, and collectivism.

How much of each is "just the right amount"? Or, to put the question another way, *where* is the "Third Position"? If *Justicialismo* were to be charted on a four-cornered diagram, with each of the corners representing one of the four basic forces, would the "Third Position" lie in the center of the diagram? According to Perón, the answer to that question is "no." He has said that "the 'Third Position' is not in any way a position of neutrality."[46] How, then, can it be located? Each of the four forces must be assigned a value. In so far as justicialist writing has attempted to do this, the general tendency of *Peronistas* is to value idealism and individualism more highly than materialism and collectivism. It will be remembered that the four forces are assumed to be in continual conflict. The "Third Position," then, locates at the point of equilibrium among the four. Since idealism and individualism are assumed to be of greater value, that is, to have greater force, than the other two elements, the "Third Position" or point of equilibrium lies closer to idealism and individualism than to materialism and collectivism. As Raúl A. Mende, Perón's minister of technical affairs, has put it:

The equilibrium is arrived at when each force expends its maximum possible energy against the maximum possible energy of its opponent.
These maximum energies logically must maintain their proportional relationships to each other.
If Force A equals 1,000 and Force B equals 100, the point of equilibrium will be C; but this point will be closer to A in the proportion of 1,000 to 100. . . .

> To give to each force . . . the possibility of its maximum expression compatible with the maximum expression of its opponent . . . is *to establish justice, to give each force its rightful place* . . . in proportion to its value.[47]

One further point: equilibrium is held to be the soul of *Justicialismo*. The "Third Position" is fluid and dynamic rather than static. "We are not sectarians, Peronism is not sectarian," President Perón has asserted. "Some say, in grave error, that it is a centrist party. A centrist party, like a rightist or leftist party, is sectarian, and we are totally anti-sectarian. For us there is nothing fixed and nothing to deny. . . . We are anti-Communists because Communists are sectarians, and anti-capitalists because capitalists are also sectarians. Our 'Third Position' is not a centrist position. It is an ideological position which is in the center, on the right, or on the left according to specific circumstances."[48]

As employed by the "new Argentina," *Justicialismo* is called upon to justify *Peronista* policies operating on three levels. First, in the area of foreign policy, *Justicialismo* is the announced *rationale* of Argentina's "Third Position" between the United States and the Soviet Union. This matter will be explored more fully in a later chapter of this book. It might be noted at this point, however, that the "Third Position," being anti-Communist and also anti-capitalist, provides the ideological context within which Perón explains his anti-Soviet and also anti-"Yankee" foreign policy. Second, the "Third Position" is the official justification for the *Peronistas'* domestic economic policies.* Peronism maintains a domestic "Third Position" between the rich and the poor. The regime says it is opposed to the "Oligarchy" and is the champion of the economically underprivileged, but neither of these groups has lost or profited in spectacular economic terms in the "new Argentina."

* In his *Argentina's Third Position and Other Systems Compared*, Leonard T. Richmond treats *Justicialismo* only as an economic system.

In effect, *Justicialismo* says in economic matters what Mr. Dooley once said of the "North American" President Theodore Roosevelt's anti-trust program: "On the one hand, bust the trusts; on the other hand, not so fast." Third, *Justicialismo* provides the ideational context for Perón's domestic political actions. Individual liberties are curtailed; federalism is reduced; political parties are restricted. But none of these, argues the "Third Position," is completely destroyed. All are saved from "extremism."

In the "new Argentina," justicialist doctrine comes completely equipped with a group of slogans which serve as battle cries or symbols behind which *Peronistas* rally. Consider some of the slogans of Peronism: "Dignification of Labor," "Elevation of social culture," "Humanization of Capital," "Faith in God," "Solidarity among Argentines." Many of these acquire their especial significance from the ideological framework of *Justicialismo.*

President Perón has declared himself to be very proud of the "Third Position," the "new Argentina's" contribution to the world of political philosophy. "When I think that we have been the first to announce this solution to men, and when I demonstrate that we have been the first to realize it, I can do no less than affirm my faith in the high destiny which God has seen fit to assign to our country," he told the congress in May of 1950. "My soul is filled with emotion when I think that the day cannot be far off when all of humanity, seeking some star in the night, will fix its eyes on the flag of the Argentines."[49]

Justicialismo *and Practical Politics*

In the sense that *Justicialismo* is whatever Perón does, it is an ingenious ideological device. Perón gives and Perón takes away, and the "Third Position" likewise does both. The reader has seen that *Peronista* policies are turned on and off, as situations may appear to demand; and *Justicia-lismo* is a doctrine of "now you see it, now you don't," a philosophy of turning things on and turning them off. Perón is primarily a successful political opportunist, and the "Third Position" is a theory of opportunism.

Justicialismo is a doctrine of the balancing of forces; in essence, the Perón regime is in itself a balancing of forces. Many people who do not know anything else about politics know that it makes strange bedfellows. Perón, like anybody else in power, finds that his regime depends for its existence on composing hostilities among various groups, and the "Third Position" is his method of persuading them to sleep with each other. The interplay of forces that brought Perón to power in the first place and the dynamic exigencies of Argentine politics are themselves an equilibrium. Perón realizes that if he is to retain power, he must preserve a peaceful working relationship, a balance, among the competing forces which make political Argentina what it is.

What is *Justicialismo?* It is more than a dubious political theory; it is a system of practical politics. *Justicialismo* is a juggler's act, a huge vaudeville performance. Perón is the clown, and Argentine special interest groups are the balls he juggles. The clown has seven balls. They are called the "army," the "Church," the "Oligarchy," the "foreign imperialist," "labor," the "interior," and the "*porteños.*" *Justicialismo* is a juggler's act: the performer must keep all seven balls in motion, and he must remain equidistant from all of them. It is, in a sense, a tragic performance if the observer harbors sympathy for the clown. The juggler must preserve his "Third Position": he dare not catch one of the balls and call it his own, for the others will fall on his head and destroy him. This is not a performance that can be terminated successfully, for it is a species of marathon. The clown cannot catch all of the balls and accept ovations for a game well played. There is only one way the performance can end: at least one of the seven balls will fall on the juggler's head. Yes, *Justicialismo* is a vaudeville performance. It is not true that *Justicialismo* is "that doctrine before, during, and after which nothing happens." Rather, it is that performance before which the seven balls had a systemized relationship to each other, during which they are kept in dizzy motion, and after which at least one of them falls on the clown. The act can end in no other way.

Justicialismo says that there are seven tyrannies. This is true. For the juggler has seven balls, and at least one of them will kill him.

Perón gives and Perón takes away. Peronism is fluid and dynamic. The justicialist technique in politics means that the regime makes a studied and systematic practice of avoiding prolonged political honeymoons with specific interest groups. The juggler's seven balls are the interest groups, and Perón cannot perform unless all of them are kept in motion. There is much talk of the army, the Church, the "Oligarchy," the "foreign imperialist," labor, the "interior," and the *porteños*. Perón needs all of them. But none of them really belongs to him, for his is of necessity a "Third Position."

Consider the interest groups. The army will probably fall on Perón's head one day, but the "new Argentina" is the army's Argentina. The military is a major bulwark of the regime, but the army is in a constant state of potential rebellion. Some of its officers hated "Evita," and some hate the workers, the *descamisados*. In truth, the army and organized labor have little in common except the accident of the revolution. Perón dare not say his regime is the army's regime, for the other interest groups will rise against him;

he dare not cling too long or too stubbornly to the others, for the army will destroy him. His is a "Third Position"; he can take no other.

Or perhaps it will be the Church that will destroy Perón. He needs the Church, but the government does not—can not—belong to the clergy. Here, too, it is necessary to juggle. Again, consider the "Oligarchy." Perón needs the landowners and the capitalists, he cannot destroy them. Without the "Oligarchy" there is no "new Argentina," just as there was no old Argentina without the "Oligarchy." He dare not throw the "Oligarchy" away, yet he cannot call it his own. And what of the "foreign imperialist"? Let the Yankee explain it himself: "Where else can you get 12 per cent on your money?"* Where is the "Third Position"? It is somewhere between more than 12 per cent ("extreme materialism") and no percentage at all ("extreme idealism"). "On the one hand, bust the trusts; on the other hand, not so fast." Mr. Dooley might well have been an Argentine.

And the workers, the *descamisados?* The juggler needs them, but they do not belong to him. And perhaps, as many Argentines predict, it may be labor that eventually destroys Perón. If it is indeed the seventh tyranny, communism ("materialistic collectivism") that terminates the performance, it will have been Perón who brought it. After all, no matter which one of the seven balls is dropped, it is the same juggler. And what of the *provincianos* and the *porteños?* They of the "interior" claim that Perón belongs to Buenos Aires; the *porteños* say, partly because Rosas represented the provinces of the "interior," that Perón reminds them of "Bloody Rosas."

Thus the seven balls. At least one will fall with lethal effect.

* See p. 256.

An intriguing question remains. Perón has said—and so it is the truth from headquarters—that *Justicialismo* envisages a temperate social order compounded of "just the right amounts" of idealism, materialism, individualism, and collectivism. How much of each is "just the right amount"? Beyond assigning greater values to idealism and to individualism than to the other two forces, *Perón does not say how much of each ingredient is the proper amount.* There is no objective standard for this; there is no quantitative formula, no mathematics, in *Justicialismo.* The "Third Position" is whatever Perón says it is; *Justicialismo* is whatever he does; and he is a juggler. Justicialist theory is, basically, a philosophy of opportunism.

Fundamentally, the process is simple. Any amount of any of the four forces great enough to overthrow Perón is "too much"; any quantity which helps him to stay in power is "just the right amount." Mathematics would be dangerous.

And how to assess *Justicialismo* as a political philosophy? Will it really become, as Perón has said, a "star in the night" for all other peoples to follow? Hear two curiously illustrious philosophers who claim no special knowledge of Perón's Argentina:

> It becomes important to distinguish between ideologies as drives and ideologies as tools. If the ideology is a drive, it dominates the minds not only of the followers but also of the leaders; if it is a tool, the ideology has consciously been used by a leader in order to enlist greater obedience among his followers or to obtain new otherwise inaccessible recruits, but the leader does not himself believe in the ideology propagated by him, unless this happens unbeknownst to himself—having repeated the same words once too often, he finally believes in them.[50]

It is somewhat difficult to imagine that Perón believes in *Justicialismo.* Perón believes in Perón.

A final word from the two philosophers:

In former times the politicians used the ideologies that already existed. Nowadays it is possible to follow Voltaire's advice "to invent God if he did not exist": it is now possible . . . to construct ideologies synthetically.

The credit for this portentious invention must go to Adolf Hitler.[51]

It remains to give this credit where it is due.

On Justicialismo *and Fascism*

The need for *Justicialismo*, advertised as a peculiarly Argentine political doctrine, was in large part created by the destruction of the Axis in World War II. Until 1945, Perón's idealogical alliance with naziism and with fascism, with Hitler and with Mussolini, was generally assumed to be a fact. But the death of the Axis left Perón hanging from an uncomfortable limb, and a primary purpose of the "Third Position" is to rescue the "new Argentina" from its wartime associations. How effective is *Justicialismo* in divorcing Peronism from fascism? To what extent is the philosophical paraphernalia of the "Third Position" a new departure in the world of ideas, how well does it disguise the intellectual climate of fascism which had originally served the revolution of 1943?

In the first place, it should be noted that naziism and fascism never were synonymous, and that from the beginning Perón's system was more Fascist than Nazi. The Perón revolution lies in the philosophical wake of the Uriburu revolution of 1930, the international orientations of which lay more to Italy and to Spain than to Germany. Moreover—and many "North Americans" misunderstand this point—the "Spain" involved is not so much the Spain of Generalissimo Francisco Franco as it is the Spain of Primo de Rivera (1923–30). When General Uriburu forced his way into the *Casa Rosada* on September 6, 1930, and heightened Argentine interest in European ideas, the first to come—and the longest to remain—were those of Primo de Rivera and of Mussolini. Hitler and Franco entered later, it is true; but they did not take root as firmly in Argentina as the ideological systems at large by 1930. Although Primo de Rivera fell from power early in the Argentine drama, many of his aides and henchmen sought refuge in Argentina and exercised a significant influence on the "Yankees of the South." A case in point is José Figuerola. An adviser to Primo de Rivera on labor matters, Figuerola left Spain in 1930 to become an Argentine citizen and aid Perón in shaping much of the social content of the revolution of 1943. Figuerola, in favor at the *Casa Rosada* from 1943 to 1949, wrote many of Perón's early speeches, was credited with being the "mastermind" of the Five-Year Plan, and was the author of much of the "new Argentina's" labor program. And—though Primo de Rivera collapsed in 1930—Mussolini, of course, remained to dominate the philosophical content of a substantial part of what was absorbed by Argentines. In a significant sense, Italian fascism provided the inspiration for the Argentine intellectual line running from Uriburu to Perón.

World War II suspended Benito Mussolini by his heels in Italy. Has *Justicialismo* hanged him in the "new Argentina"?

Argentines sometimes like to say that there are two words which do not exist in their language. One of them is "yes" and the other is "no." *Justicialismo* retains fascism and it does not. Some aspects of the "Third Position" preserve much of Mussolini's thinking. Nationalism is an illustration. "I am Italian, desperately Italian," Mussolini once said. Perón is Argentine, but somewhat less desperate. In general there is a strong nationalism in *Justicialismo*, but it is certainly not so intense as the nationalism of fascism. Again, the "Third Position" and fascism hold in common a major emphasis on the doctrine of authority or leadership. The mass of the people do not govern themselves in either fascism or *Justicialismo*. "To guide the masses one must first instruct and educate them," Perón has declared. "We must speak to them of their obligations, because in our country there is much talk of rights and little of moral obligations. We must talk somewhat more about the obligations of each citizen toward his country and toward his fellow countrymen, and forget for a time their rights since we have mentioned them often enough."[52] The "Third Position" holds that each of the four forces must be held in check by a strong authority; and that authority—*not* the mass of the people—defines the "Third Position" or the point of equilibrium. The reader may note the striking similarity between Fascist doctrine and this justicialist pronouncement: "States survive public disasters not so much because their rulers know how to govern as because their citizens know how to obey. . . . Many well-intentioned governments have fallen because of anarchy among the people, and others have achieved glory and fame because of the obedience of the governed."[53]

Benito Mussolini and Juan Domingo Perón uttered essentially similar views with respect to individual liberty, which has as little place in the "new Argentina" as it had in Fascist Italy. Mussolini attacked what he called the "materialistic doctrine of freedom"; and the following comes from the literature of Italian fascism, although it is as much a part of *Justicialismo:* individual freedom is dangerous to society because "the liberty of one will inevitably clash with the liberty of others; constant strife would arise between individual and individual with consequent loss of force and waste of the productive faculties vouchsafed to us, faculties which we are bound to regard as sacred."[54] In asserting that "in truth, whether the individual exists or not, the difference is so absolutely imperceptible in the whole of things that every desire and every complaint is ridiculous,"[55] Italian fascism undoubtedly went further than *Justicialismo* does. But in general the Fascist and justicialist ideological systems share a common hostility to the proposition of the liberty of man as an individual.

Idealism occupies a major place in *Justicialismo*. This was likewise true of Mussolini's fascism. Hear *Il Duce*'s philosophers:

> Man is above, outside, and against nature. . . . The moment that we think of man as a being gifted with the gifts of the spirit, and. therefore, endowed with the power of creation, with the ability to transcend the contingencies of his material life, with the desire to rise above the determinism of outward events and inward needs, with the aspiration toward a life which is not of this earth but belongs to the magic world of his beliefs and his dreams; that moment marks also our entrance into the realm of Fascist Idealism. . . . Life is not actually what it is, but what it ought to be; a life altogether full of duties and difficulty, which always demands efforts of will and abnegation and hearts disposed to suffer to render possible the good; the only life worthy of being lived. An antimaterialist conviction, essentially religious.[56]

Thus, both Mussolini and Perón relied heavily on idealism, although Fascist idealism was more heavily weighted toward other-worldliness and self-abnegation than justicialist idealism.

And what of the rich and the poor, of economic problems seen through Fascist and justicialist eyes? "Nobody asks me for liberty," Mussolini once said; "everybody asks me for bread." It is one of Perón's favorite quotations. "In this century we cannot admit the inevitability of material poverty . . . ; the absurdity of famines which are artificially provoked cannot last," *Mussolini* asserted. "The Fascist century maintains . . . the equality of men before labor understood as a duty and as a right."[57]

From the standpoint of ideological content, then, there

are notable similarities between the thought of Mussolini and of Perón. The parallels between Fascist and justicialist ideas are to be found primarily in their approaches to such matters as nationalism, leadership and authority, the placing of the duties or obligations of man above his rights, the devaluation of individual liberty, the notion of idealism, and some aspects of economic relationships.

However, there are significant differences between Italian Fascism and *Justicialismo*. These are likewise worth exploring.

Consider, for example, the Fascist concept of the state. Mussolini, perhaps mesmerized by Hegel, tended to deify the state, and there is no justicialist parallel to this phase of fascism. Mussolini's view of the state is indeed awe-inspiring:

> The nation is an indestructible, eternal, and immortal unity, which like all ideas, institutions, and sentiments in the world, may be eclipsed for a time, but revives again in the depths of the soul, as the seed thrown in the soil bursts into flower with the coming of the warmth of spring. . . . The Fascist state, the highest and most potent form of the personality, is force, but spiritual. This spiritual force includes all the forms of the moral and intellectual life of man. It cannot therefore be limited to simple functions of order and supervision, as Liberalism proposed. It is not a simple mechanism which limits the sphere of presumed individual liberties. It is an interior form and norm, and disciplines the whole person; and penetrates the will no less than the intelligence. Its principle, the central inspiration of the human personality living in the civil community, descends into the deeps and makes its home in the heart of the man of action as of the thinker, of the artist as of the scientist: the very soul of the soul.[58]

This is far too strong a dose of statism for the "new Argentina." Perón is a nationalist, to be sure; but he does not ride with Mussolini and Hegel as far as the deification of the state. It should be remembered that Perón is God. For most *Peronistas*, one god per system is enough; and if they recognized a second deity, her name was "Evita." Peronism loves the state, but not nearly so much as Italian Fascism did.

A second point of divergence between fascism and *Justicialismo* lies in their approaches to the question of an elite. Mussolini held that the state should be governed by a select minority, a small ruling class. Hitler's anti-Semitism was in a sense a caricature of one phase of elitist doctrine, and it has already been observed that, in the early stages of the life of the "new Argentina," some attempt was made to include anti-Semitism in Peronism. However, this was dropped from the Argentine official system after 1945. Since then, it has been difficult to find an elite, a group of supermen, in the thought of Perón. Certainly, there is no elite in *Justicialismo*. Some Argentine military men may think of the army as an elite, and some of Perón's followers may regard the *Peronista* party as an elite, but no such doctrine has yet become a part of the official apparatus. At the time this book was written, the *Peronista* party announced the inauguration of schools designed to train *Peronistas* for "leadership."* Should this program indeed get under way— and should Perón remain in power long enough—an elite might presumably emerge from it. As of 1952, however, an elitist doctrine had not yet appeared as a part of the ideological apparatus of the "new Argentina."

Considered on the basis of policies and techniques—as distinguished from ideology—there is much in Perón's practices, of course, which resembles those of Hitler and Mussolini. Conscious attempts to imitate naziism and fascism were evident in the first months after the revolution of 1943. Earlier chapters of this book have dealt with policies of the "new Argentina"—the suppression of individual liberty, the "taming" of the school system, censorship of

* See pp. 342–43.

the press and other media of communication, and perversion of the constitutional system—which are strongly reminiscent of the techniques of Hitler and Franco, as well as of Mussolini and Primo de Rivera. Perón's *techniques* rather than his ideology serve as the basis for the name-calling frequently done by his opponents. Consider the charges made by anti-*Peronista* leaders in Argentina. Enrique Dickmann: "The government of the so-called revolution of June 4, 1943, was Nazi and still is."[59] Guillermo Korn: the Perón regime "is nothing else than the attempt to rebuild a neo-Fascist empire in the rear guard of the United Nations after Hitler's defeat."[60] Alfredo L. Palacios: "The revolution of 1943 was Nazi. Its leaders admired the Prussian Army and did not for one single instant believe in the defeat of Germany."[61]

On balance, then, there is much in the ideology and the techniques—more in the latter—of the "new Argentina" that resembles naziism and fascism. To disguise this resemblance was a major purpose of the invention of the ideology of *Justicialismo*. Many Argentines believe that the justicialist disguise has not been especially effective; indeed, one of them has remarked that "if the 'Third Position' is not an improved and disguised fascism, it resembles it."[62] However, much of Peronism differs from fascism. Felix Weil has put the matter thus: "*Criollo**'fascism' is homespun authoritarianism, not imported *Nationalsozialismus* or *Fascismo*. . . . Conditions in Argentina give the *criollo* variety of dictatorship its own native tinge. The main policies, however, quite resemble the Nazi pattern."[63] And hear a "North American" political observer:

I don't think you can pin standard labels on present-day Argentina. General Perón uses parts of the program of Mussolini, techniques of Hitler, . . . the vocabulary of Marx, and a legalistic

* Used in this context, *criollo* may be translated as "native Argentine."

framework of democracy. You can't call it conventional fascism. It's far less rigid than the Nazi, Italian Fascist or even Spanish Falangist brand. You can't call it communism or socialism. . . . You have to use the name its followers use. . . .[64]

Is *Justicialismo* fascism? It is said that there are two words that do not exist in the language of the Argentines—"yes" and "no." But *Justicialismo* was invented as a disguise for what was considered Fascist; and the answer runs closer to "yes" than to "no."

13.

The Quondam Faithful

President Juan Domingo Perón's regime draws its domestic strength primarily from the political orientation of the nation's armed forces, and from the administration's ability to maintain its control of organized labor. As a political coalition, this soldier-worker alliance is at best a curious and uneasy partnership. Beyond the peculiar circumstances of the revolution of 1943, there is little in the basic Argentine pattern making for a genuine community of interests uniting the military with the labor movement. In so far as the armed services and organized labor are able to achieve a politically united front, they are the strength of the Perón government; and the extent of the dissidence within these elements is a measure of its weakness.

Men with Uniforms

The armed forces of Argentina—particularly the army —constitute a fundamentally indispensable bulwark of the Perón regime. Established by a decree promulgated in May of 1825, the Argentine Army was created within the context of a program designed to offset the strength of regional *caudillos* during the chaotic interprovincial wars.* Never more than semi-effective in serving that objective, the army

* See pp. 22–25.

has tended, especially in recent years, to give a strongly militaristic flavor to domestic Argentine politics.

The country's armed services have participated in no international conflict since the tragic Paraguayan War (1865–70). Nevertheless, the army has since become a major factor in national life. Indeed, it has been said that "no modern Argentine president would stay in power one minute without at least the passive support of the army."[1] This has been a controlling principle in contemporary national politics, although it has been denied repeatedly by the country's recent rulers. General Fárrell, who was president of Argentina from 1944 to 1946, declared that "the armed institutions are not a political force";[2] and President Perón—himself an army general, be it remembered—has asserted that "the armed forces are the synthesis of the people. They do not belong . . . to determined parties or sectors. . . . They belong to the nation."[3] Despite such contentions, it remains true that militarism is a powerful political force in Argentine affairs.

Three factors have been of primary significance in the development of the peculiar role the army has played in Argentine politics during the past generation. These factors are the circumstance that German military missions have participated in the training of the Argentine Army; the Uriburu revolution of 1930; and the chronic tendency of Argentine military officers to form political clubs and cliques among themselves.

Shortly after World War I, the Argentine government contracted for the training of its army by a German military mission composed of six officers. This mission remained in Argentina for a quarter of a century. During much of that period, the German mission was under the leadership of General W. J. Kretchmar, who, upon his death, was replaced by Colonel General Niedenfuehr. It is worth noting that a quarter of a century is, by some standards, a long time: many of the Argentines who, as young cadets and junior officers, sat at the feet of Kretchmar and Niedenfuehr were colonels and generals in the Argentine Army by 1943.

And these colonels and generals were in key command positions in that army when the Perón revolution took place. What did the Argentine Army look like in June of 1943? Hear Ray Josephs: "This is a disciplined army and it is the discipline of the old Prussian school. It is a spit-and-polish army, a proud army. . . . The goose-step, the uniform, and, most of all, the heel-clicking Prussian dogma of implicit obedience were retained and are still the dominating force. This quarter of a century influence on the highly intelligent upper cadre of the Argentine Army is still very apparent."[4] It is true that many Argentines disapproved of this aping of German militarism in the generation between the two world wars. "It is easy, and morally valueless, to maintain discipline among soldiers," an opponent of the Prussianization of the Argentine Army once declared. "It is not for nothing that a uniform is put over a man, hiding his essence and his individuality. . . . Military parades are the quintessence of the religion of externality. Parachutists parade without parachutes, tanks incapable of traveling a score of kilometers without burning up . . ., expensive but useless aircraft, students who do not study, . . . and colonels and generals on horseback with resplendent spurs."[5] Whether the Argentines who scoffed at the German orientation of their army were more sensible than those who found glory in it is perhaps an academic question: the colonels and generals with resplendent spurs, and not the civilians who wondered where the parachutists' parachutes were, made the revolution of 1943. And they freely acknowledged their sympathy toward, and their debt to, their German teachers. Listen to one colonel of 1943 whose spurs were especially resplendent, by name Juan Domingo Perón: "In the War School and in the Military College I received valuable instruction from numerous German professors. I owe them perhaps a great part of the military education I have acquired during my life, and I have a profound gratitude toward them."[6]

German training is thus one key to the contemporary political role of the army in the "new Argentina." A second is the Uriburu revolution of 1930. That uprising brought two significant changes in the life of the military. In the first place, Uriburu's rebellion transformed militarism from a covert to an open and more active influence on Argentine politics. For some eighty years before 1930, the nation's government had been essentially civilian in orientation. After General Uriburu entered the *Casa Rosada*, however, the country's administrations became increasingly military in character. Since the revolution of 1930, Argentina has had eight presidents. Six of them have been army generals.* Secondly, the Uriburu uprising achieved a somewhat dramatic alliance of the army with the "Oligarchy." It will be remembered that the 1930 revolt overthrew President Irigoyen, a Radical whose party had come into power on a program of opposition to the landowners. The "Oligarchy" supported Uriburu in ousting the Radicals, and since 1930 the military has had two openly acknowledged allegiances of significance here. One of these has been to Germany. The other has been to the "Oligarchy," from which many of the high-ranking army officers were drawn. The Uriburu revolution encouraged the first of these allegiances and formalized the second, giving the Argentine

* The generals are Uriburu (1930–32), Justo (1932–38), Rawson (1943), Ramírez (1943–44), Fárrell (1944–46), and Perón, the two civilian presidents during the period were Ortiz (1938–40) and Castillo (1940–43).

Army the peculiar political complexion it brought to the
Perón rebellion of 1943.

It is against such a background that it was said in the early
days of the "new Argentina" that "the army has . . . been
conservative and . . . it has had plenty of German influence."[7] Consider the position of the army, oriented toward the "Oligarchy" and toward Germany, on the eve of
the revolution of 1943: "The army, educated and disciplined in the Prussian military school, was seduced by the
greatness and the glory of the 'invincible' German Army;
and, believing in the triumph of Nazi-fascism in the Second
World War as dogmatic truth, many Argentine military
leaders proposed to modify the people and the democratic
institutions of the republic."[8] Such a program has, of
course, been pushed forward in the "new Argentina."
Since 1943, the army has enjoyed a larger place in Argentine political life than at any other time in the eighty years
before the eviction of President Castillo from the *Casa
Rosada*.

In the years since the Perón revolution, the army's grip
on national government and politics has been progressively
tightened. An impressive percentage of the major officials
of the "new Argentina" have been military officers. All of
the presidents and three of the five vice presidents of the
country have been army officers. The "new Argentina"
began with only one civilian in the president's cabinet (it
was remarked that "Dr. Santamarina, lone civilian member
of the Ramírez cabinet, always looks lost among all those
uniforms"[9]); today President Perón maintains a cabinet of
which an average of half the ministers are military men.
Since 1943, 45 per cent of the Federal Interventors and
provincial governors have been army officers.

Along with this domination of government positions by
the army has gone increased emphasis on the military re-

flected in such programs as enlargement of the army, expanded military expenditures, and new army-oriented governmental policies. Composed in 1943 of 3,600 officers and about 40,000 non-commissioned soldiers, the total number of men in both categories had risen to about 105,000 at the time this book was written. Military expenditures, consuming as much as half the total national budget in 1945, have in later years settled to an annual average of a little more than 25 per cent of the government's total expenses.

In the "new Argentina," the military expenditures have been devoted to enlarging the size of the army, raising the salaries of its officers and men, purchasing new equipment, and stimulating what have been called "military manufactures." According to a recently published study, the salaries of Argentine Army officers in 1948 were generally higher than the wages of officers of corresponding rank in the United States Army. Moreover, purchases of new equipment had given the Argentine Army totals of 3,600 armored trucks, 1,000 armored railroad cars, 10,000 vehicles for transporting troops, and about 700 military aircraft. The 1943 expenditures on "military manufactures" had been multiplied by ten by the end of 1949, with President Perón declaring that the preservation of Argentine sovereignty depended on the orientation of much industrial production to military purposes. Atomic experiments, including those conducted by Dr. Ronald Richter, are worth citing as leading to potential "military expenditures." Time was when the statesmen of the other republics of the Americas were alarmed by the "new Argentina's" military program. Dr. Eduardo Santos, former (1938–42) president of Colombia, asserted late in 1944 that Perón had unleashed a "monstrous and unbridled armaments race, which constitutes the greatest threat to the future of the Americas."[10] The Argentine armament program has continued in subsequent years, but the leaders of the various American governments have not declared themselves to be very worried about it since the end of World War II.*

The fabric of Argentine militarism is sewn together in three places. Two of them—German training, and the revolution of 1930—have already been located. And the third is the long-standing practice of Argentine Army officers of forming political cliques and clubs among themselves.

The process of military clique-formation is the oldest and most thoroughly Argentine of the three keys to Perón's army. Military officers have long been accustomed to forming political clubs among themselves and—even before 1930—some of Argentina's most important politicians have been army officers whose political positions were geared to their military connections. Of course, no better illustration of an Argentine political club of army officers can be found than the now-famous G.O.U., Perón's own "colonels' clique" which made the revolution of 1943. But the G.O.U. was neither the first nor the last of the Argentine Army's political clubs. Deeply imbedded in the Argentine culture, these political organizations among the military—sometimes formal, sometimes informal—have long played a part of some consequence in the nation's history. One such club made it possible for General Urquiza to rise against "Bloody Rosas" in the 1850's; others contributed to the political instability of the 1890's;† and still another was led by General Uriburu in 1930. Indeed, Uriburu remarked that his "life began with one revolution [1890] and ended with another [1930]."[11] And in the "new Argentina," the army continues to be clique-ridden.

Political clubs in the army are essentially dynamic organi-

* See pp. 414–18.
† See p. 32.

zations, and their fortunes depend in part on the interpersonal relations among the members of the cliques. Perón's G.O.U.* provides an excellent case study in the dynamics of this phase of Argentine militarism. The revolution of 1943 was, above all else, a military coup, and it produced a "gray-cloaked, booted-and-spurred government."[12] The uprising was not launched by the entire Argentine Army, but rather by a clique within it, the G.O.U. It was observed of the 1943 rebellion that "only a handful of high-ranking generals and colonels knew what was up, and many went through [June 4's] momentous events without realizing what side they were on."[13]

The G.O.U. as a politico-military clique was formally dissolved on February 23, 1944. But, as the G.O.U. was not the first such clique, it has not been the last. Political clique-formation is an integral part of the native culture of the Argentine Army. And many of the post-G.O.U. military cliques have been anti-*Peronista* in orientation. The army, too, has its "Third Position." As the army is the major bulwark of the Perón regime, so it is a leading threat to the "new Argentina." As Avalos rose against Perón, so have other generals and colonels, and so they might be expected to do so again in the future.

Consider some of the patterns of military opposition to Perón. In the years since the revolution of 1943, opposition to the regime has been expressed within the army on at least five grounds. One military clique has protested against the abandonment of the Axis and against Argentina's association with the United Nations. Another has sought the resumption of constitutional government on the basis of the Constitution of 1853. A third, active from 1947 to

---

* The letters stand for either *Grupo de Oficiales Unidos* (United Officers' Group) or the clique's slogan, *¡Gobierno! ¡Orden! ¡Unidad!* (Government! Order! Unity!). See pp. 52–55.

1949, objected to Perón's endorsement of the economic policies of Miguel Miranda. Still others, identified with the "Oligarchy" and the "foreign imperialists," resent Perón's pro-labor measures. And a fifth line of dissension within the army stemmed from the strong objection of many officers to the late Eva Perón's role in the "new Argentina." All of these military cliques have given active expression to their respective grounds for opposition to Perón, and the record indicates that the army has been anything but thoroughly loyal to the god of the *Peronistas*.

Moreover, the navy is even more politically unreliable than the army. Long involved in a somewhat acrimonious service rivalry with the ground forces, many navy officers were especially bitter toward the G.O.U. in the early stages of the revolution. Acutely aware of the dangers to the regime inherent in continued navy opposition to the government, the rulers of the "new Argentina" went to considerable lengths in their attempt to win the navy over to the military regime. A favorite device of the G.O.U. designed to buy naval support in the early phases of the "new Argentina" was to confer governmental offices upon politically connected naval officers. Thus, Vice Admiral Sabá H. Sueyro was named vice president of the nation on June 9, 1943. However, he died in office a month later, at which time the G.O.U. abandoned the idea of using the vice presidency to woo the navy. The designation of Vice Admiral Segundo Storni as foreign minister in 1943 was designed to achieve two objectives. The G.O.U. hoped that Storni would not only bring much of the navy into harmony with the regime, but also that—since he had acquired a reputation as being pro-British—he would be able to allay international distrust of the "new Argentina's" foreign policy. Both purposes failed when Foreign Minister Storni addressed a fruitless request for Lend-Lease aid to the United States. When, in September of 1943, Secretary of State Cordell Hull flatly turned down the Argentine request, Storni was forced to resign from the Ramírez cabinet. A further bid for navy backing failed when Captain Ricardo Vago, named minister of public works on October 16, 1943, departed from that post only two months later.

The regime's greatest success in winning a part of the navy was achieved through the naval faction supporting Rear Admiral Alberto Teisaire. Making his peace with the G.O.U. early in the life of the "new Argentina," Teisaire was appointed minister of the navy in February of 1944. Admiral Teisaire remained a sufficiently strong partisan of the military regime to rise to high positions in the councils of the *Peronista* party. He not only presided over the convention which wrote Perón's Constitution of 1949,* but had also been a *Peronista* senator, even served as acting president when Perón temporarily stepped down from that post during the election campaign of 1951,† and has been one of the half-dozen most powerful officials of the *Peronista* party.‡

Although Admiral Teisaire's politics carries some weight with the navy, most of its politically important officers remain basically opposed to the "new Argentina." Naval officers have given the regime cause for serious concern ever since 1943. In August of 1945, a group of high-ranking navy men formally demanded that Perón not be allowed to run for the presidency and that the "sovereignty of the people"[14] be restored. Some weeks later, eight naval captains were imprisoned for refusing to pay their respects to Perón. In September, no fewer than fifty-one highly-placed navy officers signed a formal petition urging that Perón be kept from becoming president, that "constitu-

* See p. 76.
† See p. 85.
‡ See pp. 337–38.

tional normality" in accordance with the Constitution of
1853 be restored, and that the regime cease its attempts to
"deform the real, sovereign will of the people."[15] The seamen's opposition to Perón reached its most dramatic height
during the chaotic "October days" of 1945, when the faction led by Admiral Héctor Vernengo Lima joined forces
with the army group headed by General Avalos in the latter's now-famous coup against Perón.* During the week
in which it temporarily appeared that Avalos had been successful in destroying Perón politically, at least one hundred
and twenty navy and army officers presented President
Fárrell with a five-point ultimatum demanding that he (1)
call an election within ninety days, (2) dismiss all cabinet
members who held office while Perón was in power, (3)
terminate the state of siege, (4) force Perón to remain imprisoned, and (5) turn the reins of government over to the
Supreme Court of Justice. This high-spirited ultimatum
became academic after Perón was restored to power on
October 17, 1945. The extreme nature of the navy's dissidence was made startlingly clear later in the year, when
Interior Minister Bartolomé Descalzo was compelled to
admit publicly that, although the government desired to
appoint a naval officer as Federal Interventor for the Province of Buenos Aires, *there was not a single officer in the
entire Argentine Navy available for that position!*

Let it be remembered that the men in uniform constitute
the bulk of the *strength* of the Perón regime.

Men without Shirts

In so far as it is politically organized, the labor movement
is a second major bulwark of the "new Argentina." The
government has had some success in posing as a champion
of the poor against the rich, and the country's organized

* See pp. 58–62.

workers have provided much of the political activity in support of the regime. President Perón has frequently said that his is a "labor" government, and he has expressed a strong affection for the workers of Argentina, the people whom he calls the *descamisados*.

The term *"descamisado"* has acquired widespread currency as a political symbol of large significance in contemporary Argentina. Originally, the word meant "shirtless": a leading Spanish-English dictionary translates the adjectival form of *descamisado* as "shirtless, naked, ragged," and renders the noun form as "ragamuffin."[16] Traditionally, the term as used by Argentines has borne a strong connotation of contempt and disapproval. A *descamisado* was an untidily dressed hoodlum, a member of the lower classes who knew little of the more refined social usages and manners, a man who—as the "Oligarchy" put it—was "uncultured."

The *descamisado* became a *Peronista* political symbol during the chaotic "October days" of 1945. When Perón was restored to power on October 17, labor organizations backing him played a major part in that day's events. Many Argentines who opposed Perón regarded the workers who supported him as hoodlums and ragamuffins, and called them *descamisados* by way of epithet. Commenting on the hectic activity of October 17, an afternoon newspaper at Buenos Aires declared scornfully that "a handful of *descamisados* thronged through the streets of the city, cheering the dictatorship and creating a disturbance."[17] The Peróns—especially "Evita"—were quick to seize the epithet and turn it against their opposition. It was asserted that Perón defended the poor against the rich, that his was a government of the *descamisados* against the "Oligarchy," that the time had come for a transformation of the political position of the *descamisado*.

The late Eva Perón, perhaps more than anybody else,

presided over the symbol-manipulation involved in the transformation. "The *descamisado* has ceased to be a victim of human exploitation, and has been converted into a factor making for progress, for national unity, for collective well-being," she asserted. This conversion "responds to the politico-social imperatives which place a value on the role of the workers in modern society. . . . The word '*descamisado*' . . . has been transformed into a synonym for struggle, for revindication, for justice, for truth. It has created a state of national conscience. It has been implanted in the soul of the people, like a magic impulse, to carry them forward."[18]

What is a *descamisado?* Once upon a time he was a despised and contemptible ragamuffin or hoodlum, deserving of no man's respect. But Perón is rewriting the dictionary. Today the official definition of the *descamisados*—written into law in the "new Argentina"—says that they are the "modest intellectual and manual workers organized in defense of their political, social, and economic rights."[19] And this transformation represents a principal phase of Perón's bid for a true social revolution. In a sense, the *descamisado* is the political heir of the gaucho of the nineteenth century. Eva Perón herself once pointed out that the *descamisado* "appears upon the Argentine political scene as a reincarnation of the gaucho";[20] and in many ways the *descamisado* is to Perón's Argentina what the gaucho was to the Rosas regime.*

The story of the emergence of the *descamisado* is tied to the evolution of the Argentine labor movement. And the history of the latter is essentially the history of a mushroom. In a remarkably short period of time—hardly a century— the Argentine worker evolved from slavery to participation in rudimentary industrial trade-unions. This is a road which

* See pp. 23–28.

labor in other countries of the world required many centuries to travel. While many Argentines are proud of the speed with which their labor movement has developed, that very meteoric pace may well be a significant key to the fundamental political weakness of contemporary Argentine organized labor.

Argentina's "General Confederation of Labor" (C.G.T.*) was formed in 1930. The C.G.T. opposed the Uriburu regime, which had seized power in September of that year. Indeed, the labor organization was in chronic crisis throughout the entire period from 1930 to 1943. A portion of this crisis stemmed from the struggle within the C.G.T. between the so-called "right-wing" Socialists, on the one hand, and, on the other, Communists and other elements regarded as being to the left of the Socialists. On the eve of the Perón revolution, a semi-formal division between these two labor factions took place. In 1942, union members were forced to choose between two organizations, one called C.G.T. Number 1, and the other C.G.T. Number 2. C.G.T. Number 1, led by José Domenech and based primarily on the railroad unions, was the orthodox "right wing" following Socialist leadership. C.G.T. Number 2, headed by Francisco Pérez Leirós, was essentially Communist-dominated, although it did contain many dissident Socialists.

The C.G.T., containing a claimed 330,681 members, was thus divided when the Perón revolution was launched on June 4, 1943. The rulers of the "new Argentina" moved to capture the C.G.T. in a manner that was called "identical with that employed by Mussolini and Hitler in gaining control of the labor movement in Italy and Germany."[21] In Argentina, the process was begun with two dramatic steps taken on July 12, 1943. The first of these was a decree dissolving C.G.T. Number 2 on the ground that it was Com-

* After the initial letters of *Confederación General del Trabajo*.

munist-dominated and therefore subversive. The second was the proclamation of "intervention" in C.G.T. Number 1. The latter measure had the effect of removing Domenech and other labor leaders from their key positions in the C.G.T. and replacing them with agents of the "new Argentina." On August 24, two navy captains, Andrés Chelle and Andrés Puyol, were appointed, respectively, "interventors" in the Railroad Brotherhood (claiming 15,000 members) and the Railroad Union (90,000 members). Three months later, the two railway unions were merged by a decree which relieved Chelle and Puyol of their labor assignments and named Colonel Domingo A. Mercante to replace them as the "interventor" of the newly combined railroad union.

Meanwhile, on October 27, 1943, Colonel Perón had become the chief of the National Department of Labor, and appointed as his special labor advisor Barcelona-born José Figuerola, who had discharged a similar function in the Spanish dictatorship of Primo de Rivera.* In an administrative reorganization announced on November 27, the National Department of Labor was replaced by the secretariat of labor and welfare. This larger and more powerful agency, headed by Perón and Figuerola, became the "new Argentina's" principal arm for the domination of organized labor. The secretariat, Ray Josephs said at the time it was established, "looks as if it's going to be one of the most powerful of the regime's entities and the busy colonel's make-or-break steppingstone upward."[22] That prediction was substantially correct.

These developments were frantically resisted by the pre-1943 labor leaders, but they were powerless to deter the relentless march of the "new Argentina." Three months after the revolution, Domenech and other ousted union officials presented the regime with a pitifully futile petition

* See p. 299.

for the liberation of the C.G.T. from the military. This gesture touched off a large-scale roundup of pre-1943 union leaders, many of whom were sent to concentration camps. No fewer than 130 former C.G.T. officials were jailed in October of 1943, and a month later police used tear gas to break up a workers' demonstration which had demanded the release of union officers from prison. Strikes and demonstrations involving similar demands continued throughout the remainder of 1943 and the early half of the following year. These activities were conducted on such a scale by May of 1944 that Perón publicly warned the workers that participants in additional stoppages and demonstrations would be summarily sent to join their former leaders in concentration camps in Patagonia. The warning was only semi-effective. The employees of the oil refinery at La Plata, seeking the release of their union officials, went on strike in December. This prompted the promulgation in January of 1945 of a decree branding "illegal" strikes as "crimes against the security of the state." The decree was answered on January 30 by an "illegal" stoppage of some 50,000 packinghouse workers demanding the freedom of their leaders; and in the following months, railroad and port workers staged similar strikes. This "illegal" labor activity began to taper off in May of 1945, and the events of October indicated that the regime's capture of the C.G.T. was by that time well on its way to consolidation.

The spectacular restoration of Perón on October 17, 1945, demonstrated, among other things, that he had been much more successful in dominating the C.G.T. and in securing labor support than had until then been generally supposed. According to many pre-October estimates of the situation, Perón was unpopular among the workers. On July 23, for example, Gaudencia Peraza, who had studied the condition of Argentine labor for the international leftist

Confederation of Workers of Latin America (C.T.A.L.),*
reported that 70 per cent of organized labor was not only
opposed to Perón, but even affiliated with the underground.
This figure was consistent with what the situation was
generally supposed to be, but the demonstrations of October 17, in which the C.G.T. and the *descamisados* figured
prominently in saving Perón, left little doubt that his labor-
backing was made up of considerably more than 30 per cent
of the organized workers. "It is still a moot point how much
labor support he enjoys," the *New York Times* correspondent Arnaldo Cortesi wrote on October 21, "but it is clear
that whatever support he has, whether it is great or small,
comes from the working class and in general from elements
in it."[23] And Sumner Welles, the former United States
Under Secretary of State, wrote: "The masses of the Argentine people believe that they have in [Perón], as in Irigoyen, a champion of the workingman, and a leader who
can correct the economic and political injustices which have
so long persisted in the republic."[24]

In the years since "Loyalty Day" of 1945, Perón has, of
course, expanded his control of the C.G.T. That organization claimed a membership of 800,000, or about 60 per
cent of all Argentine workers, at the time this book was
written; and the Perón regime rests primarily on an alliance
of the C.G.T. with the army. Today the C.G.T. is administered by a five-man secretariat, all of the members of
which† are staunch *Peronistas*. Eva Perón once remarked
that "the Argentine labor movement . . . is a *Peronista*
movement. It cannot exist without the doctrine of General
Perón and the doctrine of General Perón cannot exist with-

---

* After the initial letters of *Confederación de Trabajadores de América
Latina.*
† Secretary General José G. Espejo, Assistant Secretary Antonio
Valerga, Administrative Secretary Isaias Santín, Treasurer Antonio
Eduardo Correa, and Assistant Treasurer Florencio Soto.

out the support of the workers of Argentina."[25] In its capicity as a political tool, the C.G.T. has rendered much political service to Perón. This service has included not only participating in his rescue in October of 1945 and indorsing his subsequent candidacy for the presidency, but also launching his campaign for re-election in 1951 and attempting to place Eva Perón in the vice presidency.

From October of 1945 to her death in 1952, "Evita" Perón developed a special relationship to the C.G.T. To the extent that the husband-and-wife regime was a partnership, and in the sense that the army and the C.G.T. were partners in Peronism, a significant division of labor emerged between Juan and Eva Perón. The army and the C.G.T. are twin pillars of the "new Argentina." President Perón's control of the army is perhaps stronger than his appeal to the *descamisados;* and today there is little doubt that "Evita's" strength in the C.G.T. and her popularity among the *descamisados* was far greater than any influence or power she might have exerted in the army. This is a matter of significance in so far as the soldier-worker alliance is an uneasy coalition of basically opposed forces. President Perón's political machine, probably stronger among the military than among the *descamisados,* operated in conjunction with the late "Evita's" personal machine, undoubtedly far more influential among the *descamisados* than in the army. Thus "Evita" was not to be underestimated in her role in the balancing of forces that support the Perón regime. Occasionally the exigencies of soldier-*descamisado* hostility brought Juan and "Evita" Perón's political machines in momentary conflict with each other. The regime's success depends in part in its ability to play the army and the C.G.T. off against each other. This process involves an equilibrium which is rationalized in terms of the "Third Position" of *Justicialismo.*

"Evita's" appeal to the C.G.T. and the *descamisados* was thus a matter of major moment. Probably nobody understood this more fully than did "Evita" herself. "I always say that I have three loves and these loves are sincere," she once asserted. "Until the last moment of my life, these three will always be in my heart: the nation, the *descamisados* who are the forces of labor, and Perón."[26] Time was when one could stand in the *Plaza de Mayo* and listen to Eva: "I am only one more *descamisada*,* the most insignificant of General Perón's collaborators."[27] And what was the primary function of "Evita's" Foundation? She explained it herself: "The Social Aid Foundation directs all of its activity toward the *descamisado*, not as charity, but rather as justice, justice well earned in view of the many years in which it had been denied. . . . I spend every hour of the day looking after the needs of the *descamisados*, to show them that here, in the Argentine republic . . . the gulf which had separated the people from the government no longer exists; that here we are all one, working night and day for the greatness of the country and for the happiness of its people."[28] These were not merely the words of the boss' wife. They were the words of a woman who was a political boss in her own right.

Although President Perón has insisted that the C.G.T. remains a free labor organization, he has not been successful in maintaining this fiction either inside or outside Argentina. Workers' groups in other countries have frequently branded the C.G.T. as a tool of the government and have repeatedly adopted resolutions asserting that labor was no longer free in Argentina. The leftist C.T.A.L. was among the first to take this position publicly shortly after the revolution of 1943. If the C.T.A.L.'s pronouncements be regarded as

---

* "Shirtless" women—occasionally a stimulating sight to see—are called *descamisadas*; "shirtless" men are *descamisados*.

suspect because of its own political orientation, other—and more moderate—labor entities have taken similar stands with reference to the C.G.T. In April of 1944, the International Labor Office (I.L.O.), at its Philadelphia meeting, refused, by a vote of fourteen to three, to seat Argentine delegates on the ground that labor in their country was not free. And the anti-leftist Inter-American Confederation of Labor, established after World War II to offset the C.T.A.L.'s political influence in the Western Hemisphere, fell in 1951 on the question of the C.G.T. When the majority of the delegates at the Inter-American Confederation of Labor's Mexico City meeting declined to admit the Argentines, the resultant squabble produced the dissolution of the entire confederation.*

The boycott of the C.G.T. by international labor has irked Perón, and he has frequently sought foreign acceptance of his *descamisados* as a respectable and free labor organization. The most spectacular instance—and most dramatic failure—of his attempt to win international recognition of the C.G.T. came in 1947. At that time, a delegation of the American Federation of Labor (A.F. of L.), which Perón had invited to Argentina to "study" the labor situation there, published its report. The A.F. of L. group disclosed that Perón had planned their "study" for them, and that, when the delegation of "North Americans" refused to conduct their investigations along the lines laid out for them at the *Casa Rosada*, the support of the Argentine government and of the C.G.T. was immediately withdrawn

---

* Later in 1951, the defunct Inter-American Confederation of Labor was replaced by a new Inter-American Regional Organization of Workers. This organization, while it embraced both the American Federation of Labor (A.F. of L.) and the Congress of Industrial Organizations (C.I.O.) of the United States, did not have affiliates in any of the three major states of Latin America. Not only was the C.G.T. excluded, but the Confederation of Mexican Workers (C.T.M.) and Brazilian labor declined to affiliate with the new entity.

from the project. The A.F. of L. group, attempting to conduct its study without Perón's "assistance," experienced considerable difficulty in Argentina; and members of the delegation were threatened with physical violence both at Mar del Plata and at Santa Rosa. Despite official obstruction and sabotage of their study, the "North Americans" remained in Argentina long enough to discover that in the post-1943 C.G.T. "only on rare occasions have union elections been permitted, and these have been under the control of an 'interventor.' If the results were unacceptable in any way to the government, they would be annulled by the 'interventor,' who would call a new election. In the case of the railroad union, there were three elections before a directive body acceptable to the government was obtained." The A.F. of L. delegation concluded that "it is not certain whether the apparent popularity of President Juan D. Perón is due to the satisfaction of the working masses or . . . to the various techniques of psychological intimidation or coercion to which Mr. Perón has resorted."[29] Two days after the A.F. of L. report appeared, the C.G.T. was ready with a reply. "The North American delegates lie when they say that their mission was to observe the condition of Argentine labor," Perón's organization retorted. "Their presence here was for the purpose of using every method at their command to carry out all the imperialistic plans of the Department of State for penetration, . . . for dividing and suffocating the labor movement in our country."[30]

Although the main body of the C.G.T. appeared to be under Perón's control, strong indications of labor dissidence were much in evidence at the time this book was written. The most striking signs of disaffection among the *descamisados* were expressed primarily through the railroad unions in 1950 and 1951. About 180,000 rail employees defied the formal leadership of the C.G.T. to launch a series of strikes. The politics of the strikes revealed not only that the Socialists were still strong among the railroad workers, but also that there was serious conflict within the unions involved, between the followers of Eva Perón, on the one hand, and those of President Perón, on the other.* The wildcat railroad strikes gave the regime considerable concern. The president declared the stoppages to be illegal on January 23, 1951, but they nevertheless persisted. Vowing that he would "take the necessary measures to put the Radicals, Communists, anarchists, and Socialists in their place,"[31] President Perón placed the railroads under military control and rendered the strikers subject to court-martial. The strikes, which Perón branded as "of a totally and absolutely political character, . . . the product of one or two thousand agitators and 148,000 politically directionless workers,"[32] were dramatic evidence that much of the labor movement was not yet completely pacified or woven into the fabric of Perón's Argentina. When the railroad crisis subsided later in 1951, the government declared that 267 persons had been arrested in connection with the affair. These figures differed fundamentally from those collected by opposition leaders, who asserted that 25,000 railroad workers had been dismissed, and that 3,000 persons had been jailed. Moreover, it was charged that 3 prominent former C.G.T. officials—Pedro Pistarini, Bartolo Colebatti, and Carlos Necochea—had been tortured by the Federal Police because of their parts in the strikes.

The Perón regime derives its strength primarily, then, from a coalition of the nation's armed forces with the *descamisados*, the organized urban workers. Although the

* This interesting division within the *Peronista* ranks was censored from the Argentine press. *La Prensa*'s attempt to publish that information resulted in the now-famous "strike" against that newspaper launched by the C.G.T. on January 26, 1951. See pp. 211–14.

formal leadership of both of these groups is nominally controlled tightly by Perón, the "new Argentina" has seen constant indications of dissidence and disaffection in both the military and the C.G.T. To the extent that the soldier-*descamisado* alliance is an "unnatural" one, the regime is kept in a chronic state of unstable flux, in part rationalized in the justicialist context of a harmonious "Third Position" between basically opposed forces. In a very real sense, the army and organized labor are in fundamental opposition to each other, and their polarity is a significant symptom of the potential infirmity of the Perón government.

14.

The Quondam Faithful (Continued)

Organized as a political party, President Perón's followers have been known since 1949 as the *Peronista* party. This entity was formed during the course of the consolidation of the "new Argentina." With many of the original members of the G.O.U. falling from power shortly after the revolution of 1943,* Perón not only tightened his hold on the C.G.T. but also sought to broaden the base of his support through the formation of a political party dedicated to himself. Many groups—nationalists, army officers, sectors of organized labor, and even some Radicals—endorsed Perón in the early months after the uprising of 1943. The *Peronista* party was the outgrowth of his largely successful attempt to bring these divergent elements together into a political party which would both unite Perón's followers and give him more effectively integrated control over them. The *Peronista* party, serving these two purposes, today recognizes President Perón as its undisputed leader. However, as in the case of other bulwarks of the "new Argentina," the president's party on occasion exhibits tendencies to be divided into a number of mutually hostile factions.

* See p. 53.

E Pluribus Unum

The gradual unification in one party of Peron's followers was a political process which consumed the first six years after the revolution of 1943. Initially, the rebellion was the work of a military clique, the G.O.U. This organization had acted on its own in overthrowing the government of President Castillo without the active assistance or collaboration of any other political group in the country. Shortly after the rebellion, a number of nationalist organizations announced their adhesion to what they understood the principles of the revolution to be. Some time later, a small group within the Radical party cast its lot with that of the "new Argentina." These "Collaborationist" Radicals were subsequently joined by an "Argentine Labor party." The task for Perón, in the years between 1943 and 1949, was the unification of these diverse groups under the aegis of one political party subservient to him.

The nationalists were the first to be subjected to the "unification" process. Nationalist groups, springing to the support of the regime in the first months after the revolution,* brought some political embarrassment to Perón and his confreres in the G.O.U. Embracing a combined membership estimated in 1943 at 40,000, the nationalist organizations were, in the main, openly anti-Semitic and pro-Axis. This orientation was certainly shared by many members of the G.O.U. However, the international situation became such, toward the close of 1943, that it was increasingly "delicate" for the Argentine government to remain *openly* anti-Semitic and pro-Axis; and the G.O.U. saw the wisdom of at least appearing to dissociate the regime from the nationalists. In this context, President Ramírez on January 11, 1944, signed a decree ordering the dissolution of all na-

* See pp. 223–24.

tionalist political organizations. Although many of them continued to function on a *sub rosa* basis, the decree did have the effect of clearing the way for a subsequent re-orientation of the formal leadership and organization of the nationalists.

The next problem was the G.O.U. itself. The army operated with a peculiar ambivalence. On the one hand, its political action was based substantially on the process of military clique-formation; but, on the other, these cliques ran contrary to the official doctrine of theoretically unified and non-political military establishments. Moreover, the mere act of maintaining the G.O.U. as a continuing formal entity signified that it was politically apart from other elements of the army. This was, of course, in fact true; but the regime sought to deny that any such division existed among the military. Accordingly, on February 23, 1944—the day before General Ramírez resigned from the presidency—the G.O.U. was formally dissolved by its own governing board. Thereafter, the army was ostensibly unified politically, and in theory loyal to whoever held the reins of government.

One of the first political steps taken by Perón after the revolution of 1943 was a bid for more widespread support than had been represented by sectors of the nationalists and of the G.O.U. Perón sought a broadened civilian backing for his aspirations, and as early as November of 1943, he conferred with leaders of the Radical party with a view toward enlisting the support of their organization. Although the formal leadership of the Radicals issued a clandestine manifesto denying that their party had entered into any agreement with Perón, it is true that some dissident Radicals did ally themselves with his cause. Defying the main body of their party, the small sector of the Radicals sympathetic toward Perón—these came to be called "Collaborationist"

Radicals—moved toward co-operation with him after 1944.
The "Collaborationists" were led by three politicians who
until then had enjoyed some stature within the Radical
party. These were Juan Hortensio Quijano, Juan Isaac
Cooke, and Armando G. Antille. Together they launched
a campaign, early in 1945, to bring the Radical party into
Perón's camp.

In this venture, they were essentially unsuccessful. Although Quijano, Cooke, and Antille did manage to bring
some Radicals into the "Collaborationist" fold, the principal body of the Radical party remained adamant in its
opposition to Perón. Moreover, on July 24, 1945, the "Collaborationists," led by this triumvirate, were formally expelled from the Radical party. Following their expulsion,
Quijano, Cooke, and Antille became increasingly active as
political lieutenants of Perón. All three were given positions
in President Fárrell's cabinet. Quijano was named interior
minister on August 4, 1945; three weeks later, Antille became minister of finance; and Cooke was appointed foreign
minister on August 28. After "Loyalty Day" and the restoration of Perón, Quijano and Antille formally announced
on October 28, 1945, the establishment of their own political party. The "Collaborationists'" new entity was called
the "Radical Reconstruction Committee," and was dedicated to Perón's political ambitions.

Meanwhile, Perón had been working toward the use of
the C.G.T. and the captured labor movement as an organized political force. In this, as "Loyalty Day" demonstrated, he was eminently victorious. On October 17, 1945,
the *descamisados*, backing Perón, displayed their strength
as a political arm of the "new Argentina." Among the more
powerful of the elements achieving the restoration of Perón,
the *descamisados*, led by Luis Gay and Cipriano Reyes,
moved toward the establishment of a new political party.

This "Argentine Labor party" was founded in November of 1945 under the leadership of Reyes, regarded by many of the *descamisados* as a major hero of the events of October 17. Reyes' Labor party announced a platform calling for shorter working hours, labor participation in commercial and industrial profits, political rights for women, and Argentine co-operation with the other American republics.

Although "Loyalty Day" of 1945 in effect signalized the opening of Perón's candidacy for the presidency of Argentina, that candidacy was not formally proclaimed until some time later. Indeed, the presidential candidacy was announced on three separate formal occasions—by Quijano's "Collaborationists" on December 3, 1945; by Perón himself on December 11; and by Reyes' Labor party on January 15, 1946. Thus the "Collaborationist" Radicals and the Labor party became the two-pronged nucleus for the later *Peronista* party. Perón's first election to the presidency, it will be remembered, took place on February 24, 1946. Throughout that campaign, the "Collaborationists" and the Labor party were in basic agreement as to their joint indorsement of Perón for president. However, during the early stages of the campaign, there was some conflict between Quijano's Radicals and Reyes' *Laboristas* on the question of the vice-presidential candidate on Perón's ticket. On January 15, 1946, the Labor party nominated Colonel Domingo A. Mercante* for the vice presidency; the next day the "Collaborationists" named Quijano as Perón's running-mate. This discrepancy caused some embarrassment among Perón's divided backers until an agreement was reached on January 27. At that time, Colonel Mercante consented to the withdrawal of his candidacy, and the *Laboristas* announced their willingness to indorse

* See pp. 348–351.

Quijano for vice president. From the standpoint of Mercante's position, and the future of Reyes' Labor party, the agreement of January 27 was a significant forecast of things to come.

Theoretically, Perón was elected president in 1946 by a coalition of the "Collaborationist" Radicals and the Labor party. Perón himself, although he accepted the coalition during the campaign, was not enthusiastic about having to depend on *two* political parties for his electoral support. The fact that there were two parties meant potential division. The controversy over whether Quijano or Mercante should be the vice president was a foretaste of the forms that division could take. Two parties, Perón reasoned, were dangerous to the "new Argentina." It was necessary to forge a new, single, unified party of the revolution.

Accordingly, shortly after his election in 1946, Perón announced his plans for the unification of his political movement. This touched off a dramatic struggle among his followers, in which Reyes, the Labor party leader, figured prominently. When, in March of 1946, Perón proposed the formal merger of the "Collaborationist" and *Laborista* parties, Reyes protested violently against such a fusion. In the following months, Reyes broke with Perón to wage a losing battle against him. With the political eclipse of Reyes, Perón was at length able, on June 17, 1946, to announce that his followers had at last been combined in one single party.

That party was called the "Only party of the Revolution."* Proud of his achievement, President Perón asserted that the new party was in fact "the only party of the revolution. I do not accept other forces."[1] The formation of the Only party, however, worried many of the president's fol-

* The Spanish is *Partido Único de la Revolución*. The word *"único"* may be translated as "only" or "single."

lowers. As they objected to the new entity, they tended to divide into two groups. The first of these were the former aides of Reyes, who mourned his passing as a political leader. Perón was not concerned with the protests of this group, beyond taking care that its partisans did not exercise appreciable influence within the councils of the Only party. The second group voiced an objection which President Perón at length came to regard as more serious. This faction argued that "Only" was an unfortunately chosen name for the party. It was pointed out that the designation had totalitarian connotations which might harm the domestic and international prestige of the regime. The Only party suggested a one-party state. It exhumed Hitler and Mussolini. In a sense, Perón was sabotaging his own post-1945 attempts to dissociate his government from the defunct Axis. If "fascism" had suddenly become a naughty word in Argentina, the "Only party" must likewise be immoral.

Swayed by such advice, Perón late in 1948 made preparations for the "reorganization" of the Only party. It was to be "replaced" by a new organization. And that new entity was born on July 25, 1949, during the course of a huge rally held at Buenos Aires' mammoth Luna Park. Thenceforth the Only party was no more. It had been supplanted by the "*Peronista* party."

Sawdust Monolith

As organized since July of 1949, the *Peronista* party has developed a bureaucratic structure of imposing proportions. Structurally, the huge and sprawling mechanism of the party hierarchy is divided into four levels of organization. These are (1) the national, (2) the metropolitan, provincial, or territorial, (3) the regional, and (4) the precinct levels of the party.

On the *national* level, five distinct organs of the *Peronista* party have been created. These include the "Chief of the Movement," the "General Congress of the Party," the "Bureau of Party Information," the "Superior Executive Council," and the "Tribunal of Party Discipline."

The tables of the formal organization of the *Peronista* party leave no doubt that President Juan Domingo Perón is the undisputed master of the party. In his formal role as the leader of the *Peronistas*, Perón is designated by the party statutes as the "Chief of the Movement." In this capacity, he is recognized as the supreme authority of the party and has unlimited control of all *Peronista* organs. As Chief of the Movement, President Perón may countermand any decision made anywhere in the party, may supervise the selection of *Peronista* candidates and officials of the party, and has the authority to determine the agenda for the meeting of any organ of the *Peronista* party. Thus, even according to the formal tables of organization, Perón's control of his party is absolute and complete.

However, there *are* other structural units of the party. These operate under the close scrutiny of the Chief of the Movement, and all of their decisions and actions are always subject to his approval. Within these limits, the "General Congress of the Party" performs a function roughly analogous to the national convention of either of the major parties in the United States. The 376 delegates to the General Congress of the Party are elected for two-year terms— Perón may annul any of the elections—by the various Metropolitan, Provincial, and Territorial Congresses of the party.* Thus constituted, the General Congress has the authority to nominate the *Peronista* candidates for president and vice president of the nation, adopt the party platform,

* See p. 339.

and amend the *Peronistas'* tables of organization. All of these actions are subject to the absolute veto of the Chief of the Movement.

A *Peronista* "Bureau of Party Information" is attached to the General Congress of the Party. This bureau is composed of ten persons designated by the General Congress, and is charged with the production and distribution of *Peronista* propaganda. The Bureau of Party Information operates under the instructions and supervision of the General Congress of the Party—and Perón.

A "Superior Executive Council" of the *Peronista* party is on a theoretically co-ordinate level with the General Congress of the Party, but actually the council's work is of greater importance in the organization than that of the General Congress. The Superior Executive Council is composed of twenty-four members, one being elected by the *Peronista* council for the city of Buenos Aires, and one apiece by the councils for each of the sixteen provinces and each of the national territories.* Theoretically, the task of the Superior Executive Council is to carry out the instructions it receives from the General Congress of the Party. This arrangement is largely academic, however, since the General Congress—like the Superior Executive Council—is itself subject to Perón's instructions.

Basically, the council is Perón's board of advisors on domestic political strategy. It is composed of the *Peronistas* in whom he feels he can place the most trust. The party's tables of organization fix no term of office for the twenty-four members of the Superior Executive Council. Its chairman is Admiral Alberto Teisaire,† who, by virtue of this

* See pp. 133–46. The results of these elections—as in the case of all other *Peronista* party decisions—are subject to the approval of Perón.
† See pp. 76, 85, and 315.

position, wields a personal power and influence within the *Peronista* party which is subordinate only to that of Perón. Teisaire—and the other members of the council—hold office in that body at the pleasure of the Chief of the Movement.

In addition to aiding the president in the planning of *Peronista* political strategy, the Superior Executive Council operates as the agency through which Perón maintains his control of the other organs of the party. Thus the council calls the elections for the General Congress of the Party, settles such jurisdictional conflicts as may arise among *Peronista* units, inspects and regulates lesser party organs, and may "intervene" in any of them. The formal party statutes stipulate that the Superior Executive Council must meet at least once a month. Normally, it holds one meeting per week, and additional sessions are called whenever Perón or Teisaire deems them advisable.

Attached to the council and within its—and Perón's—jurisdiction is the *Peronista* "Tribunal of Party Discipline." This tribunal is made up of five members appointed for two-year terms by the Superior Executive Council. Perón, of course, controls the appointments, and may remove any member before his term expires. The job of the Tribunal of Party Discipline is to communicate the party line on various issues to the *Peronistas* in the national congress and in other government positions. Moreover, the tribunal is expected to inforce party regularity on the part of all *Peronistas*. Occasionally, the first of these two functions is more difficult to perform than the second. More than one observer has noted "the trouble . . . any *Peronista* along the line has in anticipating what the boss would like."[2] This "trouble" is aggravated by the generally recognized proposition that the *Peronistas* are "not a party in which all speak the same language. This has been verified by the

words of the president of the chamber of deputies himself*
in referring to the difficult process of amalgamating the
Peronistas: 'Some come from the right, others from the
left, others from the center, and all without a defined
orientation.' "[3] Where the party line can be ascertained and
communicated to the membership, however, the Tribunal
of Party Discipline normally has little hardship in inforcing
party regularity among the *Peronistas.* Where the line is
defied, expulsion from the party normally follows. If the
culprit persists in his anti-*Peronista* activities, he may be
dealt with by a terrifying host of sanctions and reprisals,
ranging from "contempt" charges to the *picana eléctrica.*

Two types of *Peronista* organs exist on the second—or
metropolitan, provincial, or territorial—level of party organization. This level is occupied by the city of Buenos
Aires and by the country's provinces and national territories. In each of these entities, the *Peronistas* have established a "Metropolitan, Provincial, or Territorial Congress" and a "Metropolitan, Provincial, or Territorial Council."

Each Metropolitan, Provincial, or Territorial Congress is
composed of one delegate chosen for a two-year term from
each of the *partidos* or departments into which the capital,
the provinces, and the territories are divided. These congresses nominate the *Peronista* candidates for the national
congress and for the various elective offices in the provinces,
and send delegates to the General Congress of the Party.
The composition—and the work—of the Metropolitan,
Provincial, and Territorial Congresses are under the strong
supervisory control of the Chief of the Movement.

Each organizational unit containing a Metropolitan,
Provincial, or Territorial Congress also embraces a Metropolitan, Provincial, or Territorial Council of the *Peronista*

* Deputy Héctor J. Cámpora.

party. These councils are roughly analogous in their functions to the state central committees maintained by the major political parties in the United States. Each of them composed of fifteen members elected for two-year terms by the appropriate Metropolitan, Provincial, or Territorial Congresses, the *Peronista* councils on this level are the executive arms of the party in their respective jurisdictions. Operating on instructions from the national Supreme Executive Council, they manage *Peronista* affairs in their jurisdictions and keep the national body advised of political developments in the Federal Capital and the provinces and territories.

Two types of party organs are likewise to be found on the third, or *regional*, level of *Peronista* organization. This level corresponds roughly to the *partidos* or departments into which each of the provinces and territories is divided. The two classes of *Peronista* organs on the regional level are known as "Departmental Conventions" and "Departmental Councils." The conventions, to which the regional business of the appropriate Metropolitan, Provincial, and Territorial Congresses is delegated, act on instructions received from them. The Departmental Councils bear a similar relationship to the respective Metropolitan, Provincial, and Territorial Councils, and keep them advised of political conditions and developments on the regional level.

A "Basic Unit" of the *Peronista* party exists in each of the local jurisdictions of the lowest, or *precinct*, level of party organization. This level corresponds essentially to the various voting districts. The Basic Unit is the cell of the party, and is charged with the recruitment of party members and their indoctrination in *Justicialismo* and other elements of *Peronista* thought, attitudes, and policies.

In addition to this sprawling structure, the *Peronista* party boasts a women's auxiliary organization. It will be remembered that woman suffrage became law in Argentina on September 23, 1947.* Two years later—on July 26, 1949 —the *"Peronista* Feminist party" was established. Eva Perón was its first chairman. Calling upon the nation's women to exhibit "the most strict loyalty to the doctrine, the work, and the personality of General Perón,"[4] "Evita" asserted that it was the task of the *Peronista* Feminist party to achieve four objectives. These were the strengthening of the family as a political force, the establishment of educational and cultural centers for women, the creation of a unified Argentine feminist movement, and the mobilization of women in support of the principles of the revolution of 1943. According to its organizational chart, the *Peronista* Feminist party structurally resembles the main *Peronista* party, with congresses, conventions, councils, and basic units provided for on four levels. However, that arrangement existed primarily on paper at the time this book was written. The *Peronista* Feminist party operated almost exclusively in the city of Buenos Aires, and maintained few units in the provinces of the "interior."

Despite the absence of elitist theory in the doctrine of *Justicialismo,* some case can be made for regarding the *Peronista* party as an elite. This case rests on three considerations. In the first place, the overwhelming majority of government positions in Argentina are occupied by members of the *Peronista* party. This is true whether one speaks of bureaucratic personnel, congressmen, judges, provincial governors and legislators, or municipal government officials.

Secondly, membership in the *Peronista* party is controlled. Not every Argentine can be a *Peronista,* and nobody—technically speaking—is a party member unless he has been issued a membership card. The *Peronista* party is a relatively small, and carefully screened and disciplined

* See pp. 99–100.

group of governors. In this sense, it resembles, as an elite party, the Nazi party of Germany, the Fascist party of Italy, and the Communist party of the Soviet Union. Frequently, more people want to be *Peronistas* than are admitted to membership in the party. The exact number of party members is a carefully guarded secret. The figure probably ranges somewhere between 250,000 and 300,000, or about 2 per cent of the total population of Argentina. Occasionally, when the number of *Peronistas* drops below full strength, registration is opened to permit the Basic Units to recruit new party members. Normally, it is only in those situations that persons may join the party, and even then the applicants are carefully screened. Thus to be a *Peronista* in the "new Argentina" is a very different proposition than to be a Democrat or a Republican in the United States.*

In the third place, the *Peronista* party has recently opened a school to train party members in government and leadership. The *"Peronista* Superior School" was launched on March 1, 1951. The announced purposes of the school were four in number—to develop *Justicialismo* as a political philosophy, to teach it to the party members, to train the Basic Units in techniques of disseminating justicialist propaganda among non-*Peronistas*, and to develop political leaders. "This school has a double purpose," President Perón declared during the ceremonies inaugurating the *Peronista* Superior School. "The first is the formation of justicialists and the second the exaltation of *Peronista* values to serve the justicialist doctrine in the best way."[5] Only card-carrying members of the *Peronista* party are permitted to enrol as students in the school. To the extent that its graduates

* Argentine informal parlance uses the word "*Peronista*" in a different sense than the technical one employed here. In everyday talk, anybody who supports Perón is a *Peronista;* but in strictly technical usage only card-carrying members of the party are *Peronistas.*

The Quondam Faithful

will be assigned positions of public authority and leadership, the school will contribute to the development of the *Peronista* party as an organization for the creation of a relatively small governing elite.*

This, then, is the *Peronista* party, organized for the control and training of President Perón's political entourage.

The Men around Perón

Today all *Peronistas* acknowledge the president's undisputed political leadership of their movement. Nevertheless, some of the people in the party are themselves personalities of significance in the "new Argentina." Playing admittedly secondary roles in the *Peronista* party, these figures represent the various components of Perón's political organization. And the intra-*Peronista* politics among his henchmen in part reflect the tensions among the armed services, the labor movement, and the heirs of the "Collaborationist" Radicals.

The leading *Peronistas* representing the armed forces are Rear Admiral Alberto Teisaire and Generals Juan Pistarini, Bartolomé de la Colina, and Angel J. Solari. Colonel

* The courses offered at the *Peronista* Superior School during its first year, and the "professors" teaching them, were as follows:

Course	Professor
Principles of Leadership	President Juan Domingo Perón
History of the *Peronista* Movement	María Eva Duarte de Perón
Principles of Peronism	Technical Affairs Minister Raúl A. Mende
Achievements of Peronism	Dr. Lorenzo A. García
Organization of *Peronista* and Practical Programs	Dr. Angel Miel de Asquía
Justicialismo	Technical Affairs Minister Raúl A. Mende
Political Economy	Finance Minister Alfredo Gómez Morales
The Constitution of 1949	Dr. Rodolfo Valenzuela
Justicialist Ethics	Dr. R. P. Hernán Benítez

Domingo A. Mercante also owes his political rise to the military, but his fortunes became increasingly attached to the labor movement in the years after 1943.

Admiral Teisaire, the chairman of the Superior Executive Council of the *Peronista* party, today wields an influence in that organization second only to Perón's. Teisaire has been loyal to Perón and has served him well in the years since the revolution. Born in Mendoza in 1891, Teisaire's professional life until 1943 was devoted to the Argentine Navy. He was brought into the government by the G.O.U. in 1944 as a part of that clique's attempt to offset naval opposition to the military regime. Although not entirely successful in achieving that objective, Admiral Teisaire was perhaps as effective in allaying the seamen's political hostility as any navy officer could have been at the time. Perón has leaned more heavily on the admiral as the years have slipped by, and this is reflected by the positions of responsibility which Teisaire has held in the "new Argentina." He served in the Fárrell cabinet as both minister of the navy and as minister of interior; and, during Perón's presidency, Teisaire has been a *Peronista* senator from the Federal Capital. He presided over the convention which wrote the Constitution of 1949, and since that year he has served faithfully as chairman of Perón's Superior Executive Council. From the standpoint of the Chief of the Movement, Admiral Teisaire has perhaps been the most politically reliable of the leading *Peronistas*.

So far as the army is concerned, General Juan Pistarini has not only been one of the more faithful highly-placed *Peronistas*, but he was one of the very few participants in the original rebellion of June 4, 1943, who remained in the cabinet at the time this book was written. Pistarini, who was born in the territory of La Pampa in 1882, entered upon a military career at a very early age. He studied military matters in Germany, and, on his return to Argentina, was promoted rapidly. On the eve of the revolution of 1943, he held the rank of division general and was a member of the G.O.U. He has been minister of public works ever since December of 1943. Pistarini has, on occasion, held other posts simultaneously with the public works portfolio. Indeed, his record is impressive. Since 1943, he has served as Federal Interventor for the Province of Buenos Aires, minister of the navy, minister of agriculture, minister of interior, and vice president of the nation. These posts were largely interim in nature: his chief government role has been as minister of public works, and he has held this position in the cabinets of Presidents Ramírez, Fárrell, and Perón.

Also deserving of mention as an army officer high in *Peronista* councils is General Bartolomé de la Colina. During the bulk of his military career, Colina was primarily interested in the development of Argentine air power. A major at the time of the rebellion of 1943, he was staunchly loyal to Perón and soon became a general officer. Colina was one of the military men who gave Perón political support at a time when it was most needed. During the hectic crisis preceding "Loyalty Day" in 1945, General Colina publicly asserted that Perón would be president of Argentina "no matter whom it hurts."[6] When that indeed came to be the case, Colina was rewarded for his constancy with a cabinet post of strategic influence. During Perón's presidency, the general has served as minister of aeronautics.

Among strategically placed *Peronista* army officers is General Angel J. Solari, whose political undependability has at times reached sensational proportions. An originally apolitical army man who was not associated with the G.O.U., Solari enjoyed routine success in his military career. That success resulted in his being placed in command of the military parade at Buenos Aires which, on July 9, 1949, celebrated the 133rd anniversary of General San Martín's declaration of independence. Apparently impressed with the potential political strength of Solari's positions of command, opponents of Perón approached the general with a view toward making revolutionary use of Solari's military authority. The general's reactions to these advances remained unclear when the present writer was in Argentina in 1950 and 1951. On August 17, 1950, Solari commanded the military procession which helped *porteños* observe the one-hundredth anniversary of San Martín's death. Shortly thereafter, Solari was reported to be participating in a conspiracy against the regime, and he was ordered imprisoned in September. Military pressures on Perón not only forced him to release Solari but also to name him commander of the army in December of 1950. General Solari thus occupied a strategic position of crucial importance when Perón launched his campaign for re-election in the following year. On September 28, 1951, the government announced that it had discovered a revolutionary plot in the army, and a state of siege and a "state of internal war" were decreed. After Perón's re-election on November 11, 1951, the president took advantage of his newly strengthened position to order, on November 14, a shake-up in the army, during the course of which General Solari was relieved from his command and retired from military service.

Intra-*Peronista* politics among the labor leaders also provide an intriguing key to the stability of the *Peronista* party and Perón's government. The chief protagonists in the turbulent drama within the labor wing of the *Peronista* party have been Cipriano Reyes, the late Eva Perón, Angel Gabriel Borlenghi, Colonel Domingo A. Mercante, and Dr. Juan Atilio Bramuglia. Conflicts among the chieftains of the *descamisados* have been more chaotic than elsewhere in the president's party because of two major considerations. First, *Laborista** and Socialist influence in the C.G.T. have not yet been completely eliminated. Second, "Evita's" personal political machine was more active among the *descamisados* than elsewhere in the "new Argentina," and her organization occasionally clashed with other elements of the *Peronista* party.

Much of Cipriano Reyes' story has already been told. He led the Labor party which, together with the "Collaborationist" Radicals, indorsed Perón's first candidacy for the presidency in 1945–46. After the election, Reyes broke with Perón, and the former's followers have continued to make occasional trouble for the regime. In the election of 1946, Reyes won a seat in the Chamber of Deputies, and this position gave him an effective rostrum from which to conduct his battle against Perón. This conflict frequently bordered on spectacular violence. In July of 1947, Deputy Reyes was shot at in La Plata, the capital of the Province of Buenos Aires. In September of the following year, Reyes' enmity toward Perón made startling headlines not only in Argentina but elsewhere in the world. The government at Buenos Aires revealed that it had frustrated a plot to assassinate not only President Perón but also "Evita." Fourteen persons were implicated in the affair, including Reyes and John Griffith, formerly United States Cultural Attaché at Buenos Aires. Reyes' influence has declined seriously since then, although a number of his followers and admirers are still active in the C.G.T. and the *Peronista* party.

Between "Loyalty Day" of 1945 and the time of her death in 1952, Eva Perón was a major factor in the politics of the *Peronistas'* labor sector. Her political machine, making an especially strong appeal to the *descamisados*, was

* See pp. 332–334.

most active in the C.G.T. It was once observed that, "as 'Evita' has moved in, she has surrounded the president more and more with her own men, most of them servile mediocrities ready to leap at her bidding."⁷ Notable among Eva's "men" was Angel Gabriel Borlenghi, minister of interior in the Perón cabinet. Born at Buenos Aires in 1906, Borlenghi has devoted his professional life to labor and C.G.T. affairs. By the eve of the revolution of 1943, he had acquired considerable stature in the C.G.T. He was elected to its "Confederal Committee" in 1935, and six years later he led the C.G.T. delegation at the C.T.A.L. convention held at Mexico City. With the coming of Perón, however, Borlenghi helped to swing the C.G.T. into the camp of the "new Argentina." After 1945, he attached his political star to "Evita," and became prominent among her henchmen in the labor faction of the *Peronista* party. Fighting "Evita's" battles was not an easy task for Borlenghi; but he was politically faithful to her. As the key man in her labor machine, Borlenghi carried the brunt of the *Peronistas'* struggles against the Socialists and the remnants of Reyes' *Laboristas*.

Very few *Peronistas* have been able to accomplish what Colonel Domingo A. Mercante has done. He has performed the virtually impossible feat of straddling the gulf between the army and the *descamisados*. Mercante is strong both in the army and the C.G.T. President Perón claims that the entire *Peronista* party has bridged that schism. Actually, Mercante is one of the very rare *Peronistas* to have achieved that, and today he is politically unreliable from Perón's standpoint.

Colonel Mercante, who was born at Buenos Aires in 1898, was regarded as Perón's right-hand man during the first years after the revolution of 1943. A professional soldier, Mercante was elevated to the rank of colonel shortly after the revolution. The first step in his subsequent career as a labor politician came in November of 1943, during the early stages of the regime's capture of the C.G.T. At that time, Mercante was named "interventor" of the newly combined railroad workers' union. Thereafter, his rise to power was almost as meteoric as Perón's. In April of 1944, Mercante emerged as one of Perón's two chief assistants in the secretariat of labor and welfare.* When Perón left the secretariat in October of 1945, Mercante replaced him and remained chief of that agency until January of 1946.

Until the election campaign of 1945–46, Colonel Mercante shared the belief that he was Perón's principal lieutenant. He served as best man at the wedding of Juan and Eva Perón in October of 1945. That occasion, it now appears, marked the apogee of Mercante's power in the "new Argentina." Complications soon developed, and Mercante found himself at odds with Perón on an increasing number of issues. The first of these was the question of the vice presidency for the period 1946–52. Mercante desired to be Perón's running mate in the election campaign of 1945–46; and, indeed, Reyes' Labor party nominated him for that post. But Perón felt that it was necessary to appease the "Collaborationist" Radicals, and Quijano became the vice president. Although Mercante somewhat graciously withdrew his vice-presidential candidacy and agreed to settle for the governorship of the Province of Buenos Aires, the election of 1946 signalized the beginning of his political eclipse.

It was some time before Mercante realized this himself. After the balloting in 1946, his personal political plans became more ambitious. He aimed for bigger game than either the vice presidency of the nation or the governorship of the Province of Buenos Aires. After all, there was the presidency of Argentina. Perón had been elected to that post,

* José Figuerola was the other. See pp. 299 and 320.

it is true; but his term was to end in 1952, and the Constitution of 1853 stipulated that the president would not be eligible for re-election. Mercante would wait. He would succeed Perón in the presidency in 1952. These plans, of course, depended on the continued existence of the Constitution of 1853. When, in the latter part of 1948, President Perón launched his campaign for constitutional reform,* Mercante opposed any revision which would render Perón constitutionally eligible for immediate re-election to the presidency.

The struggle over the Constitution of 1949 marked the breaking point in Mercante's relations with Perón. Mercante, desiring to be the next president, fought against a change in the constitutional prohibition of the chief executive's re-election; Perón, intending to be president indefinitely, sought a revision that would render this constitutional. During this conflict, Teisaire replaced Mercante as the president's political right-hand man. Perón, now distrustful of Mercante, saw to it that Teisaire and not Mercante would preside over the convention writing the new Constitution of 1949. And Teisaire did his job well. When the new constitution was ready for signature in March of 1949, President Perón was eligible for re-election for an indefinite number of terms.

The political pattern of the constitutional struggle was such that in it Mercante incurred the wrath of Perón. For lesser politicians, this would have meant immediate disaster. But Mercante was a man of some stature, following, and influence. It will be remembered that he had not only been "interventor" among the railroad unions, but also a major figure in the secretariat of labor and welfare. In these capacities he had built for himself a sizable entourage in the C.G.T. and among the *descamisados*. Moreover,

* See pp. 72–77.

Mercante was, after all, governor of the politically strategic Province of Buenos Aires. And, above all, Colonel Mercante was an army officer affiliated with influential military factions. Perón discovered this in October of 1950, when he endeavored to undermine Mercante's army position but learned that the colonel, like Solari, was too strong to be unseated at that time. In striking back against Perón, Mercante dealt some appreciable blows. One of them involved his role in the chaotic wildcat railroad strikes of 1950–51;[*] another centered on the presidential campaign of 1951. When Perón presented himself as a candidate for re-election, Mercante reportedly sought negotiations with the strongest anti-Perón candidate. The Radicals' Ricardo J. Balbín[†] was offered a Balbín-Mercante ticket, but this was summarily rejected for two reasons. In the first place, coalitions and inter-party tickets had been rendered difficult by the pattern of the laws in 1951.[‡] Secondly, Balbín, with the lesson of the "Collaborationist" precedent before him, preferred to run for president on an all-Radical ticket. There was little question in 1951 that Mercante had become an anti-Perón *Peronista;* but to Balbín a *Peronista* was a *Peronista.*

Another prominent member of Perón's party especially active in labor politics is Dr. Juan Atilio Bramuglia. Although he is a civilian, Bramuglia is a close friend of Mercante. This relationship stems from the early days of the "new Argentina," when both men were actively engaged in Perón's capture of the C.G.T., especially as that process affected the railroad unions. A lawyer, Bramuglia has devoted much of his professional career to labor matters. For approximately fifteen years before the revolution of 1943,

[*] See pp. 326–27.
[†] See pp. 81–83.
[‡] See pp. 361–62.

Bramuglia, then a Socialist, served as legal advisor to the railroad unions. Although he later became a *Peronista*, his pre-1943 Socialist and labor background go far toward explaining his influence among the railroad workers, his friendship with Mercante, and his subsequent clash with Eva Perón. In the first years after the uprising of 1943, Perón found Bramuglia's labor experience helpful in the consolidation of the "new Argentina." With Mercante, Bramuglia assisted Perón in the secretariat of labor and welfare in 1944. In December of that year, Bramuglia left the secretariat to become Federal Interventor of the Province of Buenos Aires. He remained in that post until September of 1945. During his stay at La Plata, the capital of the Province of Buenos Aires, he not only continued to develop his labor position but also gave the political machine in the province an orientation which aided his friend Mercante, who became provincial governor of Buenos Aires in 1946.

His work at La Plata done, Bramuglia then embarked upon a brief and curious career in international affairs. Named foreign minister in President Perón's cabinet, the former labor lawyer guided Argentine foreign policy to an uneasy *rapprochement* with the United States. Foreign Minister Bramuglia headed the Argentine delegation to the Inter-American Conference for the Maintenance of Peace and Security, which met at Rió de Janeiro, Brazil, in August of 1947 to draft an inter-American mutual defense treaty. A year later, he led the Argentine group at the chaotic Ninth International Conference of American States, held at Bogotá, Colombia. With his country occupying a non-permanent seat on the United Nations Security Council during the period 1948–50, Bramuglia attended many of the sessions of the Security Council. Indeed, he was its chairman during October of 1948, and in that capacity attempted to work out a compromise between the United States and the Soviet Union with respect to the then critical "blockade" of Berlin. Two months later, Bramuglia accepted an invitation to visit Washington to confer with President Harry S. Truman and George C. Marshall, then the "North American" Secretary of State. Bramuglia emerged from that conference to tell the press that United States–Argentine relations had become most cordial.

His international exploits having brought him considerable publicity, Foreign Minister Bramuglia returned to Argentina early in 1949 to find a cool reception at the *Casa Rosada*. His rising prestige had been accompanied by a growth in his stature among the railroad workers, the C.G.T., and the *descamisados*. As his labor strength grew within the *Peronista* party, it clashed with Borlenghi and "Evita's" personal machine. To the irritable and easily insulted "Evita," Bramuglia's rise within *Peronista* ranks was a more important question than whether or not he had been an effective foreign minister. Bramuglia was becoming too big for the *Peronista* party, especially for "Evita's" hold on the *descamisados*. Bramuglia must go. And he went. On August 11, 1949, President Perón announced the foreign minister's resignation from the cabinet.

However, Bramuglia was not as easily disposed of as that. His dismissal was followed by growing unrest among the railroad unions. His decline from favor at the *Casa Rosada* had coincided with Mercante's. Both were less bitter toward Perón than toward "Evita." Both Mercante and Bramuglia had scores to settle with the first lady. Mercante saw danger in her growing bid for the vice presidency, and Bramuglia had lost his cabinet post through his rivalry with her for leadership among the *descamisados*. Perón was aware of this two-pronged enmity and so was "Evita"; and, late in 1949, the regime embarked upon an attempt to eradicate the Bramuglia-Mercante influence from the unions. This project took the form of replacing their partisans with "Evita"-Borlenghi men in key positions among the workers. This process contributed to unrest within the unions and formed a significant background against which the wildcat railroad strikes of 1950–51 developed.

The strikes were a major crisis for the *Peronista* party. Geared essentially to "Evita's" drive against Bramuglia and Mercante, they reached their peak at the end of 1950, when "Evita" placed Pablo López, one of her "men," in a politically strategic post among the railroad workers. This appointment was acrimoniously protested by some 180,000 rail employees who walked off their jobs. Despite Perón's assertions to the contrary, the strikes were, fundamentally, an intra-*Peronista* struggle. Moreover, the strikers were more bitter against "Evita" than against President Perón. One could go to Quilmes and read the curiously prophetic placards carried by the pickets: "¡*Viva* Perón—as a widower!" Two government officials were in positions to minimize the stoppage, but they did little to halt it. One of them was Mercante, who was governor of the Province of Buenos Aires, in which a large sector of the strikes was localized. Political observers attached more than routine importance to Bramuglia's prolonged conversations with Mercante during the stoppage. Another was Colonel Juan F. Castro, who was minister of transport in Perón's cabinet, and was remarkably ineffective in his apparent efforts to terminate the strikes.* Perón was able to dismiss Castro, and this was done; but Mercante was too powerful in the army to be unseated, and little further could be done to the already martyred Bramuglia.

Life has been more peaceful in the "Collaborationist"

* So far as this writer has been able to determine, Colonel Castro's political relationship to Bramuglia and Mercante cannot be documented.

sector of the *Peronista* party. This was led in 1945 and 1946 by Juan Hortensio Quijano, Juan Isaac Cooke, and Armando G. Antille. Since then, Cooke and Antille have quietly slipped from prominence, leaving Quijano as the sole major figure in this branch of the party until his death in 1952. The venerable Quijano, who was born at Curuzú Cuatiá, Corrientes, in 1884, served Perón faithfully after bolting the Radical party in 1945 to join the "new Argentina." An attorney by profession, Quijano served as minister of interior in the Fárrell cabinet and was vice president of Argentina during Perón's first constitutional term. Some observers believe that the elderly vice president lent an air of respectability to the regime. His former connection with the Radical party was used in *Peronista* propaganda to create the impression that Quijano was only one of a large number of Radicals supporting Perón. Regardless of the effectiveness of this propaganda line, many *Peronistas* believed that Quijano did much to enhance the domestic prestige of the Perón government.

Such, then, are the men around Perón. Whether they be army or navy officers, labor leaders or parliamentarians, they do much to give political Argentina its peculiar characteristics. Like interpersonal relations anywhere else in the world, the dealings of the leading *Peronistas* with each other are fluid and dynamic, and constantly changing. The progress of events constantly alters intra-*Peronista* politics. One of these events, the death of Eva Perón on July 26, 1952, has set in motion two changes within the party of probably long-range significance for the "new Argentina."

One of these changes is the progressive dismantling of the late first lady's personal political machine within the party. This may be expected to reduce the influence of the C.G.T., and of politicians like Borlenghi, within *Peronista* councils. As the passing of Evita weakens the labor wing of the party, the influence of the military among the *Peronistas* may be expected to increase. Prediction seemed risky when these lines were written, but it did seem likely that Evita's death might bring with it a diminution of emphasis on some of the labor features of the Perón regime and a strengthening of its military overtones.

The second change relates to the *Peronistas* who had fallen from favor because of their conflicts with Evita. With her removed from the scene, it seemed likely that the way might be cleared for the return of men like Bramuglia to influence within the *Peronista* party. Colonel Mercante's political difficulties sprang in part from clashes with Evita, and perhaps Mercante's star might also rise once again. At any rate, it seemed late in 1952 that the disintegration of Eva Perón's machine would be followed by heavier military influence upon the *Peronistas*, and by the return to prominence of men who had suffered eclipse through having fallen out with the late first lady.

The *Peronista* party presents an outward appearance of monolithic unity among the supporters of the regime. This appearance, however, is largely external. Beneath the surface, the *Peronistas* are torn by the rivalries and the hostilities which have long existed among the elements comprising the "new Argentina." These divisions among the components of Peronism constitute a crucial guide to the fundamental instability of the Perón regime. The *Peronista* party is a sawdust monolith, a house of cards, and its potential fragility is a dire threat to the government of President Perón.

15.

The Otherwise-Minded

Opposition political parties have led difficult lives in the "new Argentina." They have been subjected to extremely restrictive regulation; their leaders have been persecuted, intimidated, and driven into exile; and the line between anti-*Peronista* political activity and "contempt"* or even subversion has frequently been indistinguishable. To be active among the otherwise-minded is a dangerous undertaking in the "new Argentina." Since 1943, the Radical party has been the chief opposition group in the country, and its leaders have been prominent among the sufferers of the reprisals meted out to the domestic enemies of Perón.

Status of Political Parties

Before 1943, Argentine political parties were subjected to very little regulation by the national government. Within the context of the country's federal system, a number of the provinces had pioneered in this field of regulation, which was largely ignored by the federal authorities. By the eve of the revolution of 1943, only two major pieces of national regulation of political parties had been put on the books.

The first of these was the celebrated "Sáenz Peña Law" of 1912. That legislation, designed to put an end to electoral

* See pp. 175–78.

fraud, affected political parties in so far as it restricted their participation in elections in the interests of providing for secret and compulsory voting, achieving greater integrity in the counting of ballots, and assuring representation of minority parties. Today the "Sáenz Peña Law" is regarded in most non-*Peronista* circles as a highly successful bit of legislation.

The second major pre-1943 attempt to regulate parties was an outgrowth of the Uriburu revolution of 1930. On August 4, 1931, President Uriburu promulgated a decree requiring all political parties to register with the government, submitting detailed information on their tables of organization, programs and platforms, and finances. On the basis of such information, the government was to determine which parties were legal and which illegal; and the latter were to be prohibited from engaging in political activity. The Uriburu decree, generally viewed as an instrument of dictatorship, had by 1943 been repudiated by all Argentine political groups except the Conservative party.*

"Regulation" was essentially a euphemism for the flood of decrees affecting political parties signed at the *Casa Rosada* in the early months after the revolution of June 4, 1943. The most definitive of these measures was a decree of December 31, 1943, ordering the immediate dissolution of all Argentine political parties. The new regime was opposed by the Radical, Socialist, Conservative, Communist, and Progressive Democratic parties.† The leaders of these groups, once their parties had been declared dissolved and therefore illegal, concluded that the "new Argentina" could be opposed only through underground activity, and that this could best be directed from exile.

* See pp. 386–91.
† These political parties are discussed in some detail in the latter portion of this chapter and throughout the next chapter.

Accordingly, Radical, Socialist, Conservative, Communist, and Progressive Democratic leaders flocked to Montevideo, Uruguay, early in 1944. Montevideo appeared to be an ideal site for the exiles' political headquarters. Located just across the Plata River from Buenos Aires, the Uruguayan capital was easily accessible to anybody who could get out of Argentina. Moreover, it was relatively simple to transmit communications—whether confidential material or public propaganda—across the river. Material printed in Uruguay could be delivered to Argentina for clandestine distribution there, and the exiles' radio station at Montevideo could be heard in the area of Buenos Aires and its environs.

A "Committee of Argentine Political Exiles" was formally established at Montevideo in the closing months of 1944. Led by the Conservative Dr. Rodolfo Moreno, former governor of the Province of Buenos Aires, the committee was composed of delegates from all five of the outlawed Argentine opposition parties. Until August of 1945, the exiles' committee labored to oppose the regime at Buenos Aires through printed and broadcast propaganda and by maintaining contact with the committee's affiliates remaining in Argentina. The committee was essentially ineffective in its remote-control opposition to the "new Argentina"; and today there is general agreement in assessing the Committee of Argentine Political Exiles as having failed in its work. The committee was formally abandoned on August 20, 1945. "We Argentines have not learned the lesson taught by the fighters against fascism in other parts of the world," Américo Ghioldi, a Socialist member of the committee, declared. "We find ourselves in such a nihilistic frame of mind that we are incapable of imitating the French resistance or the anti-Fascist fight in Italy."[1] Most of the discouraged exile leaders had slipped quietly back into Argentina by the end of 1945.

Meanwhile, the *Casa Rosada's* policies toward opposition political parties had embarked upon a curious path. All political meetings were prohibited by a decree of June 23, 1943, and "all political parties existing in the whole territory of the nation"[2] were ordered dissolved on December 31. These measures were followed by a decree dated January 11, 1944, specifically abolishing the nationalists' political organizations.

On December 7, 1944, President Fárrell announced the appointment of a committee to frame an "Organic Statute of Political Parties." This committee was instructed to produce a draft of a piece of legislation which would strengthen the principles of the "Sáenz Peña Law," terminate fraud within political parties, control their finances, and provide severe punishments for violators of electoral laws. The committee was composed of Doctors Rodolfo Medina, Benjamín Villegas Basavilbaso, and José Manuel Astigueta, as principal members, with Dr. Segundo V. Linares Quintana as secretary. Let it be noted that this was a distinguished group. All of them were recognized experts on the general subject of political parties, and Dr. Linares Quintana is Argentina's foremost political scientist. Moreover, the members of the committee were close students of the political parties in the United States, and drew heavily on "North American" literature in framing the Argentine Organic Statute of Political Parties.* The group worked diligently

* Readers in the United States may be interested to learn that, according to Dr. Linares Quintana, the committee wrote the statute after perusing carefully the following books by "North American" political scientists: E. McChesney Sait, *American Parties and Elections* (New York: D. Appleton Century Co., Inc., 1939); Harold R. Bruce, *American Parties and Politics* (New York: Henry Holt and Co., 1937); Charles W. McKenzie, *Party Government in the United States* (New York: The Ronald Press, 1939); V. O. Key, *Politics, Parties, and Pressure Groups* (New York: Thomas Y. Crowell Co., 1943); Robert C. Brooks, *Political Parties and Electoral Problems* (New York: Harper & Brothers, 1933); Charles E. Merriam and Harold F. Gosnell, *The American Party System*

to produce the proposed statute, which was presented to President Fárrell in May of 1945.

The measure, as subsequently amended,* provided for the control of all Argentine parties through a system of electoral courts. A Federal Electoral Court, composed of three judges and an attorney-general appointed by the president, was to be established. This tribunal was to have jurisdiction over fifteen subordinate electoral courts located in the Federal Capital and in each of the provinces, then fourteen in number. Any group of politicians desiring to form a political party would be required to pattern their organization after a structure laid down in the text of the proposed statute.† Having done this, the party leaders must then enrol at least 1 per cent of the registered voters in the district in which the party was initiated as members of the organization. Next, the organizers would be required to file with the appropriate electoral court a document setting forth the party's political program, its tables of organization, and the names of its officers. It would then be the function of the electoral court to determine whether or not the party would be recognized as legal. If this recognition were denied, the party would be prohibited from engaging in political activity. Any legally recognized party would later lose its lawful status if two-thirds of its general congress voted to dissolve the party, or if it took any of an enumerated list of illegal steps. These unlawful actions included failing to run candidates in a national election, forming a coalition with another party, opposing the constitu-

---

(New York: The Macmillan Co., 1933); and Theodore W. Cousens, *Political Organizations in America* (New York: The Macmillan Co., 1942).

    * Amendments were added on May 30, 1945, and October 13, 1949.

    † The structure to be forced on all political parties was essentially the same as the form of organization of the *Peronista* party described in the last chapter, with the exception that the other parties were not to have "Chiefs" of their "movements" or "basic units." See pp. 335-41.

tion, advocating ideologies "likely to disturb the peace,"[3] inciting violence, or acquiring international affiliations. The Federal Electoral Court was to be the judge of whether any of these violations of the law had been committed.

Once drawn, the proposed Organic Statute of Political Parties followed an uncertain course. On May 30, 1945, President Fárrell announced his approval of the statute and declared that it would enter into force the following August 1. Theoretically, this happened in August, but at that time the statute provided curious company for two previous measures which were still law. One of them was the state of siege, originally ordered by President Castillo in 1941. The other was the 1943 decree declaring all political parties to be dissolved. On August 6, 1945—five days after the Organic Statute of Political Parties had ostensibly become law—the state of siege was suspended and the resumption of political activity, but not the resurrection of the parties, was permitted. With the state of siege lifted, the opposition groups staged a huge "March of the Constitution and Liberty" on September 19.* This spectacular demonstration against the government inspired President Fárrell to reimpose the state of siege on September 26 on the ground that opposition groups had not yet learned "how to make use of the liberty restored to the people."[4] A nation-wide police roundup of opposition political leaders accompanied the resumption of the state of siege, although Fárrell insisted that these developments would not interfere with the arrangements provided for by the Organic Statute of Political Parties. Indeed, he swore in the judges of the new Federal Electoral Court on October 6, 1945.

The chaotic "October days," launched by General

* See pp. 57–58.

Avalos' ill-fated coup against Perón on October 9, interrupted the regime's plans. The opposition parties publicly
repudiated the Organic Statute of Political Parties on October 12, and three days later—while Perón was still imprisoned—President Fárrell ordered the statute repealed.
After October 17, "Loyalty Day," Perón launched his
presidential candidacy, and three considerations characterized the legal conditions under which the entire election
campaign of 1945–46 was conducted. In the first place, the
1943 decree ordering the dissolution of political parties
was rescinded on October 20. Second, the state of siege
remained in force throughout the campaign, being lifted—
and then only for forty-eight hours—on February 22, 1946.
Third, the Organic Statute of Political Parties, which had
been repealed on October 15, was *not* law at any time during the campaign of 1945–46.

Perón was first elected president on February 24, 1946,
and he was inaugurated the following June 4. On May 15,
while he was president-elect, the Organic Statute of Political Parties was again declared to be law; and the state of
siege was terminated with President Perón's inauguration.
The organic statute, in force once more, was again bitterly
attacked by the opposition parties. The law was "totally
incompatible with the free development of the parties,"[5]
according to a formal statement of the Radicals. "We will
be criticized," one of Perón's senators, Juan Pablo Ramella,
asserted, "but criticism does not interest us."[6] In the years
since 1946, the organic statute has served Perón as an instrument for keeping the opposition parties under control.

There is some utility in inquiring into the president's attitude toward the existence of political parties. The fact
that there was a time when he called his own party the
"Only party"* provides an intriguing key to his thought

* See pp. 334–35.

on the subject. However, the era of the Only party perhaps represents an extreme phase of Perón's position. At any rate, since 1948 he has retreated somewhat from the notion that only one political party should exist. His current view is that there should be only one political doctrine or program—Peronism or *Justicialismo*—and that any number of political parties is "welcome" so long as they advance that program. Hear Perón: if other parties "come to the government with our program and carry it out, they would be welcome; and if they carried it out better than we, God would praise them. We do not work for ourselves, but for the nation."[7] In other words, any party is "welcome" so long as it is a party of Peronism; and Perón would bow to anybody who is a better *Peronista* than Perón. And what of political parties that reject Peronism and *Justicialismo?* They "have no place in a constructive and useful opposition," Perón has said. "Contrary to the latter, they act on the basis of falsehoods, calumnies, and sophisms, deceiving rather than instructing public opinion. They combat the government to weaken it rather than to lead it along the true road. They do not act in benefit of the country, but merely obtain personal advantages."[8] Moreover, Perón will not settle for a political pendulum calling for the alternation in power of the *Peronistas* and other parties. He has asserted that "the structure of the state can no longer be maintained by the rotation [in power] between radicals and liberals. Administration is not enough. It is necesary to understand and to act. It is necessary to create."[9]

Within such a context, the opposition parties find themselves at a chronic disadvantage in political campaigns. *Peronista* candidates have the protection and the co-operation of the Federal Police, while leaders of other parties do not; opposition campaign propaganda is destroyed and burned; and the laws on elections—including the Organic Statute of Political Parties—are administered in a highly partisan manner. Hear the report of the opposition Radical party on the conduct of a recent election campaign: "The government participates in the electoral campaign on behalf of the official party. . . . The decrees and rules limiting public acts of campaign propaganda are applied exclusively against the opposition. . . . The destruction of the opposition's campaign signs and posters by public employees and officials continues and increases in a systematic form."[10] Since the revolution of 1943, both presidential campaigns have been conducted during states of siege in which constitutional guarantees were suspended. During political campaigns, as at other times, the press is censored, and opposition leaders expressing criticism of the regime face the likelihood of imprisonment for "contempt."* It is uniformly more difficult for the opposition than for the *Peronistas* to obtain permits for political demonstrations and rallies; and it has become virtually impossible for non-*Peronista* parties to obtain radio broadcast time during campaigns. Opposition parties, which formed an anti-Perón coalition during the 1945–46 campaign, have since then been forbidden by the Organic Statute of Political Parties to form coalitions. In the campaign of 1951, each of the opposition parties was required to run its own slate of candidates and prohibited from co-operating with any other party against Perón. Moreover, by November of 1950 no fewer than thirty-two minor political parties had been ordered dissolved in conformity with the provisions of the Organic Statute of Political Parties.

It has thus far remained true that in the elections in the "new Argentina" the ballots themselves have been counted with scrupulous honesty. But against the background of the above restrictions on the opposition groups the *Pero-*

---

* See pp. 175–78.

nistas have won overwhelming majorities in the elections. "Since I came to the government," President Perón declared in 1948, "we have seen an increase of almost 35 per cent in our electoral support. If in the election of 1946 we won all positions everywhere, in this year's elections we have again won all positions, with 20 per cent more votes than last time."[11]

With every post-1943 election producing a victory for Perón, it has become increasingly difficult for the opposition groups to operate. But those opposition parties still exist, and they are certainly worth examining.

The Radicals

Today the Radicals are the largest and probably the most powerful of the anti-*Peronista* political parties. Technically speaking, the party's formal and proper name is the "Radical Civic Union," but most Argentines refer to the group as the Radical party or as the U.C.R.* The Radicals are the oldest and most traditional of the political parties now operating—legally or otherwise—in the country. Since the 1890's, the U.C.R. has been a major force in Argentine political life, and for many people it is as difficult to picture Argentine politics without the Radicals as it is for "North Americans" to imagine what their country's politics would be like without the Republicans or the Democrats. Indeed, some of the "Yankees of the South" cannot understand how people in any country can go through life without having heard of the U.C.R. Argentines enjoy telling the story of the European immigrant who arrived in their country during the 1920's. Disembarking from his ship in the harbor at Buenos Aires, the immigrant had little idea of where the boat had taken him. Stopping the first person he met at the harbor, the immigrant asked what country he was in. Told

* After the initial letters of *Unión Cívica Radical*.

that he was in Argentina, his next question was, "And who is in power here?" "The Radicals," was the answer. The immigrant was shocked and enraged. "The Radicals!" he exclaimed. "I am in the opposition!"

It is not difficult to be in opposition to the U.C.R. Most Argentines—including many of the Radicals themselves—have taken that position at one time or another during the last generation of the nation's political history. "More than an ideology," President Carlos Pellegrini once observed, "Radicalism is a temperament."[12] What is that temperament? It is a temperament of opposition. The Radicals lead the opposition against Perón, of course; but the truth is that even before the coming of Perón the life of the U.C.R. was in essence a life of oppositionism. Founded in 1892, the Radicals have been in power only during the period from 1916 to 1930. It is worth mentioning that the U.C.R. was rarely so divided as it was from 1916 to 1930, when it was the party in power; and that the Radicals have been the most unified in the periods before 1916 and after 1930, when they have been a party of opposition.

Most non-Argentines do not find it easy to comprehend what the U.C.R. stands for in addition to oppositionism. The Radicals have been opposed not only to the *Peronistas*, but also to the Socialists* and to the Communists† and to the Conservatives.‡ But, on the other hand, there is some truth in the assertion that the U.C.R. is "the reverse of the same coin which had conservatism on its face."[13] The Radical party houses a curious combination of elements. For one thing, it has represented the "industrial and commercial interests, . . . protectionists, merchants, free-traders."[14] Also, the U.C.R. considers itself a carrier of the principles

* See pp. 378–86.
† See pp. 391–97.
‡ See pp. 386–91.

of the French Revolution and the political heir of the *por-teños'* "May Revolution" of 1810. Moreover, some Radicals have on occasion tried to make the organization something of a labor party. Thus, while the U.C.R. is frequently notable for its representation of propertied interests, there is considerable justification for Ingenieros' evaluation of the Radicals as "a progressive element in the institutional development of the country. Theirs is the party of Whigs."[15] And Weil has summarized the party's following as embracing "the urban, industrial and commercial middle class, and some worker groups."[16]

The Radical party was established in 1892 by Leandro Nicéforo Alem and Pedro C. Molina. Some years before— in 1889—Alem had joined with Bernardo Irigoyen* to form the Civic Youth Union in an expression of protest against rule by the "Oligarchy." Specifically, the Civic Youth Union sought the protection of civil liberties and the eradication of electoral fraud and other forms of official corruption. And the Civic Youth Union became the nucleus around which the larger U.C.R., then bitterly opposed to the "Oligarchy," was formally organized on November 17, 1892. The Radicals' "Organic Charter," published at that time, proclaimed that the U.C.R. would be an impersonal political association "formed to fight for the strengthening of our institutional life which would assure peace and progress to the country, for faithful observance of the laws, for the purity of administrative morality, the effective exercise of popular sovereignty, and the full recognition of the autonomy of the provinces and municipalities, fundamental bases of our system of government and national existence."[17] Other Radical pronouncements stressed the party's opposition to the landowning "Oligarchy" and antipathy toward *personalismo*, the pattern characterized by political

* Not to be confused with Hipólito Irigoyen.

adherence to leaders as personalities rather than indorsement of abstract principles and programs. The U.C.R. was to be a party of principle and not of *personalismo*.

The Radical party grew rapidly in popular support during the early years of the twentieth century. However, the organization remained an opposition party until the presidential election of 1916. Due largely to the operation of the "Sáenz Peña Law," which had been enacted four years earlier, the U.C.R. was victorious in the presidential election of 1916, which has been characterized as "the first and only honest election ever held on Argentine soil."[18] The party remained in power until the Uriburu revolution of 1930. During the period between 1916 and 1930, two Radical presidents—Hipólito Irigoyen and Marcelo T. de Alvear—occupied the *Casa Rosada*.

Irigoyen is probably destined to remain one of the most controversial figures in Argentine history. He attempted to win labor support for the Radicals, and during his first term in the presidency (1916–22) some attempt was made by the *Casa Rosada* to have pro-labor measures written into law. President Irigoyen was basically unsuccessful in his bid for a role as champion of organized labor, and his administration was followed by a general tendency among workingmen to become disillusioned with the Radical party. Irigoyen's pro-labor efforts were, in large part, frustrated by his enemies within his own party. "The Radical government was not a systematic enemy of the workers, whom it favored with some protective legislation," one Argentine has said of the Irigoyen administration. "Rather, it was indecisive, moderate, and contradictory, in consequence of the juxtaposition of heterogeneous elements in the governing party."[19] On other fronts than labor, Irigoyen was not much more successful. His rivals within his own party objected to his techniques of controlling the

U.C.R. They charged him with *personalismo*, with attempting to bend the party to his own personal ambitions; and it was pointed out that *personalismo* ran counter to the fundamental principles of the U.C.R. At length, a group of Radicals, calling themselves "*antipersonalistas*," broke from Irigoyen's leadership in 1922.

Marcelo T. de Alvear, the leader of the *antipersonalista* Radicals, was elected president of Argentina in 1922, and remained in the *Casa Rosada* until 1928. During Alvear's presidency, the *antipersonalistas* developed a strong antipathy toward the labor movement and came to be regarded as more conservative than the Irigoyen wing of the U.C.R. Although Irigoyen was re-elected president in 1928, the aged leader was unable to unite the party or to give it a definitive stand on many public issues. On the eve of the revolution of 1930, the U.C.R. was a mildly pro-labor party, with planks in its platform calling for such measures as a high tariff, opposition to British "imperialism," government control of mineral production, woman suffrage, and tax exemption for owners of small properties. The conviction was general in Argentina by 1930 that during the fourteen years that the U.C.R. had been in power the party had failed to give the country positive and successful leadership.

When General Uriburu overthrew the Irigoyen administration on September 6, 1930, the Radicals resumed the role of an opposition party, a role to which they appeared to be better adapted than to leadership of the government. Uriburu's uprising had been conducted with the support of the "Oligarchy" and the Conservative party,* and this circumstance provided the U.C.R. with convenient political symbols against which to organize an opposition. With telling effectiveness, the Radicals led the resistance against the

* See pp. 386–91.

administrations of Presidents Uriburu (1930–32), Justo (1932–38), and Castillo (1940–43). Although they gave some support to President Ortiz (1938–40), the Radicals have been essentially an opposition party since 1930. And in this capacity they were the strongest political party in Argentina on the eve of the Perón revolution of 1943.

The U.C.R.'s initial reactions to the events of June 4, 1943, were confused and indecisive. At first the Radicals appeared to indorse the revolutionists, primarily because they had deposed President Castillo, against whom the U.C.R. had conducted a bitter opposition. Indeed, the Radicals gave their "official, frank support"[20] to General Arturo Rawson, the first president of the "new Argentina." Rawson, it will be remembered, had not been a member of the G.O.U. and did not appear to be pro-Axis.* After Rawson's displacement by General Pedro P. Ramírez, the Radicals moved gradually to withdraw such backing as they had given to the new regime. By the time that Colonel Perón had emerged as the guiding figure of the "new Argentina," the U.C.R. had become fairly adamant in its opposition to the regime.

During the latter part of 1943, all of 1944, and much of 1945, Perón sought Radical backing for his presidential ambitions. Negotiations for this support were opened in November of 1943. In the early stages of this maneuvering, some U.C.R. units appeared to be receptive to a league with Perón, but the main body of the Radicals—led by the party's units in the Provinces of Córdoba, Santa Fé, and Entre Ríos—moved steadily toward a position of uncompromising enmity toward Perón. When, in December of 1943, the U.C.R. sought permission to hold a party convention so that Radical affiliates might discuss the party's political relationships to Perón, President Ramírez refused to

* See p. 49.

grant the permission on the ground that such a convention would be "inconvenient" at that time. At length, in April of 1944, the U.C.R. formally announced that it would join with other parties in opposition to the "new Argentina." This action precipitated the first of stern government measures against the Radicals, among them a decree dated June 23, 1944, prohibiting an enumerated list of U.C.R. leaders from living in the Province of Entre Ríos. Only a small minority of the Radicals—the "Collaborationists," led by Quijano, Cooke, and Antille—came to join Perón and indorse his bid for the presidency. The "Collaborationists" were read out of the main body of the Radical party on August 6, 1945.

Meanwhile, the U.C.R. mobilized for action against Perón and prepared to move in concert with the other opposition parties. In a dramatic manifesto dated March 2, 1945, the Radicals denounced the "new Argentina" as a "political system alien to the national spirit." The manifesto asserted that "we do not wish that the silence imposed [upon us] through suppression of the right of assembly and of freedom of expression be interpreted as acquiescence in facts and situations that are contrary to our historic tradition."[21] In June, the party announced its strong denunciation of the Organic Statute of Political Parties, and demanded an immediate return to constitutional government under the Constitution of 1853. Although the U.C.R. on July 21 embarked upon its reorganization in conformity with the Organic Statute of Political Parties, the Radicals made it clear that this action did not signify co-operation with the regime "in any form."[22]

The question of collaboration with the other opposition parties brought a major crisis within the Radical party in 1945. During the course of a half-century, the U.C.R. had developed a tradition of operating singly, of eschewing coalitions with other parties. This tradition was not easily broken. Some Radicals—notably the "Intransigent" wing of the party, under the leadership of the redoubtable Amadeo Sabatini of Córdoba—felt that the U.C.R. must continue, at any cost, to avoid coalitions. Others, like Dr. Enrique P. Mosca, former governor of the Province of Santa Fé, and Dr. José P. Tamborini, an ex-senator from the Federal Capital, who had been in the cabinet of President Alvear, argued that the revolution of 1943 had presented the U.C.R. with a crisis sufficiently serious to warrant breaking the tradition against coalitions. This issue was not yet decided within the party when, on August 21, 1945, Radical leaders entered into negotiations with the Socialists, the Conservatives, the Communists, and the Progressive Democrats to explore the possibility of establishing an anti-Perón coalition. The U.C.R. was among the four parties which formed a "Committee of Democratic Co-ordination" in August.* It was this committee that sponsored the celebrated "March of the Constitution and Liberty" on September 19. Although the huge demonstration resulted in the resumption of the state of siege, the U.C.R. was generally convinced by the experience that opposition could best be conducted at that juncture through co-operation with other parties.

After "Loyalty Day," when Perón became a presidential candidate, the Radical party accepted Socialist, Communist, and Progressive Democratic overtures, looking toward the formation of an electoral alliance to offer unified opposition to the "new Argentina" in the election of February 24, 1946. On November 14, 1945, the U.C.R. formally agreed to participate in that coalition, which was known as the "Democratic Union." Under the terms of the agreement for the coalition, the Radicals were to nominate both the

---

* The Progressive Democrats were not represented on the committee.

presidential and the vice-presidential candidates of the Democratic Union. Both candidates—Tamborini and Mosca—were Radicals, and the U.C.R., which had long avoided electoral alliances, found itself leading the anti-Perón coalition in the campaign of 1945–46.

The election was held on February 24, 1946. On May 15 of that year, the Organic Statute of Political Parties entered into force. It will be remembered that, among other things, that law prohibited coalitions of political parties;* and the U.C.R. and other participating organizations were forced to abandon the Democratic Union. Although the coalition was formally dead, other circumstances after 1946—particularly congressional elections in that year and again in 1948—placed the U.C.R. in the position of *de facto* representative of many of the parties of the opposition. Of the anti-Perón organizations, only the Radicals and the Conservatives† won seats in the congress. The senate was controlled entirely by Perón, but after the election of 1948, the U.C.R. held 43 seats in the 158-man Chamber of Deputies. Following the election of 1951, the Radicals, with 14 seats, were the only opposition party represented in the chamber. The opposition, then, in so far as it was conducted in congress, lay largely in the hands of the Radical party.

From the standpoint of parliamentary tactics, the U.C.R.'s formula for opposition generally involved waiting for Perón's legislators to introduce some new measure, and then to debate vigorously—and unsuccessfully—against it. This formula, of course, is open to serious censure as political strategy. While the Radicals could point to the record of debates in the Chamber of Deputies as evidence that the U.C.R. argued against almost everything Perón did, the ef-

* See pp. 361–62.
† The Conservatives were not affiliated formally with the Democratic Union.

fectiveness of this technique of opposition was at best dubious. Nevertheless, the Radicals did develop some congressional leaders who were effective in embarrassing Perón on the floor of the Chamber of Deputies. And, of course, Perón's congressmen evolved techniques of doing away with the more effective Radical deputies. These usually took the form of depriving them of their congressional immunity or expelling them from the Chamber of Deputies. The reader has already seen how such techniques were employed against Radical leaders like Ernesto Enrique Sammartino and Ricardo J. Balbín.*

The record of the U.C.R.'s parliamentary opposition to Perón has been distinguished only by the quality of its oratory. To the extent that the pattern of Radical opposition has been to wait for Perón to announce a topic so that the U.C.R. might argue against his position on it, Perón rather than the Radicals has called the tune for the parliamentary opposition. What is the voting record of the U.C.R. in the Chamber of Deputies? Ask rather what matters Perón has given them to speak and vote against. These include, for example, the substitution of Perón's new Constitution of 1949 for the 1853 document. The Radicals argued and voted against constitutional reform, both in the Chamber of Deputies and in the constitutional convention which wrote the 1949 charter. In general, the U.C.R. oratory was good. Hear a sample: the new constitution would "legalize an irritating and monstrous Caesarism, destroying in fact the judicial power as a power. . . . It will create a monarch disguised in democratic clothing."[23] Basically, this has been the unifying pattern of Radical opposition to the regime. The reader who has come this far in this book knows about a good number of laws passed by Perón's congress. The Radicals have debated and voted against almost all of them.

* See pp. 81–82 and 117–19.

On extreme occasions, the U.C.R.'s technique of opposition has involved walking out of an assembly after it adopts a Perón-inspired measure regarded by the Radicals as especially outrageous. When, for example, Sammartino was expelled from the Chamber of Deputies, the remaining forty-two U.C.R. deputies stalked out of the chamber in protest against his ouster. A few days later, they returned to the congress to continue the fight. Again, the Radical delegation to the constitutional convention walked out of that body rather than sign the Constitution of 1949. And, when the new charter provided for the extension of congressmen's terms of office, twenty Radical deputies resigned from the legislature rather than have their terms prolonged by a constitution they would not accept. "Let us close down the entire congress,"[24] the U.C.R. Deputy Arturo Frondizi suggested at the time.

Many anti-*Peronistas* have been critical of the Radicals' strategy in conducting the parliamentary opposition. This strategy has consisted primarily of following the lead of President Perón. In a sense, U.C.R. tactics in congress have been but the reverse of *Peronista* techniques. Whereas the *Peronistas* wait for the president to propose some new measure so that they might vote for it, the Radicals have in general waited for the same thing so that they might vote against it. And the *Peronistas* have uniformly commanded the overwhelming majority of the votes. On the other hand, while the U.C.R. might be open to severely adverse criticism on the basis of its parliamentary tactics, certainly the personal courage of the Radical leadership has been unimpeachable. Many outstanding Radicals have braved imprisonment and martyrdom in their battle against Perón. This is well illustrated by the hardships suffered at the hands of the "new Argentina" not only by such Radicals as Balbín and Sammartino, but also by lesser members of the party, like Eudoro Patricio Vargas Gómez, Tomás González Funes, Augustín Rodríguez Araya, Atilio Cattáneo, Silvano Santander, Enrique Isaac Sánchez Larios, Domingo Cialzeta, Teobaldo José Giménez, Moisés Lebensohn, and Luis R. MacKay.

Moreover, the U.C.R., faced by overwhelming odds, has continued to provide the *Peronistas* with their major electoral opposition. When President Perón ran for re-election in 1951, his most serious competition was furnished by the Radicals. With the Organic Statute of Political Parties in force at that time, the U.C.R. was unable to enter into a coalition with other opposition parties, as had been done in 1946. Nevertheless, the Radicals conducted a spirited campaign against Perón in 1951. In a sense, the nomination of Balbín and Frondizi as the U.C.R. candidates for president and vice president, respectively, represented a victory of the "Young Turks" over the "old guard" within the Radical party. Under the leadership of Balbín and Frondizi, the Radicals campaigned with a platform calling for resurrection of civil and political liberties, a re-emphasis on agriculture, a new minimum wage law, full employment, and nationalization of oil refineries and meat-packing plants. Despite the U.C.R's defeat in the election of 1951, no Radical could be ashamed of the showing made by the Balbín-Frondizi ticket against Perón.*

As the major anti-*Peronista* party, the Radical Civic Union is viewed with some ambivalence by the otherwise-minded. But despite its defects, the Radical party remains the chief hope of many of the Argentines who are adamant in their opposition to the Perón regime.

* An analysis of the results of the election of 1951 appears on pp. 85–86.

16.

The Otherwise-Minded (Continued)

Although the Radical party is the largest of the opposition groups in the "new Argentina," other anti-*Peronista* organizations also play important roles in the country's politics. The Socialist, Conservative, and Communist parties, each with smaller electoral support than the U.C.R., count themselves among President Perón's political enemies.* And each of these organizations has developed its own peculiar place in the patern of politics in Perón's Argentina.

The Socialists

The Socialist party of Argentina has long enjoyed a remarkable reputation among the "Yankees of the South." Many Argentines, while they might vote Radical, Conservative, Communist, or even *Peronista*, have had kind words for the Socialists. The party has been noted for the personal integrity of its leadership and for its tendency to immerse itself in doctrinal questions which delight the intellectually inclined. "The blunt truth," Weil has said, "is that the average citizen is justified in feeling that there is

* It should be noted that a Progressive Democratic party also functions as an opposition organization. This group, its strength limited to the Provinces of Santa Fé and Entre Ríos, is essentially a minor party, and is not the subject of extended discussion in this book.

virtually no difference between the Conservative* and the Radical leadership, in any case. As for the Socialists, they are different, namely, honest."[1] Who are the Socialist leaders who in recent years have given the party its outstanding reputation for personal and intellectual integrity? Américo Ghioldi, Alfredo L. Palacios, Nicolás Repetto, Mario Bravo,† and Enrique Dickmann, each a man of remarkable stature in his own way, have guided the organization during what has perhaps been the most difficult period in the history of the Socialist party. They have contributed measurably to the organization's scandal-free tradition.

They have also contributed to the doctrinal controversies which have made the Socialists a party of intellectuals who frequently find it difficult to agree among themselves, not only on the nature of social and political problems, but also on interpretations of Marxist theory. "The Socialist weakness," according to Ray Josephs, "lies in addiction to theory and philosophy and what we might call their lack of practical, sound common sense."[2] Largely because of intellectual controversies among the Socialist leaders, the party in Argentina has suffered factionalism which has resulted in no fewer than six crises since 1898 which resulted in formal splits in the party. It is not necessary to be an Argentine to understand what the Socialist Enrique Dickmann meant when he said that "Karl Marx, the great theoretician and founder of scientific socialism, instead of being a bond of union among Socialists, was—and still is—a divisive factor."[3]

Although the Argentine Socialists disagree violently among themselves as to what their party stands for, most of them would probably indorse a composite statement

---

* See pp. 386–91.
† Bravo died in 1944 of a heart attack after having been tortured by the Federal Police.

which held that their party represents, principally, two groups. The first of these includes those urban workers who have not become *Peronistas*. And the second embraces the bulk of Argentina's politically active professional intellectuals. As such, Socialist strength is concentrated in the larger cities of the country, primarily at Buenos Aires, and the party has little following in the provinces of the "interior." According to the Socialist Nicolás Repetto, "the history of the Socialist movement is the history of the fight for the political rights of the working masses, for free union activity, and for the democratization of the state."[4] In recent times—especially since the revolution of 1943—the Socialists have placed great emphasis on their desire for constitutional government and individual liberty. Indeed, one "North American" observer has remarked that "Argentina's Socialist party is probably the most truly pro-democratic group in the country."[5] If an attempt were made to line the Argentine political parties up from left to right, it would probably be discovered that there is no party of the center in the nation, and that the Socialists locate about as far to the left of the center as the Radicals do to the right of it.

The Socialists had been divided among themselves for twenty years before the revolution of June 4, 1943. That uprising, however, had the effect of bringing to the party the greatest unity it had known in a generation. The Socialists were in agreement that the Perón revolution represented a sinister threat to what they understood Argentine institutions to be. Indeed, the Socialists were among the first of the political parties to go on record as being opposed to the "new Argentina."

From the first days of the Perón revolution, the leaders of the G.O.U. recognized the Socialists as certain and uncompromising enemies of the new regime. Many of the first repressive measures taken were directed against that party. *La Vanguardia*, the Socialist organ, became one of the first Argentine newspapers to fall at the hands of Perón.* Moreover, as Perón moved to dominate organized labor, he was brought into dramatic and open conflict with the Socialists. Labor leaders affiliated with the party were among the first inhabitants of the concentration camps established in the "new Argentina"; Socialists were among the first to taste the *picana eléctrica;* and Mario Bravo, a Socialist leader who died in 1944 after a session with the Federal Police, remains one of the most celebrated victims of physical torture in Perón's Argentina.

Moreover, it was the Socialists who took the initiative in urging all opposition parties to pool their resources in a united front against the "new Argentina." On March 19, 1945, the Socialists formally invited the other opposition parties to unite in a "great national movement"[6] for the restoration of constitutional government. The party actively participated in the Board of Democratic Co-ordination, which staged the "March of the Constitution and Liberty" in September of 1945. And two months later, the Socialists invited the Radical, Conservative, Progressive Democratic, and Communist parties to join together in an electoral coalition against Perón. When the coalition—the Democratic Union—was formed, the Socialists gave it their determined support, backing the coalition's candidates, Tamborini and Mosca, both Radicals, against Perón and Quijano in the election campaign of 1945–46.

Unlike the Radicals, the Socialists have not been represented in the national congress since the revolution of 1943. Although they held seats in the Senate and in the Chamber of Deputies for the quarter-century between 1916 and 1941,† the Socialists have not won any seats in either legis-

* See pp. 215–16.
† The state of siege declared by President Castillo in that year had the effect of suspending the congress.

lative chamber since the Perón revolution. The Socialist opposition to President Perón's government has, therefore, been conducted exclusively outside the legislative halls. This opposition has primarily taken the form of attempts to retain influence within the labor movement. With the progressive capture of the C.G.T. by the *Peronistas*, this influence has waned steadily since 1943. However, Socialist strength in the labor unions, though weaker today than it was before 1943, is by no means dead, as occasional union revolts against President Perón have indicated.*

Despite the imprisonment, exile, and intimidation of many of their leaders, the Socialists have continued to participate in political campaigns against the *Peronistas*. When President Perón ran for re-election in 1951, the Socialists, like the other parties, were prohibited by the Organic Statute of Political Parties from entering into another coalition. such as the Democratic Union of 1945–46. Forced to run their own separate slates of candidates in 1951, the Socialists at that time nominated Alfredo L. Palacios and Américo Ghioldi for the presidency and vice presidency, respectively. This team put up a spirited if futile campaign against Perón and Quijano. When, on September 28, the government declared that a state of "internal war" existed, Palacios was imprisoned in connection with the excitement. Released in October, he withdrew his presidential candidacy and urged his party to boycott the election on the ground that the declaration of "internal war" had rendered effective campaigning impossible.

Although the Socialist party, like the U.C.R., is an opposition party, Socialist techniques of resistance to Perón differ fundamentally from the Radical strategy. The U.C.R.'s techniques are essentially negative in character.

* See pp. 326–27.

The Socialists, on the other hand, have developed a much
more positive program for doing battle with Perón. There
is, of course, something of negativism in the Socialist declaration that "one of the immediate and fundamental objectives" of the party is "the demolition of the theory and
practice of Perón."⁷ But this is only a small part of the
Socialist approach to the problems posed by the "new
Argentina."

It has taken the Socialists fully twenty years since the
death of Juan B. Justo, their first chieftain, to develop a
leader intellectually capable of providing the party with
guidance and direction. Américo Ghioldi now appears to
be that leader. In the years since the Perón revolution, he
has laid down a four-point program for the Socialists, and
the party, following his lead, has in general endorsed his
blueprint. The four points are worth examining.

The first of them relates to such matters as democracy
and individual liberty. "The true conflict of our age is between democracy and totalitarianism," Ghioldi has pointed
out. "Socialism will be democratic and liberal or it will not
be anything."⁸ Within the framework of the Ghioldi approach, the Socialists must press for the resumption of civil
liberties, for the restoration of freedom of the press and the
resurrection of true constitutional government. These freedoms, in Ghioldi's view, are as much in the Socialists' interest as they are to the benefit of any other sector of Argentine life.

Secondly, what about Karl Marx and the Socialists' talk
of such naughty concepts as capitalism and imperialism?
"Marxism," according to Ghioldi, "is not all of socialism.
It is a moment, a creative moment, but basically only a step.
The possibilities of the growth of socialism do not end with
Marxism."⁹ Well and good: Karl Marx died in the nine-

teenth century, but socialism must live in the twentieth. But it is not that easy to separate socialism from Marx. He did, after all, provide a theoretical construct to which the Socialists are committed and which they must use as a point of departure. How to use Marxism in this fashion? This is a lesson which Ghioldi learned sitting at the feet of Juan B. Justo. If it is necessary to cling to Marx's terminology, Justo would say, then the words should be used to mean what Marx meant by them. Within the context of Marxist theory, what does "capitalism" mean? What is "imperialism"? Do the words mean that Socialists must shake their fists at the Yankees and the British? Not at all, according to Ghioldi: the Socialists must "not make a tabu and a street slogan of the word 'imperialism.' "[10] The terms must be precisely defined. It is Peronism, *Justicialismo*, and not socialism, to pin the political label of "foreign imperialist" on the "North Americans" and the British. It is *Justicialismo*, and not Marxism, to hate the United States and the United Kingdom.

Thirdly, there is the matter of foreign policy and international affairs.* Perón has stolen Marxist terminology to justify hatred of the "Yankee imperialists," but the Socialists have not accepted the burglary. The Socialist party maintains that Argentine foreign policy must be grounded on co-operation with the United States and the other American republics, that Argentina's international destiny lies in resumption of the country's traditional role in the American family of nations. It is worth noting that today the Socialists are virtually alone among Argentine political parties in taking this position on foreign policy. The Radicals do not take it, and neither do the Conservatives. And certainly the Communists and the *Peronistas* do not.

* Argentine international relations are discussed on pp. 6–16 and 400–439.

Fourthly, one day Perón and the *Peronistas* will disappear. Then—whither Argentina? This is a question which the Socialists have faced much more realistically than the Radicals. Hear Ghioldi: "At the end of this Argentine crisis and experience, the country cannot return to 1943. No decree could turn affairs that far back!"[11] If Perón falls in the 1950's, whatever party or parties then assume the reins of government must realize that Argentina has changed during the Perón era, that the Perón revolution *was* a revolution. And today the Socialists believe that whoever governs post-Perón Argentina must realize that he will not be ruling Irigoyen's Argentina or even Castillo's, that Perón's successor must accept and build on the justicialist revolution. What changes have occurred during the Perón epoch? Many have, of course; but one is especially apparent to the Socialists. Organized labor has changed, and the lower classes have acquired a social and political consciousness they had not known before 1943. According to the Socialists, post-Perón Argentina must recognize, accept, and welcome the rise of the workingman. And, in Ghioldi's view, the test for the Socialists will be "whether or not we are in a spiritual condition to use for socialism the new forces which the revolutionary process of the last years has released, revealed, and matured. On all sides we see forces whose rate of growth has been accelerated. . . . The [Perón] revolution has contributed, to some extent, to the development of the social consciousness of many workers who had not before known even the word 'socialism.' "[12]

The *Peronistas* have captured the C.G.T. from the Socialists. Perhaps the Socialists will be able to win it back. If they can, it may well be that organized labor will be a more powerful instrument in Socialist hands than it was before 1943. Perón has, after all, "dignified" the *descamisados*.

And perhaps the Socialists will be able—no Marxist will forgive this expression—to capitalize on the Perón revolution.

The Conservatives

The student who peruses the literature in an attempt to discover what the Argentine political parties have said about themselves unearths a peculiar fact about the Conservative party, the third strongest opposition organization in the "new Argentina." The Conservatives have written very little about themselves and their point of view. Impressive quantities of *Peronista*, Radical, Socialist, and Communist material have been published, but Conservative political literature is rare. This is not so much because the Conservatives are illiterate as it is due to the circumstance that, until relatively recently, very few of them saw the necessity or utility of explaining their position. Rule by the landowners, the "Oligarchy," was "natural." It was taken for granted as a fact of life, and did not need to be explained. Just as there was no compulsion in Europe to justify the divine right of kings until that order was challenged, so in Argentina there was no cause to justify or explain domination by the landowners, the old families, the "Oligarchy." It was as pointless to write a book about that "natural" fact of life as it is to pen a treatise pointing out that the sun shines only in the daytime.

To the Argentine Conservative, the way of the world, which is so obvious that only a dense "North American" college professor would bother to mention it in a book, runs as follows. Wealth is power, and land is the only source of wealth. Argentina is above all an agricultural country, and its riches are produced on the *estancias*, the huge landed estates which form an integral part of the nation's system of landownership. And the *estancieros*, the people who own the *estancias*, rule Argentina. Q.E.D. The sun does not shine at night.

It has been said that the Radicals and the Conservatives are opposite sides of the same coin. This is true in a limited sense. Both parties represent propertied interests. But the men of wealth who call themselves Radicals derive their property not so much from the land as they do from other wealth-forms—commerce, industry, and foreign trade. The Conservatives, on the other hand, are more closely associated with the land than the U.C.R. is. In social terms, the Conservative party represents the old families, the "Oligarchy," the "two hundred families [which] make up Argentine social fabric."[13] Weil has said that the Conservatives "are the acknowledged representatives of the landed aristocracy and the other reactionary vested interests allied with this small, powerful group."[14] And Professor Macdonald has regarded the Conservatives as "less a party than a coalition of local factions having substantially the same point of view."[15]

The Conservative party has ruled Argentina throughout much of its national history. In point of fact, the Conservatives have been an opposition party only twice—during the period, from 1916 to 1930, of U.C.R. governments, and in the Perón era, since 1943. And many Conservatives hold that those two periods were aberrations in the country's history, that neither of them gave expression to the "true Argentina." What is the "true Argentina"? It is neither Irigoyen's Argentina nor the "new Argentina." It is the "Oligarchy's" Argentina, the normal or "natural" state of affairs which has been interrupted only twice—by Irigoyen in 1916, and again by Perón in 1943.

Although the revolution of 1943 drove Castillo and the Conservatives from power, the Conservative party was at first somewhat hesitant before taking its stand against the "new Argentina." A number of factors led the Conservatives to toy initially with the possibility of collaborating with Perón, as they had with Uriburu thirteen years earlier. In the first place, the policy of the "new Argentina" toward World War II did not appear at first to be substantially different from Castillo's, which the Conservatives had supported. Secondly, a number of the people active in the Perón revolution had also been associated with Uriburu. As a matter of fact, Perón himself had played a minor part in the revolution of 1930.* And, thirdly, the first president of the "new Argentina," General Rawson, was himself associated with the "Oligarchy," had not been a member of the G.O.U., and seemed politically acceptable to the Conservatives. Shortly after June 4, 1943, it was said of the Conservative party that "with a few exceptions, its more responsible leaders and affiliates have maintained a suggestive silence; there has been no statement from them on the acceptance of posts offered by the government to their prominent men."[16]

However, primarily under the leadership of Rodolfo Moreno, former governor of the Province of Buenos Aires, the Conservatives moved slowly to join the Radicals, Socialists, and Communists in opposing the "new Argentina." The Conservatives did not formally announce their hostility to the regime until July of 1945, but their position had become evident as early as December of 1944, when a prominent Conservative, former Senator Antonio Santamarina, was imprisoned after the government declared him "guilty of acts of an ideological nature in compromising himself with subversive, irresponsible elements."[17] The

* In his interesting book, *Argentine Riddle*, Weil goes so far as to advance the thesis that Perón represents fundamentally the interests of the *estancieros*. This thesis, in the view of the present writer, cannot be demonstrated to be valid.

Conservatives' formal statement of opposition to the regime was at length published on July 25, 1945.

Thereafter, the party moved to associate itself with other groups resisting the revolution of 1943. In August, the Conservatives took part—with the Radicals, the Progressive Democrats, the Socialists, and the Communists—in the Board of Democratic Co-ordination, and joined with those parties in urging the Supreme Court of Justice to assume the reins of government. With the other affiliates of the Board of Democratic Co-ordination, the Conservatives participated in September in the "March of the Constitution and Liberty"; and Conservative leaders were among the political prisoners produced by the police dragnet after that demonstration. Although the Conservatives were active in the Board of Democratic Co-ordination, they did not participate formally with the other opposition parties in the Democratic Union, the anti-Perón coalition formed for the election campaign of 1945–46. The Conservatives, however, did not nominate their own candidates for president and vice president in that campaign, thus freeing the party's affiliates to vote for Tamborini and Mosca, the Democratic Union candidates. And when Perón ran for re-election in 1951, the Conservatives were no longer faced with the coalition problem, as the Organic Statute of Political Parties had by then outlawed such combinations. In 1951, the Conservative candidates for president and vice president, respectively, were Reinaldo Pastor and Vicente Solano Lima, both members of the Chamber of Deputies.

From 1946 to 1951, the Conservatives were able to hold a small number of seats in the Chamber of Deputies, but have not been represented in the congress since the latter date. Their pre-1951 parliamentary techniques of opposition were similar to those of the U.C.R. Indeed, the Conservative legislators usually acted and voted in concert with the Radicals.

Despite the fact that the Conservatives and the Radicals generally make common cause against the *Peronistas*, it is nevertheless true that the pattern of President Perón's economic policies affects the two groups differently. It has been noted that, although both the U.C.R. and the Conservatives tend to represent propertied interests, the natures of those interests differ. The Conservatives represent the landowners more than any other economic group, whereas the Radicals speak for the holders of other forms of wealth, for the men of commerce and industry. And *Peronista* economics affect land differently than commerce and industry.* Perón has tended to neglect rural and agricultural sectors of the economy to an extent which has led many observers to find in this the basic economic weakness of the "new Argentina." On the other hand, some areas of commerce and industry appear to have benefited from Peronism. Thus the landowning "Oligarchy" has been left in a more unhappy position in the "new Argentina" than the merchants and industrialists, although land has not been expropriated on an economically significant scale.

Today the landowners and the Conservatives appear to be in retreat. "Most of them still have their land, but they're out of power and worried about the future and about breakup of their estates," a "North American" observer recently pointed out. "Perón has promised to break up big estates and turn over 'the land to those who work on it.' But very little of that actually has taken place. You can still find in Argentina a few estates as big as 200,000 or 300,000 acres."[18] Nevertheless, President Perón has said that he is "forming a new Argentina, so that there is no

* See pp. 248–57.

place for the outworn Oligarchy that betrayed the country."[19] If this indeed comes to pass, then presumably the Conservative party as it is known today might well disappear from the scene. On the other hand, future historians may demonstrate that the Conservatives signed their own death warrant as a party when they entered into league with General Uriburu as long ago as 1930.

The Communists

From the standpoint of its record since June 4, 1943, the Communist party of Argentina differs in an intriguing fashion from the other non-*Peronista* parties in the country. It will be remembered that the Socialists have been uniformly opposed to the regime since the first days of the "new Argentina," while the U.C.R. and the Conservatives took uncertain positions at first, later entering into uncompromising opposition against Perón. The Communists, on the other hand, resolutely resisted the regime from the first moments of the revolution of 1943, but *later* altered their stand to endorse a portion of President Perón's program.

It is not easy to estimate the number of Communists in Argentina. Professor Macdonald said in 1942 that "there is virtually no Communist strength in the Argentine Republic."[20] Since then, estimates of the number of Argentine Communists have ranged between 100,000 and 30,000. There has been a tendency to overestimate Communist strength for reasons which Weil has explained about as competently as any other close observer of the Argentine scene. "Vociferous intellectuals tended to give the Communist party the semblance of being a force to be reckoned with," his analysis points out. "Then, too, there is the common though unjustified tendency to lump anarchist and anarchosyndicalist groups with the Communists. Finally, all [Argentine] governments, past and present, are prone to call all dissenters 'Communists.' "[21] Although these secrets are kept by different people, the exact number of Communists and the exact number of *Peronistas* are carefully suppressed bits of information. On the basis of unofficial data assembled from informed sources, it would appear that there are probably somewhere between 30,000 and 35,000 card-carrying members of the Communist party in Argentina today. If one adds to this figure an estimate of the number of people who, while not formal members of the party, are nevertheless in sympathy with it and vote for its candidates, the combined total would probably locate between 60,000 and 65,000. The bulk of these live in the city of Buenos Aires, and many of them are associated with the labor movement.

It is now abundantly clear that the Communists vigorously opposed the regime only for the duration of the war —that is, so long as there was an Axis, toward which the Argentine regime was oriented, and against which the Soviet Union was at war. If today the Communists are censured for the 1946 change in their position, let it be noted that until that year they struggled against Perón as heroically as any Argentine political party did. Communist leaders were jailed, tortured, and exiled; and until the end of World War II, the Communist party made common cause with the Radicals, Socialists, and Conservatives against the regime. Arrests of the Communists, in high gear by December of 1943, continued for the remainder of the war. Communists were among the first inhabitants of the concentration camps, and were among the first victims of the *picana eléctrica*. Moreover, when Perón's Federal Police was established, that agency contained a Special Section devoted exclusively to making life miserable for the Communists.*

* See p. 173.

Along with the other political parties, the Communists were declared dissolved by the government on December 31, 1943. A little more than a year and a half later—on August 13, 1945—Interior Minister Quijano authorized the reopening of the Communist party's headquarters at Buenos Aires, and the Communists proceeded forthwith to co-operate with the other parties against Perón. The party joined with the U.C.R., the Socialists, the Conservatives, and the Progressive Democrats in the Board of Democratic Co-ordination, and participated with them in September of 1945 in the spectacular "March of the Constitution and Liberty." Later that year, when Perón announced his presidential candidacy, the Communists joined with the Socialists in urging the other opposition parties to pool their resources in an anti-Perón electoral coalition. The Communists played an active role in that coalition, the Democratic Union, throughout the campaign of 1945–46, giving their full support to Tamborini and Mosca, the coalition candidates.

World War II ended shortly before Perón's first election to the presidency, and a shift in the domestic position of the Argentine Communists accompanied the change in the international situation. The Axis was gone and Perón now endeavored to dissociate his government from it. With the collapse of the Axis, the Soviet Union and its western allies drifted apart; and this parting of the ways was reflected in the changing position of the Argentine Communists. The picture was no longer complicated by the Axis: Perón said he was anti-"Yankee," and the Soviet Union moved toward a similar position after 1946. Perón said he opposed the "Oligarchy" and the "foreign imperialists," and the international situation no longer prevented the Argentine Communists, in support of the Soviet Union, from joining Perón in his war against the political symbols—"Oligarchy" and "foreign imperialists"—which the Communists had long combatted before 1943. Thus the Communists returned to an ideological position in which, in a sense, they were more comfortable; and they retreated from the "strange alliance" which they had maintained from 1943 to 1946 with the U.C.R., the Socialists, the Conservatives—and the "Oligarchy." After Perón's first election, the Argentine Communist party moved away from the other parties of the opposition to adopt its own peculiar policies toward the administration of President Juan Domingo Perón.

The change was dramatically illustrated in public statements made by Communist leaders in 1945 and 1946. In the former year, while the war was still in progress, the Communists were still resolutely anti-Perón. Rodolfo Ghioldi, a Communist chieftain, asserted that the Argentine "dictatorship arms itself, intrigues, and conspires to install Nazis in neighboring state governments, seeks to divide the nations of the continent by disrupting the unity of foreign policy."[22] When, during the war, the United States Secretary of State and the British Prime Minister censured Argentina's pro-Axis policy, Jerónimo Arnedo Alvarez, an Argentine Communist spokesman, declared that "we greet the position of Cordell Hull and Prime Minister Churchill."[23] But the Communists made significantly different statements after the war. By December of 1946, the Argentine party had already moved to a position permitting the Communists to declare in a manifesto that Perón's victory in that year's election represented a triumph for forces lauded as "essentially democratic, progressive, and anti-Fascist."[24] And by 1947, the Communists had announced their position of "constructive opposition" to Perón. "Constructive opposition" signified a species of eclecticism—the Communists would support some of Perón's measures, but oppose others.

The Communists' declaration of their "constructive opposition" to the regime drew bitter criticism from the anti-Perón parties which now felt themselves deserted by the Communists. The Socialist Américo Ghioldi—who should not be confused with his estranged brother, the Communists' Rodolfo Ghioldi—asserted that "the mental attitude . . . of the Stalinist Communists is essentially anti-democratic, totalitarian, obedient to orders from Moscow, subject to abrupt changes, always ready to fabricate slogans, constantly in the act of disguising the most absurd situations and conduct with a doctrinal mask. Communist parties everywhere are political organs of the Soviet government."[25]

In their position of "constructive opposition" to Perón, the Communists live more comfortably in Argentina today than they did in the hectic years from 1943 to 1946. Some of their leaders are still arrested on occasion, and even subjected to the *picana eléctrica*, but *Peronista* persecution of the Communists is no longer conducted on as large a scale as it was before 1946. Under the Organic Statute of Political Parties, the Communists remain a legal party in Argentina. "President Perón permits them to exist legally," a "North American" observer has said, "but their meetings are regularly raided and their activities curtailed."[26] Although the Communists, like other non-*Peronista* parties, are kept carefully hemmed in by Perón, some upsurge in Communist activity in Argentina was evident by the end of 1946. At that time, a Soviet trade mission arrived at Buenos Aires. The chief of the mission, Konstantin Vasilievich Shevelev, established contact with the Argentine Communist party, and Shevelev was later named Commercial Attaché at the Soviet Embassy at Buenos Aires. Moreover, attempts have been made to use the Slavic Club at the *porteños'* capital to organize eastern European immigrants in support of Communist political objectives. The Slavic Club was under the direction of Tomás Davidoff and Pablo Shostakowsky, both residents of Buenos Aires. A "North American" correspondent, Edward Tomlinson, has recorded this account of his recent visit to the Slavic Club: "There I listen to endless speeches on dialectical materialism and foreign imperialism and the role of the proletariat and many other things which I do not understand. . . . They tell me there will come a time when I will understand and accept all these things. Meanwhile, every week there is a special assessment for this, a special contribution for that, a special tax for the other. It seems to me . . . that to be a good proletarian, one must also be something of a millionaire at the same time."[27]

There is some indication that the Communist-*Peronista* honeymoon began to wane early in 1950. In January of that year, *La Hora*, the Communist newspaper at Buenos Aires, was closed down by the government for "anti-Argentine activities";[28] and a year later the Slavic Club was ordered shuttered in an action which Radio Moscow said was taken "without any reason."[29] When Perón ran for re-election in 1951, the Communists, like other Argentine parties, were required by the Organic Statute of Political Parties to nominate their own slate of candidates. Rodolfo Ghioldi and Alcira de la Peña, the latter a woman, became the Communist candidates for president and vice president, respectively. During the campaign, Ghioldi was shot at Paraná, the capital of the Province of Entre Ríos.* Although the wound was not fatal, it was serious enough to prevent Rodolfo Ghioldi from further active participation in politics in 1951.

The Communists are in "constructive opposition" to Perón. What is "constructive opposition"? It is a principle

* See p. 84.

of selection, on the basis of which the Communists support some of the government's measures while opposing others. What is the principle of selection? Within the pattern of Argentine politics, this is answered in terms of *Justicialismo*, Perón's "Third Position." The "Third Position" stands between capitalism and communism, opposing both. "Constructive opposition" indorses that portion of *Justicialismo* which is anti-capitalist, and resists that sector of the "Third Position" which is anti-Communist. In the field of international policy, the "Third Position" endeavors to stand midway between the United States and the Soviet Union.* "Constructive opposition" supports that part of *Justicialismo* which is anti-"Yankee," and opposes that portion of the "Third Position" which resists the Soviet Union. Thus the eclecticism of "constructive opposition." It has been illustrated by Communist endorsement of Perón's policy toward the United Nations police action in Korea, and by Communist opposition against Argentine participation in the Fourth Meeting of American Foreign Ministers, held at Washington in 1951 to adopt anti-Communist measures.† Since the adoption of its position of "constructive opposition" to the Perón administration, the Communist party of Argentina has declined in its electoral support. Whereas the Communists polled 12 per cent of the national vote in 1946, they received only 1.5 per cent of the ballots cast in the election of 1951. Like the Socialists, the Communists have gone unrepresented in the national congress throughout the Perón era.

Some observers believe that Perón's policies have increased the possibility of an eventual Communist coup in Argentina. This thesis rests on the expanded political role played in the country by organized labor, and on the ad-

* See pp. 423–24.
† See pp. 424–25.

justment of the C.G.T. to authoritarian leadership and control. "If Perón ever is forced to give way to a Communist *coup*," one writer has said, "the comrades will have little to do other than drop into his chair and take over."[30] Prediction of such matters is, of course, difficult; indeed, specialists in politics have frequently been defined as those people who do not know the answers to the really important questions.

Nevertheless, the problem of the shape of Argentine politics after Perón passes from power is of crucial significance and cannot be overlooked. One approach to the question is to assume that responsibility for post-Perón government would fall into the hands of one or more of the non-*Peronista* parties. These parties—the U.C.R., the Socialists, the Conservatives, and the Communists—have now been surveyed. Which—if any—of them will inherit Perón's mantle? The Conservatives, by virtue of the flow of their fortunes since 1930, appear to be the most easily eliminated of the contenders. There is no point in denying that the Perón revolution has indeed been a revolution, and that the "Oligarchy" cannot hope to return to its position of dominance. Too much has happened since 1943—and, before that year, too much had begun happening—for that.

And the Radicals, the Socialists, and the Communists, what of them? It remains possible for the U.C.R. to inherit the Argentina of the future if the party is able to adopt a more positive program than it has displayed in recent years, and if it can bring itself to accept the social transformations of the Perón period. These are not necessarily big "ifs." The Radicals are divided on these questions, and the U.C.R. may well guide post-Perón destinies if the faction of the party which holds it to be impossible to return to 1943 remains ascendant. This faction has capable leaders—among them Arturo Frondizi, the Radicals' 1951 vice-presidential candidate—and may well fulfil the hopes of many non-*Peronistas.*

As for the Socialists and the Communists, both stand to gain from Perón's political transformation of the labor movement. Both are aware of this possibility. Of the two, the Socialists, wedded to more democratic usages and more loyal to Argentina, are stronger among the organized workers. If post-Perón Argentina does not fall to the U.C.R., then the Socialists seem likely candidates for leadership, in which case organized labor will continue to be a major political force among the "Yankees of the South." Communist inheritance from Perón remains an outside possibility. It seems likely that the Communists stand in third place among the candidates, and that they might rise to power only if the U.C.R. and the Socialists fail, and if no new party arises to take their place.

It has been noted that there is no party of the center in Argentina. The Socialists are about as far to the left of the center as the Radicals are to the right of it. But a huge gap remains in the center, and it may well be that Argentina needs a new party to fill that gap. If such an organization does not appear, then the future seems to lie with either the U.C.R. or the Socialists.

17.

Argentina and the World

Argentina's international position has acquired a novel significance in the years since the revolution of 1943. That uprising, occurring during World War II, intensified the pro-Axis direction of Argentine foreign policy; and the country remained estranged from the United States and most of the other American republics until the war thundered to a close in Europe in May of 1945. Since then, Argentine-"Yankee" relations have become more cordial, and Buenos Aires has participated in the work of the United Nations. Nevertheless, Argentine foreign policy, now rationalized in terms of the "Third Position," remains distinctive in the Western Hemisphere, and the country has not resumed its pre-Perón position in the American family of nations.

Good Neighbors

Little note has been taken of a diplomatic ceremony which took place at the *Casa Rosada* in 1939, when World War II, in its opening stages, had not yet spread to the Western Hemisphere. At that time, Norman Armour presented his credentials to President Roberto M. Ortiz as the new United States Ambassador to Argentina. Armour, a career diplomat, had previously seen service with the

"North American" diplomatic missions in Haiti, Canada, and Chile; and had taken some part in the development of President Franklin Delano Roosevelt's Good Neighbor policy. Armour found it more difficult to advance that policy in Argentina than it had been in his earlier posts. Nevertheless, his relations with President Ortiz were substantially friendly and correct.

The trouble began in 1940, when President Ramón S. Castillo succeeded the dying Ortiz in the *Casa Rosada*. Castillo pursued a policy of neutrality toward the war, as indeed the United States and the other American nations did at that time; but Castillo's "neutrality" carried with it a strong sympathy toward the Axis and a conviction that Hitler's Germany and Mussolini's Italy would win the war. When the Japanese attacked the United States at Pearl Harbor in December of 1941, nine Latin-American states* joined the "North Americans" in entering the war against the Axis, but Argentina was not among them. President Castillo, still oriented toward the Axis, continued to talk about "neutrality." And Ambassador Armour's relations with the government at Buenos Aires, remaining diplomatically correct, cooled noticeably.

Armour was still at Buenos Aires when the Perón revolution occurred on June 4, 1943, and General Arturo Rawson became the new president of Argentina. The Rawson administration was never recognized by the United States, for the simple reason that the general resigned on June 6, before Washington had an opportunity to act on the question of recognition. General Pedro P. Ramírez replaced Rawson in the *Casa Rosada*, and on June 11 the United States extended diplomatic recognition to the Ramírez regime. Armour, still the "North American" ambassador,

---

* Costa Rica, El Salvador, Guatemala, Honduras, Nicaragua, Panama, Cuba, the Dominican Republic, and Haiti.

found Ramírez' "neutrality" more vociferously pro-Axis than Castillo's had been; and United States–Argentine relations proceeded to deteriorate on a dramatic scale. With World War II in high gear, an unofficial observer reported that "Axis espionage, sabotage, and propaganda activities are still operating full blast in Argentina. Buenos Aires remains open G.H.Q. for Nazi-German, Fascist-Italian, Spanish-Falangist, and Japanese fifth-columning in this hemisphere."[1] If President Ramírez denied that he was aiding the Axis, Hitler's diplomatic service was under the impression that the Axis cause was receiving appreciable and positive assistance from the "new Argentina." "With the help of our Argentine friends and allies," Ruppert Weilheimer of the German Embassy at Buenos Aires said late in 1943, "we have been able to repel all attacks against our bridgehead in America, and we have been able to convert this bridgehead into a springboard from which we will be able to launch our attack in 1944."[2]

The "bridgehead" soon overreached itself and brought diplomatic isolation to the "new Argentina." On December 20, 1943, a Nazi *putsch*, engineered from Argentina, overthrew the government of the neighboring republic of Bolivia and endowed it with a pro-Axis regime. Argentina was alone among the American nations to recognize the Bolivian junta headed by Major Gualberto Villarroel. Ramírez, seeking to forestall the diplomatic isolation which this loneliness presaged, pleaded innocence of the Bolivian affair; but the United States threatened to publish documentary evidence of Argentine complicity in the Villarroel coup. Convinced that such publication would spell his own undoing, Ramírez promised Ambassador Armour that the "new Argentina" would clean house if the United States would not publicize the Bolivian documents. The "North

Americans" kept the secret. And Ramírez, now under inter-American pressure, and fighting his own domestic battle within the G.O.U.,* severed diplomatic relations with Germany and Japan on January 26, 1944.

Ramírez was undone anyway. The diplomatic rupture with the Axis precipitated a crisis within the G.O.U., and Ramírez was ousted from the *Casa Rosada* on February 24.

The government of the United States, now convinced that continued Argentine complicity with the Axis constituted a menace to the security of the American nations involved in World War II,† used the overthrow of Ramírez to attempt to force diplomatic isolation upon the "new Argentina." "At this most critical moment in the history of the American republics," the Department of State declared in a note to the various Latin-American states, "the government of one great republic, Argentina, has seen fit to . . . [bring] tremendous injury to the allied cause."[3] Accordingly, Washington withdrew Ambassador Armour from Buenos Aires, and refused to recognize the regime of General Edelmiro J. Fárrell, who became president of Argentina in February of 1944. Although the United States urged the other American nations to join Washington in non-recognition of Fárrell, this diplomatic isolation was not entirely complete. Chile, Paraguay, Bolivia, and Ecuador retained their diplomatic ties with the Fárrell regime.

Thus, Ambassador Armour left Argentina early in 1944. It was said that Norman Armour "has always been a strictly correct, instinctively do-the-right-thing career man."[4] Let

* See pp. 49–55.
† In addition to the nine Latin-American states which entered the war in 1941, Mexico, Brazil, Bolivia, and Colombia became belligerents in 1942 and 1943. Although they had severed diplomatic ties with the Axis, the remaining seven American republics—Argentina, Ecuador, Paraguay, Peru, Chile, Uruguay, and Venezuela—remained non-belligerents until February and March of 1945.

it be noted that, as of the time this book was written, Armour was the very last such ambassador to represent the government of the United States at Buenos Aires.

Diplomatic relations between the United States and Argentina remained severed from February of 1944 until April of 1945. During that period, the relationship between the "Colossus of the North" and the "Yankees of the South" was more strained than it has been at any other time in the histories of the two nations. The United States, deeply involved in a tragic war, and Argentina, lending "nonbelligerent" assistance to the Axis, traveled opposed roads.

Although there were no formal diplomatic ties between Argentina and the Axis after January of 1944, Axis activities were carried on in the country on a large scale. No fewer than sixteen Axis-financed newspapers* were published in Argentina, which was flooded with totalitarian propaganda. Nazis like Ludwig Freude, Ricardo Staudt, Carlos Tanke, and Heinrich Doerge played leading parts in bending the "new Argentina" to the ways of the Axis. Similar activities were engaged in by Austrians and Germans who denied they were Nazis. Consider, for example, the case of Fritz Mandl, former husband of the screen actress Hedy Lamarr. Mandl, once an Austrian munitions manufacturer, had lived in Argentina since 1938, and contributed his talents during World War II to Perón's armament program. Argentine Metallurgical and Plastic Industries (IMPA†), Mandl's munitions firm, was blacklisted by the United States as Nazi-dominated, although Mandl asserted that "no one is more interested in an allied victory than I."[5]

* Il Mattino d'Italia, Deutsche La Plata Zeitung, El Cabildo, Choque, Clarinada, Crisol, Cruz del Sud, La Epoca, La Fronda, Hechos, Mediodia, Momento Argentino, Nuevo Orden, El Pampero, El Restaurador, and El Pueblo.

† After the initial letters of Industrias Metalúrgicas y Plásticas Argentinas.

Argentina and the World

In June of 1944, the western allies succeeded in establishing a second front in Europe. Thereafter, the fortunes of World War II turned irrevocably against the Axis. By September, many leading Nazis were attempting to escape from the doomed Third Reich before anti-Axis armed forces could achieve Hitler's capitulation. A number of the Axis leaders were reported to be transmitting their funds to Argentina for safe keeping from the allies. German Propaganda Minister Paul Joseph Goebbels was said to have transferred $1,850,000 to Buenos Aires, Hitler's Foreign Minister Joachim von Ribbentrop reportedly had $500,000 there, and Admiral Karl Doenitz was likewise said to have transmitted holdings to Argentina. Nazis attempted to deliver not only their fortunes but also themselves to Fárrell's haven. Rumors that none other than Adolf Hitler himself would endeavor to escape to Patagonia were current as early as December of 1944. Two months later, Sir Robert Vansittart rose in the British House of Lords to censure the "new Argentina" for harboring Axis war criminals. Although Joseph C. Grew, then the "North American" Acting Secretary of State, declared in February of 1945 that Washington officially had "no evidence that Germans are escaping to Argentina through Spain or Portugal,"[6] reports of such operations were given prominent coverage in the anti-Axis press.

Meanwhile, the diplomatic machinery of the Americas moved to handle the "Argentine Question." Secretary of State Cordell Hull had asserted in July of 1944 that Buenos Aires had "deserted the common cause"[7] of the Western Hemisphere. By the latter part of the year, the governments of the American republics were generally agreed that diplomatic isolation of the "new Argentina" had been of limited utility, and official sentiment for placing the matter before an inter-American conference began to emerge. Secretary

of State Hull resigned on November 27, 1944. He was replaced by Stettinius, under whom Nelson Aldrich Rockefeller became Assistant Secretary of State for Latin-American Affairs. This new State Department "team" inherited
the "Argentine Question" at a time when Washington was
already committed to the decision to submit the matter to
an inter-American conference.

The story of the celebrated Chapultepec conference has
already been told.* The parley—the only inter-American
conference since 1889 at which Argentina was not represented—opened at Mexico City on February 21, 1945, and
adjourned on March 8. The conference met within the
context of a curious paradox. At the time the Chapultepec
parley was arranged for, there was general understanding
that the "Argentine Question" would be the primary business of the conference.

However, momentous events altered the nature of the
Chapultepec conference even before it opened. After the
parley was called, and just before it met, President Roosevelt, British Prime Minister Winston Churchill, and Soviet
Marshal Josef Stalin—the "Big Three" of the wartime alliance—met at Yalta, in the Crimea, to dispose of a number
of matters of greater importance to them than the "Argentine Question." One of those matters had to do with the
establishment of a postwar international organization for
the maintenance of international peace and security. It
was agreed that the charter of such an organization would
be written at a United Nations Conference on International
Organization to be convened on April 25, 1945, at San
Francisco, California. At Yalta there was disagreement on
a number of matters. One of them, relating to the projected
San Francisco conference, was the question of which governments should be represented at that meeting. Stalin, op-

* See pp. 12-14.

posed in this by Roosevelt, felt that only states at war against at least one of the Axis powers should be invited to San Francisco. Stalin won this point, and the Yalta agreement was so drawn.

Thus, on the eve of the Chapultepec conference, the Yalta decisions posed an unexpected problem for a number of the American republics. All aspired to be incorporated in the postwar international organization and to participate in the framing of the peace after World War II. But to do so, it was now necessary to be at war against at least one of the Axis powers, and seven of the Latin-American states—including Argentina—had not declared war. This was a difficult problem, and there seemed to be only one way to meet it. Between the Yalta and Chapultepec conferences, six of the "nonbelligerent" American republics—that is, all of them except Argentina—declared war against at least one of the Axis states. Ecuador declared war on February 5, 1945, Paraguay on February 8, Peru on February 12, Chile on February 14, and Uruguay and Venezuela on February 15.

And the Chapultepec conference convened on February 21. Yalta and its embarrassing aftermath—many felt that the forced declarations of war were immoral—loomed at Chapultepec to dwarf the "Argentine Question," the original purpose for which the conference had been called. The Argentine matter was relegated to a back seat as Chapultepec became an inter-American dress rehearsal for the San Francisco conference, which was to open on April 25. With the Axis on its last legs, and with inter-American resentment against the Soviet Union fanned by the Yalta decisions, a strong anti-Soviet atmosphere emerged at Chapultepec. The "strange alliance" of the Soviet Union with the West was to crumble at San Francisco; and Chapultepec likewise became a dress rehearsal for that. And the

"Argentine Question" was disposed of against such a background. So long as the "new Argentina" remained diplomatically isolated and outside the inter-American fold, the Americas would be divided at San Francisco; if Argentina could be reincorporated into the inter-American system, the Western Hemisphere would be united against communism.

At Chapultepec, the "Argentine Question" became the Soviet question. What was needed was a formula which would bring Argentina back into line with the Americas in time for the San Francisco conference. That formula was found at Chapultepec and announced there on March 8, 1945. The formula required the "new Argentina" to adhere to all of the resolutions of the conference* and to declare war against at least one of the Axis powers.

President Fárrell's government made haste to comply with the formula. On March 27—forty-two days before the war ended in Europe and five months before the Japanese surrender—the "new Argentina" declared war against Germany and Japan. "We are aware that Argentina's entry into the war could have been more timely," a British diplomat remarked, "but we are not the kind to make an issue of that."[8] At San Francisco, the Soviet delegation at first resisted the inclusion of the "new Argentina" in the United Nations, but at length agreed to welcome President Fárrell's government on condition that Britain and the United States likewise accept the Soviet-dominated Polish regime.†

---

* These included (1) agreement to stamp out the last vestiges of Axis influence in the Americas; (2) inter-American endorsement of the Dumbarton Oaks plan as the basis for the Charter of the United Nations, to be framed at San Francisco; (3) the "Act of Chapultepec," a temporary wartime instrument designed to stifle aggression within the Western Hemisphere; (4) reorganization and strengthening of the inter-American system; and (5) a series of economic agreements to raise standards of living in the hemisphere.

† See p. 16.

Thus was the "Argentine Question" settled as a diplomatic problem. Argentina became a member of the United Nations on April 30, 1945. Eight days later, Nazi Germany capitulated, and World War II ended in Europe. On June 7, British customs officials at Trinidad removed four prominent Nazis, bound for Buenos Aires, from the Spanish liner *Cabo de Hornos*. On July 10, a German submarine, the U-530, entered the Argentine naval base at Mar del Plata, in the Province of Buenos Aires, and the crew surrendered to the authorities there. A month later, a second German submarine, the U-977, likewise capitulated at Mar del Plata. Unofficial reports that leading Nazis had been taken to Argentina by the submarines could not be confirmed.

Meanwhile, Argentine–United States relations entered a new phase. It will be remembered that diplomatic ties had been severed between Washington and Buenos Aires in February of 1944. After Chapultepec, the United States and other American republics felt free to re-establish diplomatic relations with the Fárrell regime, and this step was taken on April 9, 1945. Shortly thereafter, a new United States ambassador to Argentina was named.

That ambassador was Spruille Braden, a man whom Argentines will not soon forget. Braden, who had been born at Elkhorn, Montana, in 1894, took with him to Buenos Aires a unique set of experiences in Latin-American affairs. His father had founded the Braden Copper Company, which operated in South America, and Spruille Braden first journeyed to the southern continent as a mining engineer. He worked with the Andes Exploration Company from 1914 until 1916, when he became general South American manager for the Anaconda Copper Mining Company, a post which he held for three years. From 1919 to 1933, he represented various "North American" firms doing busi-

ness in Latin America. When Franklin D. Roosevelt became president of the United States, Braden, an enthusiastic
supporter of the Good Neighbor policy, entered the
"North American" foreign service. He served as a member
of the United States delegation to the Seventh International
Conference of American States at Montevideo, Uruguay,
in 1933; and two years afterward he was chief "North
American" representative at the conference which brought
peace after the Chaco War between Bolivia and Paraguay.
Braden demonstrated remarkable perseverance in that assignment, and has been generally regarded as the man who
did more than any other single individual to end the Chaco
War. From 1938 to 1941, he was United States Minister to
Colombia; and he served as Ambassador to Cuba for four
years beginning in 1941. His experience at Havana constituted a curious entry in the annals of diplomacy. When
Braden embarked upon his assignment there, Cuba was
governed in an authoritarian fashion by President Fulgencio
Batista, who made a somewhat crude art of political manip-
ulation. Braden and Batista became close friends, and the
United States Ambassador was credited with pursuading
Batista to hold the most honest election in Cuban history
in 1944, at which time Ramón Grau San Martín became
one of the island republic's very few civilian presidents.*
The Havana episode convinced officials at Washington
that Spruille Braden was probably better qualified to deal
with Latin-American dictators than any other member of
the Foreign Service of the United States.

Then came Argentina. Today it is the truth from head-
quarters among *Peronistas* that Braden was a bad Yankee.
Among Argentines who are not *Peronistas*, Braden, like
Irigoyen, is a controversial figure. Many Argentines—of

* Batista returned to power in Cuba in 1952 in a coup d'état which
overthrew the government of President Carlos Prío Socarrás.

various political parties—say that Spruille Braden was guilty of three sins. In the first place, he made the mistake of assuming that what had worked in Cuba would also succeed in Argentina, that Perón was like Batista, that the Argentine voters would respond as the Cubans did to "North American" meddling in their elections. Second, Braden made the mistake of not being Norman Armour. Nobody has accused Braden of being "a strictly correct, instinctively do-the-right-thing career man." Braden had no objection to intervention by the United States in the domestic politics of another American republic, for the simple reason that he believed that there was no such thing as nonintervention, that nonintervention was a legalistic fiction. He argued that the size and power of the United States were overwhelming within the Western Hemisphere, and that therefore *anything* the "North Americans" did *or failed to do* in Latin America was, in effect, intervention. It followed that if the United States did not intervene in support of policies it indorsed, it thereby intervened *against* them, and that there was no middle position. To fail to intervene against Perón would be tantamount to supporting him. Third, Braden made the mistake of fighting the wrong war. The Axis was virtually dead when he arrived at Buenos Aires, where he persisted in fighting World War II for months after much of the rest of the world had stopped fighting it. Braden's activities in Argentina might have been proper if the war had still been going on. In a sense, he was repudiated by history. Although his own government's major struggle was against communism, Braden fought against the already defunct Axis and not against the Soviet Union; although his own government repudiated him at Chapultepec and again at San Francisco, Braden was never very certain that Hitler was really dead.

The war ended in Europe on May 8, 1945. Two weeks

later, Ambassador Braden arrived at Buenos Aires and commenced to fight World War II all over again. "I am not going to Argentina to establish friendly relations," he had said, "but to establish new ones."[9] At a formal reception on June 1, Braden was introduced to Juan Domingo Perón, then vice president of Argentina. The two men did not fall in love with each other, and Argentine–United States relations rapidly degenerated into a personal struggle between Braden and Perón. By July, Buenos Aires was littered with Perón-inspired handbills and posters which compared Braden with Al Capone, called the ambassador a gangster and a cowboy, and accused him of "undershirt diplomacy." A showdown between Braden and Perón was already in the making on August 17, when the Ambassador, in a speech at Buenos Aires, said things that traditionally "correct" diplomats are not expected to mention publicly. "The victorious United Nations," Braden asserted at that time, "are now being acclaimed in some high places by those who in the past had, with evident enthusiasm, attached themselves and their destinies to the Axis." He declared that a world conflict was still in progress, and that struggle "has been and continues to be between democracy and despotism, between peace and aggression." The states of the world, he affirmed, "must and will establish the only legitimate sovereignty—the inviolable sovereignty of the people."[10] So far as Perón was concerned, the Ambassador was *persona non grata*. The diplomat had demonstrated himself not to be a diplomat; Braden must go.

And Braden did go. At Washington, the impression was dominant that Braden had been successful in Argentina, that his policy was what "North American" policy should be. On August 25, 1945, Braden was named by President Harry S. Truman* as the new United States Assistant Sec-

* President Franklin D. Roosevelt had died on April 12.

retary of State for Latin-American Affairs, replacing Nelson A. Rockefeller. Now, presumably, Braden, operating from Washington, would have more power to carry forward the struggle against Perón. In one of his last speeches at Buenos Aires before departing for the United States, the new Assistant Secretary of State promised that he would continue the "task which I was discharging here. . . . The voice of liberty is making itself heard in this country [Argentina], and I do not believe anyone will be able to smother it."[11] On September 23, a group of about two hundred and fifty Argentines saw Braden off at the airport, and wished him success in his new assignment. "Wherever I may be," he told them, "I shall never forget the generous, cordial manner with which the Argentine people expressed their affection for my country. . . . The policy of the good neighbor is not made up of empty phrases."[12]

If life had been eventful at Buenos Aires while Braden was there, the excitement did not cease when he left. He was still becoming acclimated in his new post at Washington when "Loyalty Day" occurred in Argentina on October 17, 1945. Perón announced his presidential candidacy shortly thereafter, and an Argentine election was scheduled for February 24, 1946.

That election provided the frame of reference for Assistant Secretary of State Braden's approach to Argentine–United States relations. Braden's Argentine policy stood—and fell—on Perón's election in 1946. The specific vehicle of that policy was the celebrated State Department document which was officially called *Consultation among the American Republics with Respect to the Argentine Situation* and was popularly known as the "Blue Book." The "Blue Book" was frankly addressed to two publics—to the governments of all of the American nations, and to the voters of Argentina. Published on February 12—less than two weeks before the Argentine election—the "Blue Book" was designed by Braden to influence both publics against Perón. The case, as presented in the "Blue Book," rested on two charges against Perón: he had collaborated with the Axis during the war, and he had inspired many domestic "Nazi-Fascist" aspects of the "new Argentina." On these counts, the two publics were urged to regard Juan Domingo Perón as the Western Hemisphere's leading culprit.

Neither of the publics responded to the "Blue Book" as Braden had hoped. Several Latin-American governments pointed out that World War II was over, and that the "Argentine Question" was to be regarded as a wartime problem for the Americas. The issue, Brazilian Foreign Minister João Neves a Fontoura asserted in his reply to the "Blue Book," "has lost in part [its] cause of worry [in view of] the miltary victory of the United Nations over the totalitarian Axis. . . . [Therefore] Nazi-Fascist doctrines [can no longer] encounter in the Western Hemisphere a propitious climate for new and dangerous adventures."[13] The Cuban government said that the restoration of inter-American solidarity should take precedence over continuing to fight World War II; and the Chilean Foreign Office declared that the "Blue Book" had not proved Braden's case.

As for the voters of Argentina, they gave Perón 55 per cent of their votes.*

Braden was repudiated. His resignation as assistant secretary of state, accepted by President Truman, became effective on June 30, 1947.

Some parts of the government of the United States emerged from World War II earlier than other parts. Braden had represented one of the stragglers. The vanguard, on the other hand, was present at the San Francisco conference, which adjourned on June 26, 1945. The next day,

* See p. 71.

Secretary of State Stettinius resigned, and was replaced as chief of the State Department by James F. Byrnes. Under Byrnes' leadership, Washington embarked upon the long, difficult, and occasionally embarrassing road of seeking peace and friendship with Perón's Argentina. There had been no United States ambassador at Buenos Aires between September of 1945, when Braden left Argentina, and April of 1946. At that time, George S. Messersmith, a career diplomat who until then had been envoy to Mexico, became the new "North American" ambassador in Argentina. Messersmith did what he could to make peace with Perón. Messersmith spent only a year at Buenos Aires. During his period there, the United States agreed to enter into a hemisphere defense pact which Argentina would also sign, Washington released funds which had been blocked in the United States during the war, and the "North American" black list was terminated. Byrnes resigned as secretary of state in January of 1947, and Messersmith surrendered his Argentine post five months later. President Truman used the occasion of the Messersmith resignation to point out that the United States was then on friendlier terms with Argentina than it had been at any other time since the Japanese attack at Pearl Harbor.

Byrnes and Messersmith were replaced by men who continued to woo Perón. General George C. Marshall returned from China to be the new United States secretary of state, and James Bruce succeeded Messersmith as envoy to Argentina. The Bruce appointment represented a somewhat novel departure in "North American" diplomacy with Buenos Aires. Bruce was the first of a series of businessmen, none of them career diplomats, to serve one-year stretches as ambassador to Argentina. President Truman instructed Bruce to "go down and make friends with those people";[14] and the businessman-ambassador, an officer of the National

Dairy Products Company, tried to do what he was told. During Ambassador Bruce's stewardship, Argentina became a signatory with the United States to an inter-American defense treaty signed at Rio de Janeiro, Brazil; the two governments participated in the memorably chaotic Ninth International Conference of American States at Bogotá, Colombia;* Bruce tried unsuccessfully to persuade the ECA to admit Argentina, on Miguel Miranda's terms, to a role in the Marshall Plan; and Foreign Minister Juan Atilio Bramuglia was invited to the White House to confer with Truman. Convinced that he had indeed made "friends with those people," Bruce resigned as ambassador and returned to the United States to praise President Perón as "one of the nicest fellows I've ever met."[15]

Faces continued to change at Washington and Buenos Aires. In January of 1949, Dean Acheson replaced Marshall as secretary of state; and some months later Stanton Griffis, another businessman, became ambassador to Argentina. All felt that United States–Argentine relations were improving measurably. United States Senator Dennis Chavez (Democrat, New Mexico) had returned from a two-month visit to Buenos Aires to say that President Perón "certainly wants a democratic administration. . . . If you could see his program in operation then you'd see he is coming nearer to ours every day."[16]

Ambassador Griffis followed the pattern set for him by Bruce. "I will carry out my assignment from the point of view of a businessman," Griffis told newsmen as he departed for Argentina. "I do not know any better way to improve relations between two countries than by the establishment of reciprocal trade. This will be my function. I

---

* Though not on the agenda, the major event at the Ninth Conference was a spectacularly bloody uprising which had grown primarily out of a long-brewing crisis in domestic Colombian politics.

have devoted all my life to business, and it is the only thing I know."[17] During Griffis' year at Buenos Aires, the volume of "North American"–Argentine trade expanded, Braniff International Airways acquired landing privileges near Buenos Aires, and the United States Export-Import Bank loaned $125,000,000 to Argentina. Returning to the United States in September of 1950, Ambassador Griffis said that he was "very favorably impressed by the advances of the Argentine government along the road of social and economic progress."[18] In a speech before the Investment Bankers Association at New York, the Ambassador declared that Juan and Eva Perón were "tireless workers for their people," and that *Justicialismo* was directed against nineteenth- but not twentieth-century capitalism. "There is some absence of freedom of the press in Argentina," Griffis conceded. "It is true that there is some absence of personal liberty in Argentina, that there are many laws which restrict this liberty and which we would not tolerate in the United States. But it is perhaps true that Argentina is not completely prepared for what we know as integral democracy; and when I read some defamatory descriptions of honest men in our own public life I sometimes doubt that even we are prepared for it."[19] This speech was received with considerable feeling in Argentina. The *Peronista* press hailed Griffis as a good Yankee. *La Prensa*, which had not yet been suppressed, suggested that if Braden had intervened in Argentine domestic politics against Perón, Griffis was now intervening in his support. The paper concluded editorially that "it is not the task of diplomatic missions to interfere in the internal affairs of the nations where they are accredited."[20] Argentine Radicals and Conservatives feared that Griffis would receive a bullet in his head if he returned to Buenos Aires. That tragedy was averted, for the Ambassador did not return. He resigned his Argentine position on November 17, 1950, to become ambassador to Spain in an action which terminated a five-year diplomatic boycott of the regime of Generalissimo Francisco Franco at Madrid.

In 1951, Ellsworth Bunker arrived at Buenos Aires to take his post as the new United States ambassador to Argentina. This was Bunker's first diplomatic assignment; the president of the National Sugar Refining Company, he had been in the sugar business for thirty-four years. He anticipated little difficulty in carrying on in the Bruce-Griffis pattern.

Friends were being made with "those people."

On War and Peace

There are a number of places in the world where imaginations are permitted—even encouraged—to run riot, where premiums are placed on outlandish propositions. One such locality is Hollywood, California. Consider, for instance, a motion picture released by Warner Brothers in March of 1945. The film, called *Hotel Berlin*, contained a number of scenes depicting German Nazis departing for Argentina to lay the groundwork for World War III.

It is perhaps worth recording that this thesis has also, on occasion, been entertained outside of Hollywood. Thus, in September of 1944, Sims Carter, then an official of the United States Department of Justice, told a congressional committee at Washington that German industrial combinations had already completed plans to resume their activities in Argentina once World War II ended. Less than two years later, the "North American" Department of State itself pointed out that "in Argentina the Germans have constructed a complete duplicate of the economic structure for war which they had in Germany. . . . The industries essential to warfare in which experimentation in the weapons of future wars may take place and in which prototypes may be developed exist in Argentina and are controlled by Germans."[21] In the United States, this was once considered to be a matter for serious concern. "If we let ourselves be deceived into thinking that the Buenos Aires dictatorship is simply an Argentine affair," the *Washington Post* declared editorially while World War II was still in progress, "we shall be making a bitter mockery of the deaths of Americans fighting Germany in Europe before their bodies are cold."[22]

Argentina declared war against Germany in March of 1945. At that time, German capital controlled approximately three hundred and forty industrial firms in Argentina. These dealt primarily in chemicals and pharmaceuticals, electrical equipment, and metal manufactures. When Argentina adhered to the Final Act of the Chapultepec conference, that signature placed the government at Buenos Aires under obligation to stamp out the last vestiges of Axis influence in Argentina.* Although machinery for the control of enemy property was established a week after the Argentine declaration of war, the administrations of Presidents Fárrell and Perón were notably slow in moving against German-controlled firms. United States Assistant Secretary of State William L. Clayton said in June of 1945 that not one of the major German enterprises in Argentina had been eliminated at that time. Five months later, Buenos Aires had moved to "Argentinize" eighty-eight firms out of some three hundred and forty "candidates." On December 12, 1945, the Department of State charged formally that the Argentine government had violated its Chapultepec obligations.

A similar pattern characterized the "new Argentina's" treatment of the Axis agents who had carried on wartime

* See pp. 14 and 408.

espionage. Of the ninety-four such agents known to be in Argentina by December of 1945, fifty-eight had at that time been arrested on espionage charges, while thirteen had been detained without charges, twelve were still at liberty, and eleven had been ordered deported but were later saved by legal technicalities. Forty-two wartime Axis agents were deported in 1946. Of the twenty-one major agents named in the "Blue Book," the record as of January of 1947 indicated that four had returned to Germany, one killed himself, and sixteen remained unmolested in Argentina. A report published by Foreign Minister Bramuglia declared in May that fifty-two Axis agents had been deported since Argentina declared war, fourteen had escaped, and forty-three had been set at liberty with the knowledge and consent of the government of the United States.

Moreover, a number of prominent Germans who had done significant war work for Hitler went to Argentina after the war to engage in similar activity for Perón. Of these, Dr. Ronald Richter, the atomic scientist, is worth mentioning. Also worthy of attention is Kurt Tank, one-time technical director of the Focke-Wulf factory. During the war, Tank designed the famous Focke-Wulf 190 for Hitler's *Luftwaffe*. In Argentina, Tank's work was equally distinguished. In 1950, he produced for Perón's air force a jet plane known as the "Púlque II," which was capable of developing a speed of 646 miles per hour. Tank was assisted in Argentina by Adolf Galland and Hans Ulrich Rudel, both former *Luftwaffe* officials. And in 1951, Werner Baumbach, also once associated with the *Luftwaffe*, was assisting the Argentine ministry of aeronautics in the development of new rocket weapons.

In Europe, Germany has been divided between the Soviet Union and the Western powers since May of 1945. In April of 1949, a West German republic, its capital at

Bonn, was created under "North American," British, and French sponsorship. A West German–Argentine Chamber of Commerce was established at Buenos Aires late in 1950 for the purpose of restoring trade between the two to what was called a "normal" basis. A West German trade mission, headed by Dr. Günter Seeliger, arrived in Argentina in July of 1951 to negotiate a new trade agreement; it was reported at that time that "Germany is staging a noteworthy comeback in Latin America."[23] An Argentine embassy was established at Bonn on October 23, 1951. Three days later, Argentina and West Germany signed a new $308,000,000 trade agreement providing for the exchange of German industrial equipment for Argentine wool and hides.

West Germany, of course, is *west*. "North Americans" may be justified in reasoning that the strengthening of West Germany buttresses the West in general against the Soviet Union, that the Germans of Bonn are sworn allies of the United States against communism. But it does not follow that the Germans in Argentina who now tie themselves to West Germany are also sworn allies of the United States. Many of the Germans who went to Argentina before 1945 went there to turn Argentina against the United States, and many of them who journeyed to Buenos Aires after 1945 went there to escape from the control of the United States. Their love for the Yankees is certainly no greater than Perón's; and the truth is that many "Argentinized" Germans today harbor a much deeper hatred toward the "North Americans" than Perón does. A large number of Germans occupy positions of power and influence in the "new Argentina." A recent careful estimate of the Germans' role in Perón's government is worth quoting:

It's possible to exaggerate the real extent of Nazi activity in Argentina. Nazis don't run the government. Perón does. But Perón and his assistants have given many jobs to former Nazis. They are in the economic staff, in the [Federal] Police, in the army and air force. Some of the biggest *Luftwaffe* aces are now working in Argentine air force installations at Córdoba earning handsome salaries. . . .

The heart of the matter is that Nazis in Argentina potentially constitute a nucleus for resurgence of nazism, but proportionately they don't make much of a dent any more. They keep pretty quiet now.[24]

Well and good. World War II is over. But the important word in that sentence is "II." So long as Germany in Europe remains in its present condition, the Germans in Argentina may be expected to continue to "keep pretty quiet." But should Germany achieve some independence of foreign policy—and should Germany become reunited—that silence may well be broken. Let it be remembered that the line in Argentina which runs from Tannenberg* to Kretchmar† to Niedenfuehr‡ to Uriburu to Justo to Castillo to Perón remains powerful. And in Argentina that line has been *victorious*. Inability to predict what will happen to Germany is not, of course, a monopoly of the United States Department of State. It is much easier to forecast that Germany's destiny will remain a major key to the future international course of Perón's Argentina. In simpler words, the Germans may be domesticated for the time being, but they are not yet dead. It is still too early for sermons and postmortems.

And what of the Russians?

It may now be difficult for some "North Americans" to remember that the United States and the Soviet Union were still wartime allies when the Perón revolution occurred in 1943. If that revolution was pro-Axis in orientation, it was anti-Soviet as well as anti-Yankee. Whereas the United States trod the uncertain path of recognition, non-recogni-

* See p. 39.
† See p. 307.
‡ See pp. 307–8.

tion, and re-recognition of the "new Argentina," the Soviet Union did not recognize it at all during World War II. But—once again—"II" is the important word.

In April of 1946, when Messersmith began to woo Perón, the Russians embarked upon a similar project. At that time a Soviet trade mission, led by Konstantin Vasilievich Shevelev, arrived at Buenos Aires. Shevelev's contacts with the Argentine Communist party have already been noted.* He also contacted Perón, who was then president-elect. "I have maintained always that we should establish diplomatic and commercial relations with Russia," Argentine Foreign Minister Juan Isaac Cooke declared at the time. "I consider the Soviet Union as one of the world's great powers and feel that only mutual benefits can result from an interchange with it."[25] Perón was inaugurated as president on June 4, 1946. Two days later, diplomatic relations between the "new Argentina" and the Soviet Union were at last achieved.

Thereafter, Perón attempted to steer a middle course between the United States and the Soviets. After 1949, this foreign policy was rationalized in terms of the "Third Position." *Justicialismo* was anti-capitalist as well as anti-communist; and as the "cold war" developed, Perón endeavored to avoid affiliation with either the pro- or anti-Soviet camp. *Justicialismo* did not stand *exactly* halfway between capitalism and communism, be it remembered;† and Perón attempted to lean more toward the United States than toward the Soviet Union. He declared in a foreign policy statement that, if the world should become engulfed in a third general war, "Argentina will be with the United States and the other American nations."[26] Nevertheless, he insisted that "international capitalism has begun a reaction

* See p. 395.
† See pp. 291–292.

against us,"[27] and that *Justicialismo* forbade irrevocable identification of Argentina with the cause of either the United States or the Soviet Union. "There is in the world at the present time a conflict between capitalists and Communists, and we do not wish to be one thing or the other," President Perón asserted in an endeavor to clarify his "Third Position." "The Argentine people do not like extremes. We will not defend capitalism, in fact, we are dismantling it bit by bit. . . . Neither are we on the side of communism, which will fight us too at home and abroad."[28]

As United States ambassadors have done what they could to befriend Perón since 1946, so have the Soviet diplomats at Buenos Aires. This was essentially the mission of Shevelev and of Mikhail Sergeyev. And Grigori Feodorovich Resanov, who in 1951 replaced Sergeyev as the Soviet ambassador to Argentina, continued the same diplomatic pattern. If "North American" and Soviet ambassadors at Buenos Aires have been rivals for Perón's friendship, the Yankees have been more successful in this venture than the Russians.

The supremacy of the United States in the battle for Perón's favor was strikingly illustrated by the Fourth Meeting of American Foreign Ministers,* which took place at Washington, D.C., in March and April of 1951. Called in the midst of the Korean crisis,† the conference unanimously adopted the "Declaration of Washington," which committed all of the American nations—including Argentina—to the "common defense [of the Western Hemisphere] against the aggressive activities of international communism."[29] The foreign ministers also agreed that, in the event of a third world war, the Latin-American governments would themselves patrol the Western Hemisphere. This

* For a discussion of the first three meetings, see pp. 10–11.
† See pp. 427–428.

provision was designed to avoid a recurrence of the situation in World War II, when some 140,000 United States troops were required to man garrisons and bases in the Americas. Other resolutions adopted at Washington were directed toward increased inter-American production of defense materials and a rise in Latin-American standards of living.

Foreign Minister J. Hipólito Paz, who led the Argentine delegation to the Washington conference, signed these resolutions on behalf of the Perón administration. However, the Argentines were not entirely acquiescent in the work of the Fourth Meeting of American Foreign Ministers. The conference experienced some anxious moments when Paz joined forces with the Mexican and Guatemalan delegations to protest against the formation of what they called a "Pan-American army." Foreign Minister Paz asserted that any use of Argentine armed forces, "whether on a world or hemisphere basis, is governed by the National Constitution. . . . My government will not make any decision [on the use of troops] without expressly consulting the decision of the Argentine people."[30] Despite this contention, the general result of the Washington conference indicated that the "new Argentina," while clinging to the "Third Position," was aligned more with the United States than with the Soviet Union. "There were no rivalries at this meeting, no stars and no satellites, no victors and no vanquished, no winners and no losers," United States Secretary of State Dean Acheson declared at the conclusion of the Fourth Meeting of American Foreign Ministers. "We have all won . . . because we are colleagues and because our fundamental interests are common interests."[31] Thus was the course along which the "Third Position"—more anti-Soviet than anti-United States, but pro-neither—evolved in the years after World War II.

The "Third Position" has found a somewhat similar expression in the pattern of the "new Argentina's" participation in the work of the United Nations. Buenos Aires' ratification of the Charter of the United Nations was formalized on September 25, 1945. This step was heralded in some quarters as signifying the opening of a new era in Argentine foreign policy. Indeed, the "Yankees of the South" were welcomed enthusiastically into the new international organization by the other Latin-American delegations. "All Latin-American nations desire to keep Argentina in the United Nations," Colombian delegate Eduardo Zuleta Angel asserted early in 1946, on behalf of his own and other American governments. "Argentina is not menacing the peace of the world. She may be menacing her own internal peace, but that is her own concern."[32]

Shortly after Argentina's admission to the United Nations, Buenos Aires' delegates moved to assume a leading role among the Latin-American members of the international organization, and the "Third Position" was prominent in some of the work done at Lake Success. Argentine leadership among the American republics was recognized in October of 1947, when Argentina was elected to occupy one of the six non-permanent seats on the United Nations Security Council, which is charged with primary responsibility within the international organization for the preservation of world peace. Argentina was represented on the Security Council throughout 1948 and 1949. During this period, the "Third Position" achieved considerable prominence in Argentine attempts, through the Security Council, to adjust crises arising between the United States and the Soviet Union. The most noteworthy of these attempts was connected with the Soviet "blockade" of Berlin. That issue approached its climax in October of 1948, when Argentine Foreign Minister Juan Atilio Bramuglia, then the Security

Council's presiding officer, took the lead in seeking a compromise position between the two great powers.

When the Berlin question was superseded by another, the "Third Position" continued to be advanced by Argentines as a formula for adjusting issues between the "North Americans" and the Russians. With the departure of Bramuglia from Lake Success,* the primary scene of Argentine operations within the United Nations shifted from the Security Council to the General Assembly of the international organization. In September of 1949 the world was presented with the momentous news that an atomic explosion had occurred in the Soviet Union, and the United Nations was faced with the question of Moscow's possession of the atomic bomb. The "Third Position" attempted to grapple even with this issue. In the General Assembly, Argentine delegate Rodolfo Muñoz proposed a provisional international agreement to outlaw the use of the atomic bomb.

But the most significant lesson on the meaning of the "Third Position" for the United Nations came with the Korean crisis. Korea had been divided in 1945 along the thirty-eighth parallel, with North Korea under Soviet direction and South Korea under non-Soviet supervision. Official relations between the northern and southern sides of the thirty-eighth parallel were never very cordial during the five years after the division was made. And on June 25, 1950, North Korea launched an armed invasion across the thirty-eighth parallel. The government of the United States moved immediately to assist the South Koreans, and took the lead in action by the United Nations Security Council branding the invasion as aggression and organizing a United Nations police action to repel the invasion.† All members

* See pp. 352–53.

† The Soviet delegate, Jacob Malik, did not attend the meetings of the Security Council at which these steps were taken.

of the international organization—including, of course, Argentina—were requested to aid the United Nations' military action in Korea.

Whither the "Third Position?"

On June 30, the Argentine government expressed both indorsement of the "North American" action and adhesion to the decisions of the Security Council. Declaring that the United States met the crisis "with great intelligence," President Perón said that "Argentina has taken the attitude which should be taken by a member of the community of American nations." Asked what contribution his government would make to the action in Korea, Perón asserted: "I won't answer with words. Actions speak louder than words."[33] What were the actions? Foreign Minister Paz told a press conference that they would not involve the sending of Argentine troops to Korea. In an atmosphere of crisis and tension, President Perón met at the *Casa Rosada* on August 22 with Paz and with Jerónimo Remorino, the Argentine Ambassador to the United States. Remorino thereupon dashed urgently back to Washington with a message for the Department of Defense. Argentina indeed made its contribution in Korea—the contribution consisted of a number of ambulance units and $115,000 worth of food, but nothing more.

Argentine international policy since World War II has thus been characterized by a retention of German influence, lukewarm friendship toward the United States, and a hostility toward the Soviet Union which stands at approximately room temperature. This policy has been dubbed the "Third Position." Argentines are told that their nation can be proud of this policy. Of a score of Latin-American presidents, according to the *Peronista* press, the world-at-large has come to know only the name of Juan Domingo Perón. It is said that this name ranks in the headlines of the world with Dwight D. Eisenhower and Josef Stalin, and that the "Third Position" has made this kind of advertising pay.

The "Third Position": A Plague on Two Houses

The high priests of *Justicialismo* have argued that the "Third Position" is directed against both capitalism and communism, and that the foreign policy of the "new Argentina" brings frustration to both the United States and the Soviet Union. This is an argument which has not made much headway outside of Argentina. The plain truth is that the Soviet Union has not suffered noticeably because of Perón's "Third Position." If any two states have been damaged by it, those two states are the United States and *Argentina*.

What is the "Third Position?" It is the bedraggled remains of *americanismo*. Characterized as "a natural effort toward a family understanding between Latin Americans," *americanismo* was once a tendency of the twenty Latin-American states to band together for their mutual defense against threats from the outside world. So long as the United States remained associated with that outside world, Argentina enjoyed a position of leadership among the Latin-American states joined together in *americanismo*. But with the coming of the "North American" President Franklin D. Roosevelt's Good Neighbor policy, the United States sought to wrest the diplomatic leadership of Latin America from Argentina. The "Yankees of the South" have stubbornly resisted this displacement of Argentina from its traditional position of leadership among the Ibero-American states.*

Perón inherited—and has carried on—this Argentine resistance against the United States. Although this policy to-

* See pp. 6–11.

ward the "North Americans" was not called the "Third Position" until 1949, it was nevertheless evident in Perón's attitudes from the first days of the life of the "new Argentina." In May of 1944, he told the officers of the *Campo de Mayo* garrison that Argentina had succeeded in detaching Chile and Paraguay from "a bloc organized by the United States against us. . . . We can say without boasting that we have obliged the United States to mark time."[34] On a number of occasions during World War II, the fear was expressed that Argentine resistance against the Good Neighbor policy might result in a war within the Western Hemisphere. Thus, in January of 1945, Gabriel González Videla, who became president of Chile a year later, asserted that the "new Argentina" had "the sole aim of provoking a continental conflict in order to save itself from collapse . . . and Chile will be the first victim."[35]

If Argentine opposition to the hemisphere policies of the United States ever did prompt Perón to harbor aggressive designs against any of the neighboring American republics, the danger of such aggression appears to have lessened considerably since the end of World War II. Various inter-American agreements—such as the "Act of Chapultepec" of 1945;* the inter-American defense treaty, signed at Rio de Janeiro in 1947; and the Charter of the Organization of American States, framed at Bogotá in 1948—have constructed a collective security system among the American republics. In so far as these arrangements would bring Perón into armed conflict with the entire hemisphere if he attacked any American nation, this phase of the "new Argentina's" foreign policy now appears to be contained effectively. Perón has recognized this containment, and accepted it with his characteristic realism. "Are we imperialists —with only 16,000,000 inhabitants? We haven't gone crazy

* See pp. 14 and 408.

yet," he asserted in 1949. "It has been said that we want to resurrect the old Viceroyalty of the Rio de la Plata.* When they say that, I always say: 'We have lots of land and we don't need any more.' "[36]

Since the war, such aggressive tendencies as have been exhibited by the "new Argentina" have been deflected to areas not covered by inter-American collective security arrangements. Thus, Perón has entered into dispute since 1946 with the United Kingdom, contesting the generally recognized British claims to the Falkland Islands and a portion of the Antarctic. This is not the place to argue international law, but it may be worth noting at this point that most Argentines tend to regard Perón's claim to the Falklands as more valid than his assertion of antarctic sovereignty. The Argentine case for the Falkland Islands (which the Argentines call the "Malvinas") rests on the fact that the British recognized Spanish sovereignty over the islands in 1771, coupled with the assertion that Argentina has since inherited Spain's claim to the Falklands. The British, for their part, point out that Spain evacuated the islands early in the nineteenth century, and that they were fair game when the British occupied them in 1833. Perón has branded this occupation as a "usurpation," and insists that the Falklands, although they remain under effective British administration, rightfully belong to Argentina.

As for the Antarctic, the "new Argentina's" claims in this area rest exclusively on the so-called "sector theory," and not on any of the conventionally recognized or generally accepted principles of international law. The sector theory holds that a state might establish polar claims by extending to the pole the longitudinal lines constituting the state's easternmost and westernmost frontiers. This theory, which the Soviet Union has likewise advanced in connec-

* See p. 19.

tion with the North Pole, has not been generally accepted as a valid element of international law. Although it has been illegal since 1946 to publish a map in Argentina which does not show the Falklands and a portion of the Antarctic as Argentine, few non-*Peronistas* take the latter claim seriously.

In the chaotic and tragic years since the end of World War II, Argentine–United States relations have pursued a course which has troubled both the "Yankees of the South" and the "North Americans." The government of the United States has recognized the "new Argentina," later withdrawn recognition from it, and then recognized it again. This has prompted sharp criticism of the State Department from observers who charge that the Yankees have committed the sin of inconsistency.

It is, of course, easier to write a book like this than it is to frame a foreign policy for the United States. It is only in one sense—and a superficial one, at that—that Washington has been inconsistent in its policy toward Buenos Aires. Perhaps it is inconsistent to blow cold and then to blow hot, but both are only blowing, both are merely symptoms of a deeper and more significant process. And that process has been essentially consistent. The United States has been transformed from the greatest power in the Western Hemisphere to the greatest power—or second greatest—in the world-at-large. This is a change of tremendous consequence, and it has been reflected by an accompanying alteration of the Latin-American policy of the "Colossus of the North." World power politics have taken precedence at Washington over concern for the inter-American system.

Within the over-all context of world power politics, has the United States really been inconsistent in its policy toward the "new Argentina?" Consider the record from the standpoint of this larger frame of reference. During World

War II, Argentina was aligned with the enemies of the United States, and was treated by Washington primarily as an appendage of the hostile Axis. Since World War II, the United States and the Soviet Union have drifted into alignment against each other. In terms of this new alignment the place of Argentina is also new. Argentina was once with the enemies of the United States, but is no longer so committed. Whatever else might be said about the "Third Position," it is *not*—at least, not yet—a pro-Soviet position. If power politics be adopted as the operating premise, it makes sense to oppose one's enemies, and to bid for the support of states not identified with them.

As *Justicialismo* has its high priests, so has power politics. Hear a portion of the gospel: "The simple truth . . . is that in international relations one cannot choose one's friends. The ideal ally does not exist—nor is one's own country ideal by everybody else's standards—and all friends and allies have many despicable characteristics and as bad a 'record' as has, in their eyes, one's own country. The choice is one between lesser evils: whom does a country fear more, for whom does it care less?"[37] Thus the new "North American" formula. The Soviet Union is now the greater evil; meanwhile, pick Perón up and dust him off. And suppose this power-politics approach damages other elements of United States policy in the Western Hemisphere, what then? The high priests have an answer for that question, too: "A foreign policy which attempts simultaneously to solve two different and mutually exclusive problems will be vacillating, and will not, in the end, solve either. The most urgent and vital problem must be solved first. . . . Generally speaking, foreign policy can be effective *only if it is directed at one major problem at any one time*. If there are several problems to be solved at a given moment, compromise must clean the slate for the sake of the major problem's solution."[38] Q.E.D. The Soviet Union and the "cold war" must come first. Meanwhile, compromise on other matters, including Perón.

It may be true that, in the post-World War II period, the United States must hold all other problems in abeyance until it disposes of its power struggle with the Soviet Union. But abeyance is not suspended animation. The neglected questions are dynamic—they move and change, they acquire new significances. And, while the United States holds Perón in abeyance, two aspects of the "North American" position in the Western Hemisphere are moving and changing. One of these is ideological, and the other relates to the nature of the inter-American system.

Once upon a time, many "North Americans" and Latin Americans believed that the United States pursued an active interest in the progress of democracy in the American hemisphere. "North Americans" as well as Latin Americans have retreated from this belief since 1945, driven back by the newly heavy emphasis on power politics. Disillusionment on this score has crept into the literature of the Western Hemisphere regardless of the side of the Rio Grande on which the literature is published. Books and articles and speeches—be they novels, tracts in social science, or formal statements of policy—have served as an index to the course of an ideology held in abeyance. Read it in English or in Spanish. "We are not, essentially, humane people," a "North American" novelist made his hero say in a book published in 1950. "Shall we look at the degree of obliviousness, smugness, or rejection which Americans held toward the atrocities before the recent war—or hold now toward massacre and famine in India—famine in China—ruthless dictatorship in a dozen nations—Spain, for instance—Argentina—a lot more? . . . We are not humane. We are—per capita—the cruelest people who ever lived, because, unlike the poor thieves on the other two crosses—we *do* know what we do!"[39] The same point is made—albeit more gently—among the Latin Americans. "Argentines don't believe in the sincerity of" the United States, it has been observed. The Good Neighbor policy "is expected to disappear along with the Roosevelt administration, to be replaced by something akin to the old Dollar Diplomacy."[40] And how fare the Argentines who oppose Perón, the Argentines who struggle for what they call democracy, and who looked to the United States for friendship and guidance? "We still have not reached or dynamically inspired our true friends in Argentina," a "North American" observer has reported, "and the task . . . is no longer easy."[41]

And what of the inter-American system? Has abeyance strengthened it? The reader knows the story of Pearl Harbor, Chapultepec, and San Francisco—the chronicle of Armour, Braden, Messersmith, Bruce, Griffis, and Bunker. How has this strange chronicle affected the American family of nations? "It is no exaggeration to say that the United States has virtually lost its influence in the most progressive part of Latin America," a seasoned correspondent has recorded. "Bluntly, we are being made to look like louts."[42] If the government of the United States feels that it must make friends with "those people" in order to offset the Soviet Union, this has not been a secret from the Latin Americans. In April of 1951, only two months after Perón suppressed *La Prensa*, the "North American" president, Harry S. Truman, spoke at the Fourth Meeting of American Foreign Ministers. "You have affirmed our common determination to help the liberty-loving peoples who work throughout the world for the overthrow of Communist tyranny," Truman told the foreign ministers, including the Argentine. "This is proof of the vitality of free men and their institutions."[43] What did "liberty-loving" mean in that context? Latin Americans could be sure that it meant "anti-Soviet," but many wondered if it meant anything else. "The foreign ministers avoided touching on the case of *La Prensa*," *Correio da Manhã* of Rio de Janeiro noted editorially. "Freedom was sacrificed to the diplomatic convenience of having General Perón's representative sign the conference declarations. . . . Unanimity . . . was not really achieved. *La Prensa* is a reality. Perón's solidarity is at best an equivocation."[44]

World War II has divided a disturbing inheritance between the "Yankees of the South" and the "Colossus of the North." There is much talk in both Argentina and the United States of good neighborliness, and a recognition that this quality has been lacking in the recent business which each of the two states has transacted with the other. After all, the first American president to use the expression "Good Neighbor" was an *Argentine* president, Bartolomé Mitre; but this has left a negligible impression on the "North Americans." And it was a United States president, Franklin D. Roosevelt, who dedicated his administration to the policy of the Good Neighbor; but the "Yankees of the South" have fought stubbornly against that policy. Each state treats the other with suspicion and distrust; each doubts that the other can indeed be a good neighbor, for each has claimed that halo for itself.

And which has won?

The "new Argentina"? If so, it has been a peculiar victory. Perón's Argentina has clung to *americanismo* so doggedly that the rest of the hemisphere hardly recognizes it now that it is called the "Third Position." What has happened to the *americanismo* of Mitre and the good neighborliness of Argentina now that Perón has transformed them? What has become of the role of the "new Argentina" in the Western Hemisphere? Even the Argentines know

436

the answer to that question. "The foreign reputation of the republic has fallen," one of them has said. "The Argentine name is associated with decadence, fascism, and lack of liberty."[45] Can the *americanismo* of the "Third Position" be saved? Perhaps it can be preserved in the refrigeration of the Antarctic—if the British will open the door of the deep freeze. But few Argentines find comfort in the thought that the "Third Position" has driven *americanismo* to the South Pole.

Yet neither have the "North Americans" drawn solace from the contemporary state of hemisphere affairs. Since June 4, 1943, United States ambassadors at Buenos Aires have pursued three different types of politics. One of these, represented by Norman Armour, made use of only one of the proverbial three monkeys. Armour heard the evil and he saw it, but he did not speak it—to the Argentines. He was, after all, "a strictly correct, instinctively do-the-right-thing career man." And he did not intervene in Argentina's domestic affairs. The second type of policy was exemplified by Spruille Braden. He rejected all of the monkeys. He saw the evil, he heard it—and he did not hesitate to speak it. This constituted "North American" intervention in Argentine affairs, intervention *against* Perón. And the third class of United States policy—represented by the Messersmith-Bruce-Griffis-Bunker line—made extensive use of all three monkeys. This was received in Argentina as a new form of Yankee intervention—but this time *in favor of* Perón.

If it be assumed that the United States has no choice in the matter of power politics, that the struggle with the Soviet Union must dominate Washington's approach to Argentina, then which of the three types of policies just noted contributes most effectively to the process of power politics? How many monkeys, of which kinds, should be re-

cruited by the State Department for service in Argentina?
Politics, it has been said, makes for strange bedfellows,
strange alliances. If this be doubted, it might be in order to
enumerate the allies thrown together by contemporary Argentine–United States relations. These allies include abeyance, refrigeration, the South Pole—and three monkeys. If
this is not the most effective combination for the advancement of "North American" power interests, the defect lies
in the participation of too many monkeys.

One monkey is all that the United States needs in Argentina.

"Speak no evil" may serve the "North Americans" at
Buenos Aires, but the United States does not protect its
own position in also refusing to see and hear Argentine affairs. Spruille Braden did not serve the power interests of
the United States because he did not give a single monkey
the freedom of his embassy. And the Messersmith-Bruce-
Griffis-Bunker line has turned over the United States Embassy at Buenos Aires to all of the monkeys. This practice
likewise harms the position of the United States in the
Western Hemisphere. So long as Washington's duel with
Moscow sets the pattern for the relations of the United
States with Argentina, then the monkey which speaks no
evil—but *neither of the other two*—belongs with the
United States diplomatic mission at Buenos Aires. This
creature has not been alone of the monkeys there since
Norman Armour bade farewell to the "Yankees of the
South" early in 1944. "A strictly correct, instinctively do-
the-right-thing career man" is not to be sneered at. He can
enter into an effective alliance with abeyance, refrigeration, and the South Pole.

Since World War II, power politics has been the order
of the day in the Western Hemisphere as well as elsewhere
in the world. If the "North Americans" have been engulfed

by the politics of power, the United States has not been alone among the American nations in this situation. Argentina is beset by power politics as well, and the "Third Position" is little else than Perón's version of the politics of power. What does the "Third Position" mean in international politics? Let Perón explain it himself: "Argentina knows what she has got to do today, and what she will do tomorrow. She will do so in her own good time and for her own benefit—not for anybody else's."[46] Perón is right about that. In international politics, Argentina will try to do tomorrow what it did yesterday. In World War II, the "new Argentina" stayed out of the conflict as long as possible, finally to declare itself an ally of the side which had already won the war. If a third world war develops while Peronism is still in power in Argentina, Buenos Aires may well endeavor to repeat that performance. After all, it has had its advantages. Actually, there is nothing very new about the "Third Position" or power politics. The basic principles of both were announced several centuries ago by a gentleman called Niccolò Machiavelli. His little book, *The Prince*, was given to the world as long ago as 1513 by a publisher who recognized a good book when he saw one.

Notes

I. A BOOK OF INTRODUCTIONS

1. The "Yankees of the South"

1. *La Prensa* (Buenos Aires), November 23, 1950.
2. Juan Alvarez, *Las Guerras Civiles Argentinas y el Problema de Buenos Aires en la República* (Buenos Aires: Bernabé y Cia., 1936), p. 3.
3. F. A. Kirkpatrick, *Latin America* (New York: The Macmillan Co., 1939), p. 423.
4. Quoted in United Press dispatch, January 1, 1945.
5. Quoted in Samuel E. Morison and Henry S. Commager, *Growth of the American Republic* (New York: Oxford University Press, 1937), II, 513. Italics mine. See also Edward O. Guerrant, *Roosevelt's Good Neighbor Policy* (Albuquerque: University of New Mexico Press, 1950), *passim*.
6. Quoted in Associated Press dispatch, October 16, 1944.
7. *Washington Post*, March 8, 1945.
8. Inter-American Conference on Problems of War and Peace, *Final Act* (Washington: Government Printing Office, 1945), Resolution LIX.
9. Quoted in *New York Herald Tribune*, April 26, 1945.
10. Quoted in Associated Press dispatch, April 29, 1945.
11. United States Department of State, *Consultation among the American Republics with Respect to the Argentine Situation* (popularly known as the "Blue Book") (Washington: Government Printing Office, 1946), p. 86.

2. Until Perón

1. Quoted in Ezequiel Martínez Estrada, *La Cabeza de Goliat* (Buenos Aires: Emecé Editores, 1946), p. 21 n.

2. Quoted in José Luis Romero, *Las Ideas Políticas en Argentina* (México: Fondo de Cultura Económica, 1946), p. 138.

3. Ysabel F. Rennie, *The Argentine Republic* (New York: The Macmillan Co., 1945), p. 20.

4. Luis Guillermo Piazza, "There'll Always Be a Córdoba," *Américas*, January, 1950, p. 47.

5. Quoted in Associated Press dispatch, November 14, 1943.

6. Quoted in Romero, *op. cit.*, p. 42.

7. Quoted in *ibid.*, p. 78.

8. Martínez Estrada, *op. cit.*, p. 26.

9. Rennie, *op. cit.*, p. 38.

10. Quoted in Romero, *op. cit.*, p. 103.

11. F. B. Head, quoted in Eduardo Jorge Bosco (ed.), *El Gaucho* (Buenos Aires: Emecé Editores, 1947), p. 28.

12. Alvarez, *op. cit.*, p. 69. Cf. also Madaline Wallis Nichols, *The Gaucho* (Durham: Duke University Press, 1942), *passim*.

13. F. B. Head, in Bosco, *op. cit.*, p. 28.

14. *Ibid.*, p. 29.

15. José Ingenieros, *Sociología Argentina* (Buenos Aires: Editorial Losada, 1946), p. 53.

16. Quoted in Santiago Vásquez, "Confidencias de don Juan Manuel de Rosas," *Revista del Río de la Plata* (Buenos Aires), p. 599.

17. Luis Pan, *Prensa Libre, Pueblo Libre* (Buenos Aires: La Vanguardia, 1950), p. 25.

18. Ricardo Levene, *Lecciones de Historia Argentina* (Buenos Aires: El Ateneo, 1950), II, 262–263.

19. Quoted in Rennie, *op. cit.*, pp. 56–57.

20. Quoted in Romero, *op. cit.*, p. 145.

21. The complete text of Law No. 8,871 (the "Sáenz Peña Law") can be found in Ministerio del Interior, *Las Fuerzas Armadas Restituyen el Imperio de la Soberanía Popular* (Buenos Aires: Cámara de Diputados, 1946), I, 304–319.

22. Felix J. Weil, *Argentine Riddle* (New York: The John Day Company, 1944), p. 57.

23. Some confusion reigns over the spelling of Irigoyen's name. He himself spelled it *Y*rigoyen, partially to distinguish himself from Bernardo de Irigoyen, also an Argentine public figure; but government printers, following the usage rendered standard by modern Spanish orthography, changed the *Y* to *I* in all of Hipólito Irigoyen's published documents. The spelling uniformly used in this book adheres to the usage in most published material dealing with Irigoyen.

24. *Christian Science Monitor* (Boston), October 1, 1917.

25. Rennie, *op. cit.*, pp. 221–222.
26. Enrique Dickmann, *Recuerdos de un Militante Socialista* (Buenos Aires: La Vanguardia, 1949), pp. 309–310.
27. *Ibid.*, p. 288.
28. *Ibid.*, p. 295.
29. Federico Pinedo, *En Tiempos de la República* (Buenos Aires: Editorial Depalma, 1946), p. 81.
30. Quoted in Ray Josephs, *Argentine Diary* (New York: Random House, Inc., 1944), pp. xix–xx. Cf. also Karl Loewenstein, "Legislation against Subversive Activities in Argentina," *Harvard Law Review*, Vol. 56, No. 8 (July, 1943), pp. 1261–1306.
31. Quoted in Nicolás Repetto, *Labor en el Exilio* (Buenos Aires: La Vanguardia, 1949), p. 147.
32. *Corriere Diplomatico e Consulare*, Rome, January 30, 1938.
33. Quoted in Luis V. Sommi, *Los Capitales Alemanes en la Argentina* (Buenos Aires: Editorial Claridad, 1945), pp. 24–25. Cf. also Otto Richard Tannenberg, *La Más Grande Alemania* (Madrid: Editorial Artes Gráficas Mateu, 1911), *passim;* and Joseph Borkin and Charles A. Welsh, *Germany's Master Plan* (New York: Duell, Sloan and Pearce, 1943), *passim.*
34. Weil, *op. cit.*, p. 20.
35. *Deutsche La Plata Zeitung* (Buenos Aires), February 21, 1937.
36. *Diario de Sesiones de la Cámara de Diputados* (Buenos Aires: Imprenta del Congreso Nacional, 1949), I, 401.
37. Quoted in Rennie, *op. cit.*, p. 285.
38. Repetto, *op. cit.*, p. 19.
39. Pinedo, *op. cit.*, p. 186.
40. Quoted in Rennie, *op. cit.*, p. 289.
41. Quoted in Weil, *op. cit.*, p. 21.
42. Duncan Aikman, *The All-American Front* (New York: Doubleday, Doran and Co., 1940), p. 194.
43. Josephs, *op. cit.*, p. xl.
44. *Ibid.*, pp. xxx and 31.
45. Rennie, *op. cit.*, p. 301.

II. A BOOK OF ALL THAT GLITTERS

3. SOUTHERN COLONEL

1. This was one of the slogans adopted by the underground opposition in the months after the uprising of June 4, 1943.
2. Dickmann, *op. cit.*, p. 323.
3. This translation of the manifesto was made from a Photostat copy of the document. The capitalization follows the usage in

the original. An English translation of the manifesto was published in the *New York Herald Tribune* for January 15, 1946. Portions of it have also been reproduced in Russell H. Fitzgibbon, "A Political Scientist's Point of View," in W. W. Pierson (ed.), "Pathology of Democracy in Latin America: A Symposium," *American Political Science Review*, Vol. XLIV, No. 1 (March, 1950), p. 127 n; and in Michael Sayers and Albert E. Kahn, *The Plot against the Peace* (New York: The Dial Press, 1945), p. 41. Sayers and Kahn are inaccurate in dating the manifesto June 10, 1944; actually, it was distributed among the army officers on May 13, 1943.

4. Quoted in Josephs, *op. cit.*, p. 43.
5. Quoted in *ibid.*, p. 44.
6. Ministerio del Interior, *op. cit.*, I, 624.
7. Josephs, *op. cit.*, p. 136.
8. Ministerio del Interior, *op. cit.*, I, 644.
9. Quoted in Associated Press dispatch, March 19, 1944.
10. Quoted in *ibid.*, August 27, 1944.
11. Josephs, *op. cit.*, p. 140.
12. *Ibid.*, p. 136.
13. *Ibid.*, p. 137.
14. *Ibid.*, p. 83.
15. *Ibid.*, p. 93.
16. Quoted in Associated Press dispatch, October 29, 1943.
17. *Mensaje del Presidente de la Nación Argentina General Juan Perón al Inaugurar el 84º Periodo Ordinario de Sesiones del Honorable Congreso Nacional* (Buenos Aires: Subsecretaría de Informaciones de la Presidencia de la Nación, 1950), p. 58.
18. Josephs, *op. cit.*, p. 140.
19. *Time*, May 21, 1951, p. 44.
20. Edward Tomlinson, *Battle for the Hemisphere* (New York: Charles Scribner's Sons, 1947), p. 40.
21. Quoted in *La Razón* (Buenos Aires), February 8, 1951.
22. Quoted in *El Mercurio* (Santiago), November 11, 1943.
23. Quoted in Josephs, *op. cit.*, p. 230.
24. Ministerio del Interior, *op. cit.*, I, 639–640.
25. *Mensaje del Presidente*, etc., p. 57.
26. Quoted in United Press dispatch, April 16, 1945.
27. Josephs, *op. cit.*, p. 258.
28. Ministerio del Interior, *op. cit.*, I, 660.
29. Quoted in United Press dispatch, May 2, 1945.
30. *New York Times*, September 20, 1945.
31. Quoted in United Press dispatch, September 26, 1945.
32. *New York Times*, October 8, 1945.

Notes

33. Josephs, *op. cit.*, p. 187.
34. Quoted in United Press dispatch, October 2, 1945.
35. Quoted in Associated Press dispatch, October 15, 1945.
36. Ministerio del Interior, *op. cit.*, II, 79.
37. *Ibid.*, II, 79.
38. *La Prensa* (Buenos Aires), October 18, 1945.
39. Ministerio del Interior, *op. cit.*, II, 87.
40. *Ibid.*, II, 87.
41. Quoted in Riéffolo Bessone, *Los Derechos Sociales de la Mujer* (Buenos Aires: El Ateneo, 1950), pp. 23–24.
42. *Qué*, October 17, 1946.

4. The Consolidation of Power

1. Quoted in United Press dispatch, October 10, 1945.
2. Quoted in *ibid.*, August 6, 1945, and August 7, 1945.
3. Quoted in *Allied Labor News* (London), September 7, 1944.
4. *New York Times,* November 28, 1945.
5. *Ibid.*, November 26, 1945.
6. *Chicago Daily News,* January 12, 1946.
7. Quoted in United Press dispatch, January 9, 1946.
8. Quoted in *La Prensa* (Buenos Aires), January 28, 1946.
9. *New York Herald Tribune,* December 21, 1945.
10. *Ibid.*, January 2, 1946.
11. Américo Ghioldi, *Los Trabajadores, el Señor Perón, y el Partido Socialista* (Buenos Aires: La Vanguardia, 1950), p. 18.
12. *Time,* May 21, 1951, p. 45.
13. Quoted in *La Prensa* (Buenos Aires), June 5, 1946.
14. [Juan Domingo Perón], *The Voice of Perón* (Buenos Aires: Subsecretaría de Informaciones de la Predidencia de la Nación Argentina, 1950), p. 18.
15. Quoted in *La Prensa* (Buenos Aires), May 2, 1948.
16. Quoted in *ibid.*, September 4, 1948.
17. Quoted in *ibid.*, November 9, 1948.
18. Quoted in *ibid.*, November 11, 1948.
19. Quoted in *ibid.*, January 12, 1949.
20. Repetto, *op. cit.*, p. 145.
21. Perón, *op. cit.*, p. 48.
22. Quoted in *Time,* January 24, 1949, p. 29.
23. Quoted in United Press dispatch, July 3, 1950.
24. Quoted in *La Razón* (Buenos Aires), March 15, 1951.
25. Quoted in *ibid.*, April 3, 1951.
26. Quoted in *Time,* September 10, 1951, p. 44.
27. Quoted in *ibid.*, September 10, 1951, p. 44.

28. *Diario de Sesiones de la Cámara de Diputados* (Buenos Aires: Imprenta del Congreso Nacional, 1948), III, 2419.
29. Quoted in *La Prensa* (Buenos Aires), September 30, 1949.
30. Quoted in Associated Press dispatch, September 28, 1951.
31. Quoted in *New York Times*, September 15, 1951.

5. ONCE THERE WAS A LADY

1. Quoted in Jerónimo M. Peralta, *Semblanza Heróica de Eva Perón* (Buenos Aires: El Ateneo, 1950), p. 56.
2. *Time*, May 21, 1951, p. 44.
3. *Ibid.*, May 21, 1951, p. 46.
4. *Ibid.*, May 21, 1951, p. 45.
5. Quoted in *Chicago Daily News*, November 5, 1951.
6. Bessone, *op. cit.*, p. 181.
7. Alicia Moreau de Justo, *La Mujer en la Democracia* (Buenos Aires: El Ateneo, 1945), pp. 129–130.
8. Quoted in *La Razón* (Buenos Aires), July 18, 1950.
9. Josephs, *op. cit.*, p. 47.
10. Quoted in *New York Herald Tribune*, August 26, 1944.
11. Quoted in Bessone, *op. cit.*, p. 58.
12. Peralta, *op. cit.*, p. 9.
13. Quoted in Bessone, *op. cit.*, p. 192.
14. Matilde Cándida Alvarez, quoted in *La Razón* (Buenos Aires), February 8, 1951.
15. Augusta R. Carrizo, quoted in *ibid.*, February 15, 1951.
16. Quoted in *ibid.*, February 23, 1951.
17. Quoted in Peralta, *op. cit.*, p. 42.
18. *Time*, May 21, 1951, p. 48.
19. Quoted in *La Razón* (Buenos Aires), March 29, 1951.
20. *Time*, May 21, 1951, p. 46.
21. María Eva Duarte de Perón, *Mi Obra de Ayuda Social* (Buenos Aires: Subsecretaría de Informaciones de la Presidencia de la Nación, 1949), p. 4.
22. *Time*, May 21, 1951, p. 46.
23. Quoted in *La Prensa* (Buenos Aires), July 4, 1950.
24. Quoted in Luis Guillermo Bähler (ed.), *La Nación Argentina* (Buenos Aires: Subsecretaría de Informaciones de la Presidencia de la Nación, 1949), p. 279.
25. [Eva Perón], *The Writings of Eva Perón* (Buenos Aires: Subsecretaría de Informaciones de a Presidencia de la Nación, 1950), p. 18.
26. Quoted in Peralta, *op. cit.*, p. 55.
27. Quoted in *ibid.*, p. 55.
28. Quoted in *Time*, January 24, 1949.

Notes

29. Eva Perón, *Mi Obra de Ayuda Social,* p. 9.
30. Quoted in Bähler, *op. cit.,* p. 192.
31. Eva Perón, *op. cit.,* p. 12.
32. Quoted in *La Nación* (Buenos Aires), December 28, 1950.

6. INSTITUTIONALIZED LOCKSTEP

1. Quoted in *La Prensa* (Buenos Aires), June 10, 1949.
2. Quoted in *ibid.,* December 8, 1949.
3. Quoted in *ibid.,* August 6, 1948.
4. *Diario de Sesiones de la Cámara de Diputados* (Buenos Aires: Imprenta del Congreso Nacional, 1948), III, 2400–2401.
5. *Ibid.,* p. 2401.
6. Quoted in *Time,* August 23, 1948, p. 30.
7. Robert K. Shellaby, "Argentina under Peronismo," *Christian Science Monitor* (Boston), January 14, 1950.
8. Quoted in *Qué,* December 26, 1946, p. 3.
9. Quoted in *La Nación* (Buenos Aires), September 8, 1950.
10. *Diario de Sesiones de la Cámara de Diputados* (Buenos Aires: Imprenta del Congreso Nacional, 1948), III, 2400, 2403.
11. Quoted in *La Prensa* (Buenos Aires), September 30, 1949.
12. *Diario de Sesiones de la Cámara de Diputados* (Buenos Aires: Imprenta del Congreso Nacional, 1948), III, 2403.
13. Juan A. González Calderón, *Derecho Constitucional Argentino* (Buenos Aires: Laiouane, 1931), I, 315–316.
14. *Fallos de la Corte Suprema de Justicia Nacional,* Series II, Vol. 5 (Buenos Aires: Corte Suprema de Justicia Nacional, 1873), pp. 26–31.
15. *Ibid.,* Series II, Vol. 13 (1875), p. 458; and Series II, Vol. 3 (1884), p. 197.
16. *Constitución de la Nación Argentina* (Buenos Aires: Subsecretaría de Informaciones de la Presidencia de la Nación, 1949), Art. 95.
17. *New York Herald Tribune,* April 4, 1945.
18. Quoted in United Press dispatch, April 10, 1945.
19. Juan Domingo Perón, *op. cit.,* p. 89; and Alfredo L. Palacios, *La Corte Suprema ante el Tribunal del Senado* (Buenos Aires: La Vanguardia, 1947), p. 233.
20. Quoted in *Qué,* December 12, 1946, p. 3.
21. Palacios, *op. cit.,* p. 232.
22. Quoted in Josephs, *op. cit.,* pp. 39–40.
23. *Fallos de la Corte Suprema de Justicia Nacional,* Series II, Vol. 19 (1887), p. 236.
24. Readers wishing to compare the nonpolitical aspects of Argentine judicial practices with usages to be found elsewhere in

Latin America may wish to consult any of the following: William S. Stokes, *Honduras: An Area Study in Government* (Madison: University of Wisconsin Press, 1950), pp. 106–150; George I. Blanksten, *Ecuador: Constitutions and Caudillos* (Berkeley: University of California Press, 1951), pp. 127–140; J. A. C. Grant, "Due Process for Ex-Dictators: A Study of Judicial Control of Legislation in Guatemala," *American Political Science Review*, Vol. XLI, No. 3 (June, 1947), pp. 463–469; Grant, " 'Contract Clause' Litigation in Colombia: A Comparative Study in Judicial Review," *American Political Science Review*, Vol. XLII, No. 6 (December, 1948), pp. 1103–1126; and Association of American Law Schools (ed.), *Latin-American Legal Philosophy* (Cambridge: Harvard University Press, 1948), *passim*.

7. INSTITUTIONALIZED LOCKSTEP (Continued)

1. Rennie, *op. cit.*, p. viii.
2. *Constitución de la Nación Argentina* (Buenos Aires: Imprenta del Congreso Nacional, 1936), Art. 104.
3. The standard Argentine works on the interventor system are Juan Bautista Alberdi, *Derecho Público Provincial Argentino* (Buenos Aires: La Cultura Argentina, 1917); Luis H. Sommariva, *Historia de las Intervenciones Federales en las Provincias*, 2 vols. (Buenos Aires: El Ateneo, 1929, 1931); Sommariva, *Le Intervención Federal Comparada con la Norteamericana y la Suiza* (Buenos Aires: El Ateneo, 1935); and Ministerio del Interior, *Intervención Federal en las Provincias* (Buenos Aires: Talleres Gráficos de Correos y Telégrafos, 1933). Analyses in English may be found in Leo S. Rowe, *The Federal System of the Argentine Republic* (Washington: Carnegie Institution, 1921), *passim*, and in Austin F. Macdonald, *Government of the Argentine Republic* (New York: Thomas Y. Crowell Co., 1942), pp. 169–189. The best short discussion in English is Rosendo A. Gómez's article, "Intervention in Argentina, 1860–1930," which appears in both *Inter-American Economic Affairs* (December, 1947) Vol. I, No. 3, pp. 55–73, and Asher N. Christensen (ed.), *The Evolution of Latin-American Government* (New York: Henry Holt and Co., 1951), pp. 383–400.
4. *Constitution of the United States*, Article IV, Section 4.
5. *Constitución de la Nación Argentina* (Buenos Aires: Imprenta del Congreso Nacional, 1936), Art. 6; and *Constitución de la Nación Argentina* (Buenos Aires: Subsecretaría de Informaciones de la Presidencia de la Nación, 1949), Art. 6.
6. Unpublished Interior Ministry memorandum, April, 1939.
7. *Fallos de la Corte Suprema de Justicia Nacional*, Series IV,

Vol. 4, (Buenos Aires: Corte Suprema de Justicia Nacional, undated), pp. 550–563.

8. Readers interested in comparing this position with that expressed by the "North American" courts on political questions may wish to consult the opinions of the United States Supreme Court in *Luther* v. *Borden*, 7 Howard 1 (1849); *Mississippi* v. *Johnson*, 4 Wallace 475 (1867); *Georgia* v. *Stanton*, 6 Wallace 50 (1868); *Neely* v. *Henkel*, 180 U.S. 109 (1901); and *Oetjen* v. *Central Leather Co.*, 246 U.S. 297 (1918).

9. Joaquín V. González, *Manual de la Constitución Argentina* (Buenos Aires; Editorial Estrada, undated), p. 743.

10. *Fallos de la Corte Suprema de Justicia Nacional*, Series IV, Vol. 4, (Buenos Aires: Corte Suprema de Justicia Nacional, undated), pp. 550–563.

11. Josephs, *op. cit.*, p. 187.

12. Alfredo R. Bufano, *Zoología Política* (Buenos Aires: Editorial Zor, undated), p. 91.

13. *La Nación* (Buenos Aires), February 4, 1951.

14. *Ibid.*, December 19, 1950.

15. Quoted in Josephs, *op. cit.*, p. 116.

16. *Constitución de la Nación Argentina* (Buenos Aires: Subsecretaría de Informaciones de la Presidencia de la Nación, 1949), fifth transitory provision.

17. *Ibid.*, Art. 103.

18. *La Prensa* (Buenos Aires), October 21, 1949.

19. Cf. Clarence H. Haring, "Federalism in Latin America," in Christensen, *op. cit.*, pp. 336–343; and Gómez, *op. cit.*, *passim*.

20. *Mensaje del Presidente*, etc., pp. 15–16.

21. *Ibid.*, p. 6; and quoted in *La Razón* (Buenos Aires), August 29, 1950.

22. Juan Domingo Perón, *The Voice of Perón*, p. 49.

23. *Mensaje del Presidente*, etc., pp. 14–15, 17.

24. Rennie, *op. cit.*, p. viii.

25. *Chicago Daily News*, January 12, 1946.

26. Josephs, *op. cit.*, pp. 223, 187.

27. Ingenieros, *op. cit.*, p. 43.

28. Fabián Onsari, *Gobierno Municipal* (Buenos Aires: Editorial Claridad, 1941), p. 25.

29. Readers interested in comparing the Argentine situation with municipal autonomy elsewhere in Latin America may wish to consult Stokes, *op. cit.*, pp. 151–178, 265–268; and Blanksten, *op. cit.*, pp. 156–161.

30. Romero, *op. cit.*, p. 54.

31. Onsari, *op. cit.*, p. 28.

32. Macdonald, *op. cit.*, pp. 20–21.
33. Quoted in Josephs, *op. cit.*, p. 26.
34. José María Sáenz Valiente (h.), *Curso de Derecho Municipal* (Buenos Aires: Editorial Dovile, 1944), p. 86.
35. Onsari, *op. cit.*, p. 31.
36. *Ibid.*, p. 32.
37. Josephs, *op. cit.*, p. 49.
38. *Mensaje del Presidente*, etc., p. 21.

III. A BOOK OF IDEOLOGY AND POLITICS

8. PERONISM AND INDIVIDUAL LIBERTY

1. *Diario de Sesiones de la Cámara de Diputados* (Buenos Aires: Imprenta del Congreso Nacional, 1949), III, 2402.
2. Rennie, *op. cit.*, p. 352.
3. Josephs, *op. cit.*, p. 199.
4. From transcript of Radio Belgrano broadcast of September 3, 1944.
5. Quoted in Associated Press dispatch, July 27, 1944.
6. Rennie, *op. cit.*, p. 351.
7. Quoted in *La Opinión* (Santiago), January 4, 1945.
8. *Time*, October 6, 1947, p. 38.
9. Quoted in Josephs, *op. cit.*, p. 203.
10. *Constitución de la Nación Argentina* (Buenos Aires: Subsecretaría de Informaciones de la Presidencia de la Nación, 1949), Art. 15.
11. Raúl A. Mende, *El Justicialismo* (Buenos Aires: ALEA, S.A., 1950), p. 156.
12. Bessone, *op. cit.*, p. 212.
13. Quoted in *Time*, May 21, 1951, p. 44.
14. D. Yantorno, *Historia de la Independencia Económica* (Buenos Aires: El Ateneo, 1950), p. 133.
15. Josephs, *op. cit.*, p. 117.
16. Quoted in United Press dispatch, October 17, 1944.
17. Rennie, *op. cit.*, p. 44.
18. Quoted in *Time*, July 22, 1946, p. 44.
19. Ghioldi, *op. cit.*, p. 34.
20. *Ibid.*, p. 34.
21. The reader may wish to consult Ramón F. Vásquez, *Poder de Policía* (Buenos Aires: Editorial Contreras, 1940), the standard work on the police power in Argentina. For representative expressions of the "North American" Supreme Court on the police power in the United States, see the opinions in *New York* v. *Miln*, 11 Peters 102 (1837); *License Cases*, 5 Howard 504 (847); *Boston*

Beer Company v. *Massachusetts*, 97 U.S. 25 (1878); and *Stone* v. *Mississippi*, 101 U.S. 814 (1880).

22. *Constitución de la Nación Argentina* (Buenos Aires: Sub-secretaría de Informaciones de la Presidencia de la Nación, 1949), Art. 34; and *Constitución de la Nación Argentina* (Buenos Aires: Imprenta del Congreso Nacional, 1936), Art. 23.

23. *Constitución de la Nación Argentina* (Buenos Aires: Sub-secretaría de Informaciones de la Presidencia de la Nación, 1949), Art. 34.

24. Quoted in *Time*, October 11, 1948, p. 40.

25. *Anales de la Legislación Argentina* (Buenos Aires: Editorial La Ley, 1949), IX, 247.

26. Quoted in *Time*, September 18, 1950, p. 45.

27. Quoted in *La Nación* (Buenos Aires), September 8, 1950. Also, cf. *Time*, September 18, 1950, p. 45.

28. Dickmann, *op. cit.*, p. 302.

29. Josephs, *op. cit.*, p. 118.

30. *Ibid.*, pp. 286–287.

31. Shellaby, *op. cit.*, p. 3.

9. ON THE MIND OF MAN

1. Quoted in *Christian Science Monitor* (Boston), August 7, 1944.

2. Juan Domingo Perón, *op. cit.*, p. 168.

3. Quoted in *Time*, April 12, 1948, p. 42.

4. Quoted in Associated Press dispatch, September 27, 1943.

5. Dirección General de Institutos Militares, *Pensamiento y Acción de los Liceos Militares* (Buenos Aires: Imprenta López, 1948), pp. 29–30.

6. *Anales*, etc. (1944), IV, 73.

7. Quoted in *La Prensa* (Buenos Aires), January 1, 1944.

8. Quoted in Josephs, *op. cit.*, p. 322.

9. Quoted in Padre Virgilio M. Filippo, *El Plan Quinquenal Perón y los Comunistas* (Buenos Aires: El Ateneo, 1948), pp. 465–466.

10. Quoted in Josephs, *op. cit.*, p. 207.

11. Quoted in *ibid.*, p. 220.

12. Rennie, *op. cit.*, p. 212.

13. Piazza, *op. cit.*, p. 27.

14. Quoted in International News Service dispatch, July 3, 1945.

15. Quoted in United Press dispatch, October 4, 1945.

16. Quoted in Augusto Durelli, *Forma y Sentido de la Resistencia Universitaria de Octubre de 1945* (Buenos Aires: Tomás Palumbo, 1945), p. 20.

17. *Ibid.*, p. 7.
18. *New York Herald Tribune*, October 16, 1945.
19. Durelli, *op. cit.*, p. 23.
20. Ley N⁰ 13,031 ("Ley Universitaria") (Buenos Aires: Imprenta del Congreso Nacional, 1947), Art. 4.
21. Quoted in *La Razón* (Buenos Aires), April 2, 1951.
22. Quoted in *ibid.*, March 29, 1951.
23. Juan Domingo Perón, *op. cit.*, pp. 187–188.
24. Quoted in Dickmann, *op. cit.*, p. 335.
25. Quoted in *Time*, November 10, 1947, p. 42.
26. Pan, *op. cit.*, pp. 24–25.
27. C. Galván Moreno, *El Periodismo Argentino* (Buenos Aires: Editorial Claridad, 1944), p. 278.
28. Quoted in Pan, *op. cit.*, p. 112.
29. Quoted in Josephs, *op. cit.*, p. 77.
30. Decreto N⁰ 18,407 (Buenos Aires: Editorial La Ley, December 31, 1943).
31. Quoted in Associated Press dispatch, October 1, 1943.
32. Quoted in United Press dispatch, October 7, 1943.
33. *Newsweek*, May 8, 1944, p. 60.
34. *La Nación* (Buenos Aires), February 4, 1951.
35. *Ibid.*, November 6, 1950, and February 1, 1951.
36. *Diario de Sesiones de la Cámara de Diputados* (Buenos Aires: Imprenta del Congreso Nacional 1948), III, 2400.
37. Quoted in *La Prensa* (Buenos Aires), August 1, 1947.
38. Quoted in *ibid.*, July 17, 1949.
39. Quoted in United Press dispatch, August 22, 1945; *Mensaje del Presidente*, etc., p. 37.
40. Quoted in United Press dispatch, July 3, 1950.
41. Galván Moreno, *op. cit.*, p. 222.
42. Quoted in *ibid.*, p. 222.
43. Quoted in *La Razón*, Buenos Aires, February 9, 1951.
44. Quoted in Galván Moreno, *op. cit.*, p. 218.
45. *The Standard* (Buenos Aires), October 19, 1941.
46. *The Times* (London), March 8, 1951.
47. *La Prensa* (Buenos Aires), September 20, 1945.
48. Quoted in *Time*, July 4, 1949, p. 29.
49. Quoted in Weil, *op. cit.*, p. 53 n.
50. Quoted in *La Razón* (Buenos Aires), February 8, 1951.
51. *La Epoca* (Buenos Aires), January 26, 1951.
52. From mimeographed leaflet distributed at Buenos Aires on January 28, 1951.
53. Quoted in *Time*, April 23, 1951, p. 46.
54. Quoted in *La Nación* (Buenos Aires), March 13, 1951.

55. Quoted in *Time*, September 17, 1951, p. 46.
56. Quoted in Reuter's press dispatch, May 1, 1951.
57. Quoted in *New York Times*, November 20, 1951.
58. *La Vanguardia* (Buenos Aires), January 6, 1944.
59. *Ibid.*, September 2, 1947.
60. Josephs, *op. cit.*, p. 111.
61. Quoted in *La Prensa* (Buenos Aires), July 12, 1948.
62. Josephs, *op. cit.*, p. 112.
63. Quoted in *Democracia* (Buenos Aires), August 30, 1950.

10. ON HATING FOREIGNERS

1. Carl C. Taylor, *Rural Life in Argentina* (Baton Rouge: Louisiana State University Press, 1950), p. 438.
2. John W. White, *Argentina: The Life Story of a Nation* (New York: The Viking Press, 1942), p. 13.
3. Raúl A. Orgaz, *Sociología Argentina* (Córdoba: Imprenta de la Universidad, 1950), pp. 45–46.
4. Rennie, *op. cit.*, p. 62.
5. Cf. *ibid.*, *passim*.
6. Juan Domingo Perón, *op. cit.*, p. 17.
7. *Mensaje del Presidente*, etc. Italics after the original.
8. From transcript of Radio El Mundo broadcast of July 29, 1944.
9. Quoted in Rennie, *op. cit.*, p. 385.
10. Quoted in Associated Press dispatch, April 4, 1946.
11. Quoted in *ibid.*, March 2, 1944.
12. Quoted in Josephs, *op. cit.*, p. 190.
13. Quoted in *Allied Labor News* (London), August 3, 1944.
14. *El Cabildo* (Buenos Aires), December 17, 1943.
15. Tomlinson, *op. cit.*, p. 122.
16. *New York Times*, November 28, 1945.
17. Quoted in Associated Press dispatch, December 11, 1945.
18. Ministerio del Interior, *op. cit.*, II, 126.
19. Juan Domingo Perón, *op. cit.*, p. 182.
20. Quoted in *Gobernantes* (Buenos Aires), March 31, 1951, p. 15.
21. J. Lloyd Mecham, *Church and State in Latin America* (Chapel Hill: University of North Carolina Press, 1934), p. 304.
22. Rowe, *op. cit.*, p. 129.
23. Quoted in Josephs, *op. cit.*, p. 210.
24. Quoted in *Time*, January 17, 1949, p. 28.
25. Quoted in Josephs, *op. cit.*, p. 216.
26. Quoted in *La Prensa* (Buenos Aires), January 2, 1947.
27. Quoted in *ibid.*, November 17, 1947.

28. Weil, *op. cit.*, p. 8.
29. Josephs, *op. cit.*, p. 85.
30. Quoted in *ibid.*, p. 322.
31. Quoted in *New York Herald Tribune*, July 30, 1944.
32. Quoted in Associated Press dispatch, November 26, 1945.
33. Filippo, *op. cit.*, pp. 5–6.
34. Quoted in Josephs, *op. cit.*, p. 90. Italics mine.
35. *Constitución de la Nación Argentina* (Buenos Aires: Sub-secretaría de Informaciones de la Presidencia de la Nación, 1949), Art. 2. The same provision was contained in the Constitution of 1853. Cf. *Constitución de la Nación Argentina* (Buenos Aires: Imprenta del Congreso Nacional, 1936, 1853), Art. 2.
36. Josephs, *op. cit.*, p. 35.
37. *Ibid.*, p. 230.
38. Quoted in *El Pueblo* (Buenos Aires), April 11, 1948.
39. Quoted in *Crítica* (Buenos Aires), August 1, 1950.
40. Quoted in *La Razón* (Buenos Aires), December 19, 1950.
41. Juan Domingo Perón, *op. cit.*, p. 38.
42. Quoted in Bähler, *op. cit.*, p. 139.
43. Weil, *op. cit.*, p. 126.
44. Eva Perón, *The Writings of Eva Perón*, p. 32.
45. Juan D. Perón, *op. cit.*, p. 160.
46. *Mensaje del Presidente*, etc., p. 46.
47. Quoted in *La Prensa* (Buenos Aires), May 30, 1948.
48. *Mensaje del Presidente*, etc., p. 37.
49. *Corn Trade News* (London), January 3, 1951.
50. Quoted in *La Nación* (Buenos Aires), September 8, 1950.

11. The Rich and the Poor

1. Partido Peronista, *Manual del Peronista* (Buenos Aires: Editorial Ateneo, 1949), p. 14.
2. Juan Domingo Perón, *op. cit.*, p. 37.
3. Ingenieros, *op. cit.*, p. 52.
4. *Time*, August 12, 1946, p. 36.
5. Juan Domingo Perón, *op. cit.*, p. 20.
6. Weil, *op. cit.*, p. 104.
7. Francis Herron, *Letters from the Argentine* (New York: G. P. Putnam's Sons, 1943), pp. 156–157.
8. Juan Domingo Perón, *op. cit.*, p. 154.
9. *Mensaje del Presidente*, etc., p. 33.
10. Tomlinson, *op. cit.*, p. 115.
11. Quoted in *La Prensa* (Buenos Aires), April 24, 1948.
12. Quoted in *Allied Labor News* (London), July 18, 1944.

Notes

13. From transcript of Radio Belgrano broadcast of September 2, 1944.
14. Quoted in *La Razón* (Buenos Aires), March 29, 1951.
15. Quoted in *Time*, March 22, 1948.
16. *New York Times*, October 22, 1950.
17. Quoted in *New York Herald Tribune*, September 2, 1944.
18. Quoted in *La Razón* (Buenos Aires), September 5, 1950.
19. Quoted in International News Service dispatch, April 29, 1945.
20. See Russell H. Fitzgibbon, "Measurement of Latin American Political Phenomena: A Statistical Experiment," *American Political Science Review*, Vol. XLV, No. 2 (June, 1951), pp. 517–523.
21. Ingenieros, *op. cit.*, p. 68.
22. Quoted in Taylor, *op. cit.*, p. 422.
23. Juan Domingo Perón, *op. cit.*, p. 27.
24. Yantorno, *op. cit.*, p. 157.
25. Juan Domingo Perón, *op. cit.*, p. 143.
26. *Ibid.*, p. 83.
27. Peralta, *op. cit.*, pp. 25–26.
28. Juan D. Perón, *op. cit.*, p. 91.
29. Partido Peronista, *op. cit.*, p. 18.
30. Josefina Marpons, *La Mujer en América* (Buenos Aires: El Ateneo, 1950), p. 134.
31. Quoted in Ernesto Krotoschin, *Curso de Legislación del Trabajo* (Buenos Aires: Editorial Depalma, 1950), p. 333.
32. Quoted in *La Razón* (Buenos Aires), April 2, 1951.
33. Quoted in Associated Press dispatch, July 30, 1944.
34. Marpons, *op. cit.*, p. 134.
35. Juan D. Perón, *op. cit.*, p. 135.
36. First National Bank of Boston, *Behold Argentina* (Buenos Aires: First National Bank of Boston, 1950), p. 19.
37. Rennie, *op. cit.*, p. viii.
38. Josephs, *op. cit.*, pp. 156–157.
39. Quoted in *Time*, July 14, 1947, p. 32.

12. SOUTHERN DIALECTIC

1. *Time*, May 21, 1951, p. 43.
2. *Corriere Diplomatico e Consolare*, Rome, January 30, 1938.
3. *Diario de Sesiones de la Cámara de Diputados* (Buenos Aires: Imprenta del Congreso Nacional, 1938), I, 222.
4. Josephs, *op. cit.*, p. 207.
5. *Washington Post*, December 29, 1943.
6. Quoted in *Time*, May 21, 1951, p. 44.
7. Quoted in Tomlinson, *op. cit.*, p. 118.

8. *Washington Post*, January 5, 1944.
9. United States Department of State, *op. cit.*, p. 65.
10. Quoted in Associated Press dispatch, January 19, 1946.
11. Quoted in *ibid.*, March 29, 1945.
12. Quoted in *Daily Worker* (New York), March 30, 1945.
13. Juan D. Perón, *op. cit.*, p. 31.
14. Quoted in *Time*, April 18, 1949, p. 37.
15. Quoted in *ibid.*, p. 37.
16. Quoted in *ibid.*, p. 37.
17. Quoted in *La Razón* (Buenos Aires), February 23, 1951.
18. Mende, *op. cit.*, p. 102.
19. Quoted in Bähler, *op. cit.*, p. 45.
20. Juan D. Perón, *op. cit.*, p. 51.
21. Quoted in *Democracia* (Buenos Aires), August 21, 1950.
22. Bessone, *op. cit.*, p. 20.
23. *Ibid.*, p. 21.
24. Juan D. Perón, *op. cit.*, p. 90.
25. Mende, *op. cit.*, p. 47.
26. Bessone, *op. cit.*, p. 21.
27. Cf. Blanksten, *op. cit.*, pp. 12–13.
28. Mende, *op. cit.*, p. 70.
29. *Ibid.*, p. 155.
30. Juan D. Perón, *op. cit.*, p. 55.
31. *Constitución de la Nación Argentina* (Buenos Aires: Sub-secretaría de Informaciones de la Presidencia de la Nación, 1949), Art. 15.
32. Juan D. Perón, *op. cit.*, p. 40.
33. Leonard T. Richmond, *Argentina's Third Position and Other Systems Compared* (Buenos Aires: Acme Agency, 1949) p. 10.
34. Juan D. Perón, *op. cit.*, p. 133.
35. *Ibid.*, p. 69.
36. Mende, *op. cit.*, p. 83.
37. *Ibid.*, p. 78.
38. Peralta, *op. cit.*, p. 18.
39. Mende, *op. cit.*, p. 157.
40. Quoted in *La Razón* (Buenos Aires), September 5, 1950.
41. From transcript of Radio El Mundo broadcast of August 12, 1944.
42. Quoted in Associated Press dispatch, November 26, 1944.
43. Quoted in Richmond, *op. cit.*, pp. 101–102.
44. Mende, *op. cit.*, p. 106.
45. Richmond, *op. cit.*, p. 102.
46. *Mensaje del Presidente*, etc., 26.
47. Mende, *op. cit.*, pp. 94–96. Italics after the original.

48. Quoted in *La Razón* (Buenos Aires), September 5, 1950.
49. *Mensaje del Presidente*, etc., p. 28.
50. Robert Strausz–Hupé and Stefan T. Possony, *International Relations* (New York: McGraw-Hill Book Co., Inc., 1950), p. 421.
51. *Ibid.*, p. 437.
52. Juan D. Perón, *op. cit.*, p. 37.
53. Bessone, *op. cit.*, p. 212.
54. Mario Palmeiri, *The Philosophy of Fascism* (Chicago: Dante Alegheiri Society, 1936), p. 179.
55. *Ibid.*, p. 21.
56. *Ibid.*, p. 41; quoted in Herman Finer, *Mussolini's Italy* (London: v. Gallancz, 1935), p. 91.
57. Quoted in Finer, *op. cit.*, p. 500.
58. Quoted in *ibid.*, pp. 216–217; 222.
59. Dickmann, *op. cit.*, p. 328.
60. Quoted in United Press dispatch, January 17, 1945.
61. Alfredo L. Palaeios, *El Nuevo Derecho* (Buenos Aires: La Vanguardia, 1946), p. 52.
62. Yantorno, *op. cit.*, 229.
63. Weil, *op. cit.*, pp. 47–48.
64. Bernard Redmont, "Perón's Key to Power," *U.S. News and World Report*, January 27, 1950, p. 28.

13. The Quondam Faithful

1. Redmont, *op. cit.*, p. 28.
2. Ministerio del Interior, *op. cit.*, I, 646.
3. Quoted in *La Prensa* (Buenos Aires), December 21, 1947.
4. Josephs, *op. cit.*, pp. 61–62.
5. Durelli, *op. cit.*, p. 10; and Durelli, *Del Universo de la Universidad al Universo del Hombre* (Buenos Aires: Tomás Palumbo, 1947), pp. 42–43.
6. Quoted in *La Razón* (Buenos Aires), February 8, 1951.
7. Josephs, *op. cit.*, p. 25.
8. Dickmann, *op. cit.*, p. 318.
9. Josephs, *op. cit.*, p. 70.
10. Quoted in United Press dispatch, October 12, 1944.
11. Quoted in Repetto, *op. cit.*, p. 147.
12. Josephs, *op. cit.*, p. 120.
13. *Ibid.*, p. 18.
14. Quoted in Associated Press dispatch, August 5, 1945.
15. Quoted in United Press dispatch, September 24, 1945.
16. Arturo Cuyás (ed.), *Appleton's New English-Spanish and Spanish-English Dictionary* (New York: D. Appleton-Century Co., 1942), Part II, p. 165.

17. *La Razón* (Buenos Aires), October 18, 1945.
18. Eva Perón, *op. cit.*, pp. 13–14.
19. Ley Nº 13,568, (Buenos Aires: Imprenta del Congreso Nacional, 1949), Art. 1.
20. Eva Perón, *op. cit.*, p. 13.
21. Tomlinson, *op. cit.*, p. 127.
22. Josephs, *op. cit.*, p. 256.
23. *New York Times*, October 22, 1945.
24. *Washington Post*, May 15, 1946.
25. Quoted in *La Razón* (Buenos Aires), July 18, 1950.
26. Quoted in *Crítica* (Buenos Aires), August 9, 1950.
27. Quoted in *La Prensa* (Buenos Aires), February 5, 1947.
28. Eva Perón, *Mi Obra de Ayuda Social*, pp. 8, 12.
29. Quoted in *La Prensa* (Buenos Aires), March 10, 1947.
30. Quoted in *ibid.*, March 12, 1947.
31. Quoted in *ibid.*, January 25, 1951.
32. Quoted in *ibid.*, January 25, 1951.

14. The Quondam Faithful (Continued)

1. Quoted in *Qué*, September 12, 1946, p. 5.
2. Shellaby, *op. cit.*, p. 3.
3. *Qué*, December 19, 1946, p. 4.
4. Quoted in Bessone, *op. cit.*, p. 192.
5. Quoted in *La Razón* (Buenos Aires), March 2, 1951.
6. Quoted in Associated Press dispatch, September 13, 1945.
7. *Time*, May 21, 1951, p. 46.

15. The Otherwise-Minded

1. Ghioldi, *op. cit.*, p. 52.
2. Quoted in Associated Press dispatch, December 31, 1943.
3. Ley Nº 13,645 (Buenos Aires: Imprenta del Congreso Nacional, 1949).
4. Ministerio del Interior, *op. cit.*, II, 51.
5. Quoted in *Qué*, October 3, 1946, p. 3.
6. Quoted in *ibid.*, October 3, 1946, p. 3.
7. Quoted in *La Razón* (Buenos Aires), September 5, 1950.
8. Juan D. Perón, *op. cit.*, p. 49.
9. Quoted in United Press dispatch, January 28, 1949.
10. Quoted in *La Prensa* (Buenos Aires), January 18, 1951.
11. Quoted in *ibid.*, March 25, 1948.
12. Quoted in *Qué*, November 14, 1946, p. 3.
13. Rennie, *op. cit.*, p. 341.
14. Ingenieros, *op. cit.*, p. 67.
15. *Ibid.*, p. 67.

16. Weil, *op. cit.*, p. 5.

17. Quoted in Carlos R. Melo, *Los Partidos Políticos Argentinos* (Córdoba: Imprenta de la Universidad, 1945), p. 31.

18. Weil, *op. cit.*, p. 57.

19. Romero, *op. cit.*, p. 224.

20. Josephs, *op. cit.*, p. 17.

21. Quoted in United Press dispatch, March 2, 1945.

22. Quoted in Associated Press dispatch, July 23, 1945.

23. Quoted in *La Prensa* (Buenos Aires), January 20, 1949.

24. Quoted in *ibid.*, June 2, 1950.

16. THE OTHERWISE-MINDED (Continued)

1. Weil, *op. cit.*, p. 59.

2. Josephs, *op. cit.*, p. xxxiii.

3. Dickmann, *op. cit.*, p. 197.

4. Repetto, *op. cit.*, p. 185.

5. Josephs, *op. cit.*, p. xxxii.

6. Quoted in Associated Press dispatch, March 19, 1945.

7. Ghioldi, *op. cit.*, pp. 23–24.

8. Ghioldi, *Marxismo, Socialismo, Izquierdismo, Comunismo y la Realidad Argentina de Hoy* (Buenos Aires: La Vanguardia, 1950), p. 153.

9. *Ibid.*, p. 126.

10. *Ibid.*, p. 146.

11. *Ibid.*, p. 158.

12. *Ibid.*, p. 129.

13. Taylor, *op. cit.*, p. 422.

14. Weil, *op. cit.*, pp. 4–5.

15. Macdonald, *op. cit.*, p. 91.

16. R. Gröbli, *Historia de una Epoca Política* (Buenos Aires: La Vanguardia, 1948), p. 15.

17. Quoted in Associated Press dispatch, December 20, 1944.

18. Redmont, *op. cit.*, p. 30.

19. Juan D. Perón, *op. cit.*, p. 20.

20. Macdonald, *op. cit.*, p. 93.

21. Weil, *op. cit.*, p. 7.

22. Quoted in Martin Ebon, *World Communism Today* (New York: McGraw-Hill Book Co., Inc., 1948), p. 337.

23. Quoted in *Daily Worker* (New York), August 22, 1944.

24. Quoted in *Time*, December 2, 1946.

25. Ghioldi, *op. cit.*, p. 133.

26. Redmont, *op. cit.*, p. 31.

27. Tomlinson, *op. cit.*, p. 88.

28. Quoted in *Time*, January 9, 1950, p. 24.

29. Quoted in *La Prensa* (Buenos Aires), January 9, 1951.
30. Tomlinson, *op. cit.*, p. 117.

17. ARGENTINA AND THE WORLD

1. Josephs, *op. cit.*, p. 57.
2. From Photostat copy of note as carried by *La Razón* (Montevideo), January 21, 1944.
3. Quoted in *New York Times*, July 27, 1944.
4. Josephs, *op. cit.*, p. 130.
5. Quoted in Associated Press dispatch, August 28, 1944.
6. Quoted in *New York Herald Tribune*, February 10, 1945.
7. Quoted in Associated Press dispatch, July 25, 1944.
8. Quoted in United Press dispatch, March 27, 1945.
9. Quoted in *Current Biography*, September, 1945, p. 12.
10. Quoted in Associated Press dispatch, August 17, 1945.
11. Quoted in *New York Times*, August 29, 1945.
12. Quoted in Associated Press dispatch, September 23, 1945.
13. Quoted in *New York Times*, April 5, 1946.
14. Quoted in *Time*, August 29, 1949, p. 26.
15. Quoted in *Facts on File*, No. 552 (May 25 to May 31, 1951), p. 174.
16. Quoted in *Washington Post*, January 29, 1949.
17. Quoted in *La Prensa* (Buenos Aires), October 21, 1949.
18. Quoted in *La Razón* (Buenos Aires), September 24, 1950.
19. Quoted in *La Prensa* (Buenos Aires), October 29, 1950.
20. *Ibid.*, October 29, 1950.
21. United States Department of State, *op. cit.*, p. 57.
22. *Washington Post*, September 16, 1944.
23. *Time*, July 2, 1951, p. 37.
24. Redmont, *op. cit.*, p. 31.
25. Quoted in United Press dispatch, May 7, 1946.
26. Quoted in *La Prensa* (Buenos Aires), August 2, 1946.
27. Quoted in *New York Times*, April 12, 1951.
28. Juan D. Perón, *op. cit.*, p. 103.
29. Quoted in *Time*, April 16, 1951, p. 41.
30. Quoted in *La Razón* (Buenos Aires), April 6, 1951.
31. Quoted in *Time*, April 16, 1951, p. 41.
32. Quoted in International News Service dispatch, January 28, 1946.
33. Quoted in United Press dispatch, July 3, 1950.
34. Quoted in *New York Times*, May 9, 1944.
35. Quoted in United Press dispatch, January 26, 1945.
36. Quoted in *Time*, July 25, 1949, p. 24.
37. Strausz-Hupé and Possony, *op. cit.*, p. 239.

Notes

38. *Ibid.*, p. 240. Italics after the original.

39. Philip Wylie, *Opus 21* (New York: Rinehart and Co., Inc., 1950), p. 160. Italics mine.

40. Weil, *op. cit.*, p. 13.

41. Josephs, *op. cit.*, p. xv.

42. *New York Times*, April 24, 1946.

43. Quoted in *La Razón* (Buenos Aires), April 8, 1951.

44. Quoted in *Time*, April 16, 1951, p. 41.

45. Ghioldi, *Los Trabajadores, el Señor Perón, y el Partido Socialista*, p. 25.

46. Quoted in *Time*, July 31, 1950, p. 30.

Selected Bibliography

This is not an exhaustive list of books dealing with Argentine politics and government. Rather, it is a group of titles which have been carefully selected for the purpose of aiding the reader who might wish to pursue phases of the subject further than they have been carried in this book. The entries are annotated and arranged according to the three major subdivisions of the present volume.

I. A BOOK OF INTRODUCTIONS

A. IN ENGLISH

BURGIN, MIRON. *The Economic Aspects of Argentine Federalism, 1820–1853.* Cambridge: Harvard University Press, 1946.

A penetrating analysis of the economic factors involved in the nineteenth-century struggle between Buenos Aires and the provinces of the "interior."

GUERRANT, EDWARD O. *Roosevelt's Good Neighbor Policy.* Albuquerque: University of New Mexico Press, 1950.

A summary of the Latin-American policies of the United States from 1933 to 1946.

HARING, CLARENCE H. *Argentina and the United States.* Boston: World Peace Foundation, 1941.

A survey of U.S.-Argentine relations as they stood on the eve of the Perón revolution.

HERRON, FRANCIS. *Letters from the Argentine.* New York: G. P. Putnam's Sons, 1943.

A "North American's" impressions of attitudes and social life in pre-Perón Argentina.

LEVENE, RICARDO. *A History of Argentina,* WILLIAM SPENCE ROBERTSON, tr. and ed. Chapel Hill: University of North Carolina Press, 1937.

The standard text by Argentina's leading historian.

MACDONALD, AUSTIN F. *Government of the Argentine Republic.* New York: Thomas Y. Crowell Co., 1942.

A discussion of the structure of the country's government under the Constitution of 1853.

RENNIE, YSABEL F. *The Argentine Republic.* New York: The Macmillan Co., 1945.

An historico-economic analysis of the background of the Perón revolution.

TAYLOR, CARL C. *Rural Life in Argentina.* Baton Rouge: Louisiana State University Press, 1948.

The case-study method applied to selected *estancias* and other rural social organizations.

WILLIAMSON, RENÉ DE VISME. *Culture and Policy.* Knoxville: University of Tennessee Press, 1949.

A discussion of the relationship of Latin-American culture to the hemisphere policy of the United States.

B. IN SPANISH

ALBERDI, JUAN BAUTISTA. *Bases y Puntas de Partida para la Organización Política de la República Argentina.* Buenos Aires: La Tribuna Nacional, 1886.

Originally published in 1852, it exercised a profound influence on the writers of the Constitution of 1853; now regarded by Argentine lawyers as a classic.

BOSCO, EDUARDO JORGE (ed.). *El Gaucho.* Buenos Aires: Emecé Editores, 1947.

The gaucho as seen by foreigners traveling in Argentina in the eighteenth and nineteenth centuries.

BUNGE, ALEJANDRO E. *La Economía Argentina.* 4 vols. Buenos Aires: Agencía General de Librerías y Publicaciones, 1928–1930.

The standard work on the economic geography of Argentina.

GONZÁLEZ CALDERÓN, JUAN A. *Derecho Constitucional Argentino.* 3 vols. Buenos Aires: Laiouane, 1931.

The Argentine lawyer's basic handbook on the law of the Constitution of 1853.

HERNÁNDEZ, JOSÉ. *El Gaucho Martín Fierro.* Buenos Aires: Editorial Ateneo, 1950.

Regarded generally as the leading Argentine literary classic. Deals with the life and times of the gaucho. Exists in many editions.

Selected Bibliography

INGENIEROS, JOSÉ. *Sociología Argentina*. Buenos Aires: Editorial Losada, 1946.

An analysis of the evolution of Argentina's social structure, written by one of the country's foremost intellectual leaders.

Junta de Historia y Numismática Americana. *Historia de la Nación Argentina*. 10 vols. Buenos Aires: Imprenta de la Universidad, 1936–1942.

An ambitious work, embracing not only national history but also the individual histories of each of the provinces and territories.

MOYANO LLERENA, CARLOS. *Argentina Social y Económica*. Buenos Aires: Editorial Depalma, 1950.

A treatise in economic geography, containing much valuable statistical data.

ROMERO, JOSÉ LUIS. *Las Ideas Políticas en Argentina*. México: Fondo de Cultura Económica, 1946.

A significant history of Argentine political ideas.

II. A BOOK OF ALL THAT GLITTERS

A. IN ENGLISH

JOSEPHS, RAY. *Argentine Diary*. New York: Random House, Inc., 1944.

A "North American" journalist's day-by-day account of the coming of Perón.

[PERÓN, MARÍA EVA DUARTE DE.] *The Writings of Eva Perón*. Buenos Aires: Subsecretaría de Informaciones de la Presidencia de la Nación, 1950.

A collection of the late first lady's articles and speeches, setting forth the chief lines of her political thought and activity.

TAPPEN, KATHLEEN B. *The Status of Women in Argentina*. Washington: Office of the Co-ordinator of Inter-American Affairs, 1944.

A survey of this problem as it stood on the eve of the Perón revolution.

B. IN SPANISH

ALBERDI, JUAN BAUTISTA. *Derecho Público Provincial Argentino*. Buenos Aires: La Cultura Argentina, 1917.

A legal discussion of the constitutional position of the provinces in the Argentine federal system.

BIELSA, RAFAEL. *Derecho Administrativo*. Buenos Aires: Editorial Depalma, 1950.

Generally regarded as the leading work on Argentine administrative law.

Cámara de Diputados de la Nación Argentina. *Digesto Constitucional de la Nación Argentina.* Buenos Aires: Imprenta del Congreso de la Nación, 1950.
Contains the texts of Perón's Constitution of 1949 and the new constitutions of the fourteen original provinces.
LINARES QUINTANA, SEGUNDO V. *Gobierno y Administración de la República Argentina.* 2 vols. Buenos Aires: Tipografía Editora Argentina, 1946.
A detailed analysis of the constitutional structure of the government.
Ministerio del Interior. *Intervención Federal en las Provincias.* Buenos Aires: Talleres Gráficos de Correos y Telégrafos, 1933.
An official account of the interventor system.
Ministerio del Interior. *Las Fuerzas Armadas Restituyen el Imperio de la Soberanía Popular.* 2 vols. Buenos Aires: Cámara de Diputados, 1946.
The official version of the role of the armed forces in the election of 1946.
PERÓN, MARÍA EVA DUARTE DE. *Mi Obra de Ayuda Social.* Buenos Aires: Subsecretaría de Informaciones de la Presidencia de la Nación, 1949.
Eva Perón's story of her Social Aid Foundation.
SASTRE, PASTOR. *Manual de la Constitución.* Buenos Aires: Ciordia y Rodríguez, 1950.
A lawyer's guide to Perón's Constitution of 1949.
SOMMARIVA, LUIS H. *Historia de las Intervenciones Federales en las Provincias.* 2 vols. Buenos Aires: El Ateneo, 1929, 1931.
The standard work on the interventor system.
VÁSQUEZ, RAMÓN F. *Poder de Policía.* Buenos Aires: Editorial Contreras, 1940.
The most comprehensive analysis of the police power in Argentina.
VIGO, SALVADOR C. *El Régimen Municipal de la Constitución y las Leyes Orgánicas Municipales.* Santa Fé: Imprenta de la Universidad Nacional del Litoral, 1943.
A discussion of the position of municipalities in the Argentine constitutional system.

III. A BOOK OF IDEOLOGY AND POLITICS

A. IN ENGLISH

ALEXANDER, ROBERT J. *The Perón Era.* New York: Columbia University Press, 1951.
Valuable primarily for its statement of the position of the

General Confederation of Labor (C.G.T.) in Perón's Argentina.

EBON, MARTIN. *World Communism Today.* New York: McGraw-Hill Book Co., Inc., 1948.

Contains a discussion of the Communist movement in Argentina.

MUSSOLINI, BENITO. *The Political and Social Doctrine of Fascism.* London: The Hogarth Press, 1933.

Useful in comparing *Justicialismo* with fascism.

[PERÓN, JUAN DOMINGO.] *The Voice of Perón.* Buenos Aires: Subsecretaría de Informaciones de la Presidencia de la Nación Argentina, 1950.

Excerpts from President Perón's speeches and writings, containing policy statements on various aspects of the "new Argentina."

RICHMOND, LEONARD T. *Argentina's Third Position and Other Systems Compared.* Buenos Aires: Acme Agency, 1949.

Treats the "Third Position" exclusively as an economic system. Of dubious scholarship, but contains material not elsewhere available in English.

U.S. Department of State. *Consultation among the American Republics with Respect to the Argentine Situation.* Washington: Government Printing Office, 1946.

Spruille Braden's celebrated "Blue Book."

WEIL, FELIX J. *Argentine Riddle.* New York: The John Day Company, 1944.

An analysis of Argentine economic problems.

B. IN SPANISH

BIELSA, RAFAEL. *Caracteres Jurídicos y Políticos del Ejército.* Santa Fé: Universidad Nacional del Litoral, 1937.

A discussion of Argentine militarism.

DICKMANN, ENRIQUE. *Recuerdos de un Militante Socialista.* Buenos Aires: La Vanguardia, 1949.

A veteran Socialist politician's hard-hitting critique of the Perón revolution.

GALVÁN MORENO, C. *El Periodismo Argentino.* Buenos Aires: Editorial Claridad, 1944.

A valuable history of the Argentine press.

GHIOLDI, AMÉRICO. *Marxismo, Socialismo, Izquierdismo, Comunismo y la Realidad Argentina de Hoy.* Buenos Aires: La Vanguardia, 1950.

A Socialist leader's analysis of the position of his party in Perón's Argentina.

KROTOSCHIN, ERNESTO. *Curso de Legislación del Trabajo.* Buenos Aires: Editorial Depalma, 1950.
A useful summary of *Peronista* labor legislation.
LINARES QUINTANA, SEGUNDO V. *Los Partidos Políticos.* Buenos Aires: Editorial Alfa, 1945.
A history of Argentine political parties, by one of the country's leading social scientists.
MENDE, RAÚL A. *El Justicialismo.* Buenos Aires: ALEA, S.A., 1950.
The most systematic *Peronista* statement of the principles of *Justicialismo.* Written in simplified language and addressed to the Argentine lower classes.
ODDONE, JACINTO. *Gremialismo Proletario Argentino.* Buenos Aires: La Vanguardia, 1949.
A Socialist "elder statesman's" history of the Argentine labor movement.
Partido Peronista. *Manual del Peronista.* Buenos Aires: Editorial Ateneo, 1949.
The *Peronista's* manual, indispensable to the study of Perón's political party.
Presidencia de la Nación. *Plan de Gobierno, 1947 a 1951.* Buenos Aires: Subsecretaría de Informaciones de la Presidencia de la Nación Argentina, 1946.
Perón's Five-Year plan.
SOMMI, LUIS V. *Los Capitales Alemanes en la Argentina.* Buenos Aires: Editorial Claridad, 1945.
A detailed discussion of German economic influence in Argentina.

Index

Index

Index

Index

Index

Vawters, Fay, 108
Velazco, Filomeno, 58, 172–73
Velloso, Pedro Leão, 15–16
Vernengo Lima, Héctor, 59, 316
Viceroyalty of the Plata River, 19, 150, 431
Villarroel, Gualberto, 402–3
Villegas Basavilbaso, Benjamín, 360
Visca, José Emilio, 119–20, 184

Wast, Hugo; see Martínez Zuvería, Gustavo
Weil, Felix, 368, 378–79

Weilheimer, Ruppert, 402
Welles, Sumner, 279, 322
Woman suffrage; see Feminist movement
World War I, 34, 96
World War II, 10–15, 38–44, 47–49, 97–98, 278–305, 392–94, 400–411

Yadarola, Mauricio, 117–18
Yalta conference, 406–7
Yrigoyen; see Irigoyen, Hipólito

PT 44 587